CONSTANCE GARNETT

RICHARD GARNETT

CONSTANCE GARNETT

A Heroic Life

faber and faber

This edition first published in 2009
by Faber and Faber Ltd
Bloomsbury House, 74–77 Great Russell Street
London WC1B 3DA

Printed by CPI Antony Rowe, Eastbourne

A CIP record for this book is available from the British Library

ISBN 978–0–571–24560–4

For Jane
who never knew her

THE RUSSIAN TONGUE

In days of doubt, in days of dreary musings on my country's fate, thou alone art my stay and support, mighty, true, free Russian speech! But for thee, how not fall into despair, seeing all that is done at home? But who can think that such a tongue is not the gift of a great people!

Ivan Turgenev, *Poems in Prose*

Contents

Illustrations

Acknowledgements

My first thanks go to my sister Henrietta. I mentioned to her that I had been reading our grandmother's translation of Herzen, and remarked on how very well Constance wrote. 'Yes,' Henrietta replied. 'Someone should write her biography. She had such an interesting life.' I hope the reader will agree.

Many people have helped in the writing. There seems to be a law governing biographers (perhaps one might call it 'Holroyd's Law'), which states that one becomes interested in a subject only when almost all the witnesses are dead. This book would have been far easier to research – though much harder to write – if my father had still been alive. Despite the many inaccuracies in his autobiography – for he wrote entirely from memory – I have been constantly grateful for his superlative evocations of character and for his habit of preserving papers, especially for keeping undated letters in their envelopes. My son Oliver has saved me many months of tedious work by sorting and filing them all.

Constance herself kept few papers other than letters from her son. Most letters to her, even from Tolstoy and Chekhov, seem to have disappeared irrecoverably. I realise that if she had kept all her husband's letters and he had destroyed all hers I might be telling a very different story. I am therefore all the more grateful to those – acknowledged below – who have kept the papers which have made this book possible. In particular, two of Constance's nieces, Marion Gregory (Black family papers) and the late Anne Lee Michell (Olive Garnett's diaries and some other papers, now in the possession of her daughter Caroline White), have made an outstanding contribution. So too has Anna Garrett with Constance's vital letters to her mother, Natalie Duddington.

Jane Gregory's research into the history of the Blacks, much of it undertaken on my father's behalf for his novel *Up She Rises*, has provided the foundation for the first chapters.

Angelica Garnett has written for me her memories of Constance Garnett in old age and reminded me of some important things that I had forgotten.

Earlier books about the family by Carolyn G. Heilbrun and George Jefferson have provided many useful pointers, though I have always gone back to the original sources where possible. I am especially grateful to Dr Jefferson for turning over to me some of his papers. These include some relating to Nellie

Heath, which he obtained from Stella Stebbing, whom I much regret that I have been unable to trace. I hope she will accept my thanks and apologies.

With more recent writers, Barbara McCrimmon, biographer of Richard Garnett, Barry C. Johnson, editor of Olive Garnett's diaries, and Ann MacEwen, researching into her Radford ancestors, it has been a joint campaign of research, and I would like to think that I may have been as helpful to them as they have to me.

For help with Russian material I am much indebted to Tatiana A. Wolff and particularly to Alison Wilson, who has provided all the translations from Russian not otherwise acknowledged.

I have been fortunate in being able to turn for advice on medical matters to Dr John Hodgkin and Dr Stephen Tuft.

No work of this sort can be undertaken without access to a good library, and I have been particularly fortunate to live within easy reach of Cambridge University Library. I am most grateful to the staff for their help and efficiency, and was especially glad to have the use of the microfilm room.

In Russia: Galina Alekseeva of the Tolstoy Museum at Yasnaya Polyana has become a most helpful friend and (so far as the execrable Russian posts will allow) a regular correspondent; I am particularly grateful to Nelly Malinskaya for providing photocopies of Natalie Duddington's letters to the late Augusta Tovey; I have received much useful help from Michael Bird, Graham Coe, Michael Sullivan and Terry Garrett of the British Embassy in Moscow; Liudmila Grigorieva of the Moscow Museums Service; Lidia Liubimova of the Tolstoy Museum in Moscow; Yuri Ovsiannikov; Gennady Shalyugin of the Chekhov House-Museum, Yalta; O. A. Yatsenko of the Pushkin Museum, Leningrad; and the Central State Archive for Literature and Art, Moscow.

Material in the Royal Archives at Windsor is published by gracious permission of Her Majesty The Queen.

For the use of other copyright material I must thank:

The Society of Authors (Katherine Mansfield); Richard Bates and the H. E. Bates Estate; Katharine Brunt (Bréal papers); Chatto and Windus; Joy Clarke (Ursula Cox); Veronica Farrington (Pease); Angelica Garnett and Quentin Bell (Vanessa Bell); Anna Garrett (Natalie Duddington); Sir John Gielgud; Halsey Lightly and the trustees of John Galsworthy's Estate; Ann MacEwen (Ernest and Dollie Radford); Octopus Publishing Group (William Heinemann); Laurence Pollinger Ltd and the Estate of Mrs Frieda Lawrence Ravagli (D. H. Lawrence); Christine de la Potterie and Julian Gautier (Michel St-Denis).

For access to material in their collections I am grateful to:

Alexander Turnbull Library, Wellington, New Zealand (Janine Delaney); BBC Written Archives Centre; Bencroft Road Public Library, London; Berg Collection, The New York Public Library, Astor, Lenox and Tilden Foundations (the late Lola L. Szladits); Birmingham University Library (Dr B. S. Benedikz); University College, London, Library (C. J. Anderson); Bodleian Library, Oxford; British Library, Department of Manuscripts and Newspaper

Acknowledgements

Library, Colindale; Cambridge University Library; William Andrews Clark Memorial Library, University of California (Michael Hall); East Sussex Record Office, Lewes; Eton School Library (Michael Meredith); Goldsmiths' Library, University of London; Harry Ransom Humanities Research Center, the University of Texas at Austin (Cathy Henderson); Houghton Library, Harvard (Susan Halpert); Hoover Institution on War, Revolution and Peace, Stanford (Elena Danielson and Ronald Bulatoff); King's College, Cambridge (Peter Jones); Lilly Library, Indiana University (Saundra Taylor); Newnham College, Cambridge (Ann Phillips); Nuffield College, Oxford; Octopus Publishing Group Library (June Rose); Queen Mary College, London (A. G. Quinsee); University of Illinois Library at Urbana-Champaign (Gene K. Rinkel); Reading University Library (Michael Bott and Francesca Hardcastle); Record Office, House of Lords (Alexandra Wedgwood); Stanford University Library (Wojciech Zalewski); Theatre Museum, London.

For much other help of many kinds I am grateful to:

Stephen Aaron; Janet Adam Smith; Nicolas Barker; C. Hilary Bates; Lady (Susan) Bates; Anne Olivier Bell; Professor J. T. Boulton; Peter M. Brading; Nicholas Breach; Martin Brunt; Arthur Calder-Marshall; Brian Carr; D. N. Cheetham, Registrar of the Diocese of St Albans; Paul Chipchase; Major Peter Clayton; Professor Anthony Cross; Laurence Davies; Richard Davies, Leeds Russian Archive; Dr Michael Fordham; Thalia Fordham; Helen Fowler; J. J. Friedman; Patrick S. Garnett; Sebastian Garrett; Gerald Gould; A. Stuart Gray; Dr Tony Harris; Sir Rupert Hart-Davis; Colin Haycraft; Ronald Hayman; Alan Hill; Constance Hill; Michael J. de K. Holman; Michael Holroyd; Lord Horder; Enid Houghton; Rita B. Human; Peter Kaye; Josef Keith, Friends House; Peter Khoroche; Professor Mark Kinkead-Weekes; The Hon. J. S. Kirkwood; Professor Dan H. Laurence; Henrietta MacBurney; Donald A. MacKenzie; Norman MacKenzie; Lord MacLehose; Lady (Magdalene) Macnaghten; Brenda Maddox; Ellen F. Mappen; Nadine Marshall; Ernest and Joyce Mehew; the late Priscilla Metcalf; Patrick Miles; Sir Oliver Millar; Professor J. Lawrence Mitchell; Professor Charles A. Moser; Professor Thomas C. Moser; Belinda Norman-Butler; E. Winsløv Olsen; Frances Partridge; Martyn Pease; Sebastian Pease; John C. Q. Roberts, Great Britain-USSR Association; Professor S. P. Rosenbaum; Professor Roberta Rubenstein; Chattie Salaman; David Saunders; Professor Robert Skidelsky; John Slatter; Roger Smith; Mukund Sonpatki; The Hon. Oliver Soskice; Frances Spalding; Lord Stockton; Terry Tanner; Ruth Thackeray; Kathleen Tillotson; Claire Tomalin; Glyn Turton; Ursula Vaughan Williams; Professor Patrick Waddington; Professor Stanley Weintraub; Brigid Wells, Brighton and Hove High School; Lady Wright; and, I fear, some I have overlooked, to whom I offer thanks and apologies.

xi

The Garnett Family

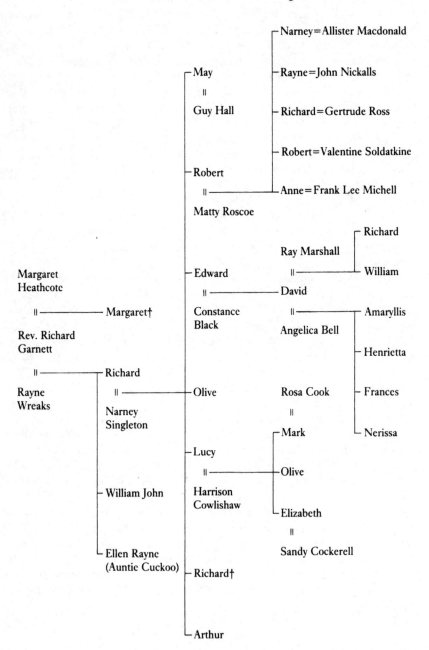

The Black Family

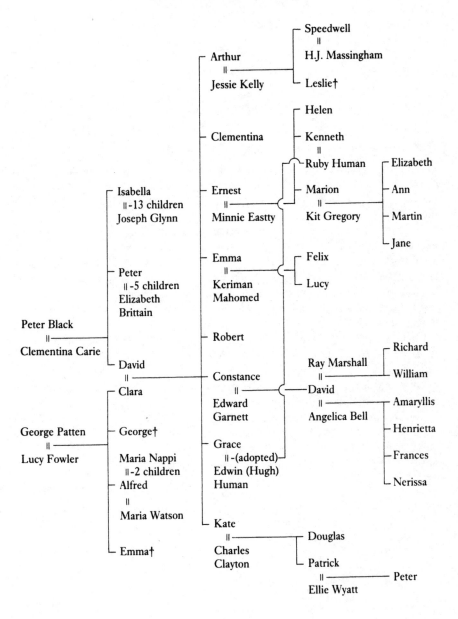

Textual Note

In spelling Russian names I have been guided by convenience rather than consistency, and have tried to provide the form that will be most familiar to the reader, using for personal names the romanisations adopted by the people themselves.

Constance Garnett was far from consistent in her private letters. Her system in her publications was influenced by the many transliterations into French that were then current, hence her use of *tch* rather than *ch*, which is now obsolete. For the inconvenience of the resulting inconsistency between my Chekhov and her Tchehov I can only beg the indulgence of the reader, who may be considered fortunate to have been spared such unfamiliar forms as Čexov and Tschechow, to name but two.

I have generally followed her practice (and that of Rosemary Edmonds in her *Anna Karenin*) of not preserving the feminine ending on Russian women's surnames.

Titles of Russian works in the Bibliography and Notes have been transliterated according to the Library of Congress system.

Contractions such as & have been spelt out.

Constance made much use of a mark somewhere between a full stop and a dash. I have felt free to interpret it as either.

All dates are in new style unless otherwise specified.

1

Antecedents

On 3 June 1831 the ships in the Russian port of Kronstadt flew their flags at half-mast. They were not saluting the death of a Grand Duke or an Imperial officer, but the funeral of a Scottish sea-captain who had died on board his ship two days earlier. His name was Peter Black, and he was Constance Garnett's grandfather. He was, like her, a pioneer in the history of Russia's communications with the West.

He was a dark handsome man, stern in command of his crew and his family, and much respected by both. He had come a long way in his forty-eight years. He had been born into a family of Forfarshire fishermen in 1783,[1] and started work fishing in open boats before he was ten. At eighteen he married Clementina Carie, a farmer's daughter ten years older than himself. She was a small woman, warm-hearted and indomitable, with her looks soon to be ruined by smallpox. They had a son, Peter, in 1803, and a daughter, Isabella, was on the way when Black was seized by the press gang in 1805. This turned out to be the making of his career. By 1812 he had risen to the rank of Master on the *Dispatch*, that is to say he had charge of all the gear and stores on board and was responsible, under the Commander, for navigating the ship. In that same year, according to family tradition, his wife, hearing that his ship was to put into Plymouth, tramped all the way there and back again from Scotland in the depths of winter. She saw him but for a single day, and it was not until the Napoleonic wars were over that their third child, David, was born on 27 December 1817 at Dysart, near Kirkcaldy on the Firth of Forth. He was to be Constance's father.

Peter Black was an able mathematician and engineer and was early involved in designing and managing the new steamships. In 1822 he took command of the *Lord Melville*, a steam-packet which plied between London and Calais. For three summers his family lived in Calais, and David learnt to speak French like a native. In 1826 Captain Black took charge of the *George IV*, which he had planned and built himself, one of the largest steamships of her day, and spent a year running a new service to Spain, Portugal and Gibraltar. In the spring of 1827, as soon as the Baltic became free enough of ice to be navigable, he took her on four trips to St Petersburg, the first regular steam-packet on this route. Sometimes the ship terminated at Kronstadt, the port on an island fifteen miles offshore which provided a deep-water harbour for St Petersburg.

This route was unnecessarily tedious and slow. There was no need to go all the way round Denmark. It was easier to take the ship to Hamburg, travel forty miles overland to Lübeck, and pick up another ship there. So in the spring of 1828 Peter Black took the *George IV* to Travemünde, the village at the mouth at the Trave, off which ships for Lübeck usually anchored. For a thousand pounds he bought a pleasant house there for himself and Clementina, and sent young David, who had had a year's schooling in London, to a boarding school in Lübeck.

The *George IV* could now ply back and forth, taking four or five days to cover the seven hundred miles between Travemünde and Kronstadt. From May to October she left alternately from either port about once a fortnight. For twenty-four Dutch ducats (about £11 10s. in the money of the time) a gentleman could travel in considerable comfort. For £10 11s. he could bring his carriage or his horse aboard; children travelled at half price, and a servant's fare was only £4 15s. Food and wine were available at reasonable rates. It was vastly preferable to lumbering across the interminable plains of Poland and the Baltic states.

There were hundreds of other ships sailing in and out of Kronstadt, but during the seasons of 1828 and 1829 the *George IV*, Captain P. Black, was the only steamship providing a regular service between St Petersburg and Lübeck. Newspapers began to print news that had come 'by steamship' – often nearly a week ahead of news that had come by land. And in June 1829 a new postal service by the same route was announced. Peter Black was providing a vital service between St Petersburg and the outside world.

In the winter the *George IV* returned to the old Iberian route, while Clementina remained at Travemünde and looked after the smallholding – for she had two cows and an orchard of fruit trees – and David learned to speak German and to skate as well as his schoolfellows. Once he skated right across the Baltic.

When Peter returned in the spring of 1830 he found that things had changed. A Belgian steamship, the *Bourse d'Amsterdam*, had arrived at

Kronstadt and was advertising a competing service. And when he returned to Travemünde from Kronstadt on 18 May he received orders from the owner, the Rev. William Jolliffe, to bring the *George IV* back to England. Jolliffe was no ordinary clergyman, but an entrepreneur who was involved in building no less than four bridges over the Thames. For the last five years he had been engaged on the new London Bridge, an enormously expensive undertaking which was eventually to cost one-and-a-half million pounds. He had run out of money and had to sell off several of his ships.

Stieglitz, the shipping agents in St Petersburg, were furious and made it plain to the public that it was no fault of theirs that they had sold tickets for a passage on a ship that was now not going to run. Peter Black must have had similar feelings. It may well have made him decide to go his own way, for on 23 September it was announced that Nicholas I, the Tsar of all the Russias, whose ice-cold eyes so alarmed the young Queen Victoria, had granted a twelve-year monopoly of steam navigation between Lübeck and St Petersburg to a new company set up by a consortium of Russian and German merchants from the two cities. Captain Black was commissioned to design and build two ships especially for the purpose, with a shallow draft so that they could steam right up the Neva. They were to be called the *Nikolai I* and the *Alexandra* after the Tsar and his Tsaritsa, and they were to be Russian ships, flying the Russian flag.

Peter arranged to build them at Blackwall. There was not much time, and the work had to be hurried on to have them ready by the spring. It was a hard and exhausting task, and not until the beginning of May was the *Nikolai I*, 533 tons, ready for sea. It was none too soon. On 17 April a salvo of guns announced that the ice on the Neva had broken up and the river was open for navigation, and by 1 May the roads outside were entirely free of ice. On 31 May the *Nikolai I* arrived in Kronstadt for Peter Black to begin his new career in the Russian merchant navy. But he was already severely ill with diabetes exacerbated by 'a foolish prejudice against much clothing'[2] and a neglect 'to protect himself properly against severe cold'.[3] On the following day he died.

The *Nikolai I* pursued her career without him. In November of that year, dangerously late in the season, she battled her way to the mouth of the Neva bringing the vast blocks of granite to form the plinth of the great column that was to be erected in memory of Tsar Alexander I outside the Winter Palace. In the spring of 1838 on her first trip south she caught fire, and Ivan Turgenev, the novelist, then aged nineteen and leaving Russia for the first time, was overcome by panic and had to be restrained by the Russian captain from forcing his way into a lifeboat. The ship was rebuilt, and with a Dutch captain continued the service that Peter had begun.

With Peter dead there was no need to stay on in Travemünde. David left the school in Lübeck, where he had received an excellent education. Afterwards he said, as people so often do, that his schooldays were the happiest of his life; and since his later years were to be shadowed by strange clouds of guilt and self-doubt, they almost certainly were.

His elder brother Peter lived in Brighton, where he had found a job as agent for the General Steam Navigation Company and Consular Agent for France. Clementina and David went to join him, and she remained there for the rest of her life.

David completed his peripatetic schooling at Brighton in the summer of 1832. About this time his sister Isabella married Joseph Glynn, an engineer who had been at school with Robert Stephenson and was as active and important in the development of marine and stationary steam engines as the Stephensons were in the railways.[4] On leaving school at the age of fifteen David made a brief attempt at a career in engineering with Glynn but soon concluded that he had no aptitude for it. He decided instead to take up the law; and the following year he was articled to Thomas Freeman in Ship Street, Brighton. He had to pay a premium of no less than three hundred and fifty pounds, which he was just able to find from the money left him by his father. He served his articles for five years in Brighton, earning nothing, and then moved to London. It took him eight years, three of them as a junior chancery clerk in London, before he was admitted to practise as an attorney, and a further year before he had earned enough to recoup his premium. Then, just as he was beginning to make a career as a lawyer, he decided to throw it up and emigrate to Canada.

David was not worried about leaving his old mother. He had a wild idea that she might follow him out when he had established himself in Canada, though she might well have preferred, at the age of sixty-nine, to have remained where she was in Brighton with Peter and his growing family.

He was not going to Canada to earn a living as a lawyer or a linguist but as a labourer on the land. He managed to find work of a kind and stuck at it for a little over a year, with his beard frozen to the counterpane on winter nights, and ploughing on summer days 'with bare feet in the hot loose black loamy soil formed of the decomposed leaves'.[5] He began to think of settling permanently and wrote home to try to raise the money to do so. He received instead the news that his mother was dangerously ill. He hurried home only to find that Clementina was already dead. He never forgave himself for having left her.

There was now no reason why he should not return to Canada, and he fully intended to do so. But his brother and brother-in-law persuaded him to stay in Brighton and to resume his career in the law, this time practising on his own. He lodged with the Peter Blacks and took an office at 56 Ship Street, but found it hard going to earn even as much as he did before he went to Canada.

He was now twenty-five years old, with a dark curly beard and the somewhat Semitic good looks one occasionally finds in Scotland. A distant cousin of Constance's who met him at dances at this time told her 'that he was the handsomest man she knew and that all the girls were in love with him'.[6] He was no libertine. His character had more of the Scottish Sabbath than of the Scottish Saturday night. Nevertheless he admitted in a memoir that in the spring of 1845 'whilst boarding at my brother's a servant girl of theirs [was] got with child by me – at least she told me so and I have no reason to doubt it'.[7] Her name was Elizabeth Viney. About this time, and perhaps for this reason, he seems to have moved out of his brother's house and lived as well as worked at 56 Ship Street.

In another part of the same house lived David Hine with his daughter; and in the summer of 1845 Miss Hine had visitors, her old friend Mrs Lucy Patten and her daughter Clara, who had come to take the sea air and convalesce after an illness.

Clara was a young woman of twenty. She was rather short, neither especially pretty nor particularly plain, though when she first met David she 'had her face swollen with toothache and tied up in a shawl'.[8] She was well-read, well-travelled and had a wide circle of interesting friends. She was intelligent, thoroughly straightforward and honest without being in the least a prig. And she had a remarkably loving and constant heart. She had never been in love before, and she fell passionately and irrevocably in love with David Black. She could hardly believe her good fortune when he admitted that he was in love with her too.

The Pattens were a family of artists. Clara's grandfather William and her aunt Mary were miniature painters. Her father George, born in

1801, was trained as a miniature painter, first by his father and then, at the age of fifteen, at the Royal Academy Schools. But miniature painting was then going out of fashion and was soon to be virtually extinguished by photography; and so in 1828 he returned to study painting in oils at the Academy. He was an excellent portrait painter, and two pieces of good luck helped to establish his reputation. Nicolò Paganini, perhaps the greatest of virtuoso violinists, and certainly the best showman of them all, visited London in 1831 and 1832 to tremendous acclaim. On the second visit Patten found an opportunity to paint his strange cadaverous face. He made a copy, and thereafter he had only to exhibit it in order to enjoy a reflection of Paganini's own notoriety. It was a most effective advertisement for his wares.

On 15 October 1839 the young Queen Victoria became engaged to Prince Albert of Saxe-Coburg-Gotha. Henry Graves, whose enterprising firm of engravers held the Royal Warrant, arranged for Patten to go to Germany to paint the Prince's portrait, so that it could be engraved and published. The portrait was 'universally approved'[9] in Germany, but the Queen was more critical, and on 17 January 1840 she noted in her journal:

I went down to look at a picture of dearest Albert's painted by George Patten . . . it is the size of life, and half length in his uniform. It is not near handsome enough, but when you have looked at it a little while, it is certainly like, but the face is too thin; it is nicely painted . . . After dinner Lord Melbourne and I looked at the picture of Albert. 'The head is like', he said, 'very good – fine expression, – melancholy' (as it is), 'which is good for a picture'.[10]

The Prince, however, thought 'The eyes look as if they were dazzled by a glare of light.'[11] But he was clearly willing to let Patten have another try, for on 14 February, only four days after the Royal Wedding, his secretary, Dr Schenck, wrote to Patten that although 'His Royal Highness's time is so very much taken up at present',[12] it was 'to be expected that at no very distant period the Prince will be more at leisure'.[13] Patten duly got his sittings, and in the latter half of March painted the Prince in his Garter robes, a fine full-length portrait now in Wellington College. This was sufficiently liked for Dr Schenck to write again on 21 June asking Patten to make a half-length copy. It was intended as a birthday present for the Prince's mother and '*must* be ready by the 11th July. The time is short but for your talent it is more than sufficient.'[14] For this rush job Patten was paid £74 16s 6d. He painted a further portrait of the Prince that summer, and it was well liked not only by Victoria and Albert but also by the King and Queen of the Belgians. He was appointed Portrait Painter in Ordinary to the Prince Consort, a post that carried no salary or special duties or privileges, but like the portrait of Paganini was useful in attracting clients.

Thackeray described the portrait of Albert in his Garter robes as 'a good downright honest *bourgeois* picture, as we fancy; or, as a facetious friend remarked, good plain *roast-and-boiled* painting'. [15] Patten was not cut out to be a Court painter, and he had no further Royal commissions. He was much more at home with prosperous manufacturers and city worthies in the burgeoning cities in the North; and they were the bulk of his clients.

It is not enough for a portrait painter to be able to catch a likeness and to present it in an acceptable form. He must also have the knack of keeping his sitters alert and interested. Once they are bored their faces go dead and he is lost. George Patten had this knack – though it may have deserted him with his first portrait of Prince Albert. He was good company. He was liked by his betters. Sir Robert Peel took to him and would come and watch him working and tell him anecdotes of Haydon and other painters. He was on friendly terms with Etty, Maclise and Landseer. He knew Cobden and the Carlyles. But his closest friends were generally men of the second rank like himself. He was elected ARA in 1837 but never became a full Royal Academician. His metier was portraits, and they earned him a good living, but he was tempted by higher things, as his grandson Arthur noted:

He painted large classical pictures which did not go off. There were especially in his painting room: Dante and Virgil, Hercules and Children, and two other subjects representing incidents in the career of some nymphs and goddesses, all much above life size. The men too brown, the women too white the backgrounds too black. [16]

These were still in his studio at his death and were auctioned off for less than a quarter of the price he had been able to command for a commissioned portrait.[17]

George Patten was perhaps a little vain of his handsome profile and his facility in extempore public speaking. He was apt to get very fussed before an important exhibition. But he was a devoted husband and very fortunate in his wife, Lucy Fowler. Constance remembered her grandmother well and was very fond of her: 'She was a little golden-haired woman, very fair with blue eyes and an exquisite rose-leaf complexion.'[18] Many years later Constance went to see George Patten's portrait of Lucy, and wrote:

My frivolous grandmother must have been a lovely woman. I am like a rough, coarsened copy of her – every feature in her face is more delicate – the skin is exquisitely fine – the hair brighter and no spectacles of course. I feel discontented since I saw the portrait again, for I ought to have been like that! [19]

George was an uncritical father to his four children, Clara, George, Alfred and Emma, and he delighted in their attainments. In 1836 Lucy sent him a batch of letters from them, and he replied: 'I *am quite satisfied* with Clara's improvement in writing and don't wish her to overwork herself, let her have *cheerful* exercise of *body* and not too much manual labor.'[20]

In March of the following year George and Lucy set off on an extensive Continental tour. They took Clara with them. George was going to improve his knowledge of the Old Masters, Lucy and Clara to see the sights. Although she was only eleven years old, Clara kept a full diary of their travels, a lively record of Italy, with much unseasonable, weather, long and uncomfortable journeys by diligence, adventures with dishonest servants and the threat of brigands.

They reached home again on 29 August, and Clara wrote a last entry in her diary:

16 days after Papa went to Liverpool alas, he bid George and Emma farewell and saw them for the last time we were taken ill of the scarlet fever the next day and that day week George died Emma was taken ill the day before and Papa was sent for and came in three days only in time to weep for Emma who died the next day here I leave off begining with pleasure and ending in death.[21]

Clara has left few other records of her childhood and youth. Wherever she may have been educated, she imbibed a lasting belief in the supreme importance of education, and acquired a good knowledge of French and Italian. Her father had a friend, John Heraud, an indigent author with far too many children to support, who was writing a life of Savonarola. Constance believed that Clara had helped him by translating the quotations from the Italian, and that her work was Very creditable for a girl of 19.'[22]

In September 1845 David Black proposed to Clara Patten and wrote to her father for his consent. She was under age, and David's income was still far short of the two hundred and fifty pounds a year they needed to live on. But he hoped that perhaps Patten, who could make as much by painting three portraits, might be willing to support them for a while. He was not. He could not understand what Clara saw in the young man, and felt that it was an infatuation that would pass off if only he took a firm enough line. Acting much out of character as a stern paterfamilias he forbade Mr Black to visit their house in London, or Clara to write to him.

From then on, throughout their tormented engagement, Clara remained constant to David, and honest though she was by nature, was drawn into one small deceit after another. For nearly four years they kept in touch through an intermediary or wrote surreptitiously and enjoyed furtive clandestine meetings.[23] David offered from time to time to cancel the engagement and leave Clara free for a more acceptable suitor. But she would have none of it. She remained constant to him, was unshaken when David's illegitimate son was born, and showed a kindly interest in the child. The rest of Clara's family encouraged the romance. Only her father remained obdurate. Even after her twenty-first birthday, when she could have married despite him, she remained sensibly aware that they could not begin a marriage with no money.

David tried to increase his earnings by translating the novels of Adalbert Stifter from German. Clara, too, began learning German, and did some translation from French. But it was very poorly paid work, even when he could find someone to take it, for 'publishers are all the same,' Clara remarked, 'The only safe way is to look upon them all as scoundrels and act accordingly'.[24]

But at last, in April 1849, Freeman & Cornford, with whom David had served his apprenticeship sixteen years before, offered him a partnership in the firm. They found accommodation in the same building, 45 Ship Street, in Brighton, and were married in London at All Souls' Church, Langham Place, on 7 July 1849.

2

Poor Connie

In leaving London for Brighton and setting up house there with her husband Clara had not entirely cut herself off from the livelier literary and artistic life of the metropolis. She still kept up with new books as they came out, looked out for reviews of her father's and her brother's paintings, went to the theatre and to hear Dickens reading his works in Brighton, and to the Annual Summer Exhibition of the Royal Academy in London. She was kept informed by her mother of what was going on in the world with news of such events as the opening of the Great Exhibition in 1851. But her increasing family kept her too busy for much more.

She had five children before Constance was born.

Arthur (born 22 July 1851) was as dark as his father and at least as handsome. He was of an enquiring scientific turn of mind, occasionally obstinate with his parents, but invariably kind and gentle to his brothers and sisters.

Clementina Maria (born 27 July 1853), as the eldest girl, was the unwilling focus of her mother's main expectations and most enterprising dressmaking. She was intelligent and persevering, with an aptitude for music and languages, and always to be relied upon for her sane good sense.

Ernest (born 30 July 1855) was a cheerful boy, smaller and less prepossessing than his elder brother. He was practical rather than intellectual, a keen gardener and accurate draughtsman, and made up in willingness what he lacked in brilliance.

Emma Louisa (born 19 July 1857) was a seven months' child. Clara had an even worse confinement than usual with her and nearly died. She was a delicate girl, rather obstinate and refractory, but warm-hearted and affectionate. She was precociously gifted as an artist, and when she was only nine her work was shown to the class as 'the result of indomitable perseverance'. [1]

Robert (born 3 January 1860) was observant, athletic, musical and ugly: 'Robbie swims like a little fish',[2] 'he is an excellent walker for a boy of his age; he accompanies us on all our long expeditions, and is always seeing something wonderful'.[3] As the one nearest in age to her he was perhaps the closest of Constance's childhood companions.

She herself was born at eleven a.m. on 19 December 1861, the only one so far to have fair hair and blue eyes. Her father did not register her birth until 31 January, and then gave the wrong date and no Christian names[4] – a strange lapse for a professional solicitor and an unhappy augury for her relations with her father, which were never to be comfortable. It was not until 18 July, when she was christened at the Chapel Royal in North Street, that she formally became Constance Clara Black.

The two remaining children, Grace Amy (born 21 December 1863) and Katharine Lucy (born 18 February 1866), always known as Kate or Katie, 'did the same things at the same time and were coupled together as the "little ones", as though they were twins, but two children could not have been more unlike in character'.[5] Grace was fair and pretty, idealistic and dreamy, but with great courage and willing to get to the bottom of things. Kate was dark and sturdy, thoroughly practical and straightforward, but with no special intellectual or artistic bent.

It is hard to see how 58 Ship Street[6] (it had been renumbered from 45 in the 1850s) could find room for this large family and a couple of servants as well as offices for the partners in the firm and their clerks, though things were eased a little in 1859 when Cornford retired and David was able to take over his office, his own becoming the family's dining room. Besides being a busy solicitor, he had from 1863 been able to increase his earnings by being Town Clerk of Brighton, and later Coroner.

He was the absolute ruler of his household. Nothing could be done without his permission, which was by no means always forthcoming. Yet he seemed remote, an outsider even within his own family. In Clara's letters to her mother she referred to him as 'Mr Black' or occasionally as 'Papa', never as 'David', although her brother-in-law was always 'Peter'.

When I first knew my father, [Constance wrote] he was already quite bald, with a splendid head fringed by white curls, an eagle nose, grey eyes, and a white beard. He was a man of absolute integrity and great humanity, and a devoted father, but we were all afraid of him, because he was nervous and irritable. He almost screamed if a door banged. We sat silent in his presence – and even when I was a woman of thirty I had to frame sentences in my mind before I could speak to him.[7]

David has confirmed this picture of himself in an account he wrote two years before Constance was born, when he was only forty-one. He was then, he said, 'nearly bald, grey headed, sunken cheeked, with long grisly beard and lacklustre eyes – irritable and selfish though still for I must not write untruly with an undercurrent of tenderness and passion that I conceal.'[8]

One of the chief objects of this tenderness was his eldest son, 'young David' (born 14 January 1846), the child of his affair with his brother's serving-girl, Elizabeth Viney. Elizabeth, if she was to continue to earn a living in service, could not look after the baby, so her mother, Jane, took charge of him. David made her an allowance of twelve shillings a month and visited the boy from time to time. He was a delicate child and seemed to be acquiring a stammer. He sometimes came to stay with the family in Brighton.

But from one such visit, probably over Christmas 1850 when he was nearly five years old, young David did not return. His father was sending him away to a boarding school at Odiham. Jane Viney was distraught:

I hope you are satisfied that I have acted a Mothers part I took him when he drew his first Breath and he is as dear as my own Life . . . I sincerely hope the person Will be Kind to him and that I shall be permited to hear from him from time to time . . . pleas to be so kind as to Let mee know how you leave him poor little fellow he will feel very strang with all Strangers . . . I cannot tell you how I feel.[9]

Mr Black was not to be moved from his purpose. Young David remained at Miss Hewett's boarding school, coming back to Brighton for his holidays. His mother and his grandmother saw him occasionally; and his father sent Elizabeth presents of money from time to time, especially when some 'heartless villain' got her with child again.[10]

In April 1860, when young David was fourteen years old, his father shipped him off to Canada to learn farming as he himself had done seventeen years before. Farm labouring, which his father had found back-breaking enough as a grown man, was even harder for a lad in his teens. All the same he stuck it out for three years, and then drifted about Canada and the United States doing various clerical jobs. When the American Civil War broke out his father begged him not to enlist on either side. 'To do so in my opinion would be little better than to commit murder. It is awful to think of the beautiful and delicate mechanism of men's bodies to be so wickedly and needlessly destroyed.'[11] Despite this injunction David was drawn into joining the Federal Army. But the heavy rains in the spring of 1865 washed away the railway, and so by the time he reached the battlefield Lee had already surrendered. Eventually he married, settled in Chicago and ran a tolerably successful colour and paint business. He sent home photographs of his wife and children, but he did not return to England, so Constance never knew him except as someone whom her elder brothers and sisters remembered with affection.

His father wrote to him with news of his half-brothers and half-sisters, characteristically showing more concern for their faults than pride in their achievements:

Arthur . . . is rather disposed to be conceited but otherwise is a very good boy, he grows tall and is now five feet six in height when he stands upright which is but seldom as he stoops a great deal . . . Ernest . . . is somewhat of a dunce but a queer boy being very unlike what you were at his age in this that he saves a good deal of his pocket money (consisting of 2d a week during good behaviour) and now has more than 11/- . . .

Clementina reads fluently any French book and speaks it pretty well – she has also (unknown to me) been learning German for the last year and reads it and has an excellent pronunciation. She also gets on well with the piano and is a decidedly clever girl – the only two faults we find with her are that she dislikes needlework and has a thick inarticulate way of speaking.

Constance (the baby) begins to call everyone in the house by their separate names although her pronunciation is obscure to those who are not accustomed to her. [She was then just over two years old.][12]

Lessons – including those in German, which David was particularly well qualified to teach – were in Clara's hands, and even with a couple of servants her hands were pretty full. Once the cook turned out to be a thief and was involved with a burglar who was sentenced to three months' hard labour. At such times Clara had to cope on her own – 'I am cook and every one is pleased when that is the case.'[13]

One of the children was always ill, and, if it was measles or chickenpox or one of the other infectious diseases, several of them were. Clara must have been particularly alarmed in 1860 when Arthur, Ernest and Emma all had scarlet fever. Fortunately it was only a mild attack; for besides the memory of losing her brother and sister she was aware, for instance, that her sister-in-law had lost all but three of her thirteen children in infancy. It was small wonder that poor Mrs Glynn took to the bottle for a while before she died in April 1859. It was indeed something of a miracle that all eight of Clara's own brood survived.

In February 1869, just as she was in the middle of brewing, the builder, who had come to investigate a dampness caused by a leaking soil pipe, discovered 'a cesspool under the middle of the front kitchen. . . . I have very little doubt it has been the cause of our all being so continually ill.'[14] Moreover, the well under the wash-house was full of dirty water which smelt horrible. So, while the builder worked in bitter winter weather, they had to keep all the windows open 'except just where we sit and as soon as we go out of a room open the window, and shut it when we come back. I have scarcely been free from headache all the week'.[15]

While none of the illnesses was fatal, some were quite serious. In November 1861, a month before Constance was born, Arthur had gone down with fever and violent pain in the back of the head. He soon recovered, but was left without the use of three muscles in the right shoulder. It was poliomyelitis. He was sent away for eight months to convalesce with George Patten, who was living in retirement at Goodrich in Herefordshire. He came back tall and strong, and by the summer of 1870 Clara was reporting: 'Arthur teaches the other two boys gymnastics. We are all surprised at the wonderful strength, ease and grace with which he does a number of things. His Papa says no one would imagine that he had not the full use of both arms.'[16]

Constance, though healthy at birth, and a cheerful good-tempered baby, soon became the invalid of the family. She developed abscesses, 'one in each leg and later one on each side of the face'.[17] She was told that one of the latter had left a scar within a millimetre of the optic nerve and might easily have damaged her eyesight. Even without this threat she was extremely short-sighted, and glaring light would make her eyes ache.

Soon after she was three she was struck with a much more serious affliction. Ernest, then nearly ten years old and away at boarding school, heard from Emma in May 1865, 'Constance goes out in a handchair' and wrote to Constance: 'I am sorry your legs are so bad'.[18] Constance's earliest memory was of 'lying flat in a long bathchair with a splint bound round me from knee to waist'.[19] The disease was diagnosed as tuberculosis of the hip-joint. The bone was operated on and weights were hung to make her legs equal in length. It seems probable that the operation was a gratuitous penance. As she was not otherwise ill it is more likely that her complaint was Perthe's disease (osteochondritis of the femoral head), which generally passes off in due course without treatment.

So for a long period [she wrote] – I don't know how long – I was lying down, often in pain, but reputed very patient and good, as I became placid and cheerful whenever I was at ease. I have no doubt I was very happy in being an object of so much solicitude and affection. An extra servant was kept in order to wheel me all day up and down the sea-front – sunshine and air even then being considered the great remedy. And my carriage was often stopped by sympathetic strangers enquiring what was the matter with the sweet fair little girl. When – I think at about the age of seven – I was completely on my legs and had to take my chance with the others, I felt the difference acutely and was often very unhappy. Arthur and my mother were always very kind and gentle to me, even when I had outgrown my privileged position as an invalid.[20]

By August 1867, four months before her sixth birthday, she was sufficiently recovered for her mother to sell the invalid carriage back to the joiner who made it. In May 1868 she was bathing in the sea; though in October her grandmother was still distressed by 'poor Constance's sticks of legs'.[21] She was to be 'poor Constance' (or 'poor Connie' – all the girls were known by their diminutives) for several years to come. Constance herself recalled that:

The family were fond of long walks into the country – and often I heard, 'Don't take Connie, she can't keep up!' and dear Arthur would say, 'Oh, I'll get her along.' I can remember his carrying me the last mile or two even when I was a big girl, eight or ten. My 'bad leg' usually began to ache before the walk was half over.[22]

Constance's legs recovered enough for her to boast in old age of her prowess as a child in walking up and down steps on stilts. But there was one further alarm. When she was thirteen she had an acute attack of rheumatism in her right leg. The pain was excruciating, and Clara was worried that the old hip-joint disease had come back. 'However,' Constance wrote, 'I recovered quickly, but probably some heart weakness dates from that attack.'[23] Throughout her life her health was not to be depended on, and these childhood afflictions must have taught her very early that it was wiser to rely on her mind than her body as a source of any pleasure or achievement.

'The notion that women have minds as cultivable, and as well worth cultivating, as men's minds' wrote James Bryce, 'is still regarded by the ordinary British parent as an offensive, not to say, revolutionary, paradox.'[24] By this standard David and Clara Black were not ordinary parents. They believed passionately in education for boys and girls alike, and thought that it was too important to be left entirely to the vagaries of schools. It began at home and was a combination of mutual aid and self-improvement.

Clementina has described how she and Arthur taught themselves to read at a very early age with the aid of a 'block alphabet':

On one side they bore a large capital letter . . . on the other, a coloured picture of some creature. Eight children, in turn, thus became acquainted with such uncommon quadrupeds as the jerboa, nil-gau, quagga and yak. The blocks were packed into a neatly made box of some solid dark wood . . . and as the twenty-six letters did not suffice to fill it exactly, the gap was supplied by other blocks printed on both faces with brief monosyllables set in rows. From these stop-gaps, I believe, I learnt to read. My mother once told me that she remembered me, as a very small child, constantly seated on the floor, grasping printed matter and demanding of my elders what this or that collection of letters spelled.[25]

With the further aid of 'a little square book, illustrated by artless woodcuts',[26] Clementina learnt to read before her fourth birthday. 'From that time forward' she wrote, 'I read every book on which I could lay my hands.'[27]

The other children learnt in the same way, though none was so precocious as Arthur and Clementina, despite having their elders to help them. Arthur became a voracious reader; Clementina was constantly 'buried again'[28] in a book, as her brothers used to say; and when Emma came to draw Constance in a typical posture it was with a book held right up to her short-sighted eyes.

Constance has described her education at home:

While the elder ones and the two younger went to school, my mother taught me herself – and all the family took a hand in my education. I used to follow my mother into the kitchen repeating my lessons while she made the pies, Arthur taught me Mathematics, Ernest taught me geography and mapmaking, Clementina taught me French and German. Arthur also superintended a certain amount of elementary science teaching and performed chemical experiments in the store-room. I had a good memory and was eager to learn. Great things were expected of me by my mother and Arthur.[29]

In the summer of 1870, when Constance was eight-and-a-half, Clara arranged for an extra servant to come in one day a week, 'then I shall be able to do more justice to Constance, for I find it very difficult to give her the 1½ hours lesson every morning, and she must have it now, for I cannot afford to pay for more instruction for her until Ernest and Emma cease to require it'.[30]

Clara taught French

by letting us read with her, translating as we went along and picking up no more grammar than was necessary in order to understand the text. She chose stories likely to interest us, so that we might be eager to continue, and we learned with her in this manner until a day arrived on which, at the end of a lesson, we fetched the book and finished the story by ourselves.[31]

Not all the experiments were done by Arthur. When Constance was eleven she found out for herself how to make a freezing mixture of snow and salt. She made ice-cream out of cream and raspberry jam, and wrote to Arthur: 'It was far superior to your chemical experiments as nothing was broken and the ice was so very nice that I quite pity you for not being there.'[32]

It is hard to see how Arthur managed to find time for any teaching at all. He had done extremely well at Brighton College, a boys' public day school, and in 1868 had come out top of all the Brighton candidates in the Senior Local Examinations – and top for the whole country in political economy. He was now compliantly working in his father's office, though his real interests lay elsewhere:

he busies himself more and more in mathematics for hours every day, and at every moment he is working out the most abstruse problems; and when he finds out fresh laws and curious facts resulting from their working he has the greatest enjoyment; only it is so far from what we can understand that he is obliged to enjoy his triumphs alone.[33]

Nevertheless:

he teaches Ernest every morning, he spends all his evenings in his office so as to be able to study quietly, and Joe Rix comes nearly every evening for Arthur to help him in his Greek and Latin, and since Halliwell [one of the clerks] left he has had more to do; and he is working as hard as he can for the University Examination which is in January. All today he has been helping Ernest with his Scripture. One thing is very gratifying, that they are all very willing to assist each other and all desirous to learn.... Constance gets her lessons regularly.[34]

There seems, however, to have been one subject upon which Constance received no lessons. 'Neither my father nor my mother' she wrote, 'ever said a word to us children about religion.'[35] David was a devout

Presbyterian, but Clara, according to Constance, 'had been brought up as a free-thinker'.[36] George Patten in his retirement was quite ribaldly irreligious, dismissing Holy Communion as an insanitary habit and much of Christianity as a fraud. But Lucy and Clara were fairly frequent churchgoers, whatever their actual beliefs. All the same there were differences with David. Early in their engagement he had marked a passage in one of Clara's letters to him:

I think you did wrong (forgive me for saying so) to engage in any discussion upon religion. It never does any good, and sometimes much harm, by making those enemies who were friends before, for persons are so much formed by early associations, education, and the different sphere of life in which they may happen to be placed, that no two persons scarcely think quite in the same way on this subject.[37]

And before they were married he extracted a promise from her: 'I will go to church once of a Sunday, and if we should have children I will give them a good foundation of religious education; and I assure you solemnly I do not make this promise merely because it is your wish, but I feel that it is right.'[38]

By the time Constance was being brought up this promise seems to have lapsed. But some of the children were instructed by their teachers at school, and others by the servants at home. As a result, before she was out of the nursery, Constance was 'distressed from time to time by the thought that my mother was possibly doomed to spend eternity in hell'[39] – not that she was entirely convinced, for Clara 'was so obviously the best and sweetest person in the world'.[40] And Constance was a precociously intellectual child:

We were given to discussing the problems of the universe even in the nursery, there was the insoluble question how God could be omnipotent since he could not make the past not have been. We were quite sure he could not – nobody ever disputed that – and it seemed to fetter the omnipotent Being in his own errors.[41]

Emma came under the influence of devout friends; and Constance sometimes went with her to little gatherings at which 'a very sweet-looking young woman who was dying from consumption'[42] read aloud to them from *The Imitation of Christ* and they 'talked of the love of Jesus'.[43] Constance too was influenced:

I read Stepping Heavenward [by Elizabeth Prentiss]. I remember my mother picking it up and reading a passage about the duty of mothers to love their children because Mary loved Jesus. 'As though mothers hadn't loved their children for thousands of years before Jesus was born!' she said, laughing . . . and I began to see that a great deal in the book was silly.[44]

And so for much of her childhood she wavered between Emma's absolute faith and Arthur's agnostic rationalism.

In earlier years, when there had been fewer children to teach, David and Clara had been able to afford occasional governesses, usually teachers who were at a loose end during the holidays. Miss Howe vainly tried to teach Clementina arithmetic. Mademoiselle Elise Bleuze had come to teach French and proved a godsend. She arrived just as Arthur, Ernest and Emma went down with scarlet fever. The rest of the children were packed off into lodgings with their new governess, and in due course returned safe and well and beginning to speak French. Mademoiselle Bleuze had one unusual asset, her father kept a high-class chocolate shop in Paris, and long after she had ceased to teach the Blacks she sent them handsome presents of Bleuze confectionery.

Emma was sent away to a boarding school in Sussex Square in nearby Kemp Town, not so much for instruction as to end the constant bickering that she seemed to provoke in the other children. Once she had gone, 'we seem now all to be at peace. The children talk and laugh but do not quarrel, and she always snapped at them all.'[45] But Emma herself was wretched. She was devoted, more than any of the others, to her mother, and was desperately homesick. When she came home for the holidays she 'sought a private interview with her father and said she *could* not go back – "Please do not ask me to go back."'[46] But he was no more to be moved than he had been by Mrs Viney. He remained the autocrat of the household.

When her brother, Alfred Patten, was about to be married to Mary Watson, his first wife, Maria Nappi, having died, Clara wrote to her mother: 'It is very kind of Miss Watson to ask for Clemie to be bridesmaid. I should like it very much and so would she, but since yesterday evening I have not found a propitious moment for asking Papa's permission.'[47] This time he gave it, and there was only the problem of Clementina's dress. 'I hope they will not have bunches behind their dress or else Clemie's will have to be made unlike the others, for I cannot bear the vulgar ugly style, and Clemie, being so short and stout, would look perfectly disfigured in such a costume.'[48]

There were other such occasions, visits to stay with their grandfather in Herefordshire and, after he died, to their grandmother in London.

There were children's parties, often with their friends the Ellises and the Rixes. Annie Rix, whose father kept a jeweller's shop, was a favourite of Clara's. She was 'so earnest and intelligent, so industrious and amiable, I cannot help wishing that Annie were a child of my own, or rather that Clemie were more like her'.[49]

On Christmas Eve 1869 'The children went . . . to Uncle Peter's, where they had Christmas tree, magic lanthorn, Clemie played quadrilles twice, and they all enjoyed themselves very much. Constance had never been out to a party before.'[50] She was just eight years old.

Uncle Peter was then in his late sixties. Constance remembered him well:

He was a charming old man with a rose-leaf complexion, blue eyes and a very kind mild expression. He played the 'cello and had a grapevine, and when we children went to see him used to cut bunches of grapes for us to take a basketful home to our mother. He was always very polite and sweet to Aunt Betsy and when she came in from a walk would go to the door to meet her and say: 'I am glad to see you home again, my love.' He spent most of his last years sitting on a cork seat by some Sussex river fishing.

Aunt Betsy looked like a Frenchwoman, with very shrewd clear grey eyes. She was very capable in a quiet way.[51]

But she had no luck with her children. One was an epileptic. One died of consumption. One married an idle impoverished husband and had more children than she could cope with. There were only two of Betsy's grandchildren whom Constance felt were worth keeping in touch with.

Peter Black used to visit his brother's family when they were on their annual summer holiday and take the boys out fishing. For these holidays the family left seaside Brighton for a whole month and went some sixteen miles inland, usually to Uckfield or to nearby Sharpsbridge. They all looked forward to it, but for Clara to hire a carter to take everything to the farmhouse was a formidable operation:

of the 12 rooms very few are furnished, only three beds in all the house, and as we shall want *nine* it is utterly bewildering to me to know how they are to be got there. Bedsheets are so heavy. Why, if we took all we wanted we should have about a ton of luggage. When we went to Mrs Jenner's we had about 16 hundredweight.. . .[52]

Constance remembered delightful days on holiday:

my mother, a stout serene figure, in a full skirt of white cotton covered with black and red sprays – walking with a slow strong step along the lanes, a bunch of honeysuckle in her hands. We children were for ever grubbing happily at a cave dug out in a sandpit – till our father stopped it (perhaps just in time to save the bank from coming down on our heads).[53]

Mrs Jenner, their landlady, was 'a tall elderly woman pale with a big nose always in black, generally with her head covered with a hat or something black'.[54] When her head was uncovered the children saw to their horror that she was bald. 'She had an old father who wore a white smock and a chimneypot hat which he kept on indoors.'[55] Clara described how 'Mr Jenner put up a swing yesterday, which is a great amusement to the little ones. It is such a pretty picture when he is at work in his carpenter's workshop with Grace playing among the shavings at his feet with the sunlight on her golden hair at the wide open door.'[56]

The children played 'prisoners' among the heather and bracken, Clementina tried to bring up some motherless chicks, which ran about the bedroom, there was a shop where striped lollipops on twigs were sold – small pleasures that Constance remembered all her life.

We children [she wrote] always went back to Brighton with a lump in the throat. I can remember the sensation of struggling to swallow my tears very vividly – and Robert and I used to distract our sorrow by making lists of the things we should take to the country next year – 11 months later. To live in the country was our idea of happiness. I believe it was largely the ugliness of Brighton that oppressed us, though we did not know that then.[57]

David was oppressed by other matters. In September 1869 he had come back 'gloomy and irritable'[58] from his annual fortnight's holiday, which he usually took with a few men friends walking in the Alps. Then in November there was a bitter row in the Town Council about the new drains. David thought the new scheme would not work – but this was for the Council, not the Town Clerk, to decide. The *Brighton Observer* printed a vicious article implying that he had acted dishonestly, and had tried to obstruct the measure after it had been approved by the Council. The *Herald* and other newspapers replied in his defence. David, who had often worried without cause, was now seriously concerned about losing his job, especially as 'Mr Hallett . . . said he should never be satisfied till he had turned out the Town Clerk.'[59]

Then, on 1 January 1870, he 'had another dreadful attack of pain'.[60] He had had one two years before, and it had been diagnosed as a gall stone passing through the gall bladder. This time it was 'very alarming, such dreadful pain in the back he really thought at one time he must be dying'.[61] He had another similar attack on 4 April 1871. And then in July 1873 Clara noted a more sinister development:

13th Sunday. First observed an uncertainty in the legs in going up and down stairs and during the week became gradually worse, and on Saturday 19th consulted Mr Humphry, who suggested lead poisoning. Walked with the assistance of an umbrella to Preston St with samples of urine for Mr Moore to test for lead but none was found in it.[62]

Constance recalled how:

my father began to have difficulty in walking and very quickly lost all use of his legs. I was in the room I remember when Clementina returned home from some absence – she had not been warned – and was terribly distressed when she walked into the dining room and found my father unable to get up to greet her. He was sent – and we all went – to Crowborough, for two months' complete rest. A specialist, Dr Radcliffe, came from London. I saw him strike a match and hold it unseen to my father's foot – which did not flinch from the flame. It was locomotor ataxy.[63]

Dr Charles Bland Radcliffe had written a paper on locomotor ataxy. He told Clara:

It is not paralysis of the usual kind because he has strength and power of motion in his legs but not power of direction . . . he had better not give up work or he will become morbid . . . so that he had better. . . go out in a chair or a fly daily.[64]

Locomotor ataxy – or ataxia, as it is now called – was recognised some ten years later to be a symptom of the later stages of syphilis; and there is little doubt that for most of her life Constance believed her father to be syphilitic. David Garnett certainly did and attributed his grandfather's extreme irritability to the emotions of a dour Scots puritan suffering for his sins and beset by guilt.

But it is now clear that David Black did not have syphilis. His condition was definitely not locomotor ataxia, his symptoms then and the subsequent history of his disease were quite different. Dr Radcliffe had made a bad mistake. So what was the matter with David Black? It is hard to say; modern medical opinion can suggest nothing with confidence; multiple sclerosis and dissecting aneurism of the aorta have been offered as possibilities.

Despite Dr Radcliffe's advice, David felt it his duty to retire from Black, Freeman & Gell, and in February 1874 to resign from his post as Town Clerk. He was persuaded to remain as Coroner, and to take the salary by way of pension; the Deputy Coroner would preside at inquests. He also received a small pension from his firm. He was then fifty-six.

The ensuing events occurred when Constance was thirteen-and-a-half. They were best told in her own words:

The first great calamity (of which I knew anything) my father's breakdown in health, was the cause of a far greater one – about a year later. He did not like anybody to do things for him but my mother – she was strong in the arms, and she lifted him from his bed to his chair and so on. During this she ruptured herself. . . .

On Tuesday [24 August 1875] my mother had taken us younger children up to Ernest's little garden plot (behind Montpelier Crescent) to tea and I remember some of the things she said to me as we walked home through St Nicholas churchyard. That night I woke up to hear my mother groaning. I was for some reason on the same floor – in one of the two back rooms, and she was in the little room opening into the back drawing room which had been turned into a room for my father. I ran to her – and I don't know what I did – got hot bottles or tried to rub her. All I know is that she was in great pain, but kept saying I must go back to bed or I should catch cold. Next day the doctor came, also my grandmother, and Clemie who was away . . . was sent for, but I don't think she arrived till Thursday. A great man was to come and operate, but could not come till Thursday. . . . I don't remember the details of Wednesday and Thursday. I had fallen asleep on Thursday evening when Emmie woke me to say, 'The operation was successful.' At six on Friday I was woken again and told: 'Make haste, dress and run for Dr Humphrey, Mamma is very bad.' Why I was sent instead of one of the boys I can't tell. I remember running through the empty streets in the early morning, by the Town hall and through that little side street Pool Valley to the doctor's in the Marine Parade. Then I remember being at home again, seeing Dr Humphrey outside my mother's room – one of the back rooms she was in – asking 'May I go in?' to which he answered, 'I don't know what they wish.' I went in. My mother, unconscious and gasping in an awful way looked quite different – sunken and grey. Grandmamma was crying on one side of the bed, my poor father, crying too (which seemed almost the most dreadful thing of all) was saying 'Oh, the little monkeys, the poor little monkeys!' – his nickname for Gracie and Katie.

In the next room Robert was sitting with a book open pretending to read.[65]

Later that day, 27 August 1875, Clara died.

'I believe' Constance wrote, 'I felt not so much personal grief, as a sort of bewildered horror. To live a single day without our mother seemed like having to live without air to breathe or bread to eat.'[66]

3

The Youngest Girl in the College

David Black had long been racked by fits of guilt and depression without reason. Now he had reason enough to last for the rest of his life. He knew that he could be nothing but an encumbrance to his family as he lay wrapped in his tartan plaid or sat upright in his huge Bath chair under a tall top hat. He knew that his disability could only grow worse – though in fact it did so only imperceptibly. He was burdened with the guilt of having been the unwitting cause of his wife's death, and later perhaps with the spurious shame of having contracted what was wrongly diagnosed as a sinful disease. He cast a pall of gloom over the household that none of his own family could dispel.

For the first years, [Constance wrote] he did little but read – every book out of the Brighton circulating libraries. He ought to have subscribed to a good library, but his great dread was leaving his daughters insufficiently provided for, and he would not even go out in a bathchair more than three times a week on account of the half-crown to the man.[1]

Constance herself was shattered by her mother's death: 'I had lost everything it seemed at once, and above all the natural confidence of all young creatures in life. It left me apprehensive, hardly daring to reckon on any happiness, and feeling that life was almost worthless because so short and insecure.'[2] It was the final blow to her religious belief. Thereafter she became increasingly sceptical of all dogma, relying upon a stoic rationalism tempered by an affectionate and generous nature.

Clementina, who was just turned twenty-two, took over the task of running the house and looking after her father and the children, 'everybody quite shamelessly took it for granted that she should be sacrificed to the family and it is sad to think how we all exploited her'.[3] Arthur gave up the unrewarding job of lawyer's clerk and earned a pittance coaching candidates for examinations in mathematics.

Constance could no longer be educated at home, and her father, prejudiced perhaps in favour of boarding schools by his own happy days at Lübeck, somehow found the money to send her away to one. She had never been to school before, though shortly before her mother's death she had attended some University Extension Lectures on Latin given by the Principal of Brighton College. She was then only twelve, while

The five or six other students were all women. We read Erasmus. I was the best in the class. My mother received flattering reports of me, and I had every influence to make me conceited. I used to have cocoa and delicious home-made cake downstairs in the room behind the kitchen before going off on the long walk and bus ride to the College, my mother sitting beside me.[4]

Things were very different now.

Annie Rix, whom Clara had found so exemplary, and her sister Mary had taken over a school in Sussex Square, and the plan was that Constance should go as a boarder and the 'little ones' as day girls. But Grace and Kate 'very sensibly took measles the first week and never went back',[5] so Constance was left on her own. She was very out of place. The other girls were a revelation to her: 'they thought and talked of little but dress and "coves", as they called young men'.[6] She hated the rules and the discipline, though she was not by nature a rebel:

I . . . took to saying 'Rien' or 'Nichts' when we were asked how many marks we had earned, to save myself the trouble of remembering how many I had lost for deportment, conduct, not speaking French or German, unpunctuality, untidiness, etc. This non-plussed the authorities, and I was once sent to bed for a whole day as a punishment – which seemed a ridiculous penalty for a grown-up girl in long skirts.[7]

Because she was an unbeliever and did not say her prayers she was not allowed to sleep in a dormitory and corrupt the other girls. She had to share a small room with the French mistress, who had her nation's horror of fresh air. When she could stand the fug no longer, Constance used to creep out in the early hours and 'sit on the stairs reading Shelley and trying to write verse in imitation'.[8]

The teaching was indifferent. Barclay Phillips, the secretary of the Local Examinations Board, old, bald and patronizing to the girls in his prize-giving orations, made them learn Euclid by heart, half a proposition at a time 'apparently supposing that understanding one was beyond our female brains'.[9] Though Constance was the worst dressed and probably the poorest girl in the school, she was so far ahead of the others in everything except French and German that she had to have most of her lessons on her own.

In the end her imagination helped her to survive. 'I became curiously popular . . . because of my ability to concoct endless romances, and there was competition to walk with me, or sit beside me.'[10]

Nevertheless she was miserable, and she was often overcome by fits of hysterical weeping. She was even tempted by thoughts of suicide, especially when the school was out walking by the cliffs along Rottingdean Road. Fortunately, after a year of this, Arthur realised that something had to be done and rescued her. In later life she said that she was glad she had had that year at Sussex Square, 'it has thrown all the rest of my life into relief'.[11]

Meanwhile there had been another great change for the Black family. In the autumn, while Constance was still at school, they moved out of 58 Ship Street to somewhere smaller and less expensive. When she returned for the Christmas holidays she found them at 40 Buckingham Place, a tall narrow house that looked as if it had been pinched between its neighbours. It was very depressing:

two wretched little rooms on each floor facing north – comfortless. There was not one room in which one felt it possible to settle down – they were all like perches. Arthur. . . had a horrible basement room (facing north too) completely lined with books. He and Ernest shared a tiny attic as a bedroom. The only place I liked to sit in was the little conservatory about 6 foot square with a grapevine in it.[12]

It seemed all the more depressing because she was so unhappy.

Arthur was able to rescue Constance from Sussex Square because there was now a much more suitable school for her to go to. On 8 June 1876 the Girls' Public Day School Company announced its plans for a new High School for Girls in Brighton. This company had been founded in 1872 to improve the education of girls by setting up public schools – that is to say they were run by an elected and accountable committee, unlike the private schools, which might be ruled at the whim of any Squeers who chose to do so. The new school was to be at Milton Hall, 75 Montpelier Street, and the committee refused to be deterred by the building still being unfinished or by a disparaging editorial in the *Brighton Gazette* which argued that High School 'seems to provide a school too high for the middle and too low for the upper class'.[13]

The new headmistress, Edith Creak, had been chosen for her academic ability, not for her age or respectability. She was still a few weeks short of her twenty-first birthday, and it was said she was worried lest the documents she had to sign in her capacity as headmistress might therefore be legally invalid. She had already had an exceptional career. Her father ran a private preparatory school at Hove, and she had been educated there in a classroom of boys – far better than she could have been in any girls' school of the time. In 1870 she won a scholarship, founded by John Stuart Mill, to Cambridge, the first woman to do so. There were no women's colleges there then, and the movement that was to culminate in Newnham College had only just begun. Anne Jemima Clough had come from Liverpool and taken a house to lodge women so that they might attend lectures. At first these had to be given especially for them, but later some of the men's lecturers allowed women into theirs. Edith Creak was one of the first five who arrived in the autumn of 1871. She was only sixteen, and the others were much older, one of them thirty. Apart from Edith, they were all good-looking women, so much so that their mentor, Henry Sidgwick, anxious for their morals, lamented their 'unfortunate personal appearance'.[14] But Edith's appearance really was unfortunate. She was large and fat and plain. Everyone agreed, however, that she was a remarkable character and a prodigy of intelligence and learning.

At first the women had no intention of sitting for the same examinations as the men, and many left Cambridge without ever having done so. But special arrangements were made, and the women were told, if only unofficially, what their examination results would have been had they been men. Some examiners would barely do that. The Newnham records report that in 1875 'Edith E. M. Creak passed the Mathematical Tripos, Class III, and the Classical Tripos. The Classical examiners objected to state what Class was obtained, but it was generally known to be Class II'[15] – not particularly good results by today's standards, but today's students do not work under the handicaps that Edith Creak had to suffer. With these grudging qualifications, and no practical experience, Miss Creak was briefly Assistant Mistress at Plymouth High School before coming to Brighton.

The new High School for Girls duly opened on 13 June 1876 for the last half-term before the holidays. There were only seventeen girls to start with, but the numbers soon grew. One of Miss Creak's first pupils recalled that 'there was not much in her manner or rules which suggested that she had ever had much to do with girls, or at any rate with girls'

Schools. There was a pleasing, easy-going way with her that put us at our ease. She came with no hard and fast rules about School conduct: these grew up with the needs of increasing numbers.'[16]

Constance has left no account of her time at the High School, which probably began in the autumn of 1876, but she was proud of having been there, and there is no doubt that it provided not only a relief from the miseries of Sussex Square, but also a partial escape from the sad cramped quarters in 40 Buckingham Place.

She was not the only one trying to get away. Robert, who was determined to be a doctor, began working as an apprentice in the Brighton Hospital at the age of sixteen. Emma soon escaped to London as a 'probationer' studying at the Royal Academy Schools and lodging over a china shop at 26 Albany Street. After a while Clementina joined her to begin a career as a novelist and social reformer. The household was left in charge of a succession of lady-housekeepers, whom Constance did not think much of, until Kate was old enough to leave school. David Black was then able to dispense with the services of these unattractive ladies, and thereafter Kate and Ernest, the most dutiful and least enterprising of the children, ran the household and looked after their crippled father.

Constance was not a particularly ambitious or competitive girl. But she was intelligent and she liked learning for its own sake. So she did well in her examinations, though she never enjoyed them. School examinations run by Oxford and Cambridge Universities had been held for nearly thirty years, but there were still relatively few candidates entering for them and not many places where they were held. Arthur had done brilliantly in the Oxford examinations, and Robert very creditably in the Cambridge. Constance sat the Cambridge Junior Local soon after going to Sussex Square and was one of the four who gained third class honours out of the fourteen Brighton girls who passed. Two years later she did much better in the Senior Local, getting second class honours and carrying off Macaulay's *History of England* and two other books as prizes. She sat the Senior Local again in 1878 and did even better than before. She passed with first class honours in Religious Knowledge, English, Latin, French, German and Mathematics. Her friend Amy Levy got second class honours, two other girls third class honours, and a further sixteen passed without honours. Miss Creak had seven successful candidates, while no other girls' school in Brighton had more than two. Constance gained a distinction in English, and her marks overall were higher than those of any of the other three thousand girls who sat the examination in England.

This had one consequence that was far more important than the usual prize-giving, with speeches by the Mayor and Barclay Phillips, at which Constance, if the *Brighton Herald* is to be believed, was once again rewarded with a set of Macaulay's *History of England*.

One day in the spring of 1879 [she wrote] – I think the Easter holidays – I was in bed, as so often, with a bad cold when a letter came offering me the scholarship for Newnham, given to the best girl in the 1st Class of the Cambridge Senior Local Examinations. . . . It was £35 for 3 years. I hurriedly dressed in a tremor of excitement and uncertainty whether my father out of his greatly diminished income would afford to let me go. [The fees then were £60 a year.] To my intense relief he seemed pleased and said that I should go.[17]

Constance went up to Cambridge in October 1879 with two other pupils of Miss Creak's, Amy Levy and Ellen Huggett, and signed the Newnham register as its 129th student. She was only seventeen. The age limit had been raised since Miss Creak's day, and she was the youngest girl in the college. She had never left Sussex until earlier that summer. A Newnham group photograph shows her as a smallish girl in a plain close-fitting dark dress, rather plumper and more full-bosomed than she was later to be, her fine fair hair parted in the centre and drawn back close to her head, and her weak eyes, usually hidden behind small unbecoming spectacles, screwed up tight against the light. It does not reveal her fair skin and fine complexion, which showed all too clearly when she blushed, as often from pleasure as from shame, but always at this stage of her life to her embarrassment, for she was still very shy and insecure.

The college had been established in Newnham Hall since 1875. Its design was in complete contrast to the uncompromising – some would say hideous – Victorian red-brick Gothic that was shortly to be erected at Girton. For whereas Emily Davies, Mistress of the sister college, intended her students to compete with men on equal terms, and if possible beat them at their own game, Henry Sidgwick, the promoter of Newnham, wanted to change the rules. Having for the moment failed to reform the Cambridge curriculum, the theological restrictions upon dons and students, and other obsolete regulations, he wanted to use the first women's college as a proving ground for his educational theories. It was to be a congenial environment, with green lawns where students could walk and talk and sit under the trees with their books; and the new building adopted the domestic Dutch style of William and Mary in red brick with neat white doors and windows. It stood four-square and alone, less than a mile from the centre of Cambridge, in two acres of its own grounds, with nothing beyond it but the flat and empty Cambridgeshire landscape. One could have been in the depths of the country. Nightingales sang. There were sheep and cattle in the adjacent fields, and within the college grounds were Miss Clough's hens and the pigs belonging to Jonathan Smith, the college 'man'.

For Constance Cambridge was a liberation. Brighton had seemed ugly to her because she was so unhappy there, and 40 Buckingham Place especially so. Now her joy at escaping from that oppressive house was not merely an emotional but also an aesthetic experience. From Newnham one approaches the old colleges by way of the Backs, one of the handsomest prospects in England. 'The beauty of Cambridge was overwhelming,' she wrote, 'it made me feel too much moved. I was constantly wanting to cry. I had never imagined such a lovely place. I had never seen a beautiful building before.'[18]

She was one of the fortunate eleven out of forty-six newcomers to be lodged in Newnham Hall. All the rest were in hostels or lodgings outside. 'It was a great delight to have a room – bedroom and study in one – to myself – and the rather barely furnished pretty room seemed to me enchanting.'[19] Another student of this time has described how these bed-sitting rooms were managed:

Getting to bed is a matter of some time here. The sofa has to be converted into a bed, the cushions changing their hue from red to white; the bureau has to be cleared for a dressing-table, and books, blotter and pens exchanged for brush and comb, hairpins etc; the screen has to be removed from the washstand and the towel-horse brought forward from obscurity; and lastly the easy chairs have to be pushed against the walls to make room for the bath, which is brought in in the morning. . . .[20]

There was a strict protocol for new arrivals, as one of them explained in a letter home:

In the afternoon I was 'at Home' and had a perfect stream of callers, all the students are expected to call on each new girl and these calls have to be returned at the end of the week; and as the wretched girls neither tell me their names nor their residences I shall have a piece of work to find out who they all are.[21]

This was made more difficult because most social life took place late in the evening, and the lights were turned off at ten o'clock. After that 'the students are left dependent upon their own lamps and candles. This increases the misery of the new student, who generally leaves a burnt-out match at every door, to denote her fruitless search for a hostess of whose name, even, she has but a rudimentary conception. . ..'[22]

Another trial was the food:

The food is distinctly not good, everyone is agreed on that; the puddings are practically untouchable, the preserved stewed fruit is often fermented, the meat is sometimes raw and generally semi-tepid; vegetables few and far between; people say they only give us what is grown in the garden; these are for the most part turnips.[23]

In other respects they were well looked after. Miss Clough was fifty-nine when Constance came up. She had a strong kindly face and dressed in voluminous clothes with a lace cap always pinned on the back of her head. To her students she was a 'dear old lady'. One of them wrote, 'During one's first two or three weeks she would come up several times to each new student's room and sit talking till she knew all about them and their surroundings; and after that she would never repeat a question nor get mistaken about any detail.'[24] She carried trays up to the sick, and was more concerned for her girls' general welfare than their academic achievements. Of the forty-six students who came up in 1879 only eleven took the Tripos.

Nevertheless Newnham was expanding. The new North Hall was opened in 1880. Women from Newnham and Girton were beginning to be accepted at Cambridge. In 1878 King's College had opened all its lectures to them. Others followed. But the girls still had to have a 'chap' – or chaperon – wherever they went. At lectures the chaperon sat at the end of the bench 'to ward off attack and prevent escape'.[25]

Constance had originally intended, probably under Arthur's influence, to take up Natural Sciences, but wisely opted for Classics and Mathematics, at which she had already shown such proficiency, although she had been studying Greek for less than a year. She soon dropped Mathematics and concentrated on Latin and Greek. She was particularly attracted by Greek. She enjoyed mastering the subtleties of its grammar and syntax. But above all the richness and beauty of its literature appealed to her aesthetic sense, and its philosophy was much more congenial to her rational and questioning turn of mind than the Religious Knowledge that she had been examined in at school.

Mathematics and Classics had always been the staple of European education, and Latin and Greek provided the key to the private club to which the civil and military rulers of the empire belonged. Latterly they had become a more serious field for academic study, and the emphasis had begun to shift to archaeology, ancient history and philosophy. But much of the teaching was still linguistic, and so Constance gained a rigorous training in the art of translation and developed great skill in expressing precise meanings.

She soon showed her abilities at Cambridge. Francis Jenkinson, who lectured on Greek, was her favourite teacher, and she, though as usual the youngest, his star pupil. 'Whenever there was a difficult, or a particularly beautiful passage,' she recalled, he would say 'Miss Black, would you try that?'[26] And when she did, the result was usually an example to the rest of the class.

Her particular friend was Edith Sharpley, another Classics student, a doctor's daughter from Lincolnshire, who was nearly three years older, though she looked even younger. She was a 'very quiet, real student scholar type – a little tired and rather frail',[27] Constance wrote, and felt herself 'a bit vulgar, bouncing and robust'[28] by comparison. Edith wrote that Constance was her 'chum in all work and in discussion of things in general'.[29] Her other friends at Newnham included two who had come up before her and were to become members of Cambridge's intellectual aristocracy: Florence Ada Brown, daughter of a Bedford minister and later wife of John Neville Keynes and thus mother of Maynard, Margaret and Geoffrey Keynes; and Ellen Crofts, who was already Newnham's lecturer in English literature and was shortly to marry the widowed Francis Darwin. In due course she became the mother of Frances Cornford and aunt of Gwen Raverat. Her niece was much struck by her advanced literary tastes and the fact that she smoked cigarettes – the only other women Gwen knew who were 'fast' enough to do so were Alice Lloyd and Jane Harrison.[30] Alice Lloyd was another of Constance's friends at Newnham. She was 'a dapper little figure' with 'bright brown eyes',[31] who became an active journalist, and under her married name of Dew-Smith wrote two agreeably dotty books on *Soul Shapes* and *Spiritual Gravitation*.

As for 'the great Miss Harrison', Constance admired her 'from my lowly distance'.[32] Jane Harrison, who had been known as 'the cleverest girl in England',[33] had taken top marks in the Philosophy Tripos of 1879 and was now studying archaeology at the British Museum. Constance remembered her as a visitor 'in the "aesthetic" dress of the period with a belt of two silver chains – the lower one round her hips giving the effect of some Greek statue'.[34] As Jane Harrison's contemporary, Mary Paley Marshall, wrote,

This was the Pre-Raphaelite period, and we papered our rooms with Morris, bought Burne Jones photographs, and dressed accordingly. We played lawn-tennis and Jane Harrison designed the embroidery for our tennis dresses. Hers was of pomegranates and mine of Virginia creeper and we sat together in the evenings and worked at them and talked.[35]

Tennis was played on some rather indifferently made courts: 'from their earliest days large stone ink-bottles have occasionally come through, and the ground has therefore not been at all true'.[36] Some students had tried to get up cricket matches, but Miss Clough disapproved and forbade them.

Social life was almost entirely within the college. New student societies, usually with bizarre names, were being founded all the time. If one was not pressed by working for the Tripos one could enjoy a 'cocoa' almost every night. Some girls did receive presents of wine and even port from their parents, but these do not seem to have formed part of Newnham's modest social life. This suited Constance well, for she was desperately short of money. Her dresses were cheap or cast-offs – never made by a dressmaker. She had no decent shoes or underclothes. And when she had to have her teeth pulled out she could afford no more than the basic half-crown fee, not the extra for the anaesthetic, 'though I was (and have always been) a fearful coward about pain'.[37] Nevertheless she enjoyed her time at Cambridge.

'The social life of Newnham was a great thing for my development,' she wrote, 'but what was most precious was the revelation of the aesthetic side of life – of which I had hardly the faintest idea except in the beauty of the country. Only at this stage I became aware that this was what more than anything else made the harmony and happiness of life.'[38] At Cambridge, by her account, what mainly moved her was the beauty of the buildings. After she went down she was far more responsive to the beauty of music and literature. Though she had an excellent sense of colour, the objects that she prized were chosen more for their associations than their looks. Moreover her sight was always too poor for her to appreciate such distant beauties as the stained glass in the windows of King's College Chapel or the details of the pinnacles around its roof. Yet the beauty of the old university was able to release those pent-up feelings that she had not dared to give way to in the last few years at Brighton. 'Almost all the while I was at Cambridge,' she wrote, 'I was in an excessively emotional state – thrilled and almost weeping with delight, or downcast and despondent to the point of despair. Though I worked at my subjects, my intellectual interests and ambitions seemed in abeyance.'[39]

Despite these overwrought emotions she survived the first part of the Classical Tripos, getting a II.3 in 1882, the university having by then agreed to class women's results along with the men's. During her final year she specialised in Greek philosophy, which must have provided some intellectual interest, whatever she may afterwards have said. She was also involved in one of Newnham's more public occasions. Besides all the activities of the various social clubs, there was an annual debate held in Hall under the eyes of Miss Clough and the rest of the staff. One gets the impression that the principal speakers were chosen by lot and the motion to be debated drawn out of a not very well filled hat. Be that as it may, in October 1882 it differed little from one debated two years before, and read 'that dramatic art is demoralising in its effect alike upon producer and public',[40] a proposition that Clara Black would have thought absurd, and even David would hardly have countenanced. Constance had to propose it, while it was opposed by her friend, Ada Radford. Ada (known to many of her friends as Audrey) had come up two years after Constance, though she was two years older. She was 'an attractive figure, with yellow hair, a pink and white complexion, very blue eyes behind steel-rimmed spectacles and hands and arms as shapely as any sculptor could wish. . . . With the merest flick of the tongue she revealed what was humorous and what was sane.'[41] Her brother, Ernest, and his future wife, Dollie Maitland, were already close friends of Clementina's. The debate must have been an ordeal for Constance, for, intelligent and articulate though she was, she was no public speaker. It is hardly surprising that she lost the motion by 47 votes to 7. However her friendship with Ada survived this unhappy evening, and she remained one of her dearest friends long after they had both left Newnham.

The following summer Constance sat for part two of the Classical Tripos. Dollie Maitland came up to see her and Ada Radford and to enjoy May Week after the examinations were over. She reported to Ernest Radford, 'Connie has finished her tripos, and seems very well: but there are several drooping people around.'[42] That was not how it felt to Constance herself. 'The actual Tripos examination,' she wrote, 'lasting 6 hours a day for 6 days, was so terribly exhausting that I felt that nothing would have induced me to go in for it if I had realised what it would be. It was like a bad illness from which one only slowly recovered.'[43] The results were published on 16 June 1883. The examiners were more than satisfied with Constance and Edith Sharpley and awarded them both First Class Honours.

This had two consequences. Firstly it confirmed in Constance's mind what she had been aware of ever since her mother and Arthur expected 'great things' of her: she was more intelligent than most other people. She had what in the parlance of the day was called a 'first-class mind', no matter that it failed utterly at a few things and never enabled her to understand, for instance, the workings of any kind of machinery. She came to her own conclusions, and her opinions were not received at second hand. This could have led to intellectual arrogance, but it rarely did so because she had no ambition to dominate other people and was still painfully shy and insecure. In one respect it made her intolerant. She hated to see stupid people in positions of authority, whether as husbands with power over wives or politicians with power over people at large.

The second consequence was that Newnham Council appointed her a lecturer in Classics. This was a temporary arrangement for Michaelmas term only. After that Edith Sharpley would take over permanently. No reason was given for this unusual arrangement. Perhaps Miss Sharpley had other commitments which made her unavailable until the New Year. Constance later wrote, 'it was a toss-up whether she or I stayed on as lecturer. I had done better in the Tripos – but she was quite obviously likely to make a better teacher. How thankful I am that she got the job! College is the right place for her.'[44] Edith Sharpley was popular with her students, who were surprised to find her 'a little thin pale girlish creature . . . so nice and clever'.[45] She remained as Classical lecturer until 1910, and thereafter in other posts at Newnham for most of the rest of her life.

Had Constance done well in her single term, Newnham might have found a means to extend her appointment. But she was not a good lecturer, and the academic life was not congenial to her. Moreover, as so often, her health let her down. She had to find another career.

4

The Nicest Set of People

Constance needed to earn a living if she was not to be a burden upon her father, and there was virtually only one career open to educated women. A few found administrative posts, but most of those who had been at Newnham became schoolmistresses. Of the forty-five who came up to the college with Constance in 1879 twenty-seven became assistant mistresses in girls' schools, and eight of those went on to become headmistresses,[1] so it was natural to assume that Constance was destined to become a teacher. But Miss Clough felt that her health was not up to working in a school, and advised her to 'go into a family'.

Robert Owen White, JP, was a wealthy cement manufacturer who had recently moved into a house at 180 Cromwell Road. He had seven children, four sons and three daughters. Constance was employed to 'stimulate the minds' of the elder girls, aged sixteen and seventeen, and to educate Olive, 'a charming child of twelve'.[2] This was probably at the instigation of Mrs White, whom she found 'much more refined'[3] than her philistine husband.

Apart from some coaching and lecturing in her special subjects, Constance had never done any teaching before. She later proved herself an excellent teacher, but at that time it was a job she had no particular taste for and was often bored by, so, until something better turned up, she did her best and gave the elder girls a course of reading based on Macmillan's English Men of Letters series and provided the younger with a thorough education. Many years later Olive White sought Constance out and told her that she had Opened her eyes to a different world – so that she believed she would have been quite another woman and her life much less interesting'[4] if Constance had not been her governess for two years. 'She probably exaggerated,' Constance remarked, 'but of course a very little turn in direction may lead to vast changes of outlook.'[5]

For this work she was paid a hundred pounds a year 'all found', not at all a bad wage. For the first time in her life she could afford some decent clothes, and she spent nearly half of her income on them. Her friends noticed two contradictory strands in her character. She liked pretty clothes and at times could be quite gay and frivolous, at others, and in other respects, she was austere and almost puritanical. She liked to say, with her unquestioning faith in heredity, that she derived these traits from her grandmothers, the lighter side from Lucy Patten and the darker from Clementina Black.

The house in Cromwell Road, large though it was, was none too big for nine Whites and several servants, and she was given a room of her own in Wright's Lane, where she could breakfast alone and have her evenings to herself. This was a great liberation, as dinners with the Whites could be a strain for a shy young woman. Once she found herself sitting next to a bishop who became so engrossed in talking to her about Greek tragedy that he absent-mindedly put his wine-glass into his coat-tail pocket. She was too shy to make any remark, and had to leave with Mrs White and the rest of the ladies before her neighbour discovered his mistake.[6]

She made full use of her evenings 'going to concerts and meetings, to my sisters and to various friends'.[7] Three of her sisters, Clementina, Emma and Grace, were already established in London with their own circle of friends, many of whom became Constance's friends also. The three Blacks had been living in rather seedy lodgings at 26 Albany Street east of Regent's Park. Emma had been the first to come to London when she won a scholarship to the Royal Academy Schools in 1877. She was a talented painter in a straightforward and unpretentious way and won a silver medal in 1878.

Clementina, who had joined her only after spending a while in Brighton, teaching and looking after the Black family, had learned to take responsibility and was the head of the little household in London. She was an intelligent and enterprising woman, with two very diverse aspects to her character and career which are well illustrated by anecdotes from her later life. When she was old and frail she took a ride on the top of an omnibus on a blustery March day and was inspired to write:

> The West wind from the ocean
> Is blowing clean and strong,
> The trees are in commotion,
> The throstle cock's in song,

And men who live in houses
Dream from behind their bars
Of battles and carouses
And nights beneath the stars.[8]

And she once went to the Houses of Parliament with her solicitor in the hopes of seeing a Bill passed. It was thrown out, and as she was leaving she said to him, 'Well, Robert, if that is the law we must change it.' And they did.[9]

Constance shared both these traits but in a different measure. Clementina only dreamed of 'nights beneath the stars', and wrote about them in romantic novels and stories – a sort of female Anthony Hope or John Buchan. But Constance's taste for adventure led her on occasion to emerge from behind her bars and make romance a reality. On the other hand, though she was always acutely aware of political questions, she made fewer forays into active politics than Clementina, who from the 1890s onwards was a constant campaigner for women's rights, and especially for women's trade unions.

By the time Constance arrived in London in 1884 Emma had left the lodgings in Albany Street. Despite considerable misgivings because she had nocturnal epilepsy and some other complaint that made her doubtful whether she was fit to bear children, she had eventually given in to his importunities and on 13 September 1883 married the Rev. James Dean Keriman Mahomed.

He was a handsome man with fair hair and blue eyes, and had it not been for his name, which he pronounced *Kree*-man *May*-o-med, one could not have guessed at his exotic origins. He was a grandson of one of the more remarkable notabilities in Regency Brighton. Sake Deen Mahomed had been born at Patna in Hindustan in 1749 and served as a surgeon with the East India Company before coming to England in 1784. In due course he settled in Brighton and began to minister to the Prince Regent and his entourage. His baths on the sea-front provided 'Shampooing; or . . . the Indian Medicated Vapour Bath' – what a contemporary called 'stewing alive with steam' – as well as 'Hot and Cold Sea-water Baths, Wooptong or Paste, Shower and Douch Baths'.[10] In 1822 he published a book on the subject full of testimonies, three of them in verse, to the remarkable cures he had effected, and a long list of satisfied customers. In due course he became Shampooing Surgeon to King George IV and died in 1851 at the age of 102.[11] His son Arthur continued to run the bath-house until 1870, when it became a hotel (now the Queen's Hotel), while another, Frederick, Keriman's father, established a gymnasium and fencing school in Hove. There the young Blacks sometimes went dancing; and there Keriman met and fell in love with Emma.

Constance thought it a disastrous match and described the six-year engagement as 'a misery',[12] adding that 'She refused him several times but he battered her into accepting him at last.'[13] A niece remembers Keriman as a kindly uncle, but there is no doubt that Constance hated him. She described him as 'huge, handsome, and stupid',[14] and wrote of the marriage that 'if my mother had been living I feel sure she would have prevented it. . . . It was unsuitable physically, morally, mentally and socially. The Mahomeds were inferior in manners, breeding and brains; and Keriman "had the skin of a rhinoceros".'[15] Constance was never a snob in the ordinary sense, being quite immune to the appeal of rank and status, and prejudiced, if anything, in favour of the coloured races, but she lived in an age before class had displaced sex as a taboo subject, and she had no inhibitions about describing people as 'refined' or 'common' if that was what she thought they were. She was, of course, writing with hindsight after Keriman had made his wife's life thoroughly wretched, and Emma had nearly died in childbed more than once. But for the moment the happy couple set up house in Lewisham Road, Highgate, where Keriman had a curacy at St Anne's, while Clementina remained in Albany Street with her sister Grace, who had joined them in 1882.

Grace, who had come to London to study art in the British Museum, was then eighteen and, as Constance wrote, was 'what is called an "idealist", which meant that she loved everything beautiful, and was almost terrified by everything ugly'.[16] She was courageous and strong-willed, and rather alarming in the way that she pursued her ideals, be they 'truth' or 'socialism', to the exclusion of all else. She was a beautiful girl with 'an incomparably more lovely face' than the celebrated May Morris.[17] Two years later Emma painted Grace's portrait, which in due course was hung in the Royal Academy entitled 'Sweet and Twenty' – though 'sweet' is not the word one would choose to describe her.

Like Grace, Clementina was often in the British Museum researching her historical novels. It was a great place for striking up friendships. In the spring of 1881 two friends of hers, Dollie and Tussy, had noticed a handsome young man in the Reading Room, and they both took the liberty of leaving their cards at his desk. He was Ernest Radford, one of the ten children of a prosperous and intellectual Baptist draper from Plymouth, and a brother of Constance's Cambridge friend, Ada. He had more or less abandoned the law to become an apostle of the arts and crafts movement and a disciple of William Blake and Walt Whitman. He lectured to great effect and wrote poetry on every occasion. Dollie Maitland (her real name Caroline was never used), who married Radford in 1883, was also a poet and writer. David Garnett wrote that 'her gay silliness was one of her chief charms, as she was seldom *purely* silly: it was almost always mixed with so much fancy, such sudden spurts of imagination, and so qualified by little gusts of laughter at herself that one would have had to be a very hard-hearted and humourless person to resist her'.[18] And D. H. Lawrence portrayed her in later years in more melancholy terms as Hattie Redburn in *Kangaroo*: 'a staunch little soul . . . with her cameo face, like a wise child . . . with grey bobbed hair, and wide, unyielding eyes'.[19] She was a close friend of Clementina's, and 'Constance loved her dearly'.[20]

Tussy was Eleanor, the youngest daughter, then aged twenty-six, of Karl Marx. She was an intelligent, neurotic young woman, a loyal disciple of her father, but with an unlucky taste in men. She had taught for a while in 1873–4 at a school in Sussex Square, Brighton, though not apparently one of those that the young Blacks went to. She may well have met Clementina there, or once again in the British Museum. At all events they became good friends, and by October 1881 Tussy was asking Clementina to sit with her mother when she was dying. Their friendship was as much literary as political, and Clementina, Ernest and Dollie were members of the Dogberry play-reading club which met at the Marxes' house at 41 Maitland Park Road.

Karl Marx died in March 1883, and Tussy had a severe breakdown. In the summer of the following year she took up with Edward Aveling, whom Dollie thought 'fit only for contempt'[21] and few of her friends could like. As a result she faded out of Clementina's life.

Much of Clementina's and the Radfords' social life centred on The Club. Clementina was president for four months in 1881 and secretary for the whole of 1884. It met once a fortnight, the meetings being alternately devoted to 'discussion and social intercourse'. The 'discussion' meetings often included a paper: Ernest's brother George on 'the historical use of the imagination' in January 1884 and William Archer, the translator of Ibsen, 'an excellent paper entitled "The Shakspere Myth"', a month later.[22] And at the social evenings someone sometimes sang. The Club had been founded as 'The Men and Women's Club' in 1880, and women were always prominent – Dollie Radford was twice elected President – and rule 20, 'Members shall be officially known by their Christian and surname without the conventional prefix',[23] seemed to show a deliberate attempt to avoid sexism.

Constance started going to The Club soon after she arrived in London, perhaps only as a guest, but more likely as a full member. In those early months of 1884 Dollie's diary records the advent of a new acquaintance, who was a 'Very interesting, and an amusing speaker' and whom she had heard at the Browning Society meeting on 22 February.[24] A week later: 'Mr. Shaw came to lunch: vegetarian fare on his account! He is a wonderful talker – very Irish – very weird in appearance.'[25] On 15 March he came to a musical evening at which Grace and Clementina were also present. On the 20th Constance called in the morning and Shaw in the evening, and it cannot have been long afterwards that Constance got to know him well.

George Bernard Shaw was then twenty-seven and had been living with his mother at 36 Osnaburgh Street for the last couple of years. He had been trying without much success to earn a living from literature, writing novels that no one would publish, and compiling a glossary and index to an edition of Thomas Lodge, a minor Elizabethan writer that Edmund Gosse had just edited. He worked in the British Museum; it was there that he had met William Archer, who was the dramatic critic of the *World*, and who got him his first regular work reviewing books and plays. He breakfasted on porridge and cocoa, dined at the Wheatsheaf Vegetarian Restaurant in Rathbone Place and occasionally took 'tea' – cocoa and brown bread – at the ABC teashop.

He turned up at political and literary meetings . . . looking like a fairly respectable plasterer, his cuffs trimmed with scissors, his black coat green with age, his boots shabby and cracked, his tall hat worn back to front because the brim was broken. The effect of his odd appearance, intensified by his angular figure and reddish beard that made him resemble a pantomime demon, was offset by his sardonic wit, the engaging Irish brogue which softened his voice, and an overt pride which saved him from being a pathetic scarecrow.[26]

A year later his ne'er-do-well father died in Ireland, and he inherited a hundred pounds. He spent fifteen of them on a new suit, a strange garment made out of undyed wool stockinette by Dr Jaeger's Sanitary Woollen System Company Limited. Thereafter he looked like a toy made for a child by an inexpert knitter.

On 10 May 1884 Shaw made his first appearance at a meeting of the Fabian Society and immediately began to influence its purpose and direction. It had been founded by Edward Pease the previous October. Pease was a shy young stockbroker who thought himself 'too conscientious when young'[27] and recalled that he 'rapidly became Secretary of whatever I was connected with'[28] – including, of course, the Fabians. The society did not acquire its name until January of the following year. Frank Podmore provided a spurious reference to Quintus Fabius Maximus, the cautious patrician commander and hero of Livy's account of the Second Punic War, who knew how to wait 'though many censured his delays; but when the time comes you must strike hard'.[29] These early Fabians consisted of 'young, earnest political novices who had no contacts with working-class life and no experience of agitation',[30] and for whom 'The notion of waiting was a good deal more appropriate . . . than was the prospect of striking hard.'[31]

There was much for these political novices to be concerned about. For instance in Ireland there was an agricultural slump, and tenants could not pay their rent. In 1880 their landlords – mostly absentee English – evicted more than ten thousand of them, the Irish responded with 'boycott, riot and murder',[32] and there were more British soldiers in Ireland keeping down the insurrection than were needed to police the whole of India. Conditions in the poorer parts of London in the pestilential 'rookeries' depicted so graphically by Doré were appalling. 'More than one Londoner in three lived in families huddled six to a room; more than one in eight died in the workhouse.'[33]

The Fabians' first tract addressed the fundamental question, *Why are the Many Poor?* They believed that competition, far from being the panacea for all ills invoked by today's conservatives, was itself evil:

Let the least depression take place in the labor market, and the worker is pitted against his fellow. The poverty of one is underbid by the greater need of another; and the competition for work reduces the highest wage of some and the lowest wage of all occupations to a pittance just above the starvation point, at which the least failure of health or work leads to pauperism.[34]

The solution was for the workers to combine in socialism, which was explained in simple terms in *What Socialism is*:

Socialism means securing equal rights and opportunities for all. The Socialists are trying to have the land and machinery 'socialized,' or made the property of the whole people, in order to do away with idle owners, and keep the whole product for those whose labor produces it. The establishment of Socialism, when once the people are resolved upon it, is not so difficult as might be supposed.[35]

But how should they ensure that the whole people were resolved upon it? Should they address themselves to the educated classes and gain their support, or should they try to rouse the unemployed? These were still fairly new questions in England. In Russia the policy of 'going to the people' had been tried only ten years before. It had become almost a crusade for hundreds of dedicated young men and women who were concerned at the plight of the people. The peasants had been emancipated from serfdom in 1861, but had been forced to buy their land and could rarely afford more than enough for the barest subsistence. To right these wrongs the young radicals 'moved out into the countryside . . . dressed like peasants or labourers, thinking high and living low, to awaken the unfortunates, point out the nature of their plight . . . and exhort them to concerted action'.[36] They were shattered when they discovered that the noble peasants were 'sly, suspicious, envious, venal and drunken'[37] brutes who reported them to the police. More than sixteen hundred of these naive revolutionaries were arrested between 1873 and 1877. The Fabians, living under an infinitely more benign regime, were content to wait, and meanwhile to hold public meetings and debates and to make meticulous analyses of the evils of society.

Even in the more prosperous parts of London, such as Constance then frequented, some evils were all too evident. Before she came up to Cambridge, and was only seventeen, Constance had stayed with John Eastty, a respectable old deacon and friend of her uncle, Joseph Glynn. He had taken her and two of his daughters to some meeting or theatre in the West End. 'We walked back very late through the Haymarket and Trafalgar Square. Girls and women were standing in rows along the walls, and every now and then one saw a man walk by them and pick one out.'[38] Constance had learned about prostitution in her Political Economy classes, where it was attributed to the pressure of population which necessitated late marriage. 'But the hideous spectacle of this coarse cynical brutality and degradation – accepted by everybody as a matter of course though never to be alluded to by any decent woman – threw me into despair. I was terrified at the ugliness of life – it seemed to blot out all beauty and romance and to make love impossible.'[39] Ugliness affected her emotionally, just as beauty did at Cambridge. But she also thought about it, and when, at about the same time, she learned about contraception she realised that it would 'be not only a way of escape from the hitherto insoluble population problem but that it might mean the end of prostitution'.[40] Nearly fifty years later she read in the *New Statesman* that the decrease in street prostitution was due to the 'competition of the amateur', and commented, 'Impossible to estimate the decrease in misery and degradation, disease and remorse, and increase in happiness and freedom, and development for women covered by this possibility of the "competition of the amateur".'[41]

Constance was attracted by socialism, though according to her son 'she had more in common with the fathers of American Independence than with twentieth century socialists'.[42] She had read *Das Kapital* carefully and had rejected Marx's theory of surplus value, believing that 'the economic interpretation of history disregarded many of the most important motives for human action'.[43] She went to meetings of the Fabian Society with Shaw, but she did not become a Fabian at this time, and apart from Shaw and Pease the earliest Fabians did not become her friends. But in May 1885 two men joined the society who were to be important to her later in different ways. Sidney Webb and Sydney Olivier were both resident clerks in the Colonial Office, but they were utterly unlike in background and character. Webb was a young man of twenty-five who had made his way by scholarships and prizes won with the aid of a brilliantly encyclopaedic memory. He was not prepossessing, and his future wife wrote: 'His tiny tadpole body, unhealthy skin, lack of manner, cockney pronunciation, poverty, are all against him.'[44]

Olivier was twenty-six; he had been 'brought up to be a gentleman and to expect service from others'[45] but had reacted against his father's stern Christianity and was 'troubled about the contrast between privilege and poverty'.[46] Shaw wrote of him:

he was distinguished enough to be unclassable. He was handsome and strongly sexed, looking like a Spanish grandee in any sort of clothes, however unconventional. . . . I believe he could have carried a cottage piano upstairs; but it would have cracked in his grip . . . he was a law to himself, and never dreamt of considering other people's feelings, nor could conceive their sensitiveness on points that were to him trivial.[47]

Graham Wallas was another early Fabian, though he did not join until a year after Olivier and Webb. He later became a friend of Constance's when he married Ada Radford in 1897. Like Webb he was an assiduous ferreter out of facts, and like Olivier he was a handsome man and a clergyman's son who had lost his faith. When he joined the Fabians he was classics master at Highgate School, but had to leave for refusing to take Holy Communion in the school chapel.

The Fabians may have been 'quite the nicest set of people' as Edith Bland asserted,[48] but they were not strong on social graces. A young guest of Edward Pease described an occasion at the Peases' when she felt she 'had been at the most . . . helpless, cold and constrained party we had ever assisted at. . . . I afterwards learned this "coldness" and absence of entertainment of guests is a Fabian attribute.'[49] Later she met Frank Podmore 'who was rude in the manner of Edward Pease and equally well-intentioned'.[50] She thought that Wallas was good-looking, but he 'behaved as if he were accustomed to being made much of, his manners were not those of one equal to another'.[51]

However, no one could call Shaw cold and aloof, and Constance found him an entertaining companion. She went with him not only to meetings of the Fabian Society but also to what she called 'the Kelmscott House socialists', William Morris's Socialist League. Morris was then aged fifty, 'an arresting figure, usually dressed in a blue serge sailor-cut suit which made him look like the purser of a Dutch brig. He had a gruff but informal sincerity which made people like him even when they disagreed with him.'[52] Yeats discovered in him 'something childlike and joyous that still leaves him my chief of men'.[53] As a boy he had been appalled at the ugliness of the manufactures at the Great Exhibition and had campaigned ever since for a socialist Utopia in which Adam delved and Eve span and there was no such thing as a gentleman. In his house he had nothing that he did not know to be useful or believe to be beautiful. His fabrics and wallpapers had become the rage at Newnham and in homes of advanced taste. Constance was much attracted by the Arts and Crafts movement, although, unlike Emma and Grace, she was no artist – nor did she ever practise any craft, unless knitting and gardening can be so described.

Dollie Radford described one of Morris's meetings in her diary for 30 November 1884. It is so phrased that one cannot be positive that Constance went there with her; but if she did not, she certainly went to others like it.

Connie Black called in the morning, and partook of a hasty mid-day meal with us. Went off in wind and rain to Hammersmith. 'Tis a place to be remembered. Came by difficult stages to Mr. [Emery] Walker's. Had tea there with him and with his wife. Afterwards we went to hear Morris lecture on Socialism, 'How we live, and how we might live'. It was a beautiful address. He is truly a poet.

Ernest spoke afterwards. Mr. Shaw and the poet Beattie [Pakenham Beatty] with him. Beattie the poet-pugilist. After the lecture we went up to Mr. Morris's house; and had some supper. His house is beautiful; and his daughter May is *most* beautiful: no wonder that Rossetti painted her so often. We did not see Mrs. Morris. Shaw was very nice: Morris talked excitedly for some time, and Beattie chattered all the time. I should like to act for that branch of the Democratic federation. Morris talked of many things and people. Verse forms – Browning – Swinburn [e] – plays – and Gladstone. Was rather surprised indeed at the way in which he did speak of Gladstone. Home very late and very wet, and more than ever convinced of the seriousness and beauty of the Socialistic movement. I do not feel this in the company of some others of its leaders – Aveling and Hyndman for example.[54]

Shaw spoke whenever he could at public meetings or debates, propounding his paradoxes with such good humour and wit that his hearers could never be quite certain whether to take him entirely seriously, so were rarely offended by what he said, however outrageous it might seem. He was convinced that much in the world of politics, social justice, religion and morals was wrong; and so was Constance. He was an immensely energetic and articulate campaigner for change, and Grace Black told him that she expected him to 'do a great deal' for socialism.[55] But Shaw was also inclined to feel that anybody who thought that the existing state of affairs was wrong, for whatever reason, must therefore be right; and this led him to be involved with Dr Jaeger, the Vegetarian Cyclists, the Anti-Vaccinationists and a host of other cranks and gadflies. For two pins he would have joined the Flat-Earthers. While he had a deep appreciation of music, he had no visual aesthetic sense and little understanding of science, but he was always ready to pontificate on them or on anything else. As Joseph Conrad remarked, 'The fellow pretends to be deep but he never gets to the bottom of things but rides off on some tricky evasion.'[56] So after a while Constance began to be disenchanted with him; and her disenchantement was complete when he told her that he would have liked to marry her if he could afford to do so, but an improvident marriage would ruin his career.

He was much given to evasive flirtation at this period of his life, and several other young women received similar declarations. But this may have been something more. Some fifty years later he told Constance's son, 'I would have married your mother if I could have afforded it, but I was very poor in those days.' David Garnett was glad not to have had Shaw as a father, but he said nothing and did not tell the old man that Constance would never have accepted him.[57]

Grace, however, might have done so. She wrote to him on 25 March 1887, 'I guessed you would think I was in love with you. So I am. . . .'[58] But Shaw was as evasive as ever, and two years later she wrote, 'Long ago I saw that my love for you was a waste of force because you were so different to me.'[59] Grace's more serious suitors were Ernest's brother, Charles, and a highly eligible young Italian, Count Francesco Papavera, good-looking, with perfect manners and impeccably socialist politics, and moreover a lineal descendant of Marcus Aurelius. Constance could not understand how Grace could refuse such a paragon, but she did.

After a year of being part of the White household Constance was able to move out from under their wing. She took on other pupils and spent only the morning with the Whites. The most important of these pupils were Tom and Antonia, the two eldest children of Charles and Mary Booth. Constance was particularly impressed by Antonia: 'Her mother was a Macaulay, and Antonia had the wonderful Macaulay memory. She used to translate Caesar, and when I set her to retranslate her version into Latin a week later she would remember every word of the original.[60]

Mary Booth, besides being a niece of Macaulay, was a cousin of Beatrice Potter who, as Beatrice Webb, was to be such a force in the Fabian Society. But Mary did not at all share the views of her socialist cousin. She was a staunch conservative, who disapproved of women's suffrage and higher education for women, was shocked by the indecencies of Voltaire and Sterne and was a devout conventional Christian. But when Constance found a sympathetic character she did not need to share opinions in order to be friends; and she took greatly to the Booths. Charles Booth was a successful and wealthy shipowner, who ran businesses in London, Liverpool and New York. Beatrice Webb, who knew him well, described him as:

tall, abnormally thin, garments hanging as if on pegs, the complexion of a consumptive girl, and the slight stoop of a sedentary worker, a prominent aquiline nose, with moustache and pointed beard barely hiding a noticeable Adam's apple, the whole countenance dominated by a finely-moulded brow and large, observant eyes, Charles was an attractive but distinctly queer figure of a man.[61]

Soon after Constance got to know him he started on the vast and influential work of social enquiry that made his reputation. Henry Hyndman, a hot-headed old Etonian member of the Socialist League, had claimed that more than a quarter of the people in the working-class districts of London lived in extreme poverty. Booth was convinced that Hyndman's figures were grossly exaggerated, and set about trying to prove him wrong. He began a massive investigation, working incognito in the East End, and employing other researchers, notably Beatrice Potter. Seventeen years and eighteen meticulous volumes later he showed that Hyndman had been more or less right, but in the process he had established social history as an exact science.

Constance did not say how she had come to know the Booths. The next, and most important, set of people she met were once again friends of Clementina's. Clementina had begun working in the British Museum soon after she came to London, and since 1879 she had been friendly with Richard Garnett. He was Superintendent of the Reading Room from 1875 to 1884 and presided benignly at the centre of that vast dome of learning. No one could have been better suited for the job. He had been working in the Library since he was sixteen and seemed to know where every book was and what was in it. He was immensely well-read, not only in English but also in Latin and Greek, and especially in German and Italian. He liked to take on a new language from time to time, as he wrote to his brother at the end of 1857: 'I am studying Danish – a very nice language – a sort of ladylike German.'[62]

He was a tall man with a scholar's stoop, and he wore an old frock-coat pulled out of shape by the books in its large pockets. His face was short and square, with a short nose and a short beard, and he wore the usual gold-rimmed spectacles of the day. His manner of speech was gentle and humorous, with the remains of a Yorkshire accent, and so measured that one could tell where each mark of punctuation was due to fall. He was invariably courteous to his readers' enquiries, however bizarre or inept. Samuel Butler, who liked to tease him, once saw him reaching up to get a book from a high shelf, and remarked, 'Why Mr. Garnett, you are the very embodiment of Milton's line "Of linked sweetness long drawn out",' adding later, 'He was much pleased.'[63]

His position in the literary establishment was similar to that in the British Museum. He was in the centre but not at the head. He knew everybody. By the end of 1885 he had written half a dozen books, edited or introduced ten, and contributed fifty-three articles to *The Encyclopaediu Britannica*; and he had just embarked on a further 177 for *The Dictionary of National Biography*. He was a sound and industrious writer of biographies and literary criticism. He wrote poetry that was so firmly entrenched in the poetic diction of his time that it was rarely memorable unless it was set to music by Elgar ('Where Corals Lie') or had some of the black comedy of his stories ('The Fair Circassian', 'The Crocodile') or was one of his better epigrams. His writings fill six columns of the British Museum Catalogue (which he edited from 1884 to 1890), but he is remembered for the tales in *The Twilight of the Gods*, with their subversive pagan morality and dry humour wrapped in the most orotund mandarin language. In view of all his other achievements one hopes that he will be forgiven for having made something of a fool of himself in being seduced by Shelley's daughter-in-law into trying to defend the poet as a pillar of Victorian respectability.[64]

The Garnetts were a Yorkshire family, and were supposed to have derived their common sense, obstinacy and unworldliness from that county. Richard's uncle Jeremiah had been the first printer, publisher and reporter on the *Manchester Guardian*, and later its editor; and there was always a good deal of that journal's liberalism in the Garnett morality.

Richard had an elder sister, Ellen Rayne, known for some obscure family reason as 'Auntie Cuckoo', and a younger brother, William John, known in Yorkshire fashion by his two Christian names. Ellen had had the unenviable task of being governess to Sir George Sitwell and his sister Florence, among others, and was consequently pilloried by Osbert Sitwell for her grotesque ugliness (she was indeed plain) and dressing so that she 'resembled a hippopotamus decked out as an elephant'.[65] William John was a harmless, hopeless character, usually in debt and never able to hold on to a job for long, whether he was mining in Colorado, a consular agent in Egypt or a music critic in Australia.

In 1863 Richard married Olivia Narney Singleton, known to all her intimates as Narney. She came from an Anglo-Irish family of fox-hunting protestants. Her father had some kind of breakdown when she was still a girl, and her mother had fled with her two children and brought them up in England and on the Continent. Narney was very sociable and had considerable charm, and was supposed to have brought into the family an Irish strain of irresponsibility and wit, none of which, alas, is particularly evident in her letters.

Richard and Narney had six surviving children, who embodied the supposed family characteristics in very unequal measure. The eldest, May (born 17 May 1864), had a fair dose of the Garnett obstinacy, but so little else that she was very much the odd one out. She was conventional, religious, a bit of a prig, and somewhat disapproving of the rest, who, in their turn, were apt to disapprove of her. Her sister Olive confided to

49

her diary that when she saw May's nature exposed it 'always sends a shiver through me'.[66]

Robert (born 27 March 1866), Edward (born 5 January 1868) and Olive (born 21 August 1871) were all well-read and bookish, but in different ways. Robert was embarking on a career in the law, and he took up collecting first editions and translating the works of Alexandre Dumas *père*. He was small and wiry, and was an entertaining talker, with a fund of good anecdotes, well told. He liked a quiet life, and his daughter in a cruelly candid memoir wrote, 'Father's dislike of giving offence was what we despised in him.'[67]

Edward, on the other hand, was a congenital outsider, never accepting received opinions and original in all his literary judgements, but continually inhibited in his own work by his acute critical sense. He loved to tease those he was fond of and was witty and entertaining in company, but apt to be morbidly depressed when alone.

Olive shared these fits of depression, but her wit was more private than Edward's. She was intellectual, observant and articulate. She longed to be a writer, and despite her extreme fastidiousness and susceptibility to Henry James she wrote well when fed by experience. She was governed by a strong moral sense of Christian ethic. Where Constance's intelligence asked, 'Is this wise?' Olive's morality demanded, 'Is it right?'

Lucy (born 22 December 1875) was not particularly bookish or intellectual, but she toyed for a while with neurotic depression, until the doctor bluntly declared that there was nothing the matter with her; whereupon she rose from her sickbed and for the next few years lived the life of a cheerful extrovert.

Arthur (born 21 February 1881) was the youngest and the family pet. He was in no way a spoiled child, suffering only from an appalling stammer. Even as a boy he was a charmer, and he grew up to be unworldly and unambitious, enjoying life and asking little of it. His adoring niece thought him 'a peach of a man'.[68]

Constance's mature judgement, written nearly forty years later, was 'There is something so individual, so racy and delicious about the Garnetts (on the male side) – the combination of extraordinary benevolence and unworldliness with deep disillusionment and the best of good spirits – and their lively minds.'[69]

One Sunday in the winter of 1885–6 Constance was taken by Clementina to 3 St Edmund's Terrace to have tea with the Garnetts. She was

David Black, Constance's father,
after he lost the use of his legs

Clara Black,
Constance's mother,
drawing by George Patten

Arthur Black

Constance, Grace and Kate Black

Grace Black

Richard Garnett, C.B., LL.D.

Olive Garnett

Edward Garnett

'Nina Lindon'

talking to May and Robert when Edward came in, and she was immediately struck by him:

a very tall, very thin boy of eighteen . . . looking as though he had outgrown his clothes and his strength. With his very bright eyes, curly head, dimples and roguish expression, he was very charming. 'A kitten on the top of a maypole,' was a happy description of him. He was at once shy and bold and very amusing. I have never seen a face so full of mischief.[70]

Many years later Constance wrote that 'he seemed to me the very spirit of youth, for ever gay and teazing . . . I used to feel as though I hardly dared breathe for fear of tarnishing the brightness of his spirit'.[71] What she does not say is that he also had an underlying vein of deep seriousness, and even of melancholy, especially when alone.

The others immediately noticed that Edward was interested in Constance. 'Edward hates visitors,' they said, 'and always has tea in Chapple's room.'[72] Chapple was 'a dear very old nurse, a tiny creature',[73] who had been maid to Narney's mother and spent her life looking after Narney and her brother and then all Narney's six children until, in old age, the Garnetts looked after her.

Edward's interest in Constance continued. She had moved out of Wright's Lane, and was sharing lodgings with Grace in Campden Hill. One evening Edward turned up there, ostensibly with a message from his sister May and stayed on for some hours. On his departure Grace said: "You say nobody looks at you when I am by, but there is someone with no eyes for anybody but you."'[74]

In the summer of 1886 the three eldest Garnetts, May, Robert and Edward, and the three youngest Blacks went on a walking tour in Sussex. It did not last more than a week at most, but 'it was a happy time for people of small means and simple tastes'.[75] Such places as Heathfield and Burwash were then small quiet villages, and 'one could walk all day on the Sussex roads meeting nothing but an occasional waggon or farmer's gig'.[76] They stopped for the night and for lunch at old inns by the way. Constance was always happier in the country than in town, and the countryside looked lovely in the perfect summer weather. She found Edward 'the most charming companion, amusing, fresh, original',[77] and by the time they got back to London they were very much in love.

5

Romance in Whitechapel

Edward Garnett had not distinguished himself at the City of London School except as a good spin bowler and a great tease. He had the usual schoolboy adventures, provoking the school bully to a fight and beating him roundly. He was an effective, if ungainly, athlete; but once when he won a race he was forced to forgo the prize so that it might be given to the boy who came in second, and who happened to be the son of the prizegiver.[1] The injustice of this rankled for the rest of his life; and if he had not already been a congenital outsider this would have made sure that he would always treat the establishment with contempt.

After leaving school at the age of sixteen, Edward had been left to his own devices. His father, having raised himself by his own efforts to a higher pitch of erudition than nine dons out of ten, did not think much of a university education. So Edward lay on the hearth-rug reading, or scoured the bookstalls in the Farringdon Road (where he once picked up a first edition of *Candide*).

Edward's father did not discourage his liaison with Constance, for, as she remarked, 'Any sensible father desires nothing better for a young son than a connection with an intelligent woman a little older.'[2] Richard had always had a marked penchant for intelligent young women himself, and had taken to Constance from the first. He was less susceptible to mere beauty and distrusted Grace's attractiveness 'because she was fanatical'.[3] And Narney was probably only too glad to have Edward out of the house, for nothing is more in the way than a horizontal six-foot teenager.

Constance did not stay long in the lodgings in Campden Hill, being driven out by bedbugs. So she moved with Grace to 7 Fitzroy Street, and Shaw arrived just down the road at No. 29 in March 1887. A few months later the three Black sisters were 'attracted by a large low-pitched room on the top floor'[4] of No. 27 in the same street, where 'we hoped by painting the floor red to give something of the look of a farm-house kitchen'.[5] It was 'a large room, thirty feet long, which they used as a combined kitchen and sitting-room; about the fireplace they fixed the woodwork of an old pew; in the large bow-window were rugs, arm-chairs, and writing-tables; and in the back of the room stood a dresser adorned with blue crockery'.[6] Grace, as the artist of the three, decorated the place, and Edward, having nothing else to do, was at their beck and call, 'painting, moving furniture and so on' – 'really a scullion'.[7]

At some time before their marriage Edward and Constance became lovers. She had no objections on principle, and she later admitted as much to her son.[8] Clementina was worried about Constance's affair with Edward and 'thought it her duty to try to check it, though it went very much against the grain to interfere in such delicate matters'.[9] May Garnett had no such scruples, as Constance wrote:

She came to see me one day when I was unwell and in bed and went bluntly to the point at once. 'Of course, you would not dream of taking Edward's feeling for you seriously' – she began. 'Of course not,' I responded faintly. She proceeded to tell me that he was a hopeless character, 'he never says a prayer' and also 'he takes after Uncle William John, and he'll never earn a living'. I was disinclined to look into the future; sure (as I thought) of the permanence of my own feelings, I could not think it possible that Edward's passion for me could last very long – and had at that time no thought of legal marriage. It seemed as though that would be 'taking advantage of him'. But May's words put rather a different face on it. If it were true that he would never be self-supporting, obviously somebody would have to look after him – and why not I?[10]

They did not in fact marry until a couple of years later. But Constance had already begun looking after Edward. She was concerned, like May, that he would never get a job. His father had done nothing about finding him a career, except to arrange for him to have shorthand lessons with the vague idea that he might become a reporter on the *Manchester Guardian* (his longhand, scratchy and dashing and well-nigh illegible, was a primitive form of shorthand already). But he did not want to leave Constance and go to Manchester. Eventually she prevailed upon his father to arrange that T. Fisher Unwin should give him a junior post in his publishing office in Paternoster Square. The story of his first day at work was an oft-told tale. Here is Constance's version of it:

It happened that I was ill and my sisters being away, Edward was staying at the flat looking after me when the day came on which he was to make his first appearance at the office. . . . He was to be there at nine – but to my consternation though I called him repeatedly, took him coffee in bed, and did all I could, it was impossible to get him off till long after that time. Finally I fetched a hansom – which seemed to me in those days a terrible extravagance – and with a sinking heart sent him off. It is quite possible, however, that this reckless unpunctuality was more diplomatic than a humble eagerness to please would have been. It probably gave Unwin the impression that Edward – though so young – was a person of consequence and this idea must have been confirmed by his studious inability to pack books, tie up parcels, etc. He had quite soon slipped into the position of 'publisher's reader', which was of all callings the one that he was fitted for by character, tastes and habits.[11]

Constance took Edward to political meetings like those she had been taken to by Shaw. After Shaw had seen them together several times he asked her who 'the pretty young man' was. She replied that he was 'A boy whose education I am undertaking'.[12] But Edward refused to be educated. He was much too sceptical by nature and always saw the difficulties before the solutions. He would not take the Fabians or the Socialist Defence League seriously, and the young lovers had a row about Land Nationalisation. Constance believed that it was the answer to the evils of landlordism. But Edward said that it would not come in England in the next ten years – 'no, nor within twenty, either'. Constance found this 'a terrible lack of faith . . . and a real grief'.[13]

Edward's response to Constance's politicking was to write a book, *The Paradox Club*, a very short novel that appeared in 1888. The framework is the love story of Patrick Weld, a young Irishman, and Nina Lindon, an emancipated woman. The plot makes the most of their mild misunderstandings. Patrick is an articulate and self-questioning version of Edward. Nina is Constance, but so idealised that were it not that the frontispiece, captioned 'Nina Lindon', is clearly a drawing of Constance, one could hardly be certain of the identification.[14] Into this are inserted some meetings of the Paradox Club, more Peacockian than Fabian, where there is much 'artificial' conversation – the sort of thing that Wilde would do better – about the relative merits of men and women, the prospects for poetry, the aims of socialism, and so on. Martell, the socialist, is a morose version of Shaw, and his comparison of businessmen and beggars is a very fair imitation of Shaw's lectures on capitalists and slaves. *The Paradox Club* cannot be taken as serious political comment. But it does throw light on Edward's relations with Constance and her socialist friends, as when he lists for nearly a page the randomly chosen socialist clichés that throbbed through Patrick's brain 'till he feebly wondered whether he was bourgeois or proletariat, or merely an overworked hind exploited by his capitalistic and marauding employer. Finally, he gave up his vain efforts to reach the bed-rock of the matter, and he sat hopeless and dazed, not daring to laugh lest Nina should think him ill-natured.'[15]

Edward himself was not always so restrained at meetings. His sister Olive described how, at a debate between Mrs Besant and Mrs Mac-donald at St James's Hall, Edward and a friend 'came and stood up at the back, and clapped furiously, sometimes doubling themselves up against the wall with laughter'.[16]

After three-and-a-half years of teaching Constance was at last offered a real job. Charles Booth recommended her to Walter Besant for a post in a new project in which he was deeply involved, and which had rather surprisingly come into being. Besant was a small stout man with a bushy beard and a brusque manner. He had succeeded as a man of letters more by energy and generosity of spirit than by any great literary talent or sensibility. He was deeply interested in the history of London and very knowledgeable about its topography. He had come to the conclusion that the way to regenerate the impoverished East End was not by the usual charitable works – hospitals, orphanages, almshouses – let alone by economic or political action, but by providing a place for healthy recreation of all kinds, what he called a Palace of Delight. To this end he had published a novel, *All Sorts and Conditions of Men*, in 1882. His angelic heroine, Angela Messenger (the word 'angel', one recalls, means 'messenger'), has inherited a prosperous brewery in the East End, and is concerned to put her money to good use. She has finished her time at Newnham, and turns her back on the academic life. The college and her friend Constance Woodcote, a mathematical bluestocking, are presented as objects of some ridicule; even the architecture is mocked as 'a palace built in the conceited fashion of the day'.[17] So, leaving behind all thoughts of political economy and the classics, she goes to the East End, where she disguises herself as a dressmaker, employing seamstresses in an Utopian commune, where an old sailor reads aloud while they work, and there are compulsory breaks for tennis and gymnastics. This rather thin and sentimental story is spun out with a sub-plot of would-be Dickensian characters until, at the end of the three-decker novel, the Palace of Delight is brought into being.

The book was an immediate success. It caught the mood of the time and did not disturb Victorian prejudices. Miss Messenger, even when disguised as a dressmaker, is always recognised as a lady. There is no suggestion that by owning a brewery she was exploiting the workers, or that drink might be corrupting her customers. There is no picture of the real squalor of the East End, though Grace Black did suggest to Shaw that 'if Walter Besant could be got at, he could soon be made a thorough socialist – And his books are exceedingly popular'.[18] His campaign for a Palace of Delight was taken seriously, and adopted by the establishment.

A bequest of 13,000*l* left in 1841 by John Thomas Barber Beaumont . . . with the object of providing 'intellectual improvement and rational recreation and amusement for people living in the East End of London,' was made the nucleus of a large public fund amounting to 75,000*l*, which was collected under the direction of Sir Edmund Hay Currie, with Besant's active co-operation, for the foundation of an institution on the lines which Besant had laid down.[19]

The Drapers' Company, which had a long history of charitable works in the area, provided the funds for a technical school. Luncheons were held at Mansion House, Oscar Wilde applied for the secretaryship (but did not get it),[20] and the Prince of Wales laid the foundation stone on 28 June 1886.

A little less than a year later, on Saturday 14 May 1887, Queen Victoria drove seven miles, through streets decorated in a sort of preview of her Golden Jubilee, from Paddington Station to Mile End. There she opened the first phase of the People's Palace, the Queen's Hall, a huge over-ornate barn, designed by E. R. Robson, and decorated with twenty-two statues of worthy queens, from Esther of Persia and Boadicea to Maria Theresa of Hungary and Louise of Prussia.

The next phase was to build a library, and Besant, as Chairman of the Library Committee, was looking for two young women to work as librarians. Despite his prejudice against Newnham and bluestockings called Constance, and her complete lack of experience, he offered Constance one of the jobs, and she was delighted to accept. But there were as yet no books and no library to put them in, so she could not start until the autumn.

Meanwhile she and Edward watched the procession of the Jubilee itself on 21 June. They walked down Tottenham Court Road and Charing Cross Road to the thickly sanded processional route and joined the immense multitudes of good-humoured excited people who had come to watch the gorgeous pageant. The soldiers were 'dressed in brilliant colours, with lots of glittering gold facings on their uniforms.

. . . We agreed that the finest figure in it was the German Emperor all in white and gold – looking like a medieval knight.'[21]

Despite her radical politics Constance shared the views of many of her generation about that Jubilee summer:

It was a wonderful time – and looking back, I feel that it celebrated the moment of the greatest prosperity of the country – that England's greatness touched its high watermark that year. Hope and faith were in the air. It seemed that such immense strides in wealth and power – and above all in humane culture and science – had been made in those fifty years that it was quite reasonable to hope that only a little more time and effort might establish permanent peace and prosperity everywhere, and abolish poverty, disease and ignorance.[22]

While waiting for the library at the People's Palace to open, Constance continued to teach classics to Tom and Antonia Booth. She had spent ten days of April at the Booths' country house, Gracedieu, near Coalville in Leicestershire, and then was there the whole time from 6 August to 3 September. It was not all work, and she was roped in to play cricket with the 'young things'.[23] She must have missed Edward at Gracedieu: 'I was very much in love at the time and I remember succumbing to the temptation of talking about Edward to Mrs Booth – an awful crime in my own eyes, for we had agreed not to tell anybody of our feelings for a time.'[24]

Constance started work at the People's Palace towards the end of September. She was Joint Librarian with Frances Low. Neither of them had any training for the job or experience of librarianship, but there were only a handful of women in the whole country who had. Besant was unusually enlightened in choosing women at all. Nevertheless Constance thought

it was an absurd thing to appoint inexperienced and untrained girls to manage a public library and reading-room – and particularly absurd to appoint *two* of them with equal authority. My colleague Frances Low was a rather fickle and capricious young woman, not at all easy to work with. She would agree to some arrangement – even suggest one – and I would find next day that she had changed her mind, undone all my work and done something quite different.[25]

They had as yet no proper premises, only temporary accommodation in a corner of the Queen's Hall, and only a motley collection of books that had been donated, 7,332 in all, of which some three thousand had been given by Isaac Pitman of Bath, the inventor of Pitman's Shorthand. They had barely a week to make a provisional catalogue before the library opened on 30 October. Constance said that they had 'no notion how to compile a catalogue. We made one by the light of nature and a very bad one it naturally was.'[26] This may have been true of their first hasty catalogue, but in fact their methods were closely modelled on those of the British Museum, and Constance took advice from Richard Garnett.

It was hard work, but they did not both have to be on duty together, and Constance was able to go on teaching the Booths one morning a week. The library could not as yet open in the evenings, the most convenient time for working people, because the Queen's Hall was liable to be in use then for anything from a Cat and Rabbit Show to a full orchestral concert. The job was not particularly well paid, the two librarians each got eighty pounds a year, and out of that Constance had to pay for her food and lodging.

Carl Heath was a relative of the Easttys of Bermondsey and a friend of Edward's who became a Quaker and devoted himself to the peace movement and so came to know Gandhi. He 'knew something of social work in the East End'[27] and found Constance 'two tiny rooms in College Buildings, in Wentworth Street, just behind Toynbee Hall'.[28] College Buildings were new industrial dwellings, built as a private speculation in 1866. 'They were amongst the most original in appearance at the time, exhibiting Gothic tendencies, with plenty of detailing in terra cotta',[29] for, as the *Builder* reported, 'An attempt has been made to avoid the barrack-like appearance too often characteristic of this class of dwelling, as it is found that the rooms let more readily when a more cheerful appearance is given to the exterior.'[30] Constance described it as 'a pretty red brick building, with five storeys of tenements, two sides of a square, and enclosing a good-sized asphalted court'[31] and said that in summer it 'was very pretty, with its red bricks and white stairs and balconies and flowers in most of the windows'.[32] She wrote about life in blocks of model dwellings, signing herself 'A Lady Resident' in the second volume of Charles Booth's *Labour and Life of the People of London*, so we have a very full description of what her everyday life was like:

My dwelling consisted of two tiny rooms, about 9 ft. square, opening into one another. The front door, with its separate number and knocker, opens out of the front room into a common open balcony; and the back door out of the back room into a tiny private balcony, about a yard or so square, leading to the sink, &c. These little balconies are often turned to good account with flower boxes and hanging baskets, and one woman had rigged up a pigeon-house, and kept pigeons very successfully there. Each tenement is complete in itself, except for the want of a tap; to fetch water the tenants have to take their buckets to the common tap on each balcony. Though so small, the rooms are fresh and very clean, brightly coloured and painted once every year. The asphalted court provides a large and safe playground for the children, and the flat roof is utilized for washhouses and a drying ground. Each tenant is bound in turn to clean and whiten a part of the balcony and stairs, and each in turn on her fixed day enjoys the use of a washhouse and the roof to dry her clothes. These common rights and duties lead, of course, to endless contention.[33]

She also gave a 'short sketch of an average day', a sample of which may be quoted here:

In the afternoon a certain torpor falls upon the Buildings, only broken by the jingling cans and cat-calls of the afternoon milk-boys. But this is the favourite time for the women to call upon one another, and I can catch various fragments of conversation relating to the bad turn Mrs. D.'s illness is taking, to the uncalled-for visit of the curate to a lady who dislikes curates, to the shocking temper of little Maggie (Mrs. C.'s child), who is reported to be the tease and torment of all the children in the place.[34]

She discussed the character of the different buildings, which depended more on the class of inhabitants than on architecture: 'It is curious, on the principle of "like to like," how quickly a Building forms for itself a certain character – Jews' Buildings, rowdy Buildings, genteel Buildings, &c., all being estimated as such by public opinion.'[35] By these criteria College Buildings seem to have been genteel, though one might have expected them to be Jewish, since Wentworth Street was a Jewish area. Like its neighbour, Middlesex Street, better known as 'Petticoat Lane', it was a busy and mainly Jewish market. Here is how it looked a few years after Constance lived there:

Each ground floor is a shop, and the kerb on either side of the road is cumbered with stalls. As you worm your way through the press of people it is easy to imagine that you are in a foreign city. On every side are un-English faces, un-English wares, un-English writings on the walls. The accents of an unknown tongue assail your ears.[36]

A later writer called Wentworth Street 'a painter's paradise';[37] and in *The Paradox Club* Edward had Lofthouse, the over-aesthetic poet, exclaim:

I went down Wentworth Street last May, and saw a mass of colour as brilliant as the gleaming mackerel the hawkers were crying. Hundreds of women with pink, or buttercup yellow, or olive green, or dark blue shawls thrown over their heads, Jewesses with dark brown hair, Irishwomen with those exquisite deep blue eyes and black eyebrows, were sitting in the doorways, or standing at the stalls, bearing the chaff of the men good-humouredly. Oh, the colour in those piles of blood oranges![38]

Between Wentworth Street and the People's Palace there was a mile and a half of the broad highway of the Whitechapel and Mile End Roads. These also had their markets frequented by immigrants of all kinds, but especially Jews who had fled in large numbers from persecution in Russia and Romania. In the reaction that had set in after the assassination of Alexander II in 1881, there had been appalling pogroms and a deliberate policy of persecution of the Jews. K. P. Pobedonostsev, the Procurator of the Holy Synod and 'evil genius' of the Romanovs,[39] expressed the hope that 'one-third of the Jews will convert, one-third will die, and one-third will flee the country'.[40] Only the third part of his wish was fulfilled. Some two million Jews left Russia before the end of Tsardom, mostly to America. And during the 1880s the number of Russians in England increased by twenty thousand. Most of them were Jews, and most of them settled in the East End of London.

Constance, with her taste for adventure, found this exotic world a 'new interesting life that seemed intensely romantic'.[41]

College Buildings were, if anything, slightly nearer to Edward's office at 26 Paternoster Square than to the People's Palace, so, as Constance wrote, 'When I could get back in the middle of the day we lunched together and all the weekends he spent with me'[42] – not that she was entirely free, for the library was open all week, and the librarians generally took turns with Sunday duty.

Constance had found a worthwhile job, feeding the minds of the East Enders. But the technical college that might improve their chances of employment was not yet open, and many of them were out of work. There were protest marches, which had led to a riot in Trafalgar Square in February 1886; windows were smashed, and the middle classes were alarmed into giving generously to the Lord Mayor's relief fund. Charles Warren, a hawkish ex-soldier, took over command of the Metropolitan Police, but the marches continued, and Warren over-reacted. He closed Trafalgar Square to the meeting on Sunday 13 November 1887, and had two thousand police and four hundred soldiers standing by with live ammunition to keep it closed. In the inevitable clashes that resulted the demonstrators were routed. 'We *skedaddled*,' Shaw wrote, 'and never drew breath until we were safe on Hampstead Heath.'[43] It became known as 'Bloody Sunday', though nobody was killed, and other far bloodier Sundays were to follow elsewhere. But on the following Sunday the police beat up a bystander so severely that he died. Socialism had its martyr, and William Morris wrote his 'Death Song' for the funeral procession. The Fabians had learned, as one of the characters in *The Paradox Club* put it, that it was folly to 'conclude that the way to Utopia is to march along in a street procession with red flags',[44] and that like Fabius they must wait 'most patiently'.

A month after these events Constance went to spend the Christmas holidays with her family at Brighton, where David Black spread his usual pall of gloom, as she wrote to Edward:

Things at home are rather depressing. I don't know how it is that a family of people who taken separately have many good points can be so cold-blooded and disagreeable when they are taken collectively. There is a kind of deadly coldness, and a sort of strained unnatural feeling about us all from Papa even to Katie and me who are quite thawed when away from home.[45]

She must have been glad to get back to the library, even though it was still in its inconvenient temporary quarters. The new library building was completed in June 1888, and formally opened by Princess Alexandra on 15 August, but the transfer of books and fittings took a long time, and it was not ready for the public until 18 October.

It was a smaller version, seventy-five feet in diameter, of the Reading Room of the British Museum, octagonal instead of round, and with a vaulted dome derived from Prior Forcer's fourteenth-century kitchen at Durham. Two metal galleries, reached by spiral staircases, gave access to the bookstacks on the wall, and a funicular railway brought the books on overhead wires from the assistant at the bookstack to the librarian's desk at the centre. This alarming contraption, capable of carrying a hundredweight of literature at a time, must have been far more distracting than the occasional chattering women and girls about whom the librarians were apt to complain.

High above the bookstacks bland busts of Chaucer, Shakespeare, Milton, Dryden, Johnson, Scott, Byron and Wordsworth looked down upon the readers, who generally preferred less exalted fare: Dickens, Rider Haggard, Dumas, Kingsley, Stevenson and Mrs Henry Wood. Darwin was also surprisingly sought after. The East Enders might look like 'rough lads' but they were remarkably well behaved. Some of the younger ones could not resist trying to get a rise out of the lady librarians. 'Facetious youths, when asked their name, will think it a stroke of wit to reply, "Jack the Ripper," or "Ally Sloper," but these light sallies must be discouraged before they become subversive of the gravity of other readers.'[46]

This was uncomfortably near the bone. The first of Jack the Ripper's victims, Mary Ann Nichols, a pauper prostitute like the four others, was found hideously disembowelled on 31 August 1888 almost exactly haif-way between College Buildings and the People's Palace. The fifth, Mary Jane Kelly, on 9 November, about two hundred and fifty yards north of Wentworth Street, and the remaining three, in September, formed a ring at varying distances around College Buildings. These grisly events hardly disturbed the genial calm of Besant's *Palace Journal*, which has only one brief reference to 'the late Whitechapel murders';[47] nor does Constance mention them in her memoir.

She did, however, move out of College Buildings that autumn to new lodgings in Royal Mint Square, probably No. 212. This can hardly have been to get away from the Ripper, for her new rooms were only half a mile from the sites of his third and fourth murders. Nor were they any more attractive than College Buildings. But Royal Mint Square housed a colony of her friends. Her youngest sister, Kate, had married Charles Clayton, an architect, in March of that year, having hitherto lived in Brighton and looked after David Black. Now Grace had taken over that chore, and Edward and Constance and the Claytons and Olive Dymond, an old Newnham friend and a new colleague at the People's Palace, had all come to live in Royal Mint Square, just behind the Royal Mint itself.

It was a much bigger development than College Buildings, and despite 'curious architectural qualities', being 'much ornamented with porches and bay windows' and 'even an occasional coarsely detailed Ionic column,' it 'was a very poor example of private development'.[48] The rooms were larger and better fitted, and the rents were higher, than at College Buildings, but it was a gloomy place, with an asphalted square where 'a few miserable shrubs flourished, or rather decayed' and 'steep ill-lighted staircases and dark narrow corridors'.[49] Whereas College Buildings were 'built to admit as much air and sunshine as possible',[50] Royal Mint Square was designed to exclude them. 'I think,' Constance wrote, 'the great difference I noticed in the cheerfulness and temper of the children must have been largely due to this cause.'[51] There was little of the neighbourly feeling of College Buildings; and it must have rated in her classification as 'rowdy Buildings'.

Nevertheless she was happy there. She and Edward were, as their son wrote, a 'carefree couple'[52] at this time in their life. And her position at the People's Palace was much improved in October when Frances Low resigned and she was promoted to Head Librarian, with an increase of salary to a hundred pounds and two other sub-librarians, Olive Dymond and Minnie James, working under her. Miss James was a dynamic and intelligent young woman, 'pretty, vivacious, piquant, with a decided opinion on many subjects',[53] as well as being a dedicated librarian.

The library was now in good hands, but it still had barely ten thousand books, though there was supposed to be room for a quarter of a million. Apart from the eight or nine hundred pounds a year spent in running costs, it had no funds. For books they were still dependent on gifts, and the books that people give away are too often those that they do not want to read. The People's Palace was never short of religious tracts and Latin prosodies.

Constance had found a far more congenial career than teaching, a worthwhile job, and one that she enjoyed. Despite her shyness she got on well with readers and staff, and was well liked. In February 1889 *The Queen* published an article, 'New Career for Women: Librarians', in which she set out the attractions of the job for women, despite its 'modest remuneration', and argued that it was a career that they were particularly well suited for. She described in some detail exactly what the work involved. There were problems and snares in classification: *Soap* was not a technical work but 'a romance by Constance MacEwen'[54] (the first of the operas?), and *The Story of a Popular Delusion* was not a work of fiction, but a polemic by Shaw's friends, the Anti-Vaccinationists. Books must be catalogued under author, title and subject, both generic and particular, as she demonstrated with *One Hundred Ways of Dressing Oysters* by Mrs de Salis – a not entirely fictitious title. And readers unfamiliar with libraries must be steered to the books that will suit them. Above all the librarian must have 'a sympathetic tolerance of the never ending irregularities and mistakes that must be made by young and inexperienced readers; without some stock of patience and sense of humour she will not always be equal to the demands made upon her'.[55] She ended with a plea for proper training for women librarians, for, as she later wrote to Richard Garnett, 'My own case taught me that the management of even the smallest library wants an apprenticeship.'[56]

By now she had completed that apprenticeship and was on top of the job, so that readers of the *Palace Journal* of 17 July 1889 must have been surprised to see her referred to as 'Miss Black (whom everybody who knows the Palace will be sorry to lose)'.[57] She had resigned in order to marry Edward, leaving Olive Dymond to complete the preparation of a printed catalogue for the press (it was published in September), and Minnie James to take over the running of the library. But even she could not manage without adequate funds, and the People's Palace had already begun to decline by the time Olive Garnett took a friend to see it on Whit Sunday 1892:

The only signs of activity we found were in the Reading Room and in the Queen's Hall where a school and a few people were looking at a puppet show to an accompaniment of Ta-ra-ra-boom-de-ay by a melancholy man. Everything else was shut up, no one about. . . . I fear the gigantic scheme is a gigantic failure.[58]

The technical school, however, went from strength to strength; and it gradually absorbed the failing Palace. By 1905 it had become the East London College, and in 1934 was refounded as Queen Mary College. It is now a major School of the University of London and has an international reputation, especially in science and medicine. Little remains of the old People's Palace except Robson's original frontage and the octagonal reading room, which remained part of the college library. Books – more than a quarter of a million of them – and readers overflowed into the adjacent rooms and even into the cellars below, until in the autumn of 1988 they were moved to a bigger and better library on a new site to the east, leaving the old octagon embedded in acres of glass and concrete as a fossil of Victorian good intentions.

6

Marriage and Motherhood

Edward and Constance were married at Brighton Register Office on 31 August 1889, with Ernest and Grace Black, and Charles and Kate Clayton, as witnesses. Constance's career as a librarian had come to an end, though not quite in the way that David Garnett said when he wrote, 'after three years, they decided to have a child. Constance resigned her job several months before my birth.'[1] In fact David was not born until two-and-a-half years later. But he may well have been right in believing that Constance was going to have a child. She could have told him that she had left the People's Palace to have a baby; and he drew the wrong conclusion.

In the surviving letters there are, as one might expect, no more than hints upon such a matter. A fortnight after the wedding, on 14 September, Edward wrote rather peremptorily to his father, who was already on his way to visit them, to put him off:

We are going up to London to-day to see a doctor with whom we have an appointment. Nothing is really the matter, only a slight operation is required. I should not mention the fact, if it were not necessary to explain our departure – and it certainly need never be referred to again.[2]

This secrecy implies that it was no ordinary operation. And if Constance had had a miscarriage, and it was 'incomplete', she might well have needed a 'slight operation' of curettage to complete it and return her to health. In the event she wrote to her father-in-law in the following May: 'The trouble of which I told you in the autumn is now at an end and we are most thankful to say without the necessity of an operation to which in fact Edward would never have consented, as it seems to be often injurious and always unsatisfactory.'[3] Curettage is not now thought to be injurious or unsatisfactory, but it sometimes was in the 1880s.

This might explain why Constance left the People's Palace so unexpectedly. For Besant could hardly have objected to her continuing her career as a married librarian – as indeed her son believed she did. All that Constance said by way of explanation was 'we wanted to save up and take a cottage in the country'.[4] But even though 'economy and clever management became a passion (satisfying the instincts inherited from Scottish peasant forebears)',[5] they cannot have saved much to offset the loss of Constance's hundred pounds a year; and Edward at this time was earning not much more.

In Henhurst Cross they found their perfect, if tiny, country cottage. It was south of Dorking on the edge of the estate of Broome Hall, the country house of Frederick Pennington, who had been Liberal MP for Stockport. His wife was an ardent suffragette, and they were an enterprising couple, pioneers of lawn tennis (Gladstone first saw the game played on the lawn at Broome Hall) and later of motoring. They were distant relatives of the Yorkshire Garnetts, through whom Edward presumably heard of Henhurst Cross. It was an idyllic spot (and indeed apart from the traffic on the A29 it still is). It is a small upright Victorian cottage built of stone, with latticed windows, tall chimneys and pretty fretted barge-boards on the gable ends.

Behind the cottage there was a garden and a small orchard, with the land falling away sharply to a copse full of bluebells and a stream at the bottom. There was one house across the road, otherwise around them nothing but woods and meadows and the park of Broome Hall. After one spring visit Olive Garnett wrote:

I shall not forget the bridal blossom of the blackthorn rising in fairy array amid the gray green foliage of willow and ash. The sunsets behind Leith Hill, the primrose copse, the wind flowers, or opening cowslips in the meadow, nor my own happy peaceful lying down to sleep. The friendly birds, the robins in the kitchen, the bullfinch outside, the larks in the fields and the solitary woodpigeon's note. All these were lovely.[6]

And even in late January, only a week after there had been skating on the lake in the park, Constance could write: 'It has been most lovely weather . . . the birds are singing and some I fear are rushing into improvident marriages already'.[7] In summer the nightingales sang so much that Clementina told Richard Garnett they 'distressed my peace of mind as a labour agitator by toiling in their vocation for twenty hours out of the twenty-four'.[8] Country life, however, had its disadvantages, as Olive noted on another occasion. Despite there usually being a cat in the house, the mice here are most rampageous, occasionally they get into the wars as when Edward and Connie . . . found one preserved in a jar of treacle or when Mr. Rose caught four at once in the bread pan and executed summary justice on them, but generally they go scott free. They had a feast the other night. Knocked over a dish of haricot beans, lifted up a heavy earthenware cover and reduced a number of biscuits to crumbs, nibbled through an unbaked pie and committed other enormities. The wild creatures are becoming bold, the rabbits are actually burrowing under the parlour window and are expected to come up through the floor.[9]

Ever since her childhood holidays at Sharpsbridge and Uckfield Constance had wanted to live in the country. Now she had all the time in the world to work in the garden, and apart from occasional sick headaches was healthier than she had ever been before. She worked as hard as her Scottish peasant forebears, uprooting useless old trees, planting new ones and breaking new ground for the kitchen garden. Soon she was in thrall to the vegetables, as she wrote to Narney in the spring of 1890:

It is rather amusing how one comes to subordinate the household to the garden. In February I had greens (which neither of us care much for) for dinner fourteen times, because I wanted to get the cabbage ground ready for another crop. Now we are eating leeks steadily on the same principle, but we both like them so we don't complain of that. We are both entirely rustic now and think of little but slugs and bullfinches and the need of rain.[10]

She was indefatigable in harvesting the hedgerows; on one September day in 1890 she picked twenty-seven quarts of blackberries.[11] For the rest of her life her household was one where 'there was always jam making and fruit picking to be done' and 'the raspberries had more than their ordinary flavour'.[12] Later she became passionate about her flower garden. But she was too lacking in sensuality ever to be a good cook by Garnett standards; her husband and her son were both far better. In London she had done all her own housework, now various country girls came in to help her, among them Alice Rice, one of a family of nine from Coldharbour, an agreeable mile-and-a-half's walk away. Edward was much taken with her brother David and got him a job at Fisher Unwin, where in due course he became London traveller and a well-known figure in the book trade.

Otherwise they had few neighbours. Young Fritz Pennington would drop in with a pheasant when he had been out shooting, or bring round a Northern Garnett who happened to be staying; but Edward and

Constance did not mix much with local people. They remained outsiders in the country.

They had hardly settled into the cottage before Constance lost an old friend. On Friday 13 September 1889 Clementina wrote to Grace that Amy Levy 'had got charcoal, shut herself into a little room and so painlessly killed herself during the night'.[13] Constance commented bleakly: 'What a sad end to her sad life. I can feel no grief for her, poor girl, for I know she had twice made the attempt before, and one cannot wish to prolong an existence as joyless as hers was. But her poor mother – I cannot bear to think of her.'[14]

Amy Levy had always had a 'total inability to derive pleasure or consolation from the extraneous circumstances which would have brightened the lives of others'.[15] As she wrote in a dedicatory poem to Clementina:

> Evil I see and pain; within my heart
> There is no voice that whispers: 'All is well.'[16]

She had an utterly uncompromising view of the world:

> Never ask for bread, get a stone instead,
> Never pretend that the stone is bread.[17]

This had produced some fine poetry, but in the end it had done for her.

One might have expected Christmas at Brighton with the Blacks to be another bleak experience, but David Black took to Edward no less than Richard Garnett had done to Constance; and his presence lifted some of the 'cold-blooded and disagreeable' atmosphere that Constance found so oppressive. Edward encouraged the old man to talk about his experiences in Canada, and took down what he said. Just as the Blacks became friends of the Garnetts in London, even Keriman and Emma being occasional visitors, the Garnetts were a great acquisition to the Blacks. A year or so earlier Ernest Black had started converting some old railway carriages at Holmbush, some ten miles from Brighton, into rudely thatched dwellings, known as the Huts. These became a joint resort for holidays for the two families, and eventually a regular dwelling for Arthur Garnett and others.

Some time around the Christmas holidays Constance went to London and saw Barnum and Bailey's 'Greatest Show on Earth'. Thirty-eight years later she recalled Barnum as 'frankly and consciously a rogue',[18] but the show was 'stupendous – I nearly fainted – like the dream of a mad megalomaniac circusman'.[19]

Edward had rooms in College Buildings, where he stayed for his three days a week in town. He walked the mile and a half to Holmwood Station on Wednesday mornings and got back to Henhurst Cross around eight o'clock on Friday evenings. He was hardly out of the door before Constance was scribbling little notes of love and concern, often in pencil, hastily to catch the post. Edward kept them (but only one or two of his replies survive). They are rarely dated more than 'Wednesday' or 'Thursday' and have few external references to enable one to be certain when they were written. Nevertheless one can see at once that Edward and Constance were no longer such a 'carefree couple' as they had been when she had to carry the responsibilities of a full-time job. Now, with only a cat for company, she had time to worry, and seemed to need to receive – and to give – constant reassurance that they were both happy in their new situation. Hitherto she had been the dominant partner, 'looking after' Edward and educating him. Now she was his 'girl', the little wife staying at home, while he was the breadwinner in town. Edward was no more cut out for his new role than she was for hers. He was by nature a feckless husband. It was typical that he should forget Constance's birthday and Richard should remember it; and that Constance should write to her father-in-law, 'after a vain search for your letter, I conclude it is in Edward's pocket, the usual fate of my property, if I let it fall into his hands'.[20]

On his days at home Edward was reading manuscripts for Fisher Unwin and trying to write a third novel. His second book, *Light and Shadow*, had come out in 1889. It was far more shadow than light, and was described by the *Athenaeum* as 'an almost subjective nightmare of a single mind' rather than 'a story of action and incident'.[21] It was not a success. As to the third book, Constance wrote to her father-in-law:

I am afraid . . . he is trying to do something so difficult that he can hardly hope to be even moderately successful. However I have not said this to him, for after all he must write after his own impulse and it would be foolish to discourage him. Very likely as he gets on with it, the idea may take a different shape, and it may work out into a success of another kind.[22]

Edward remarked, 'When I succeed best, I find I am not writing a *novel*, but a sort of prose poem.'[23] And when it eventually appeared in 1894 that is what his next book, *An Imaged World*, turned out to be.

But while he was making slow headway as a novelist, he soon established himself in his true metier as a critic, writing about De Quincey for *Atalanta* and reviewing books for the *Speaker*. In the summer of 1890 he wrote to his father: 'I have had an idea in the back of my brain for a long time that it is not impossible to put criticism into living form, or rather, that it is one's duty to try and do so.'[24] This became his life's work.

In February 1890 Constance learned that Richard Garnett was to be promoted to Keeper of the Printed Books at the British Museum upon George Bullen's retirement, and in congratulating him wrote: 'Of course it was a foregone conclusion, but my mind has the unfortunate, dreary peculiarity of refusing to rejoice in any future event while there is even the thousandth chance against it.'[25] It was one of her few superstitions. The outward effect of this advancement was that in June the Garnett family – except, of course, for Edward – all moved from St Edmund's Terrace to the Keeper's official residence on the east side of the Museum facing Montague Street.

Meanwhile at Henhurst Cross in the spring of 1890 Edward and Constance had a constant stream of family visitors: Narney and Arthur, Chapple with Olive and Lucy, Robert Black, who was rarely able to escape from his duties at Brighton Hospital, and 'Gracie and Mr Human'. Grace, during her banishment to Brighton, had been secretary of the Labour Bureau, organised a union for underpaid laundresses, and fallen in love with Edwin Human. Constance thought he had 'a particularly pleasant voice',[26] but was nonetheless surprised that he should be preferred to the 'romantic suitor', Count Francesco Papavera. Human, always known to his friends as Hugh, was an engineer doing experimental work on torpedoes, a friend and former colleague of Charles Clayton, and had been a neighbour of Edward and Constance in Royal Mint Square.

Constance paid occasional visits to London, to see Lily Langtry in her own production of *As You Like It* in March – 'very jolly and thought her very good' – and to *Tannhäuser* at Covent Garden in September.[27] In August Edward and Constance went with the Holman Hunts to spend a week with the Booths at Gracedieu and invited Antonia and her mother back to the cottage in October. With congenial visitors there was a great deal of radical talk. When Olive came to stay Constance reported to Richard: 'We enjoyed her visit and miss her very much. We showed her no mercy, but attacked all her views and opinions in a heartless way. She was very well able to defend herself and the established order of things from our revolutionary onslaughts.'[28] Olive's diary records how she spent Friday morning darning socks and the afternoon gathering 'autumn leaves berries etc. to fill vases', but when Edward got home they talked 'all the evening about false ideas of morality'.[29] She was always liable to be upset by Constance's scepticism – 'Many things she has not settled'[30] – but later admitted: 'Connie always presents matters in new lights, and makes one feel the force of her intellect'[31] and even exclaimed, 'How conscientious she is and how very slowly she arrives at her conclusions!'[32]

New friends came to stay. Lina Eckenstein, feminist historian and writer of children's books, came more than once and brought her nieces. With her too they 'talked and talked till quite late about the relations between men and women etc.'.[33]

Just before Christmas 1890 Edward wrote to his father about another new friend, 'a young Irish poet for whom I have conceived an affection'.[34] This was W. B. Yeats, who was then twenty-five. He had recently published his first book, *The Wanderings of Oisin*, and was shortly to let the Garnetts read the manuscript of a poetical play, *The Countess Kathleen*, which Edward thought 'most original . . . in quite a new manner'[35] or, as Olive put it, 'very good and weird, I think'.[36] Edward had made friends with him in London, and 'they'd walk from his digs to Edward's digs and back again, all night long, absolutely forgetting everything in the most natural way'.[37] Yeats was then so poor that he 'used to have to black-up his heels so as to cover the holes in his stockings'.[38] Edward went on to tell his father about Constance and Yeats:

One result of my Irish friend's visit has been to stimulate her taste for the marvellous. Yeats is an adept in Occultism, well, hardly an adept, but a *chela* at any rate, and Connie insists that she is going to study Astrology. To which I reply she must sit at your feet; I rather think you once offered to teach her.[39]

This was Edward at his most mischievous. Nobody could have been more rational and less likely to succumb to a taste for the occult than Constance. Edward was no more to be believed than when, some forty years later, he signed a French hotel register as the Bishop of Chichester.[40] Richard, on the other hand, perhaps as a result of his lack of formal education, was most susceptible to the charms of the pseudo-sciences. His stories reveal considerable knowledge of necromancy; so much so that T. E. Lawrence wrote that 'the learned Doctor would have been in some danger' of being arraigned for witchcraft 'if the nineteenth century had been the ninth or the seventeenth'.[41] He was a practised astrologer, cast horoscopes for his friends, and even wrote on astrology under the anagrammatic pseudonym of A. G. Trent. Edward was thus deftly teasing both his father and his wife.

Richard was always generous to the young couple, though he did not make them a regular allowance. Edward told him, 'Connie manages so admirably with the little I earn, that in spite of my inertia, we are not likely to come to grief'.[42] But she found it hard to do so when the house was full of guests. In one month in the summer of 1890, instead of spending the usual £2 10s on food (the same amount as Edward earned for a review in the *Speaker*), she laid out £6 and warned, 'we cannot afford much of this princely hospitality'.[43] Richard gave them well-chosen presents of books for Christmas and birthdays, as well as un-birthday presents – a sewing-machine, which saved Constance much eye-strain, in the spring of 1891 – and money for holidays; all of which were gratefully accepted, though one present of money in March 1891 was not spent but inaugurated the fund for '"The Thatched House" – a home to be created'.[44] They could afford to do this because, as Edward wrote to his father, 'I am now getting 4£ a week from Mr Unwin – a sum which I am quite content with. I pointed out that 2£. 6/ – a week was inadequate payment for the headwork I have been doing for some time for him, and I offered at the same time to take a further quantity; and he accordingly met my wishes in a kind and liberal spirit.'[45]

In March 1891 Constance wrote to her father-in-law that she would 'come to town next Monday for a week or ten days to effect a household removal on a small scale – from College Buildings to 24 John Street, where we have taken two very nice rooms from quarter day. . . . John Street has many advantages; among the chief, it is very near you.'[46] The following year, after they were well established, Olive noted that 'The new rooms are charming, prettily papered and painted, there is new furniture of simple make and good colour. How much Edward's taste and how much Connie's one can hardly tell.'[47]

In September 1891 Constance told her father-in-law that she was 'hoping to bring you a little grandchild early in the spring'.[48] He responded at once with a present of a 'bamboo lounge' – what now would be called a reclining chair. She was by then four months pregnant, and had 'never been in better health and spirits than the last few months'.[49]

One reason for her good spirits was that she now had some real intellectual exercise, which she had lacked ever since she left the People's Palace. As she wrote:

One day in [June or July] 1891 Edward on coming back from London told me 'I have met a man after your heart – a Russian exile – and I have asked him down for a weekend.' This was Felix Volkhovsky, who had recently escaped from Siberia and he soon became a great friend. He had no home and (I forget whether at his suggestion or ours) it was arranged that he should make our cottage his headquarters.[50]

Edward and Constance were already interested in Russian literature: Edward had written an informed critique of Charles Edward Turner's *Modern Novelists of Russia*, which he felt failed to show 'how they have successfully widened the whole scope and aim of the novel',[51] and Constance had been reading Turgenev in January 1890, probably in French. The young Garnetts were therefore predisposed to be attracted by this new Russian friend. Edward's family had long been sympathetic to political exiles. Richard's mentor at the British Museum was Antonio Panizzi, a refugee from Italy. Karl Marx had been a reader at the British Museum from 1850. Richard was unaware of this when he gave the first volume of *Das Kapital* a cautious review in 1868,[52] but later came to know him well, though Marx never became such a close friend as the 'Anarchist Prince', Kropotkin. 'Political exiles and revolutionaries were thus nothing new to Edward', as his son noted.[53]

Volkhovsky was then aged forty-five, and had with him his ten-year-old daughter, Vera. Ever since his days as a law student at Moscow University he had been in constant trouble with the authorities. He had founded the 'Rouble Society', which, with subscriptions at a rouble a head from like-minded intellectuals, published simple tales designed to appeal to peasants, encourage literacy, and put across an anti-Tsarist message. It was part of the movement of 'going to the people'.

Volkhovsky was arrested three times on suspicion of belonging to 'a secret society', and also of being supposedly involved with a charlatan called Nechayev who managed to convince both the genuine revolutionaries, such as Bakunin, and the authorities that he had an enormous subversive underground network and that bloody revolution was imminent. Volkhovsky was imprisoned three times without trial (when eventually he was tried he was acquitted) and suffered six-and-a-half years of solitary confinement in the Peter-Paul fortress. His sufferings there made him permanently deaf. In the winter of 1877 to 1878 he was arrested with 192 other young people. The spectacular trial merely publicised their revolutionary ideals. Many were acquitted but were mostly picked up afterwards and sent into 'administrative exile' all the same. Volkhovsky spent eleven years in Siberia, the youngest of his three daughters died, and his wife committed suicide.

He escaped from Russia to England by way of Vladivostok, Japan and Vancouver. Vera, who was his second daughter, got out by a subterfuge. Michael Hambourg, a professor of pianoforte at the Moscow Conservatory, had brought his son Mark to London in 1889 to exploit his talents as a musical prodigy. He had left his wife behind in Russia with his other three sons and his daughter to follow later. Their passport listed all five Hambourg children, though Mark was in England. So Vera was shorn of her long hair, dressed as a boy, and successfully smuggled out of Russia disguised as the pianist.[54]

In London Volkhovsky at once began working on the émigré journal, *Free Russia*, and later ran a Free Russian bookshop in Augustus Street, Hammersmith. His career shows the remarkable durability of ordinary human foibles. One might suppose that no one could survive what he had come through without becoming either a saint or a moron. But Constance wrote:

He was a curious mixture – on one side, a fanatical almost Puritanical revolutionary, pedantic and strict, and ready to go to the stake rather than disown or disguise opinions really of no practical importance, scrupulous, – on the other hand, pleasure-loving, vain, rather intriguing, a tremendous 'ladies' man', a first-rate actor, fond of dancing. One day he was a pathetic broken down old man – very sorry for himself – the next day he would look 20 years younger, put a rose in his buttonhole, and lay himself out very successfully to please and entertain.[55]

Olive noted, 'I should have imagined he was a Russian' and remarked on his 'expressive brown eyes and thick straight falling hair'.[56] Although his 'terrible deafness. . . made him a rather tiring companion,'[57] he joined wholeheartedly in their conversations, for he had a good command of English. His Russian friends said that he was just like Rudin, the eloquent hero of Turgenev's novel of that name,[58] who, as Edward put it, 'is a theorist and has never really understood human nature. . . . He lives only for his ideas. . . . He is a master of words, but he cannot act.'[59] Olive spelled this out to her father:

It seems that it is a Russian characteristic to live in a world of theories and to talk of them with great ease as one would ask for a piece of bread and butter. Volkhovsky indeed breathes theories. I think that this must be good for the national character, and it certainly trains the mind and makes life much more interesting. . . . When Volkhovsky is here we live in quite a little Russian world. It is so curious to awake from Siberia to a Surrey lane.[60]

This was most congenial to Edward and Constance, who grew very fond of Volkhovsky and put him and Vera up, not only at Henhurst Cross, but also in their London rooms in John Street. 'He insisted on paying for his board (unlike most Russians he was of a very independent character and strictly honest about such matters).'[61]

Constance was very grateful to him for two 'great services': he made her go for 'rather long walks' in the later months of her pregnancy, to the great benefit of her health, and perhaps of the child's, and he 'suggested my learning Russian and gave me a grammar and a dictionary, and the first story I attempted to read – one of Stankevitch's'.[62] Such was Volkhovsky's influence that Olive too started 'learning a little Russian'. As she told her father, 'it seems an opportunity not to be lost for acquiring the pronunciation, and I can go on with translation when I come home. The elements of Russian seem to be very easy, but I believe that there are "states" of the verbs which come later and are horribly difficult.'[63] Olive was referring to what are more correctly known as 'aspects' of the Russian verb. Her grandfather, the Rev. Richard Garnett, defined the two aspects in one of his formidably learned articles for the Philological Society:

The verb in the Slavonic languages presents some remarkable phenomena . . . a regular, perfectly philosophical distinction is made between perfective and imperfective verbs, that is, between those expressing an action completed at once and not repeated, and those denoting continuance or reiteration. Thus *to dig*, implying a continued action, is regarded as imperfective; but *to bury*, which is done only once to the same subject, is a proper perfective.[64]

Compared with most European languages Russian has few tenses, but this lack is supplied by the 'aspects'. In Russian one is less concerned with a fixed point in time before or after which something is said to happen, than whether it is a continuing or a completed action. Jane Harrison, whose prowess in Greek Constance so much admired, gave a lecture soon after she had taken up Russian, in which she asserted that the Russian language 'clings to the imperfective at all costs', and boldly argued that this was due to an inherent trait in the Russian character, and one that was particularly strong in Dostoevsky. It explained why 'he is not concerned either to approve or disapprove; he has not got there yet . . . the action is never complete; we have no statement of results, no moral judgment; all the people are still alive and may do anything at any time. That is what is so exciting.'[65]

Be that as it may, it was precisely the complexity of the language that Constance found so exciting. She started translating Goncharov's novel, *A Common Story*. 'The first sentence took hours to puzzle out, but I soon advanced to translating a page a day, writing it out as I deciphered it.'[66]
By January 1892 she was able to write to her father-in-law:

I do a few pages – some four or five – of a Russian novel every day, but want a dictionary still for every sentence; and I think it will be some years before I have, as you say, 'mastered' the language, even in the sense of reading it as fluently as French. The idea of speaking it has faded away before an increased knowledge of the subtlety of the language.[67]

This exercise was only partially interrupted by the imminent arrival of David or Narney, as they had decided to call the child. He or she was due in February 1892, and from her mother's and her sister Emma's experience Constance had reason to fear a difficult childbirth. And 'as the only doctor in the Henhurst Cross district was reputed never to arrive until everything was over, as he was a sensitive man and hated seeing women suffer',[68] she thought it wiser to trust to old Dr Humphrey, who had known her all her life (and whom she had run for when her mother was dying), and to go to Brighton before the end of January. At this critical time Edward caught influenza, and for a while was so seriously ill in London that Constance feared it must be typhoid. Even when he was well enough to travel he kept away for fear of infecting his wife and the unborn child.

Constance could only wait, work at her Russian and keep out of the gloomy house in Buckingham Place as much as she could. On 6 February she wrote to Edward, now certain that the child would be David (or 'Hob') rather than Narney:

I have been keeping to my little time table today – went down early to the Pier and sat there a long while, conning my Russian grammar part of the time, but idling for the most part and watching the waves – it was low water and calm – and thinking of my little Hob and how he must grow up without any of the Black coldness, or the Northern Garnett obstinacy. I am praying he will be a warm-blooded impulsive romantic independent muddle-headed boy – full of spirits and sympathetic – nearly all his father with only the smallest grain of his mother and perhaps a little of Gracie in him. Anyway he will be healthy and manly for certain. . .. But I am sure nothing will happen for ages. Hob is so contented where he is and shows no sign of wishing to make a move.[69]

The baby was indeed long in coming. 'Edward . . . says that he begins to think Narney or David must be a Garnett, she or he procrastinates so.'[70] Edward had recovered enough to be at Brighton when at last Constance went into labour. It was, as she had feared, long and difficult. On 10 March, after a stormy night, Edward was able to telegraph his father: 'David Garnett arrived safely last night. Constance all right.'[71] He hastened to send his father the wherewithal to cast a nativity: 'The time of birth was a quarter to twelve (at night) exactly, Greenwich time. The doctor used chloroform and instruments, or no doubt it would not have taken place until well into Thursday (this) morning.'[72]

David Garnett's horoscope when it came was drawn up with legal formality in a fine copperplate hand by James R. Wallace ('Mercury') of Halifax. It could hardly have been gloomier:

The Nativity is an unfortunate one. It is bad enough to have Saturn in the Midheaven, even if he be void of aspect. But here he casts his bad aspects wholesale, as he squares Mars in the 2nd house, opposes Jupiter, Mercury, and the Sun in the 4th, and is in semi-square to the Moon also.[73]

Consequently the 'native' was in danger of death by accident, to say nothing of financial loss and bankruptcy; in short, 'This is not a nativity which promises honour, authority, or public esteem, and the native should not seek to enter public life.'[74] The only helpful advice that 'Mercury' could give was: 'My opinion is, that he should keep to his birthplace, Brighton, and engage there in something relating to the sea, or to liquors and liquids, matters connected with bathing, boat-hiring, aerated water-making, dealing in liquors, etc.'[75]

Fortunately nobody took much notice of this solemn tosh, least of all the 'native' himself. He was from the first a sturdy healthy baby, as his mother had predicted. It was only some months later, after he had cut his first tooth, that Constance admitted, 'I am terribly afraid there is really something wrong with his sweet little eyes. . . . I had a fearful pang – it struck me at once that he looked as if one eye were blind.'[76] It was not. But he did have a defect of his eye muscles, due, so Constance was told, to damage caused by the forceps at birth. It did not cause a squint, but merely prevented him from looking out of the corners of his eyes. Far from being a disfigurement, this meant that he had to turn his head and give you his full attention, and many people found his candid gaze most attractive.

As Richard's first grandchild he was doted on not only by his mother but also by all the rest of the Garnetts, especially Narney. He was given various saccharine pet-names (which out of respect for his memory will be left in decent obscurity). These were eventually extinguished when he was given two volumes of Caldecott's picture books:

the picture of Baby Bunting crawling on the floor in his rabbit skin provoked such adoration . . . that a rabbit skin was eventually cured with alum and saltpetre and made into a little cap for me to wear, as a result of which I was promptly called Bunny by the village boys, and Bunny I have remained.[77]

In character he turned out very much as Constance had hoped, except that he was not without his share of 'the Northern Garnett obstinacy'. Neither Edward nor Constance had the least doubt that there was such a thing as a 'Black' or a 'Garnett' with immediately recognisable characteristics. This, as much as any incipient strains in their marriage, is illustrated in a legendary exchange:

Edward: 'Alas and alack, I have married a Black.'
Constance: 'Oh damn it, oh darn it, I have married a Garnett.'[78]

Constance thought of herself as a 'Black'. 'I am cold-hearted but benevolent' she remarked to a friend, who wrote: 'But that was not true: her heart was not at all cold, and she was capable of deep and powerful feelings. In actual fact she had a passionate temperament, but only those close to her understood this – the rest saw her only as "gentle, patient, reserved and shy".'[79]

Constance was slow to recover from her ordeal. Nine days after David's birth she wrote to her father-in-law that she was 'well enough to write a pencil note at last' and 'To-day I am at last to be allowed to leave my bed and lie on a sofa in my room; tomorrow I shall be allowed an armchair' and added, 'I feel so intensely happy and thankful all has gone so well; and now we have nothing to fear in the future and everything to look forward to, I used to think Edward and I could not possibly be happier; but now we seem to be achieving the impossible!'[80]

This was an illusion. Much as she may have worried before the child was born, she must soon have realised, like every other normally affectionate parent – and she was more than usually affectionate – that once a child is born it 'entwines itself into your tenderest guts',[81] as her own child was to put it, and your peace of mind is thereafter at risk. Indeed within a few days of her euphoric letter to Richard she was writing at length to Edward:

I had a long talk with the old doctor yesterday. He was very sympathetic and nice. The moral of his remarks was – that I must expect now to feel middle-aged – that a certain spring of youth etc is always lost in childbirth – that one can never look at life in the same way again. But all the same I think – and I have meant to talk to you some time about it – that looking on it dispassionately on the outside – for both our sakes – it is very important to our happiness that I *should* get back a little of the keen edge of my feelings again. I am always trying to work up my feelings – trying – and oh so unsuccessfully! – to feel excited (for instance about the Huts, about your work, and in all our desires – such as to try to want to see Sarah Bernhardt). The only thing that I can do in which I really feel satisfied is in *doing* things – working at my translation – making Baby a frock etc. Of course you know I do get a great great happiness out of Baby and I never felt a tenderer love for you. But it is a passionless unegoistic love. . . . It isn't for my sake I say this really, chiefly – it is because I seem to see you tied for life to a middle-aged dreary resigned woman – wet-blanket on everything – I want to be young a little longer![82]

She was only thirty (Edward was twenty-four); and she was impatient to feel the return of sexual love – for that is surely what she is describing – and 'desperately anxious to get home to our cottage (Brighton is a hateful place)'.[83] But she remained in Brighton for Grace's wedding to Hugh Human on 31 March. Grace made it an austere occasion, 'You see she won't have money spent on flowers and she won't have her presents here and she won't have a "breakfast" so there really won't be anything bridal or festive to carry it off.'[84] But Richard Garnett came and partook of the 'cold collation' beforehand, and 'He has such a delightful way of always seeming pleased with any entertainment' that he and Edward did something to break 'the monotony of our Scotch and Dutch dulness'.[85] Grace and Hugh went to live in a 'very poky little flat'[86] in Holbein Buildings near Sloane Square, and Hugh, in deference to Grace's pacifist principles, gave up his job working on torpedoes and had to look for something else.

About a week later, and four weeks after giving birth to David, as Constance recalled:

though I felt very weak and disjointed, I went back with the baby and David Rice's sister Alice. Unluckily at the station I had to run for the train, and this was followed by troubles that caused me discomfort on and off for thirty years afterwards, and made it necessary for me to lie down almost all day for a long time.[87]

This was almost certainly a prolapse of the uterus. Today this would be treated with remedial exercises and minor surgery. But then the patient was prescribed constant rest, and Constance also had the disagreeable experience of having to wear an internal 'support'. Her disability did not make it any easier to cope with 'the received practice to feed babies at first every two hours day and night'.[88] Edward and Constance were 'poor sleepers at the best'[89] and even with the help of a nurse girl 'David drove us almost gibbering the first six months of his life'.[90] Other things conspired to increase their burdens at Henhurst Cross:

That summer there was an extraordinary drought. I believe there was no rain in the late spring and early summer for twelve weeks. Our well ran dry – every drop of water had to be saved. We got a kettle or two a day for drinking from a neighbour, and Edward brought pailsful from the stream which shrank and shrank till there were only a few muddy pools. Water was so precious that after being boiled and washing the baby's bottles, it had to wash his clothes, and only then was used for washing up our crockery, and then our dirty hands.[91]

It was a wonder that they did not all die of typhoid. Constance gradually recovered most of her health. But David Garnett wrote, 'My parents never shared a bedroom in my memory',[92] and at some point their marriage seems to have become virtually celibate. If this did not happen in the summer of 1892, Constance clearly foresaw that before long it might, as she told Edward in a letter that accurately spelled out the rest of their marriage:

I want to tell you how dear you are to me. I am frightened sometimes that . . . because one side of passion seems to have died away for a while in me, you may begin to doubt my love. Dear one, do believe that my heart is full of tenderness and love and gratitude to you; and no new interest – not even my little beebi – can ever make that less. . . . I want to make you happy without clogging you and hampering you as women always do. I know and see quite clearly that in many ways we must get more separate as time passes but that need never touch the innermost core of love which will always remain with us.[93]

7

The Gentle Nihilist

Some time in the summer of 1892 Volkhovsky took Edward and Constance to 31 Blandford Road in Bedford Park, Chiswick, to meet the editor of *Free Russia*. His real name was Sergey Mikhailovich Kravchinsky, but he was always known by his revolutionary *nom-de-guerre*, Stepniak, or 'man of the steppes'. They took to one another at once, and this meeting was, as Constance said, One of the most important events of my life'.[1] By 11 August she was writing to Edward: 'A letter from Stepniak yesterday – and another from his wife and him today – both quite affectionate and evidently anxious to come to us at once. . . . Mrs Stepniak asks if there is a room, a tent or a stable in our neighbourhood where they could stay a fortnight.'[2]

She later wrote of Stepniak:

He was of medium height and burly with very broad shoulders, a dark beard, dark eyes, a big forehead and a broad Russian nose. He was very strong and he had the gentleness, the quietness, which so often goes with great physical strength in men. He had also great warmth of heart, often found among Russians, and a genius for drawing out the best qualities of the people around him, and this warmth of heart and interest in other people seemed as though they were part of his physical make-up. Just as his broad powerful hands seemed able to understand material without any trouble, so that he could make anything he wanted, of wood, or leather, or metal, so his warm heart enabled him to understand all kinds of people, and to set them on the road they should follow.[3]

And in her unfinished memoir she wrote of him:

He had the perfect intellectual honesty so rare in the English. At the same time he was undisciplined, incapable of living by rule. His 'softness' made me despair; he was shamelessly exploited by the other Russian exiles, and often did injudicious things, simply because as he said '*Ya nikogo ne mogu obidet* [I can't bring myself to hurt anyone].' To my horror I found that he habitually carried books out of the British Museum reading room at the lunch-hour, and I could

81

not make him feel that it was a crime, since, as he said, he always took them back.[4]

He was good with children, though he had none of his own, and David liked to be carried on his broad shoulders. Edward once fantastically declared: 'A goddess fell in love with a bear – and so was born Stepniak.'[5] Constance thought this a very good pedigree, but David, who was then not yet four years old, had somehow come to hear of such terrible bears as those that revenged themselves on the children who mocked Elisha, and after pondering the matter said, 'That bear that was Uncle Stepniak's Dad was a *good* bear.'[6]

In conversation he was irresistible, 'the only man who ever succeeded in reducing Bernard Shaw to silence'.[7] In his best known photograph he seems to be trying to beat one into submission with his thunderous brow, and Olive Garnett wrote: 'he overwhelmed us not only morally and mentally but physically. In argument he comes up and literally towers over one.'[8] On the other hand she recorded only one occasion when 'gloomy, suffering, frowning, he looked more like that photograph of him which I have than I have seen him look yet'.[9] And Bernard Shaw, who knew him well, wrote:

No doubt his massive head, his black hair, his powerful shoulders, his immense concentration of expression, used to impress people and even overawe some of them. But if he ever made any deliberate dramatic use of his formidable aspect, I never detected it. On the contrary, his charm in private intercourse was that he betrayed the heart of an affectionate child behind a powerful and very live intellect. . . . At first I used to wonder how far Stepniak's way of contracting his neck between his shoulders with a sort of shy, nestling action, and looking up at you in an irresistibly disarming way, was due to the fact that he was struggling with a language other than his own; but I gave up that theory on observing that it was the same when he spoke Russian.[10]

His wife, Fanny (*née* Lichkus), had been a medical student in Russia, where she was imprisoned for trying to get into a trial with false papers. She had had a daughter when they were in exile in Switzerland, but the baby was premature and lived for only a few days. According to David Garnett, Fanny was 'a birdlike, fuzzy-haired Russian Jewess, impulsive, passionate and apt to fly into sudden tantrums'. And he adds, 'She was . . . violently jealous of every woman he met, including Constance.'[11] On the other hand, it is fair to say that Olive's diary (admittedly self-censored of 'painful' material) gives no hint of these tantrums, and describes several occasions when Fanny Stepniak had every excuse for

Sergey Stepniak   Fanny Stepniak   Felix Volkhovsky

Nellie Heath   Constance with David

Henhurst Cross

The Cearne

showing jealousy, but did not do so. On the contrary, she completely accepted Stepniak's adoption of the younger Garnett girls as his 'dear daughters' and always remained on affectionate terms with them. Her relations with Constance were far less comfortable, and though they remained friends for life, Fanny was apt to be touchy and to take offence at trifles.

Stepniak allowed himself to be called a Nihilist; but he was very different from Bazarov in *Fathers and Children*, with whom Turgenev established the term, if he did not coin it. Bazarov believed in nothing, rejected all received opinions, spurned the arts, and sought scientific truth by dissecting frogs. But the term Nihilist had become attached to the more active revolutionaries, and Stepniak had let it stick. He had, however, a deep sympathy for the arts and considerable knowledge of music and literature. 'It is still a grievance', Olive noted, 'that people will insist on regarding him as a political character and not as a literary critic',[12] 'writing novels is what he really enjoys'.[13] He felt that force of circumstance had obliged him to become a political character as well as an artist, just as it had done Shaw. Socialism for him was a matter of morality rather than economics.

Stepniak had taken refuge in England in 1884 and been very active in propaganda against Tsarist autocracy, as both a journalist and a writer of books. In 1890 he founded the Society of Friends of Russian Freedom – the secretary, as usual, was Edward Pease. In August of that year he began bringing out a monthly journal, *Free Russia*, which soon established itself as an accurate source of information that the Tsarist regime would have preferred not to see reported, as it was quoted in the British press. At the end of the magazine there was usually a full-page advertisement in French for the British-made 'Cyclostyle'. Then, as now, in the struggle against tyranny the pen was mightier than the sword, but the copying machine was mightier than either.

At the end of 1890 Stepniak went to America, where George Kennan's damning exposés of the exile system in Siberia had been appearing in the *Century Magazine* for the last three years, and had aroused much sympathy for his cause. There he gave some fifty lectures, making converts and setting up an American society, which did not, however, last long after his return to England. Despite his hesitant English and strong Russian accent (his private letters are written in much less practised English than Volkhovsky's), Olive thought he lectured 'delight-fully, as if he were having a confidential talk with his hearers',[14] although on a later occasion he 'laboured very much to explain his meaning'.[15] But then, if Bernard Shaw is to be believed, 'the longer he lived in England, the less he thought about the difficulty of the language, and consequently the worse he spoke it'.[16]

Stepniak in England was 'very careful not to offend English prejudices',[17] demanding no more for Russia than an end to autocracy and the iniquitous exile system, an amnesty for political prisoners and the institution of a constitutional monarchy with a parliamentary democracy on British lines. Although he was an active supporter of the Fabians, Stepniak was by now so far to the right of some of the more hot-headed socialists that Shaw thought he was almost a Liberal.

But in his earlier career, about which he rarely spoke, there had been events of a far more revolutionary nature. He was born in 1851,[18] the son of an army doctor, and graduated from the St Petersburg Artillery School in 1870. Soon afterwards he joined the revolutionary Tchaykovsky circle, and in August 1873 was one of the first to 'go to the people'. Being good with his hands, he was able to get work among the peasants as a sawyer. The ordinary people liked and trusted him, and so he was unusually successful as a propagandist. When he was arrested he was set free by the very peasants who were supposed to be guarding him. He fought for six months in Bosnia-Herzegovina, using his artillery training to help rebels against the Turks. But the rebellion was crushed; and in 1876 he went to Italy and engaged in revolutionary activity there until he was arrested with a revolver in his possession and imprisoned. In gaol he learned Spanish and Italian (he already had a working knowledge of English, German and French), and translated works from Italian. On 9 January 1878 King Victor Emmanuel died, and his successor, Umberto I, declared a general amnesty on his accession, and so Stepniak was released.

While he had been away the revolutionaries had brought off a remarkable coup in Russia. The trial of the 193 (Volkhovsky had been one of them) had aroused public sympathy for the cause, but had not made the authorities any less repressive. The governor of St Petersburg, General Trepov, was particularly brutal and had one prisoner, who refused to take his hat off to him, flogged so unmercifully that he went mad. In revenge for this act, which was not only brutal, but illegal under Russian law, Vera Zasulich, a veteran revolutionary at twenty-six, queued up at the usual time for petitioners' visits, and when it came to her turn, took two shots at the governor. The first time the pistol misfired. The second time she hit him in the pelvis. She was of course arrested, but the authorities, hoping to deflect public odium from themselves, did not treat it as a political crime, and had her tried by jury, who they felt sure must convict her. The judge, however, was scrupulously impartial, despite pressure from above, and the defending counsel managed to turn the trial into a choice between Zasulich and Trepov. The jury preferred Zasulich. They simply ignored the evidence and found her not guilty. By the time the police were ready to arrest her again she had gone into hiding, and before long she was safe in Geneva.[19]

Tolstoy thought it was 'a harbinger of revolution'.[20] Dostoevsky, who was present at the trial, incorporated much of what he saw into *The Brothers Karamazov*. Stepniak, who was not, was inspired to emulate Zasulich. He felt that the autocracy was now an absolutely arbitrary tyranny 'which was not supported, and did not wish to be supported, by the nation, or by any class, or by the laws which it had made itself'.[21]

Against such a Government everything is permitted. It is no longer the guardian of the will of the people, or of the majority of the people. It is organised injustice. A citizen is no more bound to respect it, than to respect a band of highwaymen who employ force at their command in rifling travellers.[22]

Stepniak found an opportunity to emulate Zasulich. General N. V. Mezentsev was Chief of Police in St Petersburg. When prisoners in the terrible Peter-Paul fortress went on hunger-strike and demanded to be moved somewhere where the conditions were less appalling, he merely said, 'Let them starve. I have ordered their coffins.'[23]

On 15 August 1878 it was reported that Ivan Kovalsky, a student from Odessa University, whom Stepniak had known in the Tchaykovsky circle, had been executed for armed resistance to the police. Stepniak decided to retaliate by assassinating Mezentsev. On the following day Mezentsev was taking a morning walk in Mikhailovsky Square with a retired colonel called Makarov. He was met by

an unknown young man of medium height, dressed in a grey overcoat and wearing glasses, who . . . threw himself at him, struck him in the chest with a dagger and ran round the corner into Bolshaya Italyanskaya Street. Makarov chased after him, shouting 'Stop him!' and hitting out wildly with his umbrella; at that moment another young man with a black moustache, in a long dark blue coat and a round black beaver hat, fired at Makarov almost point-blank but did not hit him, then both the murderers jumped into the droshky, probably their own, standing in the Italyanskaya harnessed to a black horse . . . galloped off along the Malaya Sadovaya and were hidden from sight.[24]

Stepniak justified his action in a pamphlet, *The Assassination of General Mezentsev*, dedicated to 'the sacred memory of Ivan Martynovich Koval- sky', which is better known by its sub-title, *A Death for a Death*.

A reward of 50,000 roubles was offered, but Stepniak eluded capture, living in St Petersburg with false papers as an 'illegal person', a way of life described in some detail in *Underground Russia* (originally written in Italian as *La Russia Sotterranea*). In that book Stepniak did not acknowl- edge his hand in the assassination, but merely wrote of it with approval, and praised the self-sacrifice and daring of the terrorists – who, unlike those of today, were content to murder only those directly concerned in the Tsarist oppression rather than slaughter the public indiscriminately. His aim was

to reconcile Europe to the bloody measures of the Russian revolutionaries, to show on the one hand their inevitability in Russian conditions, on the other to depict the terrorists themselves as they are in reality, i.e. not as cannibals, but as humane people, highly moral, having a deep aversion to all violence, to which they are only forced by governmental measures.[25]

Once he had published *La Russia Sotterranea*, where he first used the name 'Stepniak' – without any Christian name or initials – he was never known as anything else, and evaded questions about his revolutionary career. But he was momentarily caught out at a press reception on his arrival in New York on 30 December 1890. The journalists were generally friendly, but then:

'Have you ever killed anybody?' mildly inquired one of the journalists.
Stepniak opened his eyes at this question, as well he might, but he answered it promptly in the negative.
'I didn't suppose that you had,' said the inquirer.[26]

The friendship between the Garnetts and the Stepniaks prospered. By the middle of October Constance was going once a week to the Stepniaks to read Russian. He encouraged her to pursue her translations, and it was due to him that she began to have a sense of vocation to translate Russian literature, and Edward to promote it. The Stepniaks became part of the family. Unlike Volkhovsky, who had begun to get on Edward's nerves and to irritate Constance with his demands for devotion, Stepniak asked nothing from them except that they give of their best. His intentions were entirely benign. But he put further strains on their marriage, for there is no doubt that during the next few months Constance fell 'more than a little' in love with him.[27] Quite how serious it was is impossible to determine. Very few of their letters survive, and when writing to Edward, usually very affectionately, she never mentions Stepniak other than as a good friend whom they both shared. But it was generally believed afterwards by Constance's friends that she had been in love with Stepniak. They were equally sure that it did not become an 'affair'. She had no objection in principle to women having extramarital affairs, but, as her son said, 'She did not make such experiments herself.'[28] And she probably still had little desire for sexual love.

All this put even further strains on Edward, and he 'took it very hard',[29] but he 'admired and appreciated Stepniak's strength and goodness',[30] and 'he showed his character by being immensely sympathetic' to him.[31] Moreover, in their different ways they inspired one another. When Edward was working well Constance told Olive that 'Stepniak inspired him, and that they mutually encouraged one another'.[32] And on 26 November 1892 Stepniak told Olive 'as a great secret that while he was at the cottage he had the idea for a short novel, he has made . . . Edward . . . the hero, imagining what he would have been had he been a nihilist. He wrote the whole thing in a fortnight about 15,000 words'.[33] This is perhaps his short story, *Domik na Volge* (*The House on the Volga*), in which the description of the hero, Vladimir Murinov, is certainly reminiscent of Edward.[34]

Stepniak passed his Russian friends on to Constance, so that before long she was complaining to Olive that whereas Olive was 'very fortunate to know such a large number of young men, all rather above the average', she herself hardly knew 'any even now, except Russians'.[35] Stepniak would ask her to talk Russian or French to visitors who knew no English. She found herself having to entertain a Russian diva, Madame Sviatlovsky, who was appearing as the old nurse in the first London production of *Eugene Onegin* at the Olympic Theatre.[36] Later Olive called at the flat in John Street and came upon Constance talking Russian to 'a very pleasant motherly middle-aged woman, like . . . the best type of French peasant woman',[37] who was a trained nurse and midwife. This was Sofya Nikolaevna Lavrov, a fervent disciple of Bakunin. She had abandoned her husband, a retired army officer,[38] in order to be a revolutionary. Her sister's brother-in-law was Peter Kropotkin. Kropotkin was a prince by birth, from one of the most aristocratic families in Russia. He was born in 1842 and brought up at the court of Nicholas I. He had a distinguished career as a geographer before becoming the apostle of philosophic Anarchism. With the help of Stepniak and

Madame Lavrov he made a dramatic escape from prison in Russia, was later imprisoned in France, and settled in England in 1883. David Garnett remembered 'this extraordinary man' as 'a very familiar figure in my youth':

He was rather tall and always wore a frock coat. He had eyes which gleamed with perpetual excitement behind steel spectacles, he was bald but had by far the largest beard I have ever known – a beard which fanned out to his shoulders on each side and covered everything down to his solar plexus, and he never stopped pouring out a torrent of ideas. . . .

He radiated benevolence: he was entirely unselfconscious, he was unaware of time and of practical life. He liked to stand up when he was talking and he often walked about the room gesticulating with a forgotten cup of cold tea in one hand. . . .

Disbelieving in God and every code of morality, he was profoundly convinced of the inherent reasonableness and goodness of all mankind, which needed only to get rid of the whole of its inheritance – to shed not only kings and queens and capitalists, but gold and silver and copper, churches and bishops and vestments – to stand forth in all its natural majesty, magnanimity and truth. All that was needed, he believed, was a thorough spring-cleaning for mankind to live in perfect peace and happiness thereafter.[39]

Princess Kropotkin, as she liked to be called, though Kropotkin had renounced his title and there is some doubt whether he had actually married her, for any form of legal marriage was against his principles, was 'a short ugly Mongolian looking woman',[40] for whom Constance felt a 'distaste'[41]; and David thought their daughter Alexandra was a 'pest'.[42]

Kropotkin's Anarchist views were shared by the children of William Michael Rossetti, who had taken over the Garnetts' house in St Edmund's Terrace when they moved to the British Museum. Olive, Helen and Arthur produced an Anarchist magazine, *The Torch*, which they printed in the basement and sold on the streets and at May Day rallies in Hyde Park. In December 1891, when the eldest of them was only sixteen, they had shown Olive Garnett their statement of 'principles', on the strength of which she had become a 'member', and they had taught her to set type.[43] But since then she had come to think that their hopes of converting the upholders of authority – the army, the police, the prison warders – to Anarchism were naive. She remarked of the young Rossettis: 'Poor children they want so much to know some desperate characters and no one will introduce them'.[44] And when Edward and Constance spent an afternoon at the Garnetts' residence in the British Museum talking Anarchy, French Revolution etc.' with Olive and Helen Rossetti, Olive Garnett commented: 'I was glad that they should meet, the humorous way in which E. and C. conversed with them delighted me; my moral conversations compared with their more delicate method seem brutal.'[45]

But not all their friends were Russians or Anarchists. In October 1892 they had a visitor at Henhurst Cross who was to become as important in her way as Stepniak. This was Nellie Heath. She was then aged twenty, a younger sister of Carl Heath who found Constance her rooms in College Buildings, and she had met Edward and Constance briefly when Constance was working at the People's Palace. Nellie's Christian names were Ellen Maurice, but she was never known to the Garnetts as anything but Nellie, though some of her French friends called her Ellen. Her mother had died before she was nine years old, and her father, Richard Heath, took his young family to live in France, where Nellie went to school. Heath was a devout Christian socialist, who held an almost mystical view of the brotherhood and the sufferings of the working man. He had himself begun life as an artisan, an engraver by trade, whose job it was to convert the rough sketches of 'our correspondent' into printable and often very striking illustrations for the magazines. Nellie was also an artist. When she left school she had come back to England, where she had studied painting under Sickert, for whom she developed a violent but unrequited 'crush'. In her prime Nellie was a painter in oils of scrupulous honesty and fidelity. She shared something of her father's altruism and saintliness, and was 'religious but without overt religious affiliations'.[46] David Garnett wrote of her:

The first impression was of extraordinary softness, a softness physically expressed at that time in velvet blouses and velveteen skirts; a softness of speech and a gentleness of manner and disposition which made it difficult and painful for her to disagree with, and impossible flatly to contradict, any statement made to her. . . .

But under this softness was an iron will-power. . . .. She would not be driven; she refused, in spite of her extreme gentleness, to be coerced.[47]

Nellie's visit to Henhurst Cross was a happy occasion, they went 'shopping in Dorking and were so fortunate as to find a magnificent circus perambulating the town'.[48] It was also a turning point in Nellie's life. She would always remember when she came that time to Henhurst Cross. She felt that the little Garnett family was 'something so peculiarly lovely' and loved all three of them ever afterwards. She was especially attached to the little boy, who was for her 'quite separate from other children'.[49]

David had always been a happy distraction from Constance's work at her Russian; now he was becoming a positive hindrance. Olive described him about this time as

a delicious little rogue . . . a regular little country urchin, with flaxen floss silky hair, lily skin and rosy cheeks. He has a most humourous expression when amused, and is full of life and spirits, never still for a moment so that he requires constant attention. He is without fear, and the natural phenomena around him give him constant occupation in experimenting – chiefly with his mouth.[50]

And Constance confirmed this when she wrote to her father-in-law to thank him for a birthday present of *Peer Gynt*:

David is very well and boisterously active. His capacities for mischief are developing rapidly and I foresee that some discipline will be required before long to keep the little person within bounds. Temptation takes the form at present of books and manuscripts. The imp is never so happy as when he gets hold of some unobserved and he is a formidable destructive critic – quite merciless in his treatment of them.[51]

For Christmas they once again went to Brighton, where the little boy charmed his old grandfather and 'trotted round my father's couch, not in the least shy or frightened of his great bald head, white beard and ivory white face'.[52] It was the Humans' last Christmas in England. Sydney Olivier in the Colonial Office had arranged for Hugh to be appointed head of a technical college in Colombo. He and Grace, who had 'become a model wife and will not do anything without consulting her husband',[53] were due to sail from Tilbury Docks to Ceylon on the *Oratara* on 12 January.

There was a larger party than usual for Christmas. Arthur Black was there with his wife Jessie and his two children, Speedwell, who was five years old, and Leslie, a baby of fifteen months. Arthur, who was remembered as 'dear Arthur' for having been so kind to Constance as a child, had not been involved in his sisters' social life in London, and when Speedwell had come to stay at Henhurst Cross it was without her parents. Arthur had taken an external degree in mathematics at University College, London, in 1877, and though he did well and was a favourite pupil of W. K. Clifford, professor of applied mathematics, he had not fulfilled his earlier promise. He did interesting original work, but it was not published. He did not get any kind of academic post, but earned an obscure living coaching private pupils in mathematics, and had recently begun teaching at the School of Science and Art in Brighton.

He seems to have led a lonely and isolated life, a consequence probably of an unfortunate marriage. On 29 January 1886 he had been married in church, despite his agnostic convictions, to Jessie Kelly, a bootmaker's daughter from Kew. He was then thirty-four and she was eighteen. Jessie Kelly has left little trace of herself. David Garnett believed that Arthur's marriage was due to 'a crazy idealism'. He wrote, 'He went with a prostitute and then believed it was his duty to "save" her. That is my interpretation and I think it was my mother's also.'[54] On the other hand, Marion Gregory recalls that Jessie's daughter Speedwell once denied hotly that her mother had been a 'fallen woman'. If Arthur was 'making an honest woman' out of the girl he had seduced – unlike his father with Elizabeth Viney – she was not pregnant with their first child, who was not born until twenty-one months after the marriage.

Arthur and Jessie were on record as an affectionate couple, but for whatever reason, social disparity or lack of common interests, Jessie was unhappy and neurotic, and by the end of 1892 she had become subject to attacks of violent hysteria. She was 'such an untidy body'[55] and so neglected her home and her family that she made it impossible for any servant to live in the house at 27 Goldstone Villas, and Speedwell was taken away to live with Clementina as her adopted daughter.

On Thursday 19 January 1893 Edward wrote to his father from Brighton, whither he must have hurried that same afternoon:

A very terrible thing has happened. Arthur Black has killed his wife his boy and himself.

He was undoubtedly insane at the time. His wife, whom he had always treated too well, drove him to madness, by her drunkenness.

The inquest will be held today or tomorrow.

The Blacks are here.

I write a line in haste to say that the matter had better not be discussed before strangers and servants and that the halfpenny papers be kept out of the house.[56]

The inquest was held by Mr Bedford, the Deputy Coroner for East Sussex, on the following day. The official records have been lost, but it was very fully reported in the Brighton newspapers, from which the following story emerges.

Arthur did not turn up for the first day of school term, Tuesday 17th. Mr Miller, the school secretary, wrote to him at once, of course without result, and so on Thursday he went to 27 Goldstone Villas. When he got no reply he reported the matter to the police. They sent a detective, Walter Parsons, who, having likewise knocked in vain, fetched Ernest Black, and together they broke through the window on to the area, though the garden door seems, by Ernest's and the detective's accounts, to have been unbolted. Inside they found the baby, Leslie, in his nightdress, lying in a pool of blood on a mattress beside the bed. He had a wound at the back of the neck apparently made with a knife, and his skull was broken. They hurried upstairs and were met by 'the feet of some person protruding from the doorway of the back room on the ground floor'.[57] This proved to be Jessie Black. She was lying on her back, and her head 'appeared to have been smashed by some blunt instrument'[58] so violently that there were brains as well as a pool of blood on the floor. She also had a wound in her neck, which the police surgeon, Edward Treves, who had not yet done an autopsy, thought was probably caused by a bullet. Ernest and the detective then followed a trail of blood up the stairs to the next floor, where in the room that had been Arthur and Jessie's bedroom, Arthur was lying in his nightshirt face downwards on the bed. He had been bleeding from the nose, and there was a bullet wound in the right thigh which the police surgeon said could not have been self-inflicted. On a small table by the bed there was a revolver with four chambers discharged and two still loaded with their cartridges, a blood-stained coal-hammer and knife and a collection of medicine bottles, some of which had contained chloroform. Arthur had drunk it and it had killed him; it had also, according to the police surgeon, caused the bleeding from the nose. There was no suicide note, only 'an unopened letter in the letter-box from the little girl [Speedwell], stating how happy she was'.[59]

The verdict of the jury was that 'the mother and child came to their death by the hand of Mr. Black, and that Mr. Black destroyed himself whilst of unsound mind'.[60] This was the inevitable formula for any suicide. It was taken up by Edward in a letter to his father of 20 January: 'Most likely the verdict is correct – certainly Arthur was insane.'[61]

But if he was indeed insane, what had driven him to madness? At the inquest Ernest, and particularly Elizabeth Eastwood, 'nurse and charwoman', testified that Arthur was 'always patient and kind towards' his wife.[62] She on the other hand, although she 'always spoke of her husband in the most affectionate terms',[63] was, according to Ernest, 'one of those weak-minded eccentric women, almost hysterical, liable to all kinds of fancies; and she was a very jealous woman'.[64] Mrs Eastwood spoke of her fits of hysteria in which

she would walk and rave about the house, tear up and down stairs, and sometimes no one could pacify her. It didn't matter to her whether people were in the house or not. Mr. Black would have to leave them and go to her. Her screams were so terrible that the neighbours each side were alarmed. When she had these fits she had all kinds of queer delusions. She told me on one occasion that someone was strangling her. I only came to the conclusion that it was a delusion.[65]

Although Edward and Ernest were agreed about her drunkenness, Mrs Eastwood had never seen her 'the worse for drink',[66] while Arthur was 'a total abstainer'.[67] In short, the evidence tended to show Arthur as kindly, balanced and sane, while Jessie was hysterical, slovenly and perhaps inebriate.

A neighbour, Mrs Ellen Bird, testified to hearing two shots in Arthur's bedroom – but only two, and no screams – at seven-twenty on Tuesday morning. Another neighbour, Florence Evans, swore to having seen Arthur in Goldstone Villas around six-thirty on Wednesday evening, although Mr Treves thought he must have been dead by then. The charwoman, who may well have been dramatising her story after the event, said that on Saturday Arthur 'had a very wild look; in fact, if I had not seen him on the previous Wednesday and then found him very much altered, I should not have known him'.[68] She remarked that he seemed much changed, and he replied, 'Yes, I am; I have enough to make me.'[69] But he gave no indication what had happened between Wednesday 11th and Saturday 14th to effect such a terrible change in him. And there are other puzzles: Why had Mrs Bird heard only two shots, when four chambers in the pistol had been fired? Whose blood had left the trail upon the stairs? And did Mrs Evans really see Arthur in the street on Wednesday evening after two shots had been fired?

Edward wrote of the inquest that 'the whole thing was so hastened through that several very curious features in the case were not gone into'.[70] This is so much the language of Sherlock Holmes, whose 'Adventure of the Cardboard Box' was appearing in that month's issue of the *Strand Magazine*, that one almost expects the great detective to take over and explain all. Without such superhuman aid, no post-mortems except on Arthur, and no opportunity to cross-examine the witnesses, it seems impossible to resolve all the inconsistencies and produce a coherent explanation.

J. E. Bush, the Deputy Coroner for Brighton, who represented Arthur's relatives at the inquest, 'submitted that the evidence was just as strong in favour of the mother having slain her child in a fit of jealousy, and the husband might then have taken her life'.[71] This was the version that Arthur's niece recalled; and it is probably what Constance believed. But she said nothing. The skeleton was pushed into the family cupboard and the key turned in the lock. Even David Garnett, who liked to think himself open about everything, refused to have it mentioned. Olive, who was staying at Henhurst Cross when the tragedy occurred, excised all mention of it from her diary, but overlooked one loose scrap of paper, which reads:

saying that 'it was not fair to her'. Thus he was almost isolated, and succumbed in the end in a way which had [be]en already foreshadowed in the minds of his friends [72]

Speedwell, the sole survivor, was brought up by Clementina. On 15 January, when her father was probably lying dead in Brighton, Clementina had taken her to see the Garnetts at the British Museum, and Olive found her 'a tiny child, pretty, very shy to-day, and like the little girl in Sir Joshua Reynolds' picture, who is holding the mouse-trap'.[73] And after her parents' death the other Blacks, especially Kate, continued to make much of her.

Arthur died intestate, but in a draft will he bequeathed his manuscripts to Constance.[74] In due course she and her brother Robert set about trying to get some of them published. They were sent to Karl Pearson, whom Constance had known ever since the days of The Club. He was impressed by Arthur's work on the mathematics of animal evolution, but felt it was 'undesirable to go into his mathematical treatment so long as I am busy on the subject myself' [75] and passed it on to Francis Galton, the most distinguished geneticist of the day. Galton was impressed by Arthur's ability, but found his mathematics difficult to follow. In the end only an extract of his work was published, despite Constance's plea:

It is very painful to think that work, which is all that remains of his very rare and original mind, should be altogether lost and wasted. If what he has done, could be of any value as a basis, or in any way embodied in another man's work, I should be for my part, as I know he would have been, quite content.[76]

But it was not, and the manuscript of his *Algebra of Animal Evolution* was lost. Some account of his other work Of high quality' was given in a brief paper by Donald A. MacKenzie in 1977.[77]

After a later bereavement, in infinitely less shocking circumstances, Constance was 'so numbed, so stupefied by the suddenness and awfulness of it'[78] that she could not 'face it or realize it at all'[79] for nearly two months. But Arthur's crime and death remained always too awful to be mentioned, perhaps ever to be faced at all. Somehow, despite the numbness and shock, she disciplined herself with her usual stoicism to work harder than ever at her Russian. On the verso of the scrap of Olive's diary that seems to refer to Arthur and Jessie, Olive wrote: 'We discussed "Dimitri Roudine" which Connie is going to translate and for which Stepniak is to write a preface.'[80]

Dimitri Roudine is the French title of the novel by Ivan Turgenev usually known as *Rudin*. Turgenev, who had been dead for nine years, had lived for much of his life in France. He had authorised and supervised, if not actually written, French translations of his works himself. Without ceasing to be a Russian he had become an honorary Frenchman. When Henry James published a collection of essays and reviews entitled *French Poets and Novelists* in 1878, he included a piece on 'Ivan Turgénieff'. English readers were as likely to have read his works in French as in an English translation. This gave some legitimacy to the practice of doing English translations from the French version – though hardly to the New York edition of *Rudin* of 1877 'translated from the French and German versions'. Turgenev visited England a dozen times, and met many of his English contemporaries, of whom Richard Garnett was probably one.[81] He had acquired a considerable reputation in England, and had been given an honorary degree at Oxford and been shown round Newnham by Jane Harrison. But there were few good English translations direct from the Russian, and nothing approaching a collected edition.

The man who should have undertaken this was W. R. S. Ralston. He was employed to work on the Slavonic collections in the British Museum, where he had been promoted to the upper section of the first class of assistants over the head of Richard Garnett in 1857. He was an excellent linguist and published a translation of Krylov's *Fables* in 1868. He made friends with Turgenev and visited him in Russia. He was assiduous in promoting Turgenev as a writer and producing him in society. He translated *A Nest of Gentlefolk* in 1873 under the title of *Liza; or 'A Nest of Nobles'*. Turgenev thought it 'exceptionally well translated'.[82] But though Ralston became Turgenev's bear-leader whenever the novelist was in England, he failed to establish himself as his official translator.

He had a row with his superiors at the British Museum in 1875 and had to resign; he did not translate any more Turgenev.[83]

Turgenev's novels, with their artistry in drawing character and their realism which trod a middle path between the French tendency towards cynicism and salacity and the English obsession with moral improvement, appealed to Edward's taste. In them, as in those of the other great Russian realists, people, as D. S. Mirsky has said, 'are not good or bad; they are only more or less unhappy and deserving of sympathy.'[84] This was exactly Edward's own view of the world, and what he wanted to set up as an example to English writers. For Stepniak they were also precious in that they 'laid bare and predicted the progress of the most formidable social and political movement in modern Russia . . . a decade before its birth'.[85] For Constance the subtlety of Turgenev's writing and the beauty of his style, particularly in descriptive passages, were a challenge. It was one that should have daunted her, and she would hardly have accepted it without Stepniak's persuasion. A year later, when she was starting on her second volume of Turgenev, she wrote to Olive, 'oh! it is difficult. I am amazed now at my impudence in undertaking it, and Ralston is so good, that I must make a decent job of it somehow'.[86] She may not have realised, when she started on *Rudin*, with no publisher as yet in view, that she was embarking on the rest of Turgenev's fiction, but it was something that both she and Edward believed should be done. An undated letter of hers to him of about this time does not refer explicitly to translating Turgenev, but it reads exactly as if it did: 'I see something before me very clearly that I want to do above all things and I know it is what the whole bent of your nature urges you towards too. So we have a common object to work for together – besides Bunnie.'[87]

8

'You must go to Russia'

Olive Garnett was twenty-one when she first met Stepniak in the autumn of 1892. She had been to lectures where he had appeared on the platform, but it was only on 20 October that Edward and Constance invited her to John Street especially to meet him and Fanny. Stepniak, perhaps teasingly, talked of marriage and free love, and Olive was irritated and refused to be drawn. But then he began to discuss her writings with her and asked her to write for *Free Russia*. 'I went home,' she wrote, 'revolving great moral and literary schemes and burning to have my little say. I felt very virtuous *very*. I mean I want to be and with God's help I *will*.'[1]

From then on she became increasingly intimate with the Stepniaks. There was another important meeting at John Street six months later. By then she had written a novel called *Provincials*, and Edward had read it. She read aloud what she called '*the* chapter' and 'Edward and Connie and Stepniak commented as we went along'. Stepniak 'put his finger on the weak points, and at once seized on the interest of the situation, and in short taught me a great deal'.[2] At the same time she was exasperated because she felt that she was

being 'soothed and patted on the head' and not allowed to have any feelings or ideas of one's own. . . . Stepniak and Connie cannot but regard me as a baby, of Edward I have the lurking suspicion that he is just as much a baby as I am. Yes, they were all very kind, and Stepniak was most careful to assure me that I need have no scruples about bothering him as going into my work was almost as delightful to him as creating his own. . . . Stepniak advised me to study Turgueneff, and to come to him in difficulties. . . .[3]

The relations between a fledgling writer and an experienced critic analysing her work are very like those between a patient and a psycho-analyst, so it was not surprising that Olive, like so many patients, fell in love with her analyst. Stepniak, for his part, indeed found it delightful to work with Olive, and had less time to give to Constance. It was now Fanny, not her husband, who went 'to the cottage to help Connie with her translation'.[4]

Constance had been very low and prostrate with toothache, and had spent March in the country recovering. Then there was a plan for Edward and Constance to spend May in Paris with the Stepniaks,[5] but now the Stepniaks dropped out. Whether it was to be more than a holiday is not clear, but Paris in the spring has a reputation as a tonic for lovers, and they were much in need of one.[6] 'Connie bought some very nice things to go to Paris with'[7] and they persuaded May Garnett to go to the cottage and look after David. But on the morning of Sunday 7 May old David Black 'died peacefully in his sleep' and they were 'telegraphed to immediately' to come home.[8] A few days after Arthur's death Edward had written to his father: 'Mr Black bears it wonderfully. So far he has shown great strength of mind, but I am afraid he will only realize it later. Now it is a sort of *narrative* of the end of Arthur's troubles to him.'[9] He did indeed soon begin to realise it, and he never recovered. He was seventy-five, and he had been bedridden for nearly nineteen years. After leaving small bequests to his American grandchildren – whose father, 'Young David', had predeceased him – he left his money to be divided equally between his eight children, Arthur's share being left in trust for Speedwell. In due course Constance received about a thousand pounds, a substantial contribution towards the fund for 'The Thatched House'.

The visit to Paris was not a success and had only exacerbated the differences between Edward and Constance. She told Olive:

She did not enjoy Paris very much, the food did not agree with her, and the cynical materialism and indecency of the people sickened her. She saw a good deal of the students and their mistresses and way of life and thought the absence of idealism and commonplace immorality horrible. She said she did not mind so much if people occasionally overstepped limits, but to dwell in a dead level of materialism, and for young people to take their pleasures as old people take theirs seemed shocking.[10]

They completed their interrupted holiday by going with David to stay at Charles Radford's house near Yelverton in Devon. Ernest Radford was also there, apparently in excellent health, although he had recently been in a mental hospital and out of action for about a year.

David Garnett tells how Ernest had come to stay at Henhurst Cross, probably late in 1891, at a time when

There had been a murder in the neighbourhood for the change of half a crown, and the murderer was still at large. As Edward had to be in London one or two nights a week, leaving Constance alone, he bought her a Derringer pistol.

One of the visitors. . . was Ernest Radford. . . Ernest, who was in an odd frame of mind, picked up the pistol, told Constance that it needed mending and that he would take it to a gunsmith, and put it in his pocket. On his return to London he called on an editor who had rejected some of his poems and fired a shot at him. Ernest then spent a year in an asylum, after which he recovered.[11]

There is no mention of this strange story of the murderer and the pistol in the letters of the time, but Ernest certainly did have a serious breakdown in March 1892, from which he was still recovering in January 1893. By the summer he seemed a fit man compared with Edward and Constance, who were both poorly. Ernest wrote to Dollie from Devon: 'I think Garnett a very nice young fellow. I wish he could look less ghastly. Connie is concerned about his Physique.'[12] And Constance's own 'internal trouble' was playing up. She wrote to Olive who was at Henhurst Cross with Lucy and Fanny Stepniak – the cottage was always being lent to friends and relatives when they were away:

I am lying down all the time here and I think I am better – but I am anxious to go on so as to give myself a chance of getting right. We have a nice big Devonshire girl here who takes Bunnie all day and night. As long as I do *no* walking or lifting or housework I am all right, but even ten minutes' walk brings on the weakness again. I am meaning to go to a specialist when I can manage to be in London again – but I don't know when that will be. . .. Edward is learning tennis and driving and enjoying himself very much. Ernest Radford is here – he takes me out for the most delicious drives in a dear little trap just like a comfortable easy chair on wheels. The country is wonderful.[1]

They all three came back from Devon looking 'splendidly well, so brown'.[14] But this was merely skin-deep. Only the baby was really well. David was now 'a very good humoured, sweet tempered boy, but very obstinate, and needs the constant attention of one person'.[15] He learned to tease his mother before he could talk, pretending to pick up a pin or to have some other forbidden object in his little fist, but when his fingers were forced open there was nothing there. He thought this a great joke.

Three days after their return Constance was again complaining of 'internal trouble'.[16] Her rest had relieved the symptoms but had done little to cure the problem, for it was the antithesis of the modern treatment, and six weeks later she was having trouble with her internal 'support'.[17] The mental stresses of their marriage had not gone away; and they could hardly forget the terrible things that can happen to minds under stress when they had such recent and dreadful precedents as Arthur's and Ernest's insanity – a reminder that could only increase the stress in their own.

Despite her 'internal trouble', and despite – or perhaps because of – her increasing desperation, the summer of 1893 was an extraordinarily active time for Constance. On 14 April she was elected to the Fabian Society, which she had taken an interest in for the past nine years without actually being a member. She had been proposed by Eustace and Margaret Hartley, who had become regular friends of the Garnetts during their visits to John Street. Hartley was in his early thirties, a tea dealer in the City and a charming if slightly desperate character. Olive observed: 'The Hartleys have a very "advanced" atmosphere about them, all the latest literary and social gossip . . . it seems as if only by keeping himself in full swing, laughing joking talking etc that Mr. Hartley can endure life'.[18] Constance liked Hartley, and found him a reliable ally for her social plans. No doubt Stepniak also had had a hand in her joining the Fabians. He was a Fabian himself and shared many of their views, while they actively supported the Society of Friends of Russian Freedom.

In the eight years since Constance had first started going to meetings with Shaw the Fabian Society had firmly established itself. It now had over three hundred members and was 'no longer an exclusive debating society: they were suddenly faced with a chance to become a serious political body – a chance which they had not sought and did not wholly comprehend'.[19] While Webb sought with some success to 'permeate' the Liberals and influence their policy, the provincial branches, especially in the industrial midlands and north, had become more active in working-class politics. These new working-class socialists were mainly concerned with their rights, whereas the original Fabians were actuated by a sense of duty.

The Fabians had had some success in working for rights. In 1888 Annie Besant, then a member of the Executive, had discovered the appalling plight of the girls who made matches for Bryant and May. They worked for fourteen hours a day for five shillings a week, and, unprotected from the poisoning effects of phosphorus, developed a horrible condition which they called 'fossy jaw' and which made their teeth fall out. Annie Besant encouraged them to strike, and when they did so the Fabians, with considerable help from Clementina Black and her Women's Trade Union Association, helped them to carry on until they succeeded. After three weeks they were able to return to work with considerably improved conditions, if only slightly better pay. But the real victory was for trade unionism itself. The match-girls had won widespread sympathy. They had 'caught the dry tinder of men and women who had previously seen no hope of improving their lot'[20] and other successful strikes followed.

Constance kept on with her work of translation – still without any definite prospect of publication for *A Common Story*. And she had been thinking of writing something of her own, as Olive reported:

She has a novel in her head which she wants to write. But if she hasn't written it by the end of the year she wants me to write it. She told me the first chapter. It has a strong 'advanced woman', Cambridge, flavour. She says that she lacks just my gift [for] telling a story, which if she had she could do wonders with. She writes heavy inferior George Eliot style.[21]

She finished *Rudin* on 6 July and asked Edward to get her *A Sportsman's Sketches* – presumably just to read, for she did not begin translating it until the following year. On the same day she wrote Edward a letter of terrible bitterness.

Edward, as his son recalled, was apt to be 'irritable and neurotic and became easily exasperated by his wife and child'.[22] And at this time he had some cause for exasperation. He was highly sexed and could never have been happy if his marriage had become celibate. Constance was loving and affectionate, but more and more as a mother loves a son than a wife a husband. Edward was also frustrated in his own writing. His prose poems, as Constance had long ago seen, were 'so difficult that he can hardly hope to be even moderately successful'. His literary gifts were on a large scale. He could see what was wrong with a book and how to put it right. When Ford Hueffer wrote an impossibly woolly life of his grandfather, Ford Madox Brown, 'Edward talked extremely well, brilliantly, and gradually evolved something practical out of the vagueness'.[23] But, unlike Constance, to whom the right word came quickly and almost unerringly, Edward found the process of writing a constant struggle, and his large critical sense only inhibited him. He may even have realised that his sketches were not going to be even moderately successful; one could not make literature out of atmosphere alone – or, as Olive put it bluntly, there were 'too many adjectives'.[24]

In this unhappy mood Edward was unbearably cruel to Constance, and she wrote him her bitter letter. She did not, however, post it, but nor did she destroy it; so it still lies in its unstamped envelope with the rest of the family papers. It seems certain that Edward must have read it; and it was not something he could easily have forgotten:

I read Tolstoi's Boyhood etc yesterday and liked it very much more than when I read it before. How well he analyses. Here is a passage which struck me 'She would sigh as if enjoying her grief and give herself up to the contemplation of her misery. In consequence of this and sundry other instances of her always considering herself a victim a *kind of intermittent feeling of calm dislike* began to be noticeable in his treatment of his wife – that *restrained dislike for the once-loved being which betrays itself by an unconscious desire to say something disagreeable* to him and to her.'

That is just what I see so clearly in you now. . ..

The consequence of your critical attitude is to make me shrivel up and feel I must not stir hand or foot for fear of making things worse. Love certainly makes people better than they were without it; when it is withdrawn it is not only the character that is seen clearer, it also deteriorates generally. At least I feel myself so soiled and spoiled, so degraded in my own eyes, and every hour in such a false position. I am constantly courting the love of a man who treats me with obvious contempt; naturally I try to console my pride by thinking it is more for his sake than mine.

When you are away I can take interest in outside things and work and regain my self-respect. When you are here, I am apt to alternate between trying to excuse your attitude to me by humiliating myself in my own eyes, and then at intervals simply hating you for it, which makes me much more miserable.

What I want is work and independence – to regain my self-respect. If you would manage to let us see little of one another for some time, there might be a hope of getting into a new and better relation to one another. We are both too sore from too much friction to be able to be natural. If we could be more apart, and keep at a distance when we meet, we might come to realize what is precious in what is left to us and to forget a little some of the pain and desecration and want of mutual respect which is spoiling everything for us.[25]

The crisis was far from over when, on 29 July, Stepniak telegraphed Constance to 'come in her best dress'[26] and wrote to Olive, 'We have Vladimir Korolenko with us – the author of the Blind Musician, [which Stepniak had translated] the first of the novelists of our generation and a most delightful man' inviting her to 'come in the evening to meet him'.[27]

Korolenko had been exiled to Siberia in 1879 'by pure mistake', as Constance afterwards put it, and had lived for a year with the Yakuts – One of the happiest years of his life', he told her. 'All the other exiles died, but the women put a taboo on Korolenko – and no wonder, his good, candid, intelligent and handsome face must have won hearts anywhere in the world – and so he was fed and cared for, and lived in an ice hut round a paraffin lamp, and eat Yakut food.'[28]

In 1885 he was allowed to return, and settled in Nizhni Novgorod, two hundred and forty miles east of Moscow, where he married and began to make a name for himself with stories, many of them inspired by his experiences with the Yakuts, and some of them translated by Stepniak and published in *Free Russia*. In 1891 he achieved notoriety by being one of the first to alert the world with his articles in *Russkie Vedomosti* that large areas of Russia, especially those south of Nizhni Novgorod, were threatened with serious famine. This was only partly due to the failure of the season's crops. It had also been brought about by acts of government policy. When the serfs had been emancipated in 1861 they had been obliged to compensate their owners by buying their freedom, and few of them had been able to acquire enough land for more than the barest subsistence, so they had always been vulnerable to famine. Moreover the finance minister, I. S. Vishnegradsky, deliberately put the main burden of taxation on the peasants. He was determined that the Russian economy should catch up with that of the West; and he attempted to do this not by building up an industrial base at home but by importing ready-made machinery from abroad and capital mainly from France, and paying for it with exported grain. In the first half of 1891 more grain was sent out of Russia than in the previous two years. Mountains of it were piled up at Königsberg waiting for the German trains to take it onward, while in Samara and Ryazan peasants were starving, and in their weakened state dying of cholera and typhus. Korolenko had made himself 'politically suspect' by exposing this scandal. But he had not set out for England and America as an exile; he had come to see the freer countries for himself, and to return to Russia. He was taking a risk by spending most of his time in London – he was there from 16 to 23 July – in the company of such a conspicuous revolutionary as Stepniak.

When the guests arrived at Blandford Road they found 'a tall powerful looking man, with a fine expression, handsome features and black hair and a square black beard. *Very* quiet in manner, with great power of observation. He reads English but does not understand one spoken English word.' Constance 'was able to hold a conversation with him in Russian, but – perhaps mercifully – the other English had to content themselves with looking at him'.[29]

In other respects it was an unhappy evening. Constance was in a desperate state of mind. Stepniak had been spending a lot of time with Olive, discussing and criticising her writings, and she felt herself neglected. When he and Fanny made much of Olive and introduced her as his 'daughter', Constance was overcome with jealousy, an emotion that she despised as 'the beginning of the end of love',[30] and burst out to Olive: 'I feel very sore, Stepniak doesn't think anything of me now. You are just in the hey-day, wait a bit and you will be in my position.'[31] Stepniak, who was sitting with Olive and Fanny, did not ask her to join them, but just said to her, rather severely, 'Oh, you must go to Russia.'[32] And when Constance suggested that she might be arrested he pooh-poohed the idea. Olive found all this most upsetting, and Edward was equally unhappy. He 'didn't seem to be specially friends with anyone, he spoke only to men'.[33]

On the following day 'Connie came to dinner'[34] but Olive did not record the conversation. Two days later, on Tuesday 1 August, 'Connie came to the house for a moment but had a bad sick headache and went away quickly. Edward looked very pale and nervous.'[35] And on the Wednesday

Connie came and talked of . . . how men, artists especially like Stepniak, admired a girl because she wore a pink ribbon and thought her quite ideal until they discovered she was an ordinary mortal and then if she had not the virtues and qualities they admired, woe betide her etc. And I said 'quite so'. And she said . . . wasn't I afraid to see people again when they admired me for fear of disillusioning them?

And I, feeling that after all something more than a pink ribbon links Stepniak to me, said 'Oh no, I want to see them very often so that by the time the first fancy dies I may have replaced it by something more substantial, for after all the worst of us must have at least one good quality.' And she said 'Yes, but suppose the person doesn't happen to care about that particular quality?' and I knew she was thinking of E and herself. She allows that lately they have both been very morbid and depressed. . . . I am so sorry for Connie and I want to be sympathetic, but she prevents me by her uneasy manner. . . . When people are passing through phases if they would only recognise that they are, and set to work at something useful and different till they come out at the other side, as they are sure to do in time, what agony they would spare themselves![36]

The Tuesday of Constance's sick headache was also May Garnett's wedding day, and that none too auspicious occasion may well have helped to cause it. May had been engaged for four years to Guy Hall. May's niece, Rayne, described him as 'a stupid man with a slow drawl then fashionable. He was handsome with a straight back to his head like a

Prussian officer, blue eyes and a fine golden moustache. He smelt of cigars and wine.'[37] Nevertheless she could not help feeling sorry for him. Like Uncle William John, he seemed unable to get a job except at the end of a long sea voyage and was constantly in debt. He had spent most of their engagement working in a bank in Rio de Janeiro. In March 1891 Edward wrote to his father urging that something be done to sort out Guy's affairs and get them married so that 'May's nature would be ripened and softened by happiness, and Guy's simplicity of heart would work towards a close union.'[38] More than a year later Olive was observing that May 'ought to marry immediately'.[39] When eventually they were married, Guy still could not find a job in England, and so, although he had promised May that he would not go back to South America, and had told her he had 'made arrangements for getting rid of my return ticket',[40] there was nothing for it but for him and May to do so.

Edward was as wrong about May and Guy as she had been about him and Constance. Unhappiness hardened and sharpened May's nature, and Guy lapsed into drink and idleness. When eventually he returned from Brazil he 'confided to . . . Edward . . . that he had contracted syphilis'.[41] At its worst moments Edward's marriage was never such a disaster as May's.

All too many of Constance's letters to Edward are undated, so that it is often difficult and sometimes impossible to reconstruct the pattern of their relationship. Nevertheless it is clear that by early August the worst of their crisis was over. Though Constance's letter of 6 July must have left a lasting wound, it may also have cleared the air; and less than a month later she was regularly writing, 'I long for you to be home.'[42] Other undated letters may refer to this period, as when she writes, 'Your sweet tender generous little note is so like you – and it touches me so. We will be good and think of each other.'[43] And once on a printed letter-heading from John Street, where she had had to go off alone: 'I think you felt me rather cold to go off like this without you – but, dearest, such absences make one feel just how dear, how precious our love is to us. Other interests – even other love – cannot alter it.'[44] This is one of the few possible references to her love for Stepniak.

When she wrote that she longed for Edward to be home she often invoked little David, for instance when they had Emma Mahomed and her daughter Lucy staying at Henhurst Cross:

There's not a scrap of pugnacity, or sulkiness, or malice, or selfishness in him. When Lucy torments him, his face falls and he may weep; a minute later he will kiss and be friends. I never saw a little child so free from the desire to snatch away another's things, or keep his own to himself. How happy we are to have such a little sweet for our own. Make haste home. . ..[45]

She adored her child, yet at the same time she was making plans to leave him for a month or longer, now that she had a nurse, Jane, who was living at the cottage and could be relied upon. When Stepniak had said, 'Go to Russia,' at the party for Korolenko, his manner may have been dismissive, but he was talking about a serious project and one in which he had a serious interest. Back in October 1892 he had told her 'that if she would only go to St Petersburg and go into society she would be the rage'.[46] She had been immersed in Russian life and literature for the last two years, but she knew Russia only at second hand. She wanted to see the reality 'simply in order to train herself in Russian ways, outlook, language and atmosphere in preparation for the task of translating . . . its literature'.[47] But there were other reasons. Stepniak always had need of innocent-looking emissaries to carry letters and books that could not safely be sent through the censored mails, and perhaps also to take money collected by the Society of Friends of Russian Freedom to help Russian political prisoners and exiles to escape.[48]

Constance, despite all her recent ill-health, had not lost her taste for adventure. To travel to Russia in any circumstances was then a considerable adventure, and to do so when there were Tsarist agents in London, who could easily have known of her relationship with two of the most conspicuous enemies of the regime, one of whom was wanted for murder, could have been dangerous. But Stepniak, as we have seen, merely pooh-poohed the idea of her being arrested.

Some time in the early summer, on a visit to the Stepniaks, she had met Zinaida (Zina) Vengerov, a young woman of twenty-six who was 'translating the Egoist into Russian and she is going to take Connie with her to see Geo. Meredith'.[49] In return Constance took her to see Ada Rehan in *Love in Tandem* at Daly's Theatre. Stepniak said Miss Vengerov was 'the very person to look after Connie in Petersburg' and 'Stepniak . . . and Fanny . . . both evidently think it would do Connie good to go'.[50] By the end of July it was 'practically settled' that she should go 'to Russia in October for six weeks'.[51]

Meanwhile she had a lot of work to do. She had at last found a publisher. Heinemann had accepted her translation of *A Common Story*, William Heinemann was just turned thirty and had been running his own publishing firm for only three-and-a-half years. His father was

German, and he had been partly brought up in Germany. As a result he was an 'internationalist by habit and inclination, a good linguist, fond of foreign literature, music and art'.[52] He brought a breath of continental air and energy to the staid world of respectable English publishing. One of his first books was a life of Ibsen, he had started an 'International Library' of translations of foreign classics, and he published the translations of Ibsen by Constance's old friend William Archer. *A Common Story* was a natural addition to his list, and to her 'intense joy'[53] he gave Constance forty pounds for it.

Heinemann also gave her an immediate commission to translate another book. He had discovered that Deibner in Berlin was bringing out a Russian text of a new book by Tolstoy which had been prohibited in Russia by the censorship, and he made arrangements with the German publisher to acquire the first sheets off the press, and also the rights in the book in so far as Deibner owned them. He was apparently unaware that Tolstoy had long since authorised an American edition of his works, which was published in England by Walter Scott, and had sent the text to the translator so that it could constitute the twentieth volume. The new work was entitled *The Kingdom of God is Within You*; and it was the latest broadside in Tolstoy's campaign as a moralist. Reviewing Louise Maude's translation of *Resurrection*, Edward wrote:

There are two men in Tolstoi, the artist and the moralist, always grappling. In early years the artist got the moralist under him and held him down, without silencing his voice, and the lucky world saw the great light of *Anna Karenina* and *War and Peace*. Then the moralist came uppermost. . . .[54]

Tolstoy was sixty-five, and with his long white beard he already looked like a patriarch. He made a brave attempt to live as a simple Christian, wearing peasant dress, working in the fields and making his own shoes (not half so well as Stepniak could make them), and doing all the other menial tasks in a life of total abnegation, while the rest of Yasnaya Polyana went on as usual around him. In the end, as A. N. Wilson has put it, 'Tolstoy's religion is ultimately the most searching criticism of Christianity which there is. He shows that it does not work.'[55] But in 1893 he was still trying to make it work.

The Kingdom of God is Within You was an angry book by an angry old man: angry at the injustices and miseries that he saw around him, especially in his beloved Russia; and angry because he had preached much the same sermon before and nobody had taken any notice. The gist of his fulminations was that the crux of Christ's teachings lay in the Sermon on the Mount, especially in the injunction, 'Resist not evil', and that they had been perverted and diluted in the explications of the Apostles and the Church. Since temporal authority had been set up at least on the pretext of resisting evil, it was acting in defiance of Christ's command, and of course to take up arms for whatever cause was sinful. So long as Tolstoy was cataloguing the obscenities of war and the evils perpetrated by those in power he had a strong case. But he had nothing to offer in their place but anarchy, and logically he was in a paradoxical position, for if resistance to evil was in itself evil, then it was evil to resist that resistance. By his own precepts Tolstoy should have kept quiet and suffered the evils of the world to continue. But meekness was not in his character.

Naturally such a subversive work, deliberately offensive to all authority, could not be published in Russia, and there was all the more interest in it elsewhere. Even if Heinemann did not know of the rival edition, he had every reason to get his own out quickly. Constance had to put aside the Turgenev and set to work on Tolstoy. By 22 October she was hoping to finish it within a week.[56] But before the week was out she wrote to her father-in-law:

I am working tremendously hard. A second volume of the Tolstoi has turned up and I am proceeding with it now, but whether there are other volumes and if so whether Mr Heinemann wants me to do them I don't know. It is delightful to have more work. On the other hand it can hardly be finished within next month; and [it] is certainly not a work which could be admitted into Russia, and I shall be sorry if my visit should be deferred. So I am feeling altogether rather unsettled and uncertain.[57]

In the event she did not get away till the end of the year. Meanwhile she was able to report that 'Edward has just received an inconclusive but favourable reply from Dent. I think it is pretty certain he will take the book on Edward's terms; I feel very much delighted at the fact.'[58] Dent did indeed take Edward's volume of prose poems and brought it out the following year with illustrations by William Hyde.

At last they were beginning to 'come out at the other side' of their unhappy phase. Until she took up the Tolstoy Constance had been working at her translations of Turgenev without a publisher committed to taking them on. Some time in the summer of 1893 she wrote to Fanny Stepniak:

Edward is very hot about a scheme for a complete edition of Tourgueneff –
and he thinks if we don't make haste it will be too late perhaps. So he wants to
get an answer from Stepniak to several questions about it. Will you try and
make him write to Edward about it? I know the most awful task you can set a
Russian is to ask him to write a letter, so I came today in the hope of wringing
a verbal answer out of him. Edward wants to know the total amount *about* of
Tourgueneff – how much there is besides the 13 vols which have already
appeared in English. I enclose his note on the subject.

  Could it all be got into 10 vols and would Stepniak write a critical introduction
for £20, and a brief preface to each vol. for £4 (£60 altogether if 10 vols)? You
see if Edward gets it all worked out in detail as to cost – size of matter etc – he
can present a definite scheme to Unwin – which he can pass on to another
publisher if refused by him. If we delay that shark will have worked out in his
pottering way some cheaper scheme for utilizing the wretched translations from
the French – and a bad edition will appear just fit to cut out all chance of a
good one – also neither you nor we shall have any hand in the matter! [59]

Unwin turned down the plan, but Heinemann was prepared to take it
on. 'There is no work I should like so much;' Constance told her
father-in-law, 'and it would mean employment for a year or two.'[60] She
wrote to Stepniak:

Now that I have a prospect of permanent work as a translator, it is absolutely
necessary I should have help I could reckon upon in correcting my work. I
should like to make a definite *business* arrangement (paying a certain percentage
of what I receive to my coadjutor.) Could you undertake to do this for me? . . .
I should like to do my work with you – but if it is taxing your time too much, I
will ask Volkhovsky (but his deafness would make it much more difficult for
him) Edward says 5 per cent but I think that's too little![61]

They settled on twenty per cent, but Heinemann was uneasy about
having the introductions written by Stepniak, as Olive noted:

he is afraid of his politics. He would rather get Björnsen, or Henry James to do
the work. Edward has made an overture that Stepniak's name shall appear at
the end of the introductions, not be advertised at all. Of course, as Connie says
she will not have half the pleasure in translating if Stepniak has no share, the
idea was his, and no one else can give the facts about these epoch-making
novels as he can. Other writers may write their critical introductions, they cannot
write the critical-historical introductions that he can, which will make the edition
unique.[62]

  Edward's plan was adopted in that Stepniak's introductions were not
mentioned on the title-page, though they were sometimes referred to in
advertisements. But, of course, Constance could not proceed until she

had finished her translation of Tolstoy and had returned from her visit to Russia; and her plans still could not be settled. On 7 December she had not received the last instalment of Tolstoy's manuscript, and until she had finished it she could not leave. Then she had a nasty dose of influenza. Olive went to see her and found her health much recovered, but she 'explained that she was in a very bad temper and was delighted to see someone outside the sphere of if'.[63] She had good reason to be annoyed. Zina Vengerov had gone back to St Petersburg promising to confirm the details of the visit, but had not sent a word to her, though she had written to Fanny Stepniak 'saying that she is disgusted with Petersburg and dreads my coming, the literary people all get drunk and she is afraid I shall be disappointed'.[64] Constance was very angry with her.

Olive's comments are unusually severe:

She is bent body and soul upon getting on and making money and owns that at present she feels uncomfortable and unsettled. She evidently wants to be absolutely independent of everyone and to do that she must be financially independent. Certainly in some ways she is very admirable even if one does not agree with her premises, one must admire her logic and admit its soundness. People when they are no longer useful are dead leaves in her path.[65]

Constance had been financially independent in London before her marriage, and in her bitter letter to Edward she had spoken of the need for independence. In a discussion of marriage and women's rights she had said that 'till women were on the same money basis as men it was hopeless to talk of their rights, they simply did not exist'.[66] But she had not taken up Russian merely in order to make money. Her remuneration as a translator was not much better than it had been as a librarian. How she treated her friends will become evident in due course.

She spent the afternoon of her thirty-second birthday, 19 December, with the Stepniaks making plans for Russia. Richard Garnett had already given her one vital piece of equipment, a fur cloak which was made to Stepniak's specifications, and which she told her father-in-law was 'altogether a perfect success and very, very warm. I can turn up a lappet which comes up to my eyebrows, while the skirt reaches down to my toes. I should think I could go to the North Pole now with impunity.'[67]

She spent Christmas Day at Henhurst Cross in beautiful weather with David, who kept up 'an incessant little chatter and in stout gaiters and galoshes he runs about the garden and woods in the most absolutely independent way'.[68] It was not until the 27th that a 'satisfactory' letter from Zina at last arrived and Constance could make firm plans. David Rice found out the train times from Thomas Cook's, and she planned to leave 'on Sunday evening next [31 December 1893] from Holborn Viaduct via Queenboro' Flushing and Berlin'[69] for St Petersburg.

The last days before Constance's departure, when she was busy sorting out all her commissions and messages for Russia, were overshadowed by an irritation and a crisis. She had completed her translation of *The Kingdom of God is Within You* and handed it in to Heinemann. He had not yet had time to bring out the book, but had sold extracts to the *New Review* for their January issue. These had been set from uncorrected proofs, and other papers had got hold of them, had picked up the errors and published 'depreciatory paragraphs'.[70] A more serious worry was that the *Daily Chronicle* of 26 December carried a long account of a visit to Tolstoy at Yasnaya Polyana by their St Petersburg correspondent, William Steveni, which included the words:

The Count did not speak very hopefully of the forthcoming English translation of his new book, 'The Kingdom of God Within Us.' [*sic*] It appears that it was not translated direct from the Russian, but from a French edition, which appears to be very imperfect. Apparently, the American edition of the book will be the best; for it is being translated from the original MS. by an American lady, Miss Delano of Boston.[71]

Heinemann hastened to write to Tolstoy, who replied in English on 5/17 January 1894:

I never sell the right of translation of my books and everybody is welcome to translate and to publish them. . . . I am very glad to hear, that the translation has been made from the Russian and hope, that it will be very good.

I have no reason nor right to excuse [*sic*] you of anything improper. . ..[72]

To prevent ignorant critics repeating these calumnies, Constance was trying to write a translator's note to disarm them. She never found it easy to write such notes, and was relying on Stepniak to help her. They had only two days in which to get it done before she left for Russia. When the book eventually came out in February 1894, handsomely produced in two volumes, with the signature, 'Leo Tolstoy', blocked in gold on the front by way of authentification, it included a note from the publisher: 'This version of Count Tolstoy's work has been made directly from Russian advance sheets sold to me by the publishers of the Russian original.' Constance's note began by introducing the book, and concluded rather brutally:

One word as to the translation. Tolstoy's style in his religious and philosophical works differs considerably from that of his novels. He no longer cares about the form of his work, and his style is often slipshod, involved, and diffuse. It has been my aim to give a faithful reproduction of the original.[73]

Constance saw herself as a translator, not as an advocate. Her task was to present her author's arguments with absolute fidelity, not to state his case in the manner most likely to convince his English readers.

The crisis was also provoked by the *New Review*. In the opening pages of the same issue there was a thoroughly alarmist article, 'Anarchists: Their Methods and Organization'. It was in two parts, the first by 'Z' and the second by 'Ivanoff'. There was little doubt that the articles had been planted, if not written, by P. I. Rachkovsky, the head of the Russian foreign secret service, with help from Olga Novikoff, an assiduous apologist of Tsarist Russia, who liked to think of herself as the 'M. P. for Russia' – oblivious to the implied insult to democracy. As long ago as 1886 she had maintained that the revolutionaries were criminals, and that 'in England some of them – like the murderer of General Mesenkov [*sic*] – are leaders of a portion of "public opinion"'.[74] According to the *Daily Chronicle* the *New Review* article was not original, but a mere abridgement of an anonymous pamphlet that had been in circulation two years before.[75]

The second part, by 'Ivanoff', repeated this attack on Stepniak. It did not say outright that he was the 'murderer of General Mezentzeff', but left little doubt of it in the reader's mind. Stepniak had never admitted to having killed Mezentsev, but he had written in such extravagant praise of this 'act of heroism' in *Underground Russia*[76] that his silence seemed as much due to modesty as to caution. Constance probably had at least a shrewd suspicion that her friend Stepniak was none other than Kravchinsky the assassin, and thought no worse of him than he did himself. She certainly brought David up to believe that Stepniak had done no more to be ashamed of than any soldier on active service who kills an enemy. But to many of his other friends at the time it must have been a considerable shock, and to all of them it was a cause for alarm.

On Thursday 28th Constance spent the early evening with Stepniak working on the preface for *The Kingdom of God is Within You*, but did not tell him that she had seen the attack in the *New Review*. Afterwards he and Fanny were due to go on to see the Garnetts at the British Museum, but it was a miserable foggy night, and Fanny stayed behind. At the residence they had an even more miserable evening. Olive, even though she only knew of the article and had not yet taken in the full force of its implications, could not bring herself to mention the subject to Stepniak. But it was clear from his mood that he knew of it, for this was the occasion on which he was 'gloomy, suffering, frowning, . . . more like that photograph of him which I have than I have seen him look yet'.[77]

Olive spent the morning of Friday 'in blissful ignorance'[78] shopping for Constance at the Civil Service Stores, and only in the afternoon did she get hold of a copy of the *New Review* and read the article. It was a great blow to her. It was a setback to the cause of Russian freedom, and 'Selfishly, I feared that I might lose "my Stepniak" – the artist – in the Stepniak I do not know, the nihilist, terrorist and — —'.[79] She could not bring herself to write the word 'assassin'.

In the evening there was a farewell party for Constance with Christmas pudding and champagne at the flat in John Street. Olive and Lucy arrived to find that Eustace Hartley was there with Nellie Heath, Fanny Stepniak and a couple of other friends. There was a lively general conversation until the arrival of Stepniak and Edward, who had been dining out together. Thereafter Olive was wretched:

There was loud talk, laughter, but we all 'felt' uncomfortable. I did not know who in the room knew of the article, or that Connie had already taken Lucy aside to tell her that Fanny did not know and was not to be told. My only comfort lay in Fanny who was so sweet and good to me, and who sat hand in hand with Lucy on the divan. I happened to sit next to Stepniak, and I could not speak to him. . . . Did he think I knew, or pity my innocence?. . . We all drank champagne. Stepniak smoked.[80]

Edward's reaction, as it had been at that other unhappy party for Korolenko, was to tease Olive, but without his usual wit, and in what she thought was 'very bad taste'.[81]

Meanwhile Constance, as well as preparing for her journey, was having to cope with the crisis. On Saturday she went to lunch at the British Museum, and Olive recorded their 'frank talk':

1st. About last night and the awkwardness, the bad taste, Edward, Hartley etc. She says after *all* Hartley *is* reliable in practical matters, and Edward is just a bundle of paradoxes whom *no one* can possibly understand. 2nd. About Stepniak. She promised to tell him to-morrow that Lucy and I had read the article and 'if every word of it were true', and if that being so, we were bound in sober reason to condemn, we were none the less the same towards him as we had ever been, regarding the whole affair as one past, and removed from the sphere of our comprehension – except in one particular, which – whatever the motive [–] must forever be a source of regret. As for himself personally – as ever – in him we have implicit confidence. He on his side says that there have been far worse things said of him and that he denies nothing and never has denied anything. [82]

This was the line that he took when he was given an opportunity to write a reply 'Nihilism: As It Is' in the February issue of the *New Review*, the ownership of which had just been taken over by Heinemann.[83] It was the mildest of answers, intended to show that he was a reasonable man in whose mouth butter would not melt. He worked on the article with Olive, and asked her 'About the general, what have I said?'

'You have said neither one thing nor the other,' Olive replied.

'That is as I intended.'[84]

The storm, as Olive hoped it would, blew over.

Sunday was Constance's last day in England. She dined at the British Museum, wearing 'her money and keys round her neck'[85] ready for the journey. She told Olive

that on reflection she should not tell Stepniak that we had read the article, because she had read the accusations in a book long ago, and everyone was supposed to know. I was glad because I have calmed down . . . the emotions of Friday evening etc . . . were real enough at the time, but, I agree with her, better buried on one's own breast. Of Edward she quoted 'How can I know what I think until I hear what I say?' Of herself 'How can I tell what I feel until I see what I do?'[86]

Constance could not stay long. She bade them an affectionate farewell 'a little, not much excited' and 'hurried back to John Street to correct proofs with Stepniak'.[87] Edward, who had been spending the day at Limpsfield visiting Sydney Olivier, returned in time to see her off at Holborn Viaduct on the first leg of her long journey to St Petersburg. And Olive ended her account of Constance's doings in her diary for the last day of 1893 with the words, this time unqualified by any mention of dead leaves, 'How admirable she is in many many ways!'[88]

9

Russia in Winter

Constance took the train from Holborn Viaduct to Queenborough on the Isle of Sheppey late on New Year's Eve 1893. She sailed on the night boat to Flushing, and thereafter for two days and nights she was on the train to St Petersburg.

It was midwinter, the time when the bitter continental cold keeps one cooped up within one's railway carriage. The windows frost over on the inside, and one can see out only by scraping a peephole – and then only if the outside is clear. If the train stops for any length of time porters in thick coats and earmuffs come round with mops and buckets of hot water to swab down the windows, but soon they are as opaque as ever. The nights are long, and during the short daylight hours, even if one can make out the landscape through the frosted glass, there is usually little to see but the interminably flat and snowy wastes of East Prussia, Poland and the Baltic States. So one is more than ever conscious of one's fellow travellers.

Constance found it 'very exciting all the way',[1] despite suffering because 'Two awful Roumanian merchants – perfect mountains of fat – travelled in the same carriage – they kept fingering my coat, my skirt, etc, – and saying that they could see that it was English – it was such good material.'[2] They had the same horror of fresh air – especially as it was below freezing – as the French mistress with whom she had shared a bedroom at her Brighton boarding school. 'Every time I opened a window or even a ventilator in their absence they shut it up when they came back.'[3]

As they approached the Russian border she must have been anxious about getting through the customs, then no less formidable than they have been since. Besides lists of information to be obtained about Turgenev, and commissions to be undertaken for the Kropotkins, she was carrying letters from Stepniak to Korolenko, which, though no doubt disguising both their identities, might still have compromised her had they been found. She may well also have had a copy of Stepniak's book, *Underground Russia*, which had at last come out in Russian, and certainly found its way to Tolstoy at about this time; and according to one account she also had a considerable sum of money in ten-pound notes intended for famine relief.[4] She got into conversation with a French hairdresser going out to St Petersburg who 'was a little anxious because he knew no Russian. . . . So I undertook to speak for him and he in return carried my bag'[5] when they changed trains at the frontier at Wirballen (now Virbalis). 'As he told me his autobiography, I told him – in answer to his questions – that I was married and had a little son.'[6] After they had safely got through the Russian customs and were settled in the Russian train,

two big handsome Russians in fur caps and shubas kissed each other at the carriage door and one got in. I was tired and pretended to be asleep. Then the Frenchman, apparently unable to contain his wonder, began telling the Russian gentleman that here was a young Englishwoman who had left her husband and child to go to Russia. 'Avec?' enquired the Russian expressively. 'Non, c'est étonnant – seule!'[7]

She had left London on Sunday night, and arrived at St Petersburg on Wednesday morning. Zina Vengerov and Minsky, a poet who was married to her niece, were at the station to meet her, but they did not find one another at first, and Constance 'engaged a porter and a cab and got my luggage myself. The common people speak Russian quite as clearly as educated people and they are clever in understanding me, but they always smile so much at me, as if I were an amusing baby trying to talk.'[8]

She was not staying with Zina, but in a lodging that had been found for her in a handsome, if somewhat austerely neo-classical, block on the Moika canal. This suited her 'as it will make me a little independent – and as they don't get up till 12 I shall be able to get some work done here every morning'.[9] She described to Edward her lodging, number 6 at Moika 16: 'The houses here are built like old English inns with a yard in the middle and contain many separate dwellings – as though one numbered Royal Mint Square as one house.'[10] She had a 'very nice room indeed, large and airy. . . . It has deep low windows with window seats, solid farmhouse furniture and the floor is the colour of red-bricks, so the whole effect is like an old fashioned English farmhouse room – very clean – rather bare.'[11] This was agreeably reminiscent of her old rooms in Fitzroy Street, and she slept well on that first night in St Petersburg.

She awoke refreshed to find her arrival recorded in the *Novosti i Birzhevaya Gazeta*:

Staying in Petersburg at the present time is Miss Constance Garnett, the daughter of the celebrated English poet, Dr R. Garnett, who is in charge of the library section of the British Museum. The young writer, having graduated at Cambridge University, has learnt Russian well and is currently engaged in translating our classics. Her translations of Goncharov (*A Common Story*) and others are excellent. The object of Miss Garnett's visit is to acquaint herself with current Russian literature.[12]

She was excited by her first impressions of Russia in winter:

The climate is delicious – imagine zero Fahrenheit – that is 32° below freezing – and I have not had cold hands or feet since I left London. And the keen crisp frosty air makes one feel excited and vigorous. You would be always in the street – so picturesque and full of life – the queer little sledges about as big as goat chaises with rough shaggy ponies so prettily harnessed and everywhere the delicious sound of metal on the frost like the clink of skates. . . . One is so near the ground that one is not afraid of being upset, and that is lucky, for the drivers do their very utmost to upset each other. The streets are wide and monotonous – electric light – snow everywhere, and sledges scudding about – bells ringing. The only hideous incongruity – tramcars![13]

She found it 'rather difficult to tell the men and women apart as all wear such voluminous garments that they look like stout women';[14] nevertheless, she thought,

All the men look handsome or at least interesting out of doors from their very grand and becoming dress. It is rather a shock when they take off their splendid big shubas and you see a little shrimp emerge who might be a London clerk. Their caps are very jolly – and big – come right over the ears and forehead and are of soft fur such as beaver.[15]

She was taken to meet Zina's relatives, including 'an enormously fat sister, mother of Bella who was married to Minsky. . . . The ladies on that occasion were all so fat that I felt like a sylph – you could hardly have encircled any of their waists with both arms.'[16]

Friday was Christmas Eve by the Russian calendar, and all entertainments were closed for the Christmas holidays, so she could not go to the theatre, but Zina took her to a Christmas fair:

The shops are concentrated in a sort of market – and thousands of Xmas trees are there – such a pretty sight – the country people selling them – and the eager

Russian children and the fat bargaining mammas – all buying and selling is done by bargaining – no fixed prices for anything, and the Russian ladies pride themselves on being good 'higglers'. There are delightful wooden toys made by the peasants. I shall bring Bunny a little toy sledge and giggy [gee-gee].[17]

She makes no mention of the handsome baroque palaces on either side of the frozen Neva. Perhaps they were no more to her taste than the neat Regency houses of Brighton. She was finding plenty of other things to enjoy, but already she was feeling 'homesick in spite of all these excitements'[18] and beginning to worry about the child she had left behind. 'You can't think,' she wrote to Olive, 'how one wants letters when one is 1600 miles away and has a small son at home.'[19] After ten days she had had a letter from her father-in-law, but not a word from Edward, and only one postcard from Jane who was looking after David. She was desperately worried. Letters took only two or three days, although all hers were opened (the posts and the censorship were efficient in those days). 'What does it mean?' she wrote to Edward. 'Can Bunnie be ill and you are afraid to tell me?' She signed herself bluntly, 'Yours, C. Garnett' she was so upset and angry at his lack of consideration.[20]

Then at last, a fortnight after she had left England, she was able to write, 'I can't tell you how glad I was to get your letter yesterday – I was ill in bed all day with a fearful sick headache and to have something from home was a great comfort.'[21] David was, of course, in excellent health and spirits, and in danger of nothing more serious than being 'completely spoiled' by his doting aunts and grandparents.[22]

Among Russian literary people she found 'a great interest in English life, education of women, politics, education of children etc and often am somewhat abashed to find people knowing more about England than I do myself.'[23] 'The interest in English literature is much greater here than in England.'[24] She asked Edward to have copies of *An Imaged World*, which she herself longed to see, and his father's *Poems* and *The Twilight of the Gods* and indeed any of Fisher Unwin's books sent to the *Vestnik Evropy* for review. Constance's brain, as she wrote, was 'seething with literary schemes.'[25] One of these concerned Anton Chekhov.

At a literary party she met Baroness Ikskul von Gildenbrandt, a friend of Chekhov's, who spoke English perfectly and knew 'a great deal more of our literature and politics than most English people'[26] and who told her about Chekhov's latest work. Back in England Constance and Edward had thought of trying to get Fisher Unwin to publish a new story by Chekhov. By 1893 he had established a reputation in Russia as the first writer of his generation (he was thirty-two, Tolstoy was sixty-five) on the strength of his tales and a few plays, though his three dramatic masterpieces were still to come; yet he was still barely known outside his own country. The story that the Garnetts had in mind to translate was 'Ward No. 6'. It is set in the squalid quarters for lunatics in a provincial hospital, and it tells how the doctor in charge becomes so obsessed by his philosophical discussions with one of the inmates, a man with a highly original intellect despite his persecution mania, that he neglects his duties more and more until he becomes certifiable as a lunatic himself. 'Ward No. 6' caused a considerable stir when it came out in Russia. Some readers saw it as a cautionary tale showing what happens if one takes Tolstoy's gospel of non-resistance to evil too literally, others as an allegory of the condition of Russia. But Chekhov was the least political of authors; as a writer of tales he took things as he found them, as a doctor he worked endlessly to alleviate individual suffering. In 'Ward No. 6' he is examining the precarious division that separates a doctor from his patients. Fisher Unwin must have considered it too morbid a tale for English palates.

In St Petersburg Constance learned from the Baroness about a series of articles by Chekhov appearing in the *Russkaya Mysl* in the autumn of 1893. In 1890 he had astonished his friends by deciding to go and investigate Sakhalin, the Russian island north of Japan that served as a penal colony even more remote than Siberia. With no official permit and 'no credentials but his card as a newspaper correspondent',[27] and fatally infected with tuberculosis, he set off on the three-thousand-mile journey by train, boat and coach across the continent to Sakhalin.

He stayed three months on the island, traversed it from north to south, made a census of the population, talked to every one of the ten thousand convicts, and made a careful study of the convict system. Apparently the chief reason for all this was the consciousness that 'We have destroyed millions of men in prisons. . . . It is not the superintendents of the prisons who are to blame but all of us.'[28]

Even for Chekhov 'In Russia it was not possible to be a "free artist and nothing more".'[29] It was three years before he completed his reports. Although they were accepted by the authorities, and were dry and factual in tone, they were as damning as anything that George Kennan had written about the exiles in Siberia.

Constance thought Edward should 'make haste and secure a translation'[30] of Chekhov's narrative as it would be more acceptable to the English than 'Ward No. 6': 'The same artistic and realistic treatment which the English public could hardly accept because of the horrible subject in fiction is acceptable in a narrative of fact, and it might be a way of introducing him and paving the way for his stories.'[31] But nothing came of it.

The novelty of St Petersburg literary life did not last long; and whether or not Zina had been right to say that the 'literary people all get drunk',[32] there is no doubt that Constance soon began to be disappointed in them and exhausted by the hours they kept:

This life would soon be the death of me. . . . Here people drag on a miserable existence without air, exercise or proper sleep, living in rooms so hot that my spectacles are always steamed, and eating all the while hot meat (and hardly anything else!) three times a day. They are all dull, pessimistic and sleepy all day – about ten they begin to wake up and to drive about and pay calls – for someone to drop in at one or two o'clock is quite common.[33]

Stepniak had said that she would be 'the rage' in Petersburg society.[34] Constance told Edward that she was beginning to 'go' in Petersburg, and sent him an example of her fan-letters, adding:

Do not imagine this kind of thing puffs me up and makes me vain of being a 'success'. These people are so deadly blasé that they will give anything to get a new person to speak to – that is all. . . .
   [Russia] teaches me to value the simple English virtues one has been taking for granted all one's life. It seems to me that I have been living in a select circle of angels. . . without knowing it! The process of reasoning – 'If I do *this*, *that* will follow, and *that* will be a disaster for me or for others' – is a logical process that not one in ten Russians has ever been through in his life, and the wholesale misery all round from sheer stupidity and recklessness is the thing that strikes me most.[35]

But among these society people there were some who were not 'deadly blasé', and who became lasting friends, Madame Evgeniya Arseniev, for instance, whose husband, Konstantin Konstantinovich, edited the great Brockhaus Russian encyclopedia. She introduced Constance to 'a most interesting girl'.[36] Aleksandra Alekseevna Shteven was an energetic young baroness who owned considerable estates at Yablonka in the Arzamas district, a hundred versts (seventy miles) by sledge south-east of Nizhni Novgorod. She had a strong social conscience and had founded no less than thirty-two schools, much to the annoyance of the indolent local priests, who thought that they had a monopoly of rural education. Miss Shteven (she seems not to have used her title) took to Constance at once, and after the briefest acquaintance invited her to come to Yablonka, calling at Tver and Moscow on the way. She would also be able to visit Korolenko at Nizhni Novgorod.

On Sunday 21 January the two young women, still almost total strangers, set off from St Petersburg on the night train. Constance could not sleep because the Russian girl talked all night, yet was still fresh and ready for a busy day in the morning. At Tver they rode through the snow to visit a school for priests' daughters. Sasha Shteven and the headmistress at once 'fell to talking nineteen to the dozen',[37] while Constance, breakfastless, was ready to faint with exhaustion. They helped her to the headmistress's private room, but still gave her nothing to eat or drink.

I remember [Constance wrote] there was a glass of cold milk and some buns on the table – probably put there for the lady's lunch. I longed to take them but my manners were too good. Presently I heard a rustling sound – and, horror! – black beetles were running over the plate and the buns! This was the model school, the pride of Tver![38]

Eventually she was given food and drink and recovered enough to be shown round the dormitories 'where the beds stood not a yard apart, and the double windows all sealed up for the winter'.[39] She asked about playgrounds and games, and was told that the girls would not go out of the doors – except to church – until the spring.

Sasha Shteven also had business in Tver with I. I. Petrunkevich, an important figure in the zemstvo movement. When serfdom was abolished, and landowners were no longer autocrats on their own estates, local elected assemblies, known as zemstvos, were set up in their place. The government, however, came to distrust them, limited their powers, and obstructed the excellent work they were trying to do in local government, health and education. Thus provoked, the zemstvos provided an important movement for greater freedom and democracy.

In the evening the two women continued their train journey to Moscow. There Sasha went to stay with a friend, while Constance put up at the Hotel Rossiya. She was enchanted with the city. 'I have never seen anything that has made on me such a striking impression. . . . I don't believe Athens or Constantinople even could be more attractive, and I am sure they could not boast of such a marvellous variety of interest.'[40] But it was only on her return journey, a fortnight later, that she described what she found so delightful:

In the morning it was snowy and horrid, but in the afternoon the sun came out and then all the city shone out with glittering gold domes and spires, and the infinite variety of delicate colouring everywhere, and the rooks cawing over the crosses high up against the sky. Every day I still have here I shall spend the mornings in walking or sledging about the town, so as to try to print my impressions forever on my mind. Walking is a difficult matter though as there is a horrible thaw and a foot deep of soaking filthy slush covers the street. That is just Russia! The exquisite poetic delicate spire against the tender pearly sky – and underfoot filth indescribable![41]

Soon after her first arrival in Moscow she went to see Tolstoy in his town house, a two-storeyed wooden building in Khamovniki, and at once came under the spell of the old genius: 'He made a great impression on everybody who saw him for the first time. His piercing eyes seemed to look right through one and to make anything but perfect candour out of the question; at the same time there was an extraordinary warmth and affection in them.'[42]

She did not stay long, but he invited her to come to supper on the following day. There she met his wife, Sofya Andreevna, a handsome middle-aged woman, whom she later described as 'a Philistine, admirably qualified to be the wife of the Mayor of Brighton'.[43] Tolstoy's elder daughter, Tatyana, and his brother, Nikolai, were also there. She partook of an excellent supper with his family, while Tolstoy himself, in accordance with his principles of the simple life, ate nothing but porridge, which Tatyana cooked for him on an oil stove. Constance was therefore rather surprised when the old sage told her that while she was in Moscow she must on no account miss going to the picture gallery, for she 'thought he had renounced such vanities'.[44]

He was very anxious to see her translation of *The Kingdom of God is Within You*, and said that he liked the English translations of his works much better than the French. She must have reassured him that she had proved a fit translator, for he pressed on her another book of his which he said was 'the cornerstone . . . of all his philosophy',[45] and which he wanted her to translate. This was *The Four Gospels Harmonised*, which Constance described as

an unfinished work, written 10 years ago – now for the first time being printed – in three vols about 300 pages each – consists of texts in Greek, with the old and T's new version – printed in three columns side by side – followed by some pages of commentary. It is very interesting and would no doubt find many readers in the religious world. But it would be *very* difficult to translate, as the

Russian *old* version is often so different from our English, and the shade of distinction between the old and new versions would be very hard to render.[46]

Apart from the difficulty of translating it, she was already pledged to get on with the Turgenev, and Heinemann was pressing her. She wrote to Edward:

if H. is willing to let the vols. come out one every *three* months that is what I should prefer; and if so, fix it and I can feel perfectly safe of adhering to it. A vol every two months will mean that I can do nothing else. But if he insists on one every 2 months, we must agree. But if possible make the three months arrangement.[47]

If she were to undertake Tolstoy's *Gospels* for Heinemann it would mean 'deferring the Turgenev for some three or four months later'[48] – a remarkably short time in which to contemplate translating a work so full of unusual difficulties. Nor did it seem likely that Heinemann would want to take a book so much more suited to a specialist religious publisher. Tolstoy wanted to have her answer as soon as she came back from her visit to Yablonka, and she thought she would have to 'return it with thanks'.[49]

She left for Nizhni Novgorod with Sasha Shteven by train on the evening of Sunday 28 January. The journey took fifteen hours in 'an infamous smelling stifling third-class railway carriage'.[50]

Constance did not, alas, set down her impressions of Nizhni Novgorod, an exotic city on a great bend of the wide Volga, to which merchants came in autumn from all over Asia to a fair so vast that according to Alexandre Dumas it attracted its own settlement of four thousand prostitutes.[51] Constance said that she could have written a long letter about the city, now deep in winter snow, 'but I must keep all that till I get home. It's impossible to describe all one's impressions . . . you know I never write a diary.'[52]

She arrived at Nizhni Novgorod on Monday morning and spent that night at a hotel. Then she went to deliver letters from Stepniak to Korolenko, who lived with his wife, Evdokiya Semenovna, modestly with only one servant in rented accommodation. She was welcomed warmly and asked to stay the night, although the Korolenkos were 'feeling completely overwhelmed, shaken by misfortune'.[53] When Korolenko was in America he had suddenly been overcome with anxiety about his family, and had set off home to Russia. The day after he reached Paris he heard that his two-year-old daughter had died. When he got back to

Russia he fell ill, his other daughter caught diphtheria, and when Constance arrived a nephew living in the same house had just died and a niece had only recently escaped from death's door. As Korolenko wrote to Stepniak, 'It really seems as if the Lord is venting His wrath upon us.'[54]

It was hardly surprising that Constance thought that Evdokiya Semenovna, a handsome woman, always severely dressed in black, with an attractive pale and 'exquisitely refined' face looked so 'very worn and sad'.[55] Nevertheless she had a delightful evening with the Korolenkos, while Sasha was up till one o'clock in the morning 'racing about Nizhni seeing people about her business'.[56] Korolenko told her about his happy life in exile and showed her his drawings of the Yakuts, while from Evdokiya Semenovna she learned something of her history:

[She] was one of the Ivanov[sky] family of which every member – including a little brother of twelve – had served time in prison. She said her two years in the Peter-Paul fortress was a great benefit to her. She had a kind good old gaoler who procured mathematical books for her, so that she was able to pass her exams and take her degree at once on coming out. And the rest from the terrible over-excitement of revolutionary activity had been good for her nerves.[57]

The following morning Constance woke at seven; and by eight she and Sasha were on their way in a covered two-horse sledge 'cleverly made of rough poles of wood'.[58] The driver, 'such a delightful typical peasant tucked us up as if we were babies, and smiled with delight when we declared we were as comfortable as possible'.[59] Constance's comfort had been assured by a friend of the Korolenkos' called Popovich, who had been visiting them the previous day, and had pressed on Constance 'his huge black sheepskin shuba'.[60] She felt she was 'rolled up like a bear' and was 'very thankful to be rolled up in so many layers – not only because of the cold',[61] but also because she was thoroughly padded against all the jolts and jars.

Constance had always imagined that:

sledging was like being drawn about in a chair on the ice on a pond or river – Not at all! It is much more like being at sea, and at first I was afraid it would produce the same effect – Happily the absolute impossibility of being ill had a deterrent influence and I managed to suppress my feelings.[62]

For the first 'twenty miles out of Nizhni there were still hills and black forest to be seen on the horizon – snow of course everywhere – overhead a leaden sky – inky towards the horizon – which seemed to threaten more snow'.[63] But after that there were only 'A few birch trees marking the road – and telegraph wires to show us we were not quite away from civilization',[64] and then just rods stuck in the ground to mark what passed for a road. All the same they were constantly wandering off it, which was no disadvantage: 'It is a great deal more comfortable when one is off the road as the snow is more even there – on the road it is in hillocks and ruts and we have to keep throwing ourselves to one side or the other to prevent the sledge being quite over.'[65]

Every twenty versts or so they stopped to change horses, and when Sasha calculated that they had gone half way, they halted at the posting station and ordered a samovar; 'it is a small room very warm and *fairly* clean, distantly related to a 3rd class waiting room and a rather dirty farm parlour. There we unpacked our provisions and had dinner. I don't think I was ever so hungry.'[66]

In the afternoon Constance dozed, and was 'too tired to take much notice of anything',[67] but she woke up when they met another sledge bearing two dead bears. 'Our driver was so delighted just like a child. He stopped our horses that we should stand up and see them. It seems there are bears in the forests still and the day after tomorrow Sasha's brother-in-law is going with some neighbours to hunt a bear.'[68]

Sasha told her that there were also wolves in the forest. Constance thought she was a 'nice plucky girl',[69] for she spent a great deal of time driving about at all hours in a tiny sledge, accompanied only by a boy of fourteen, and once she had seen four wolves. She did not turn back, that would only have encouraged them. The correct tactic, as soon as you notice that you are being followed by wolves, is to stop the sledge and drive them off with cracks of your whip. The longer they follow a sledge the more dangerous they become. [70]

There were dangers enough without benefit of wolves 'simply from the state of the roads – especially as the earth has a way of cracking open across the road – and the crack gets bigger and bigger till it becomes a sort of ravine'.[71] Sasha had 'had some very thrilling adventures and once was very nearly frozen'.[72]

Besides changing horses at the posting station they also changed drivers. And in the afternoon they had 'a rather cross and depressed driver' who probably had 'an agreeable engagement for the evening and to go off 30 versts at a moment's notice did not suit him at all. So he said he did not know the road and to prove it, he lost his way before long.'[73] They went six miles out of their way. They were already delayed because they had not been allowed to take the direct route as 'the roads were too bad', and this had added another fifteen miles to the journey. Evening came on, but there was always some light from the white snow. When Constance peeped out of the sledge:

I could see now nothing but plains of snow – before and to the right and the left – not a landmark anywhere – and not a sound except the tinkle of our bell. I resigned myself to the position and nearly went to sleep leaving my fate contentedly in the hands of our driver – who was almost weeping – and the cheerful Sasha, who was by now congratulating herself on having brought enough provisions to enable us to be another 24 hours getting home if necessary.[74]

After 'hours of jolting and swearing at the horses and getting out of the road and finding it again'[75] they reached a village, where the driver bargained for fresh horses, and 'a peasant with an ivory face and jet black hair and beard, rather like some picture I have seen of John the Baptist'[76] invited them into his izba:

It was like stepping into a hothouse. I was blinded by the steam on my spectacles at first, then I saw the interior of a Russian izba for the first time. Two women and several children got up from the lockers on which they had been asleep. All of course were wearing their ordinary day clothes – mostly of homespun linen – and kerchiefs on their heads. In the middle of the fearfully hot airless hut swung a sort of large birdcage covered with a large red cotton cloth, and from it came the miauling of a baby. Sasha gave all the bread she had left to the children. They eat it at once as though it were cake. I could not stay more than a few minutes in the izba – I was afraid of fainting – so I went out and sat in the sledge where the temperature was somewhere about zero under the immense dark blue starry sky. The peasant directed our driver. I remember one of the women ventured to put in advice – and was at once told to hold her tongue – that this was not a woman's business.[77]

They put on an extra horse in front in tandem with the other, for the tracks were too narrow for two to go abreast. But the driver's whip was too short to reach the front horse, which perversely kept trying to turn back, and once even tipped them over: 'the driver shot off into the snow and I fell slowly and comfortably in my feather-bed wrappings upon Sasha. The peasant was up in a minute and pushed the sledge back again.'[78]

They did not reach Yablonka until after midnight. There Constance found a household 'out of a Russian novel'.[79] Besides Sasha's Finnish stepmother, there were the grandmother, the governess and children and even the family idiot – an extraordinary creature who can read – and even French and German – and can tell you what day of the week was March 3, 1854 or any date you like to mention – in about three minutes, but who is yet terribly and obviously an idiot. He is a man about fifty and is part owner of the estate.[80]

It all seemed quite medieval. There was even a 'dragon' that had attacked 'and *this is a fact* killed some women and children – but no one could find out what it was'.[81]

On her first afternoon at Yablonka Constance went for

a lovely drive with Sasha in a sledge to a neighbouring village – sunshine and blue sky – towards sunset the most marvellous delicacy of colouring. The scenery is like our Sussex downs, somewhat *flattened* and on an immense scale, nothing but snow slopes and plains and a few birch-trees here and there. The izbas are built of wood. . . rather neatly finished and pretty. But the villages look poor and desolate through the absence of trees and hedges and gardens and creepers. The houses just stand about in the snowy wilderness with nothing to veil their nakedness.[82]

Sasha also took her to see one of her schools, where the peasant children 'paying where possible a few kopecks'[83] were taught to read and write. But the fetid air indoors was more than Constance could stand, so she came out and made acquaintance with some peasant women and asked to see their izba.

I have never seen such poverty as these poor creatures live in, such filth and such utter want of care and comfort, and yet the strange thing is that they are not brutes, but far more sensitive and intelligent than our country labourers. . . . The Russian peasants are very inquisitive about foreign countries and very nice to strangers, and these women were so eager to question me, and to hear how people live in England. Their faces are so bright, and they are so ready to laugh; and yet nearly everyone here looks ill – especially the children – it is the effect of the years of famine. Children born in the worst year – if they lived at all – were found to be sickly, as the mothers had no milk or next to none. Most of the people are good-looking but often hideously disfigured by syphilis which is prevalent and not being treated in any way has awful results. Perhaps it may be one of the causes of the superior nervousness and sensibility of the people though. The children are as nervous and responsive as the children of our most intellectual classes.[84]

She was shocked to meet a boy who had been orphaned after his mother had lain ill for eleven weeks before dying without once having been seen by a doctor. She learned how every day during the famine the Shtevens had baked a hundred loaves of bread for the peasants, who 'divided what they had to the last – and when they died it was not by ones but by dozens'.[85] The peasants knew that some of the grain had been sent to them by the Quakers in England, and when cholera followed they believed that the English had sent it; so Sasha took Constance about and showed her to the peasants 'as living proof that the English people were good'[86] and would never do such a thing. She also visited a gipsy encampment 'where she saw a tame bear sitting outside one of the huts with one of the gipsy babies in its arms. The baby was fast asleep and the bear swaying rhythmically.'[87]

She stayed at Yablonka for a week, and then on Wednesday the 7th Sasha took her to Arzamas, a substantial town some fifty miles away, and there engaged a sledge that was going to Nizhni Novgorod that night with only one other person in it besides the driver, a young merchant who 'was so nervous at this close juxtaposition with a heathen heretic woman that he kept crossing himself and muttering prayers'.[88] By two o'clock in the morning Constance was so tired and so perished with cold, despite her two shubas, that she preferred to spend a disagreeable night in a squalid posting station, rather than continue the journey. There she was separated only by a screen from a drunken traveller, who called himself a 'government inspector' and kept hawking and spitting when he was not snoring. She spent a dreary night, but when she looked out of doors at first light she was enchanted: 'a peasant came out and went to a well – all the shadows were bright blue on the snow – it seemed so romantic – like a dream – to be so far away from everyone, a complete stranger in this new world – it was uncomfortable and I was tired – but inwardly thrilled all the time'.[89] She had some tea and ate her sandwich rolls. The 'spitting gentleman' insisted on coming with her to Nizhni Novgorod and sharing the cost. But just before they reached Korolenko's house he got out and slipped away without paying.

Korolenko was distressed by this behaviour, and related the story at length, along with an account of Constance's work in the East End and her impressions of poverty in Russia, in a newspaper article about her visit.[90] He gave her a long letter to take to Stepniak as well as copies of his book *The Famine Year* and his latest collection of stories. The letter concealed Stepniak's identity, but was openly revolutionary in tone, concluding with a grim account of the aftermath of the famine and a foreboding of its recurrence in the future: '"crowds of beggars will stretch out along the roads", but this time there will be no carts of free bread coming to meet them. I do not wish to prophesy, but I do think this is how it will happen, and it will be a terrible time.'[91]

With this compromising cargo hidden in her luggage Constance returned to Moscow. There she enjoyed the beauty of the city, absorbing as much of it as she could, going to the picture gallery and being struck by the works of Repin: 'He is very fine, but terrible, terrifying in his realism.'[92]

She had a 'fruitless expedition'[93] to see Tolstoy in Moscow: 'These prophets are dreadful people to deal with. He has gone into the country with his whole family and will not be back for a week – so it is impossible to talk things over in regard to his book. But I shall see the Countess on Tuesday.'[94] She told Tolstoy that she could not take on the *Gospels* 'as Mr. Heinemann could not, I think, publish a purely theological book and I am pledged for the next few months to work for him'.[95] She passed it on to Charles Edward Turner in St Petersburg, who agreed to do it, while at the same time Tolstoy offered her the reversion of his 'great social novel',[96] *Resurrection*, if Turner did not want to do it. Nothing came of this either.

By now she was longing to be home again. She had a vivid dream of Bunny in the train from Nizhni Novgorod to Moscow: 'it must be real' she thought, 'because I am *touching* him – one can't dream the sense of touch. . . . I don't think I have ever dreamed with such conviction before.'[97]

One of Constance's reasons for coming to Russia was to improve her spoken Russian. Shortly after she had first arrived in St Petersburg she had written to Edward: 'I shall work very hard at my spoken Russian and directly I can understand conversation I shall rush back to my little son.'[98] Once during those first days with Zina she had found herself alone with Nikolai Konstantinovich Mikhailovsky, a distinguished philosopher and friend of Korolenko's, and from shyness and lack of confidence in her spoken Russian was unable to communicate with him at all, and they sat together in embarrassed silence, though she had conversed happily enough with Korolenko five months before.

It may seem strange that she should have already completed translations of three very different books and yet was diffident about going shopping alone in St Petersburg. She could talk French fairly fluently and German quite adequately, but she did not consider herself a 'linguist',[99] and she had learnt Russian, as she had learnt Ancient Greek, as a written language. Her training in Greek was far more thorough than in Russian, and she had been taught not only to translate but also to compose verses in dead languages. Yet even the most eminent of her Cambridge tutors might have been tongue-tied in the presence of Plato and hesitated to go shopping in the agora of Ancient Athens.

Even after a month in Russia she had to confess:

It is disappointing that I still cannot follow a conversation in Russian, and can speak only a little better than when I came. But I have learnt and seen so much of Russian life that I feel I could hardly have spent my time better. And I have made such nice acquaintances that I shall want to come to Russia every year.[100]

It was not until her return visit to Moscow that she was able to write:

I think I am now just beginning to understand and speak Russian. Everywhere I receive compliments on my accent, but the construction of the sentences – almost always in the impersonal, and in the general, like Latin – and so much more positive than ours – is still very difficult for me.[101]

Constance had originally intended to pay a visit to Kronstadt to see her grandfather's grave, but she was told that she would never be able to find it in the deep snow, and she abandoned the idea. She went to St Petersburg on 15 February, and after a few days there set off on the long journey home. But when she reached the frontier at Wirballen she was detained. They put her alone in a waiting room. She called – as she had learned to do from Sasha – for a samovar; and while she waited she burned Korolenko's letter, and no doubt any other compromising papers, in its flame.[102] Eventually 'she was told that they thought the stamp on her passport was incorrect but, after telegraphing St Petersburg, had been informed that it was in order'.[103] She was allowed to proceed, and reached home on Saturday 24 February.

On the following day Olive reported: 'Connie looks very well, absurdly young-looking for thirty-two.'[104]

10

An Unsettled Year

Richard Garnett had been of much practical help to Constance in her travels, giving her the shuba and allowing her to draw money on Russian branches of his bank. But he could not share his son's and his daughter-in-law's passion for Russian literature, and had been anxious about her journeying alone so far into a barbaric country. On the same day that she left Moscow for Yablonka he expressed his concern in a typical sonnet:

> Dove that of old, fraught with the olive-spray,
>   Toldest of Earth arisen from the flood,
>   And how the grove in ancient station stood,
> And badest man take courage and be gay:
> Vain for green leaf this January day
>   To search the savage waste of Scythian wood,
>   Yet thither wend, of Clara's ill or good
> Bringing back tidings on thy westering way. . . .[1]

(His poetic conventions required the second person singular and that Constance be referred to by her second name.)

Everyone was glad now that she was back. When she and Edward went to lunch at the British Museum on the day after her return, he was wearing a new suit, and she had brought them back presents from Russia. Besides toys for David there was 'a box of sweetmeats' for Narney, 'cranberries coated with sugar', and for Olive 'a delightful hood with long tails, made of fawn coloured cloth trimmed with gold braid, it is Circassian and all classes wear such; ladies at the theatre and children going to school. . . .'[2] They made her 'talk incessantly of her adventures',[3] and when she had talked all afternoon she went with Edward to the Hartleys and began all over again.

The talk was not only of Russia. Constance was in a restless mood. She had 'plans'. She wanted to leave the flat in John Street and to set up house in Hampstead, with the Stepniaks and the Steffens somewhere nearby. Gustaf Steffen was a young Swede of twenty-nine who had trained as a mineralogist, but was by inclination a social historian and reformer. He joined the Fabians and worked in London, studying conditions in British industry and writing political journalism. He and his wife, Oscara, became close friends of the Garnetts for a while until he left London in 1897 to go to Italy.

The Hampstead plan came to nothing, but Gustaf Steffen found a house, 12 Lion Gate Gardens, less than two hundred yards from Kew Gardens, which he thought would 'do for them all'.[4] It was a severe gabled building of no particular charm, but with a fair-sized garden, and it was no more than ten minutes' walk from Richmond Station; 'the only drawback at present known is that it has no copper'.[5] There were 'gas fittings' to be seen to; and Ernest Black would deal with the 'drains etc.' He had been a practising architect for some time now, but only after David Black's death had he been released from bondage to his ailing father. It was not long before he was engaged to Minnie Eastty, a daughter of the Blacks' old family friends.

The Garnetts and the Steffens would share servants, 'Edward could boat on the river'.[6] It all seemed 'very satisfactory',[7] and the house was 'bright and airy' inside, and the 'paint and papers, and fittings charming'.[8] But it would hardly bring Constance any closer to Stepniak, and Olive was right to remark, 'I wonder what the Stepniaks will say', [9] for it was essential for Constance to be near Stepniak so that she could consult him easily about her translation. She was back at work on Turgenev within ten days of her return.

Both versions of *The Kingdom of God is Within You* had come out while she had been away. Heinemann had tried to stop the Scott edition from appearing, by claiming that in 'publishing' Deibner's Russian edition in London he had established exclusive rights to the book. This was sharpish practice, and it failed. The two translations came out together and had to sink or swim on their merits. A reviewer in the *Academy*, who claimed to have read the French and German versions, took the occasion to compare the two English ones. He found fault with Aline Delano for translating the text without properly considering what the author was trying to say, and praised Constance in comparison. He thought Delano's version of the sub-title, 'Christianity not as a mystical doctrine, but as a new life-conception' was 'very Teutonic', whereas Constance's 'Christianity not as a mystic religion but as a new theory of life' was 'intelligible' and 'in sensible English'. To point out errors of this kind' he added, 'is not hair-splitting, but log-cleaving, a performance little to our taste.'[10]

Nevertheless he split a few more such logs. It was, as he said, a tedious business, but it did show how poor some of the earlier translations were, and why Constance's were better, even on the most basic level.

Constance's routine of translation was beginning to be established. She would read through the Russian, looking up the unfamiliar words and phrases and noting the English in pencil between the lines, just as she had done in her Greek books at Cambridge. Russian novels were usually paper-bound, and by the time she had finished with them they were often just a stack of loose sections. Then she would set to and write out the translation fairly rapidly. David has described how he

would watch the changing expressions on her face, eager, frowning, puzzled or amused. The Russian words were translated not only on the foolscap sheet of paper in front of her, but into English features of flesh and blood. Her face was so expressive that I could guess at the emotional tension of what she was reading.[11]

In her prime when Constance had become more confident in her work, D. H. Lawrence described her as,

sitting out in the garden turning out reams of her marvelous translations from the Russian. She would finish a page, and throw it off on a pile on the floor without looking up, and start a new page. The pile would be this high . . . really almost up to her knees, and all magical.[12]

And when she had completed a sufficient batch she would go through it with a Russian friend before it went to press.

The task of the translator is free of the chief frustration of the creative writer. One can set oneself a stint of, say, five thousand words a day, and one knows that when it is completed there are another five thousand words waiting to be tackled the following morning. Constance's 'will power where translation was concerned – so many pages a day whatever might be – was inflexible'.[13] Of course there are constant difficulties in trying to find the right words in English, but one never has the mental block which would later hold David up for weeks at a time unable to proceed with a novel, or Edward for hours with a review.

In the spring of 1894, besides her work and arranging about the new house, she had a fairly busy social life. She went to some of the 'Sunday Popular Debates' organised by J. T. Grein at which Stepniak and Volkhovsky spoke. She started going to a course of four lectures on

Russian literature that Stepniak gave on successive Wednesday after-noons at Miss Chadwick's in Campden Hill. But at the third of them, on 14 March, Olive found her much agitated. She gave Olive 'a letter from Edward to read, in which he said that he felt too ill and nervous to come up this week'.[14] Constance would have to carry out the move from John Street without his help. Edward was on the verge of some kind of nervous breakdown. He had been moody and unhappy for some time, and he had been unable to bring himself to write regularly to Constance in Russia. From St Petersburg she had written to him on 7 January a long letter full of love and concern for their relations and for his physical and mental health:

Dear one, we know each other so well; we have been so close in the past that we never ought to lose what is precious to both of us. Only let us be honest and give freely what we still can give each other. There could be no reason for coldness for neither of us asks more than that. You think me colder than I am, because I am timid with you, and increasingly timid, and the first condition for all happy relations is absolute freedom to be oneself.

Write to me how you are in health. . . more and more clearly I see that you ought never to lose sight of the necessity of building up your nervous health. . . . You ought to make that an object always present to you – and to try to get over insomnia and nervous irritability now while it is still possible by putting yourself in the best conditions of fresh air, early hours etc. In a few years it would be too late, and you would have become a pessimist, a slave to your moods, dependent on stimulants for sleep and work. . . . I want to see you become healthy and happy and manly – instead of peevish, and irritable and nervous. I could not bear you to become to Bunny what our father was to us, poor man, when we were children, through his nervous irritability. You know anyone who cannot be freely approached because of the possibility of throwing him into a bad temper or nervous agitation, becomes more and more isolated. . . . If you are not careful that will happen to you. . . .

I want you to make the best possible of your life. You are something very rare and you have something worth prizing and perfecting. It is terrible to think of your sinking into something inferior to what you have been, getting less and less self-control, weaker, more moody. You have a strong will and could exercise self-control, but you will not recognise the necessity – that is the danger. Forgive me this long lecture. . . . Dear one my heart is full of tenderness for you, of true and unselfish love for you.[15]

Now Edward was 'advised to take an entire rest'.[16] Fisher Unwin gave him two months' holiday 'to go abroad in if he likes'.[17] But, as Olive reported:

He has decided not to go with Hartley to Cornwall but simply to stay all the time at the Cottage, doing nothing as far as possible and in cheerful society. He thinks that Lucy, Fanny and I will be nice quiet companions as Connie cannot leave the new house. Connie does not want him to be left alone, Jane is leaving and so Baby will have to be at Kew with the Steffens' servants and her. . . . I promised to go and ask Fanny to go next week. Connie is busy packing for moving and is overtired. Lucy went to help her.[18]

But Fanny's general servant 'vanished', [19] and she could not come to the cottage until later. Olive spent much of April with Edward at Henhurst Cross. The weather was 'most glorious, quite extraordinary'.[20] Edward, who was thoroughly run down, suffered from a swollen cheek, not mumps but an abscess. However, he gradually recovered his spirits, and he and Olive had 'long moral discussions'; [21] Edward was all for 'spontaneity, nature, impulse, change'; Olive for 'solidity, intellect, reliability, truth'.[22] At the end of six weeks she wrote that Edward 'is very much better, quite different ever since I have been here; his stay here has been most successful, I consider, and so has ours. . . . I have seen Edward in his trying moods now and I understand him much better and his affairs generally.'[23] But she did not commit her understanding to paper.

Edward then went off to spend the remainder of his rest-cure at an ancient farmhouse next to Tarr Steps, an immemorial clapper-bridge of huge stones beside a ford in a wooded valley on Exmoor, an even more attractive place then than it is now as a National Trust beauty spot. And then it had the advantage of a railway station at Dulverton, an easy six miles for such a walker as Edward.

Meanwhile Constance was being elected to the Executive Committee of the Fabians. When this was first mooted, Graham Wallas consulted Shaw, who replied with uncharacteristic curmudgeonliness:

Mrs Garnett has done nothing for the Fabian; and there is not the smallest reason to suppose that she has any other object in Executiving than to be in the fashion. However, I have no objection whatever to her coming on; she and I were acquainted formerly. But I wont manifest in her favor or in anyone else's without much further consideration. There is, I hear, some question of getting our names to use as supporters &c. If I am not to do that for Galton &c, I shall certainly not do it for Constance.[24]

It was quite true that Constance had not done much for the Fabian Society, though when she returned from Russia the *Fabian News* reported in the column 'What Members are Doing': 'Mrs. Constance Garnett, the translator of Tolstoi's last great social work, has just returned from

Russia, where she has been studying the economic position of the peasantry in the famine districts.'[25] She may indeed have submitted a report or given a talk to the Fabians about what she saw at Yablonka, but it sounds more as if they were appropriating her journey to the society's purposes, just as they appropriated Tolstoy's fundamental Christianity to socialism. On the other hand she never cared a rap for fashion, and was far too unambitious to have engineered her own election.

There were fifteen members on the Executive; and when the ballot was counted the first eight places were taken by old members – headed by Shaw with 336 votes. Constance came second of the four new members with 259, and Ramsay MacDonald scraped in with 195.

James Ramsay MacDonald was a young Scot of twenty-seven with a 'fine voice, an excellent presence and a resonant turn of phrase', [26] who by hard work had made some progress in a career in politics without yet being sure where he was going. He had been a Fabian for seven years and considered himself a socialist, but nevertheless tried to become the Liberal candidate for Southampton. Constance liked him and they remained friendly for many years after they had both left the Fabians.

Shaw had long since ceased to be an engaging curiosity, and was becoming a serious political and literary figure. *Arms and the Man* opened on 21 April, just at the time of the Fabian election. The Stepniaks had a box at the first night, and Fanny wrote to Olive:

It was great fun, the actors played well and the piece was accepted with acclamations, cheers and great applause. B. Schaw made a short speech. He appeared in evening dress irreprochable and all the ladies, including Dora Forbes, got into ecstasis. Connie (the new member of the Fab. executive) came down with Hartley into our box from the gallery. We had many distinguished visitors in our box during the intervals, amongst them the authors of '*Obsessions*' and '*the other way round*'.[27]

Dora Forbes, the pseudonym of the male author of *The Other Way Round*, and Guy Walsingham, the pseudonym of the female author of *Obsessions*, are fashionable writers in Henry James's story 'The Death of the Lion', which Olive had been relishing a few days earlier with Fanny at Henhurst Cross. They may possibly be private nicknames for real people, but it seems more likely that Fanny was just joking about the high literary society in which she found herself. All one can say for certain is that there was 'a real Bulgarian admiral'[28] in the Stepniaks' box.

Arms and the Man was successful enough for Shaw to open his first bank account. 'It showed him that he could achieve success at the box office without abandoning his moral purpose and that he could educate more effectively with humour than with sermons.'[29]

The main concerns of the Fabians at this time were the perennial question of Land Nationalisation, about which Edward had been so sceptical, and the Eight Hours Bill. Many workers – like the poor match-girls – were working fourteen hours a day, and some even longer, and there was a well-established movement to restrict all employment to eight hours a day. The Trade Union Conferences in recent years had voted overwhelmingly to promote a Bill making it illegal for any workers to be employed for more than eight hours except in trades where a majority of the members petitioned to be exempted, and this had been taken up in a modified form by Gladstone.[30] In 1894 it was the chief goal of the Labour movement.

Constance was absent on 27 April from the first meeting of the Fabian Executive to be held after her election. But on the afternoon of Sunday 6 May she was in Hyde Park with her friends to see the annual May Day parade, 'the fifth of the great legal eight hours demonstrations'.[31] An immense procession came in from Hyde Park Corner, 'bands playing, banners waving', [32]

there were the Tailors, the Bricklayers, the Cigar Makers, the Ironfounders, the Amalgamated Carpenters and Joiners, and suchlike older and skilled unions, side by side with the Dockers, the Gasworkers, the Builders' Labourers, the Navvies, and the Carmen. Radicalism was not absent. The Hatcham Liberal Club sent up two brake-loads of its members.[33]

There were a dozen platforms, and the Fabians had one of them – 'a waggon picturesquely adorned with evergreens and red twill in which Pease stood upright, as if he were posing to Walter Crane for his "May Day" picture'.[34] There were also Fabian speeches from Enid Stacey and the Rev. Stewart Headlam; and as usual the wittiest and most notable was from Bernard Shaw. Olive and Arthur Garnett were given a bundle of Fabian tracts to sell and went round crying 'Price one penny!' and 'exchanging friendly words with the other vendors' until Edward arrived and spoilt their sport by buying up their entire stock.[35]

When the speeches were brought to an end at five o'clock – Shaw's was 'cruelly cut short by "Time's up"'[36] – and they all dispersed, Lucy Garnett walked home with Edmund Houghton, a Fabian of thirty-one, whom Constance and the Hartleys clearly had 'plans' for with regard to her. But the plans were no more successful than such things usually are.

Lucy fell, not for Houghton, but for his friend Harrison Cowlishaw, an architect and fellow Fabian, who shared rooms with him in Lincoln's Inn. Harry, as he was always known, was a craftsman by inclination. He liked to wear a smock and aimed to make himself a master of all the crafts at the architect's service.

During May and June Constance attended six out of eight of the meetings of the Fabian Executive Committee, and was elected to the Women's Tract Committee. She also found time for a good deal of social life, as well as getting on with her translation. On the Friday before the May Day demonstration she had been with Hartley and Houghton and Olive and Lucy to the first London performance of Ibsen's play, *The Wild Duck*, put on by J. T. Grein for the Independent Theatre Society at the Royalty Theatre. She 'had a real passion for the theatre'[37] and was sympathetic to Ibsen. She had been in the country the previous March trying to get well after toothache and depression when Elizabeth Robins played Hilda Wangel in *The Master Builder*. But she heard about it from David Rice who 'went and said the pit was in fits of laughter at many of the finest passages and began to go out about five minutes before the end' and she wondered how Miss Robins could 'feel it worth acting before such wretches'.[38] She did not, alas, record what she thought of *The Wild Duck*. The critics were puzzled, but Olive at least 'enjoyed the performance immensely'.[39]

On 24 May she went with Edward and a party of friends to hear Sydney Olivier read *A Freedom in Fetters*, a problem play of tangled sexual morality.[40] Olive, who considered herself 'the nearest thing to an average Britisher' present at this first reading, was upset by it and thought it 'A most unpleasant situation, staging well treated.' 'There was scarcely any humour in the play, or wit, and no passion,' she observed, adding hopefully, 'But I suppose the actors put that in.'[41]

At the end of May Edward, his brother Robert, Houghton and other friends attended the sale of the effects of Ford Madox Brown, who had died in October 1893. He was an old family friend, and when Edward had published Grace Black's collection of stories, *A Beggar*, in 1889 he had drawn a carefree colophon of Edward in the character of Autolycus, which Edward afterwards used as an occasional bookplate. At the third day of the sale, the 31st, Edward bought a square piano by John Broadwood for twelve shillings, a gothic oak dining-room table made at William Morris's workshops and some Morris chairs.[42]

And on 16 July Constance and Edward went to the Hartleys to hear

Fanny read Stepniak's play, *The Convert*. Constance may well have had a hand in translating it from Stepniak's Russian.[43] Mrs Richard Garnett and William Archer 'had places of honour on the sofa',[44] and there was a large party of friends, from Edward Pease to Zina Vengerov, to hear it. Fanny read well, but the audience was unmoved and gave it a rather blank reception. Olive felt 'a vague sense of surprise and disappointment'.[45]

At Lion Gate Gardens there were several visits from Lucy, and, as had been promised, trips on the river. Richmond had displaced Henhurst Cross as home, which was fortunate, because the Broome Hall Estate, which owned the cottage, had, so Olive told Constance, 'been sold to a Mr Alexander Shipley for £100,000',[46] and the future of their tenancy was in doubt.

Meanwhile another of Constance's translations had been published. While she was still in Russia Heinemann had announced that *Rudin* was to be 'looked for some time in May, hardly sooner'[47] and would be followed by Turgenev's other 'continuous tales'. By July the book was out, and notices were beginning to appear. The anonymous reviewer in the *Daily Chronicle*, the Liberal paper that was the Garnetts' regular reading, was full of praise:

It is only of late years that translation has been regarded in England as a reputable art. . . . Translations are no longer executed by people who are equally ignorant of the language from which and into which they are translating. Perhaps, then, we may regard it as a merciful interposition of providence that Turgenev, half of whose charm resides in his gracious silver-tongued style, should have been preserved from the translator-traitor of bygone days. . . . The complete translation projected by Mr. Heinemann has been entrusted to Mrs. Constance Garnett, and could not have fallen into better hands. If in subsequent volumes Mrs. Garnett can keep up to the level of excellence attained in 'Rudin' we shall have to thank her for one of the best series of translations in the language.[48]

And generally the new edition was welcomed (though it did not in fact claim to be complete except as regards the novels). But the *Daily Chronicle* was not so kind to Edward, and had printed a 'slashing' review of *An Imaged World* on the previous day. It was headed 'Prose, Poetry or What?' and was so vicious that Olive thought it was 'written probably by Henry Norman in revenge for T. F. U[nwin]'s having refused his wife's MSS on Edward's advice'.[49] The *Bookman*[50] was only slightly less hostile. Even friendly reviewers did not know what to make of Edward's 'series of love-poems in dithyrambic paragraphs . . . using nature and man, town and country, . . . with intense subjectivity'.[51] Ernest Rhys managed to praise them for attaining 'something very like what in the case of Welsh preachers is expressively termed the "hwyl"',[52] but thought that William Hyde's wash drawings were more successful than Edward's text. Yeats, writing anonymously in the *Speaker*, let his friend down as lightly as he could: 'There is enough of poetry in this remarkable book for many poems, and yet it seldom perfectly satisfies the artistic conscience or quite lays asleep the thought that we will forget it when it is thrust into the shelf'.[53] And in Yeats's hands, cut to the hard bone and shorn of all needless rhetoric, they might indeed have been fine poems.

This very unequal reception of their work would have tested a marriage that was much more secure than Edward's and Constance's. Fortunately Edward, although he could not heal himself, was beginning to develop an almost unfailing touch in diagnosing the health of others. While the door to his own creative writing was being closed, another was about to open.

Fisher Unwin was very partial to series in which he hoped the weaker titles might ride off on the backs of the stronger. The most familiar of these was the Mermaid Series of unexpurgated reprints of old plays, but there were also the Adventure Series, Cameo Series, Overseas Library and several others, among them the Pseudonym Library, which Unwin considered his 'first success', [54] though Edward must have the credit for the choice of titles. It ran to fifty-two volumes in the first four years. They were small and shortish books in a distinctive tall and narrow format 'and typographically attractive at the price of eighteen pence'.[55] They included works by Yeats, Olive Schreiner and Constance's eccentric Newnham friend, Alice Dew-Smith, published of course pseudonymously, as well as several collections of Russian short stories.

On 5 July, a Polish sea-captain, who had for some time been signing himself Joseph Conrad, and who was living in London after serving fifteen years on British ships, though rarely at the level for which he was qualified, sent to Unwin for inclusion in the Pseudonym Library a long novel entitled *Almayer's Folly*. It sat in the office until 8 September, when the author, growing impatient, asked for a decision or to have it back. It was much too long for the Pseudonym Library, but it was far too good to reject, as W. H. Chesson, one of the readers at Unwin, realised as soon as he read it. 'It must be submitted to Mr. Garnett,' he wrote.[56] Edward was impressed, but he was uncertain whether the English was good enough for publication. Constance 'was far more sensitive to language and to the beauty of a writer's style than Edward',[57] so he showed it to her, saying that 'it was the work of a foreigner and asked her opinion of his style'.[58] She thought that Conrad's foreignness was a positive merit, and gave it her imprimatur. Unwin took it on and persuaded Conrad to accept a paltry twenty pounds for the rights.

It was not until November of 1894 that Edward and Conrad first met. It was at the National Liberal Club. Edward's memory was of

a dark-haired man, short but extremely graceful in his nervous gestures, with brilliant eyes, now narrow and penetrating, now soft and warm, with a manner alert yet caressing, whose speech was ingratiating, guarded, and brusque turn by turn. I had never before seen a man so masculinely keen yet so femininely sensitive.[59]

Many years later Conrad described his view of the occasion:

I saw a young man enter the room. 'That cannot be Edward so young as that', I thought. [Edward was eleven years his junior.] He began to talk. Oh yes! It was Edward. I had no longer doubt. But I was too frightened to speak. But this is what I want to tell you, how he made me go on writing. If he had said to me, 'Why not go on writing?' I should have been paralysed. I could not have done it. But he said to me, 'You have written one book. It is very good. Why not *write another?*' Do you see what a difference that made? Another? Yes, I would do that. I *could* do that. Many others I could not. Another I could. That is how Edward made me go on writing.[60]

This was the beginning of the most fruitful of literary friendships. For nearly thirty years Edward not only made Conrad go on writing, but assuaged his self-doubts and kept him on the right track with a constant stream of sympathetic criticism. The story is charted in detail in Conrad's letters, edited with an introduction of brilliant percipience and precision by Edward after his friend's death, and has been a subject of study for academics ever since.

But for the moment, in the summer of 1894, Edward was still somewhat in the dumps, and they were all unwell. Constance went down to the cottage to rest after her rather hectic spring. David became very ill with continual diarrhoea. She could not sleep. She felt she would 'soon be utterly broken down if I go on like this. I have had no peace of mind since I left Russia somehow, and I feel I have been losing ground in health steadily in spite of all efforts.'[61] Edward's abscess had not recovered but only grown worse, and he had gone to Brighton to see if Robert Black could operate on it and the sea air would help him recover. They were due to go and stay with the Richard Garnetts at their usual holiday resort at Charmouth in Dorset, but Constance suggested delaying it until September, 'when your father and mother would be away; as that would make no extra work for servants then'.[62] Narney replied on 7 August: '*My command* is to come down on 15th all three of you. The sooner Edward better. . . . The weather is delightful – now – and the bathing is excellent. . . . We can all look after Bunnie. He need be no trouble at all.'[63] But they were all too ill for the command to be obeyed. Just as Edward was beginning to recover, David's condition grew worse. 'I believe he would have died' Constance wrote, 'but for Valentine's Meat Juice (some preparation of raw blood) sent us by a nurse, Mary Belcher, at that time a great friend of Edward's.'[64] And she herself, as usual in the autumn, was afflicted with sick headaches.

By the time they were well enough to go to Charmouth David was 'almost a skeleton'.[65] There 'he plumped out again like a balloon'.[66] Although Dr and Mrs Garnett had already left, there was still a large party. Besides the younger Garnetts, there were Bertha Garraway, Charlie Garnett from Yorkshire, and the Kerbey boys, wards of 'Uncle Edward' Singleton, Narney's brother. Olive had had a severe depression, amounting almost to a breakdown, in the summer, so she too was convalescing.

Constance spent her time bathing and translating. She finished *On the Eve* and started on *Fathers and Children*. It was the first time that David had had a seaside holiday: 'he paddled and was very happy'.[67] A man brought a dancing bear through the village. David was fascinated – as he always was by bears.

Meanwhile there was a crisis over the introductions to Turgenev. Edward's compromise had been accepted by Heinemann – if not entirely by Stepniak – and *Rudin* had appeared with no mention of Stepniak on the title-page, but only his signature at the end of the introduction. He and Constance felt that this was shabby treatment, and he told her that he did not want to write any more. Edward therefore proposed that he should write them himself. Meanwhile Stepniak suggested that they should be written by Edmund Gosse or George Moore. Nothing could have been more calculated to strengthen Edward's resolve to write them himself. He had a 'lifelong prejudice against what he called "academic critics"',[68] and shared Olive's contempt for Edmund Gosse. ('Mr. Gosse' she once wrote, 'made a greater fool of himself than usual. His speech was in such execrable taste that it was torture to have to sit still and hear it.')[69] Heinemann had felt it necessary to get Gosse to write a preface to Constance's translation of *A Common Story*, which had yet to come out; it was a very uninspired piece of work, and was dropped when the book was reprinted. As for Moore, Constance was fond of quoting her father-in-law's assessment: 'A bit of a goose and a bit of a genius.'[70] She thought that *A Mummer's Wife* was a work of genius and could hold its own with the French and Russian novels, but that some of his other works had a 'curious lack of distinction'.[71]

Constance, however, felt that if she could not have Stepniak to write the introductions she would prefer to have none at all. Perhaps she saw, if only unconsciously, that Edward's involvement could be a threat to her independence – not that she put it like that to him. She told him that he had enough to do without having to find something new to say about each volume:

You want to keep all your energies for work you care for and really feel drawn to. I know if you did the work ever so slightly and quickly I should like it a great deal better than a preface by a fool like Gosse and his tribe. But I would rather have a foolish preface by Gosse than a slipshod one by you, or a good one that cost you time and trouble. . . .

What I have decided is this – to write to Heinemann that S. refuses to write more under present conditions and that the other volumes must appear *without prefaces*. He will probably be glad to let the matter rest there – and it will be infinitely the best solution. *If* he says we have agreed to furnish prefaces and must do so, then we can revert to your plan, or better still get him to offer the work to the ever willing and fluent Gosse. . . .

I shall see Stepniak this evening; but I shall insist on his having his preface ready for vol. II in case it is wanted – if H. does not agree to dispense with prefaces.[72]

Heinemann did not agree to dispense with introductions, and Constance had to be reconciled to Edward writing them. By the end of October she reported to her father-in-law: 'Edward is making rough notes for his preface to "On the Eve;" and we get very great pleasure reading through the translation together, as a preparation for it.'[73] As it turned out, Edward was better suited to introduce Turgenev to the English than Stepniak was. Stepniak wanted his readers to read Turgenev in order to understand Russia; Edward wanted them to appreciate Turgenev in order to understand how novels should be written. His prefaces were well received and helped to establish his reputation as an authority on Russian literature in parallel with Constance's as a translator.

What with David's illness and convalescence Constance was absent from all the meetings of the Fabian Executive between July and November. Then in mid-November she became a regular attender again. She went to a meeting of Clementina's Women Workers' Union, but was saved from unwittingly appearing at a 'loyal' Russian gathering by another sick headache.

They spent Christmas at Richmond. David's grandmother gave him a rocking-horse. He was christened Chopper, and became almost a creature of fable, as Constance reported to Narney in due course:

Chopper by the way is the hero of an epic. David composes the incidents and his Mum strings them into doggerel – Hyde is to illustrate them! Here are some lines

> When Daddy-Dumdy-Dee is cross
> And Mum's at work or ill
> I saddle Chopper my good horse
> And ride off to Leith Hill.
> We trot along the roads so fast
> That people cry as we go past
> 'I never saw a horse go faster,
> I wonder who's that Gee-gee's master.'
> 'I'm David Garnett, Chopper's master!'
> I shout and gallop on the faster. . . .[74]

On the Saturday after Christmas Constance and Oscara threw a big children's party at Lion Gate Gardens. Everybody came. The Mahomeds and the Claytons were there, the Hartleys, Olive and Fanny Stepniak and other Russian friends. It was a beautiful day. They danced round the tree, pulled crackers and 'tried fortunes'. It was the Garnetts' last Christmas in town, and a happy end to an unsettled year plagued by illness. Nevertheless Constance had managed to translate some two hundred thousand words and published four volumes, and had already established her reputation as a translator.

11

The Dear Little Cearne

On 24 January 1895 Constance told Olive that by a new arrangement with Fisher Unwin Edward was 'guaranteed not less than £350 a year, possibly more, and five per cent on something or other', so that she felt quite rich with her earnings as well.[1] *On the Eve* was due to come out in March. By then she would have published six volumes in just over a year. For the Turgenev translations she was paid a fee of nine shillings per thousand words on publication (about thirty to forty pounds a volume) with a royalty of ten per cent on sales over two thousand copies. Out of this she paid Stepniak one-fifth of her earnings for his help in checking her translation.[2]

Constance had also inherited about a thousand pounds from her father's estate. She was therefore able to think seriously about 'The Thatched House' and was 'very anxious to build a house'[3] – a proper house not a cottage – in the country, especially as Edward had 'now only to go to the office on Thursdays'[4] to report on the manuscripts that he had read during the rest of the week.

On the evening of that same 24 January Edward and Constance went to the St James's Theatre to see *Guy Domville*, Henry James's play which had had a disastrous first night three weeks before. The wretched author had been led on to the stage to be hissed, but the play had nevertheless continued its run, such was George Alexander's loyal following, and the interest that this scandal had aroused. Unfortunately Olive, the diarist of the family, who later developed such a devotion to Henry James that she was moved to write, 'Henry James seems to obsess me, or is it the spring coming?'[5], did not go with them, and we have no record of what they thought of the play.

They then went down to Henhurst Cross for the weekend. 'It was very cold at the cottage but very jolly',[6] since Lucy had come down with Harry Cowlishaw to discuss plans for the new house. Lucy had been spending a good deal of time with Harry recently and had adopted his

Arts and Crafts point of view. Olive, a little wistfully perhaps in view of her own unhappy amours, thought that Lucy looked blooming and happy. Cowlishaw was planning to set up 'a workshop somewhere in Holborn where he means to have a loom for weaving, dyeing apparatus, plastering etc'; [7] and Lucy was to have a latchkey to it, apparently with her parents' approval, although she was not actually engaged until Harry had a formal interview with Richard Garnett on 18 June.

Cowlishaw at this stage in his career was still totally committed to William Morris and in love with medieval rusticity. According to David Garnett he had never built a house before, and 'The first plan was for a great hall open to the roof, in which the family should eat and sleep, with a solar chamber on one side. There was to be a central open fire, with louvres in the roof instead of a chimney.'[8] Edward and Constance had the sense to reject this archaic notion, and Cowlishaw produced new designs which were pronounced 'delightful' and which he said could be 'worked out at a cost of £700 only'.[9] It was not after all to be thatched.

They also had to find a site for the house and decided not to be too far away from a small colony of Fabians and their friends already established near the Chart Woods a mile or two east of Oxted and close to the Surrey-Kent border. Henry Salt, a Fabian who had been a master at Eton but had resigned 'in protest against working with "cannibals in cap and gown," deciding to devote his life to vegetarian and humanitarian causes, and opting for the Simple Life on a hundred pounds a year',[10] had settled at Crockham Hill, south-east of the Chart. Sydney Olivier had returned from a stint of duty as Colonial Secretary in British Honduras in the spring of 1891 and enlarged a cottage near Limpsfield Chart into a house called the Champions for his wife and four daughters; and Edward Pease and his wife Marjorie had settled among hopfields at the Pendicle a short walk away in Pasten's Road.

Edward thought that the Olivier girls would make good friends for David, and both he and Constance were much attracted by the woods at the Chart:

Limpsfield Chart in those days was a scattered hamlet with cottages clustering behind a big wooden windmill on the edge of a strip of common. There was a smithy opposite a large pond, now dried up, and there was no church. The common was bounded on the south by fields falling steeply away and giving a splendid view which extended from Crowborough Beacon in the east to Hindhead in the west. Clayton Mills on the Sussex Downs and Blackdown near Haslemere were visible to the long-sighted.[11]

Constance, of course, was far too short-sighted ever to appreciate these remote splendours. The southern side of the Chart Woods plunged down to meet a line of pasture fields known as Scearn Bank. 'These fields were sheltered by the wall of forest. The branches of great beeches and tufted larches hid the roots of those rising behind them, and, along the edges of the meadows, banks of primroses reflected the pale sunlight of the spring.'[12] Edward chose half the topmost field as the site for their home. It was indeed a most beautiful site, but by no means a convenient place to build a house. As David wrote:

Nobody would have thought of building a house half a mile from any highroad, approachable only by a rough cart-track through a lonely waste of woodland, in the time of Jane Austen or even of George Eliot. It was remote from a village and was not part of any existing community. . . . Instead there was a great horizon, solitude, and the encompassing forest which may have given these fields their name – for they are encerned or encircled by the woods. My parents might have been the pilgrim fathers building a blockhouse in New England. They were indeed pioneers, who would not have been happy in a community, or on the outskirts of one. Their choice of a site was due to an awareness that they did not belong, that they rejected and did not wish to fit into the Victorian social hierarchy.[13]

On the other hand the Limpsfield Fabians, who were likewise rebels, but were less insulated from the outside world by the woods and their own natures than the Garnetts, took an active interest in local affairs: 'In the early Nineties the Fabians, led by Olivier swept the board in the local parish elections and for some time after this Marjorie Pease was a leading figure in local politics.'[14]

Constance duly bought the site – the deeds were in her name, her address grandly given as 'British Museum, London W.C.' – from the Leveson-Gower Estate for three hundred pounds, quite a lot of money in those days for just over half an acre of meadow. The Stepniaks remarked that 'now that the Edward Garnetts have become landed proprietors, bourgeoises, we can abuse them!'[15] and encouraged Olive to tease them, though they were by no means the first Fabians thus to abandon the strict path of socialism.

In March, impatient to be on the site before the builders had even started, they rented a cottage at Froghole, a mile or so to the east. It was 'a tiny old cottager's cottage with worn doorstep, worn floors, low ceilings and warm chimney corner, cool within, cheerful without',[16] but David remembered it as 'overrun by rats'[17]. There was no room for friends and when Olive came with Arthur and her friend Bertha King they had to stay in another cottage nearby. She was no less delighted with it than she had been with Henhurst Cross:

The glorious view over the plain there came as a delightful surprise after the shady winding road and we fell in love with our cottage and Froghole generally. I was especially delighted with Arthur's room across the landing from ours, with its doorway reached by a ladder from the garden and framed by the boughs of an apple tree, and with its other doorway into the upper floor of a mysterious looking oast house. Our own airy bedroom with its magnificent view through tiny panes and the cool red brick floored rooms below charmed us also.[18]

But while Olive was charmed, Constance found her cottage inconvenient for her work. 'I am longing for a study to myself' she told her father-in-law, 'free from the scrimmage of meals and Bunnie. On dark days one cannot see to sew and hardly to write in this little room.'[19] After six months of working in these conditions her weak eyes were 'rather troublesome' and she was 'forced for some time to lay aside all reading and writing'.[20]

Printed Russian is not kind to the eyes at the best of times. Whereas the roman alphabet, in its minuscules, has ascenders and descenders (what used to be called 'pot-hooks and hangers') to twelve out of the twenty-six letters, the cyrillic alphabet as then constituted had only four out of thirty-five. As a result, even when written in minuscule, Cyrillic looks rather like something typewritten in roman capitals. The words form themselves into long rectangular blocks, rather than the more easily recognisable irregular shapes in roman. One need only compare a word in roman minuscule with the same written in small capitals (e.g. legibility/ LEGIBILITY) to get a visual impression of the difference between roman and cyrillic. One must not push this argument too far – Russian scholars do not all suffer from eyestrain – nevertheless it would be a great service to Russia to reform the design of its alphabet, which could easily be done by adapting its far more legible, but much less used, cursive 'italic'.

Constance still had to make visits to London. She attended all six of the meetings of the Fabian Executive in January and February, but no more. When the time came for re-election in April she asked not to be nominated. She still supported the Fabians, and remained a member, but the pressure of her work was increasing, and she had got nothing done in March because she was ill and too busy moving house. She did not go to the annual May Day parade in Hyde Park, where Olive saw only Bernard Shaw of 'all our friends who attended last year'.[21] Constance had a 'conference' about Turgenev with Sherwin Cody, an American journalist who combined reviewing fiction for the *Saturday Review* with being a cousin of Buffalo Bill. She even invited him down to Froghole. She went to London in order to befriend Tolstoy's niece, who was visiting Cambridge.

She was working hard. *On the Eve* came out in March. When Olive read it she wrote, 'the translation seems excellent to me but Connie says it seems to her to grow worse as it goes on and there are shocking misprints'.[22] There were the proofs of *Fathers and Children* to be seen to, and she was busy with the two volumes of *A Sportsman's Sketches*, which, with its rich descriptive passages and specific vocabulary, she found one of the most challenging of Turgenev's works to translate. For all this she had to have regular sessions with Stepniak to go over her translations and resolve her 'difficulties'. The Garnett residence in the British Museum provided a convenient place of assignation for these meetings, until the Stepniaks decided to take a cottage near the Chart Woods. It was even smaller than the one at Froghole, 'a tiny little box of a cot',[23] no more than half a small cottage with one room up and one down, in Pasten's Road, almost next door to the Peases.

Thereafter Stepniak was at hand when Constance needed his help. They could go over her translations together in the orchard at Froghole,[24] and had by now established a regular working relationship, unfraught by outbreaks of undue emotion. Olive, on the other hand, after her crisis of the previous summer, was having to resign herself to seeing much less of Stepniak than before. He suggested that she should 'go into a family' in Russia, as Constance had done with the Whites in Cromwell Road, and found some people in Odessa who seemed willing to have her. Olive 'had a great struggle, rapturous moral victory and decided then and there to go to Odessa and obey Stepniak forever in everything good'.[25] Constance gave her advice and encouragement about going, and helped her to improve her Russian. The Odessa plan fell through, but she did not abandon the idea of going to Russia.

Olive had 'always been curious'[26] to see Stepniak in the country and hoped that it would do him as much good as it did her. But he was constantly being 'urged by Fanny to shut himself up to produce',[27] and Constance felt that if Fanny needed money she should translate herself. As for Stepniak, there was 'a falling off in the quality of his work'; he 'wanted a new life, to elope with someone, not to be set down to work'.[28] This was speculative 'talk' at its most theoretical. It was not the time for

Constance to be thinking of eloping with him herself when she and Edward were so committed to rooting themselves in the soil of Scearn Bank field, and if Stepniak had run off with someone else it would have been a dreadful hindrance to her work. Olive found all this upsetting: 'Connie generally has this effect on me when she "talks" about things'.[29] Constance herself soon came to dislike this kind of 'talk'. A few years later, when she read Henry James's novel, *The Awkward Age*, she commented, 'the whole thing is a magnificent study of the vice of that mixture of gossip and psychological analysis, which spoils every natural impulse – and which is by the way *our* prevalent vice'.[30] Fanny meanwhile was so 'conscious of household cares as not to be able to shake them off'. Olive found that 'keeping the cottage tidy and cooking took all her time, and all the while I was there about an hour and a half she continued to chop the meat in a bowl'.[31]

Poor Fanny was also encumbered with some Russian Armenians – Avetis Nazarbek, his wife Murro and their two children – who had fled from the atrocities of the unspeakable Turk and were battening on the Stepniaks. They can hardly have found room to stay in the Stepniaks' minute cottage, but they were always about the house. At first Olive was fascinated by them:

The Armenian gentleman is very wonderful to look at, small and slight with an ivory complexion, dark eyes and masses of coal black hair, rather long . . . like a very pretty waxwork, one wants to stick a pin into him to see if he will call out. He is a poet and poses with a distingué air. . . .. His wife, very elegantly dressed in the French style, is also goodlooking, sallow complexion with liquid brown eyes and dark brown hair. They speak no English but have come over to enlist English sympathies with their countrymen so they are trying to learn.[32]

Their children talked 'Armenian to their parents, Russian to Fanny, Greek when they don't want to be understood'.[33]

Thus, within a few months of their arrival at Froghole, the Garnetts were already beginning to attract foreigners to the Chart. The country people, who were unused to strangers, and were still learning to accept the first Fabian colonists, must have looked on them with the simple wonderment of American savages meeting the first Europeans. They were far more disconcerting than the waiters from Italian restaurants who occasionally prowled the Chart woods in search of chanterelles and other edible fungi. (Edward, incidentally, when instructed by Fanny Stepniak and other foreign ladies, became a keen and expert fungivore, but Constance was no gourmet, and could not share in the passion for mushrooms which in Russia reaches almost to the status of a religion.)

By late May the site of a new house, which they named after Scearn Bank, but for some reason spelt 'Cearne', had been pegged out on the ground. On the evening of the 20th Edward took Olive and Arthur to look at it. It was still

a buttercup meadow, on a slope with a copse rising behind to north and east and the magnificent view spread out to the south and west with undulating hilly ground between. The cuckoo called and cows with tinkling cowbells were driven in for the night. We wandered from peg to peg, imagining the rooms, the verandah, the kitchen garden and the rest of it.[34]

The building was founded with due ceremony:

In a large cornerstone we had a hole made and in it put today various little articles which might be of antiquarian interest in centuries to come. With these we put a document composed by Edward and carefully written out on parchment. In it he describes the site and gives its ancient name – and then makes brief sketches of himself, David and me, Harry and Lucy, our parentage, and our favourite authors and musicians. Then in a very fine piece of rhetoric he winds up by a brief summing up of our aspirations and a hope that the posterity who read the document have outgrown them and risen to higher things. What a delightful find for the year 2995![35]

They suffered the practical difficulties that pioneers might expect in building a home:

Since there was only a rough woodland track leading to the site, all the building materials had to be carted on tumbrils, which were tipped back with their weight resting on skid-beams as they came down the steep hillside. The wheel of one went over the edge of the track, and the whole thing crashed down the hillside, killing the shaft-horse. All the stone for the house was hewn out of the quarry on the Chart common, and the larger pieces for the fireplaces were carved in the quarry by the master mason.[36]

The building stone was deliberately not squared up, but left rough cut in pieces of irregular shape but fairly standard size that must have taken some skill to fit together into vertical walls with rectangular openings for the doors and windows, which were of iron with smallish rectangular leaded panes. There were two chimneys. They had lids on the top and smoke-holes at the side to prevent the wind coming down the hillside causing a downdraught. The wrought iron hinges and door-latches were made at a smithy on the site, and Cowlishaw himself decorated the largest bedroom with hoops of Burne-Jonesian briar-rose in the plaster on the sloping part of the ceiling.

There was no water, and 'a well had to be sunk . . . before building could be begun'.[37] As the site was on a well-drained slope, the well-sinker had to go down a long way; and before he reached water the sides began to fall in, not having been properly shored up. Eventually, at sixty feet, he found a good supply of water, 'but with an iron sediment'.[38]

Building was still incomplete when Olive visited Froghole in November. David was by now three-and-a-half years old, and had the wit to wind his arms around her neck and say, 'Dear Auntie Olive, I love you better than all my aunties' ('The Irish rascal!' she exclaimed in her diary), and after an early supper they took a lantern and 'strolled off to the site':

A crisp starlight night for a ramble, but Connie had blistered her foot and held my arm all the way, as in turn we swung the lantern over the heath, under the pine branches and through the copse. Then a stumble over builder's paraphernalia and lantern held now to a window, rafter or a chimney nook, or a loose plank. No staircase as yet but we sat atop of a ladder and saw the stars shining serenely in the sky-roof. Well might Connie and Edward be proud and me admiring and Cowlishaw admired.[39]

On the following day they went again in daylight: 'To the beauties of the house were added this time the beauties of the garden, with Bert at work in it; the men in the wind putting tiles on the roof, red against the unpolished tortoiseshell of stonework and green of dark firs behind.'[40]

The house was due to be completed soon after Christmas, and a great housewarming was planned. Stepniak 'promised to get a bear's ham from Russia for the occasion'.[41] But there was to be no housewarming and no bear's ham.

In the autumn of 1895 the Stepniaks had gone back to London, and were now living at 45 Woodstock Road, just round the corner from their old house in Blandford Road. On Saturday 21 December Stepniak had a meeting at 56 Rylett Crescent, less than half a mile away in Shepherd's Bush, with Volkhovsky and Egor Egorevich Lazarev. Lazarev had been one of the accused at the trial of the 193. He had been an active revolutionary in exile in France and America, and a somewhat inefficient manager of the Free Russia Press Fund. The meeting was to discuss plans for a new journal which would bring together the socialists and the liberals in a single national front against autocracy, and which Stepniak was to edit. But much remained to be settled, and they decided to reconvene on Monday morning. Stepniak duly set out on foot on the 23rd. At the end of Woodstock Road was the single track of the North

London Railway Company and a crossing consisting merely of a stile over the fence. There was a clear view of the track for several hundred yards, so it was thought that pedestrians could be safely trusted not to cross when a train was coming. When Stepniak reached the stile that morning a train was approaching. He took no notice. The train driver blew his whistle and the stoker shouted, but Stepniak kept on going. The driver braked hard with his powerful vacuum brakes, but it was too late. The train went over Stepniak and could not stop until his body was under the second carriage. He was killed outright. It must have seemed that he deliberately tried to kill himself. But he had no reason to do so. 'His friends knew the explanation: the noise in the Turkish prisons had been appalling and he had developed the power of being able to shut out exterior sounds when he was thinking. In a state of concentrated thought he could, at will, make himself actually deaf.'[42] Olive had also noticed it and wrote: 'He has the faculty of retiring into himself when bored and forgetting his surroundings. "How else could I endure English dinner parties?"'[43]

Volkhovsky arranged the funeral. On Christmas Day he wrote an affectionate reply to Ada Radford's letter of sympathy and added a postscript:

The funeral takes place on Saturday. The body to start from 45, Woodstock Rd at 12. Friends – Russian and Foreign – to follow till the top of the Street, when they leave the cortège for Waterloo Station. The body shall be met by all mourners and friends at W. Station at 1.30. Short Speeches to be delivered. At 2.45 the body leaves for the Crematorium.[44]

The ceremony at Waterloo was almost a state funeral. 'It was a significant and striking spectacle,' the *Times* wrote, 'this assemblage of Socialists, Nihilists, Anarchists, and outlaws of every European country, gathered together in the heart of London to pay respect to the memory of their dead leader.'[45] There was a red flag draped in black, and a large wreath from the German Communist Party. There were speeches in English, French, Italian and Yiddish. Volkhovsky spoke 'under much emotion',[46] and the other speakers included William Morris (making his last public appearance out of doors before his death in the following October), Kropotkin, John Burns, Keir Hardie, Eleanor Marx and many others. Some two hundred people accompanied the cortège to the crematorium in Woking, where 'The weather was very unfavourable, and much discomfort was experienced from the steady fall of rain and sleet.'[47]

Fanny Stepniak followed the coffin all the way, but as to Constance and Olive the contemporary accounts give no clue. It seems possible that Constance was among the mourners, and probable that Olive was too overwrought to appear in public. She wrote cryptically to Lazarev, 'I rejoice that He rests. I can do that for him in spite of my unspeakable anguish and I hope that all his friends will do the same.'[48] And her niece recalls: 'Like primitive people in bitter grief, Olive cut off all her hair.'[49]

Constance was no less anguished, but, as at the time of her brother Arthur's death, was more reticent. She left no explicit record of her feelings, but, as David wrote, 'Stepniak's death was a blow from which it took my mother long to recover. But it only cemented more deeply friendship with his widow, Fanny . . . and with other Russians, particularly those who had been close friends of Sergey's.'[50] It also strengthened her resolve to carry on the task which he had set her. She needed all her resolve, for she was up to her neck in work, with the two volumes of *Virgin Soil* to be done; and in the middle of the tragedy she had to provide some sort of Christmas for her beloved son. She also had to arrange the move into the Cearne, which took place late in February.

The house as eventually built was L-shaped, of two storeys, with a windowed attic above for storage and, where the land fell away, a low cellar that served to house garden tools – Chopper's stable. To enter the house one went up three stone steps in the angle on the L. On the right was a long open porch where one might sit and look out south-west over the view, while bats roosted in the roof above. On the left was a massive door, studded and hinged with heavy iron as if for a castle, which swung easily to let one into the house. At first one stepped into the large dining room, which filled the left-hand wing. It housed the Broadwood square piano, which neither of them played – Constance's fondness for music was purely as a listener – and the heavy oak dining table with its ecclesiastical legs and impractical bevelled edges, both of which had belonged to Ford Madox Brown. But later two tall seats – 'settles' they were always called – were put in facing into the dining room. The space above them was boarded off up to the ceiling, and with a door between them they formed the wall of a passage from the front door to the back. A step to the right was a plain staircase leading away, and round to the right the door into Constance's study, lined with bookshelves, and with easy chairs covered in her favourite peacock blue on either side of a poky inglenook and an open fire. Cowlishaw liked to expose heavy square beams whenever he could, but deliberately cut them short so that they had to be supported at the ends by projecting stone corbels, roughly cut like all the stonework, which threatened to brain any unwary visitor approaching the fire. Beyond the staircase were a kitchen and scullery. And just outside the back door was a privy, with the basic necessities provided by a bucket of ashes and an old copy of the fat illustrated catalogue of the Civil Service Stores, which Dr Garnett, as an eminent civil servant, encouraged his friends to patronise, and which once rivalled the better known Army & Navy Stores. Upstairs there were four bedrooms, and in due course a bathroom so narrow that one could only just squeeze alongside the bath, and which had a folding seat on the back of the door that could be set up only when the door was closed. Edward slept at the far end of the west wing, and Constance's bedroom was halfway along the south one – even at Henhurst Cross they had had separate bedrooms – and the best bedroom, the south one, decorated with Cowlishaw's briars, and looking out on to the view, was reserved for visitors. The pictures were more interesting than decorative, and not helped by being framed in funereal black. The floors downstairs were of the red tiles that always made Constance feel at home, or well scrubbed light oak blocks, and in many of the windows there were rather uncomfortable window-seats of bare wood. Stone and wood were generally left unpainted. Everything was hand-made: where the latches had not been wrought by the smith they had been cut out of wood by the carpenter. There was nothing exceptional about the proportions or design of the Cearne – indeed some of its features were distinctly perverse – its attraction lay in the wholesome honesty of its workmanship and materials. As one of Constance's nieces wrote: 'through a deep porch, unstained oak, bare floors and deep window seats all gave off a delicious aroma of wood-smoke, apples and country sweetness'.[51]

For the new house they 'bought a fat little Welsh pony, named Shagpat, and a governess cart, and engaged a lad of 18, Bert Hedge-cock, to look after it and the garden, and help Alice Martin in the house'.[52] This brought 'a full realisation of our new grandeur' to young David, who remembered on his fourth birthday, a week or so after they had moved in,

strutting up to the stable in a new long coachman's coat, talking to our new man, Bert Hedgecock, while Nettle, a pretty red bitch, played about us – my dog. Bert was grooming Shagpat – my pony. The sense of property was intensely developed, and I was conscious of being monarch of all I surveyed.[53]

A week later, on 16 March, Conrad came to see the Garnetts' new house and to let them see his new fiancée, Jessie George. But they did not have much time for such pleasures. They 'had only been three weeks in the house and had not even got up curtains in the windows, when Edward was taken ill with typhoid'.[54] How he had been infected was a mystery; the well had been given a clean bill of health, and the drains were 'above reproach'.[55]

Typhoid fever was then a very serious disease from which many people did not recover. Edward ran a high temperature, and became feverish and even delirious. Constance believed that in typhoid the walls of the intestines become 'as thin as paper'; and even if this is not literally true, they become quite unable to tolerate any kind of solid food. With the help of a professional nurse Constance looked after Edward herself. He was kept alive on liquids and dosed so heavily on quinine that it made him quite deaf. The crisis cannot have lasted long, but during those few days, which felt like months, Constance must often have thought that she was going to lose him as well as Stepniak. The fever was slow to subside, his temperature fluctuated, down one day and up again the next. When Robert Black came to see him at Easter he told Constance, 'He has had a great escape and now we have nothing to do but be very quiet and patient for a few weeks, and all will go well.'[56]

For the first fortnight he was not allowed any visitors. When Fanny Stepniak offered to come and help, Constance was obliged to put her off: 'the house must be kept quite still. I sit with him all day. He likes to have me with him – he is so weak and lonely.'[57] She told Fanny that 'there is a little new cottage at Crockham Hill to let – new and not very pretty but convenient . . . you would have to *make haste* if you wanted to take it or it will be snapped up. Cottages are so scarce.'[58] The rent was five shillings a week, and Fanny took it.

To add to her own worries Constance had to ensure that Edward had none. They would be 'attended with risk. He must see no letters, hear nothing but good news.'[59] It was an impossible task. Edward began to 'fret a good deal about money . . . so unlike his usual happy-go-lucky way in such matters',[60] whether Hyde had been paid for a picture, how they would manage without his own earnings. 'As he is paid by the manuscript he will lose more than two-thirds of April's and also of May's salary – about £35 altogether.'[61] The nurse had cost ten pounds, and Constance had only fifteen pounds in the bank – having laid out so much on the Cearne – and was not due to get any more until *Virgin Soil* was published in the autumn. Richard Garnett, when applied to, allayed this immediate worry.

In the middle of all this Constance had an 'awful scare' about David. 'He complained of headache and stomach ache, I took his temperature and found it was 102-2°. You may fancy my terror. I thought he was in for it too.'[62] But it was only tonsillitis, aggravated by a chill on the stomach. Constance had to conceal it from Edward and 'chatter away glibly to him of what Bunnie is doing in the garden, while the poor little duck keeps as quiet as a mouse in his bed upstairs'.[63]

Edward's mind was still too feverish for him to read for more than a few minutes at a time. There was no question of him tackling the manuscript of the beginning of *The Rescuer*, which Conrad sent to him on 13 April, desperate to know 'Am I mindful enough of Your teaching. . . . Am I blessed? Or am I condemned?'[64] He could only look at pictures in illustrated magazines 'to get through the long dreary hours'.[65] His bed was raised on to a platform so that he could see out of the window 'and (when the door was opened) into the room beyond and this of course tends to raise his spirits'.[66] His insides were too frail for the grapes sent him by well-wishers in the British Museum, but not for Spey Royal whisky, 'the sort he likes best', which he was prescribed every six hours,[67] or for Burgundy 'which does a great deal to keep him up – it is the only thing he is ready to take as much (or more) of as the doctor allows'.[68] He was much less happy with his insipid semi-liquid food. When Mary Belcher, the friend who had already saved David's life with Valentine's Meat Juice, and whom he was normally very fond of, brought him tapioca pudding, he threw it at her and it stuck in her hair. This was a sign that he was beginning to be like himself again. So long as he was really ill he had been a wonderfully good patient, though he was irritable and impatient when in health.

As he recovered he was moved from a bed to a couch, and could 'hobble round the garden with a stick, of course very slowly and with difficulty'.[69] David was sent away as soon as he was well enough to recuperate at the seaside at Brighton and later at the Huts with Ernest and Minnie Black, who had married in 1894. But then the maidservant, Alice Martin, went down with tonsillitis, and even Bert Hedgecock had severe sick headaches. Somehow Constance survived in tolerable health, though more than a little exhausted. Fortunately Grace Human was home on leave from Ceylon, and could do the housework while Constance rested and recuperated. On this visit Olive found Grace 'charming, though not nearly so goodlooking, perhaps sweeter than ever' and 'leaning towards Theosophy'.[70] But Edward thought she rapidly got rid of her 'Indian air' and looked 'fresh and bonny'.[71]

Olive, of course, was a visitor, staying not at the Cearne but with Fanny Stepniak, who had already moved into the cottage at Crockham Hill. Olive and Fanny, barely four months after their bereavement, were surprisingly cheerful together: 'we have tremendous appetites, all *three*, for we have Fanny's dog as well. We are also in wonderfully good spirits, everything seems to amuse us somehow, everything seems to have a humourous side; and I'm sure I hope we may continue to think so. I suppose we are in a state of reaction.'[72]

Fanny's relations with Constance were still edgy. She had taken over her husband's role in checking the translations because she desperately needed the money, though she was 'unsuited to the task' as 'she soon got bored'.[73] When Constance, who was apt to be tactless, 'in the simplicity of her heart . . . meant to be charitable'[74] and offered to increase the fee from one-fifth to one-third, Fanny was deeply wounded.

At the beginning of June, while still at Crockham Hill, Olive had an invitation to go to Russia and be an English miss in the family of the cultured and wealthy Madame Arseniev, who had introduced Constance to Sasha Shteven. Constance wrote that the Arseniev household was 'conducted after the style of the best aristocratic families in England' – not that she herself had the least experience of such families. She thought Olive would find the life 'a trifle stiff and ceremonious at first, but they are such thoroughly good kind people that she can hardly fail to be happy with them'.[75] Olive felt it was Stepniak's wish that she should go, and left for Russia on 11 August, having first attended her brother Robert's wedding to Matty Roscoe on 26 June. There was no question of Edward being well enough to do so, though he was at last able to start writing to Conrad about *The Rescuer*, while Constance worked on the proofs of *Virgin Soil*.

By the autumn, as Edward recovered, and began to be able to work normally again, life at the Cearne settled into what became an established routine. Edward went to London on Thursdays and came down again on Fridays. For the rest of the time he read manuscripts at home.

He always sat up late reading or writing. This was almost always in the long stone porch of the Cearne, where he had a long wicker chair in which he lay working. On the low stone wall beside him he had a wooden packing case with the side towards him removed and a hole burned in the top. In this stood the little copper lamp for which Stepniak had forged him a tripod of iron.

Edward worked at night partly because he suffered from sleeplessness . . . He made up for not sleeping at night by going on sleeping in the mornings, long after the rest of the household was astir. Frequently he did not come down to breakfast until eleven, and in the morning hours it was of the first importance that no noise should be made which might awaken him.[76]

Constance saw to it that David learned to be a silent child. He has described how she, unlike Edward, was an early riser, and before getting down to work on her Russian,

used to get up by half-past six or seven in the spring and summer, and we soon sat down to our breakfast of porridge, with milk for me and coffee for her. Her day contained so much that I cannot easily fit it all in. First thing in the morning she used to go round the garden, while the dew was still on the plants, and collect those miscreants, the slugs. There was a moment of self-indulgence, for the serious day's work was before her. Some of the housework had to be done, then I was called in and my lessons started. . . .[77]

She taught him, as her mother had done her, in the interstices of her own work. At first it was for no more than ten minutes a day. David was reluctant to learn his letters, but under pressure he caved in, 'All right, I will learn to read. But when I have learned, I never, never shall.'[78] Nevertheless by early November Constance was able to report to his grandfather that he could 'read all words of three letters. He seems to learn fairly quickly – and is very clever and sensible in practical things.'[79]

He was, as he remarked, 'an observant little boy',[80] and much of his real education lay in the observation of the plants and creatures that lived in the Chart Woods. He ran wild in them, and by the time he was seven he knew them by heart: 'I learnt to remember every tree and stone and turn in the paths. These memories are still with me, and I can remember exactly where scores of trees stood that have since been felled, and the stones and roots which stuck up in paths that have been abolished or transformed.'[81] He became a thorough countryman in a way that neither of his parents were, and so by inclination and experience a naturalist. Near the end of his life, Jonathan Raban in summing up David's literary achievement perceptively remarked that for him 'literature is only a hair's-breadth away from the natural sciences'.[82]

For the rest of her life Constance thought of the house by the Surrey woods as home. And whenever she was away it was not long before she wished to be back at 'the dear little Cearne'.[83]

12

Visitors and Colonists

Constance noticed a change in Edward after his escape from typhoid. She wrote to Volkhovsky on 17 September: 'Edward has quite regained his old health – more than his old health in fact. But I think his illness has left other effects – on his mind I mean. He takes life more seriously and is more inclined to prudence, though he seems livelier than ever on the surface.'[1] He was now 'more ready to be apprehensive about money'[2] than she was, though he still could not be entirely relied upon to post a letter or pass on a message. Money was indeed a serious worry at this time. They had started life at the Cearne in rather too extravagant a style. In the spring of 1896 Edward had been unable to work, and in the autumn Constance was more than usually afflicted by sick headaches, and got little done. *Virgin Soil*, which came out in September, completed the series of Turgenev's novels, but not the entire edition, for there were still the volumes of stories and sketches to follow; and these were only a selection of all those that Turgenev had written. Constance found *Dream Tales and Prose Poems* particularly difficult to translate, but had it done by the end of the year.

Ever since she had tried to get Chekhov's Sakhalin articles published in English she had considered it her business not merely to translate what came her way, but to bring the most important Russian literature to English readers. She was, however, too short of money to turn down any of the 'jobbing' translation that Dr Garnett put in her way. She even agreed to translate a collection of letters that Turgenev had written in French. She knew the language well, but, as she told her father-in-law:

I shall very much dislike the job. Nothing is a more difficult and ungrateful task than translating French into English and none of the letters seem to me worth preserving. There is a collection of most interesting letters of Turgenev to Herzen and others published in Russian and those I would gladly have undertaken.[3]

The French translation fell through, and the Russian letters did not come her way. But then she heard of the latest event in Chekhov's career.

Anton Chekhov was considered in Russia to be the leading writer of the younger generation – he was one year older than Constance – and had been awarded the Pushkin Prize for Literature as long ago as 1888. His reputation was based on his short stories. His short farces were popular, but his longer plays had not succeeded. The first production of *Ivanov* had lasted only three performances, and *The Wood Demon* (an early version of *Uncle Vanya*) ran for a week. On 29 October 1896 the Aleksandrinsky Theatre in St Petersburg put on his new four-act play, *The Seagull*. He had agonised through a week of rehearsals, and even more through the first act of the performance. It was the custom to give the first performance of a new play as a benefit for an actor, and in this case the beneficiary was the comedienne, Elizaveta Levkeeva, who was not in *The Seagull* but was appearing on the same stage in a vaudeville to follow. Most of the audience had come to be amused by her. They had expected also to be amused by Chekhov, and were bewildered and then hostile at being treated to a drama of non-drama, a tragi-comedy of failure and inaction. It was a disaster, but not quite such a disaster as it seemed to the author, who fled in misery at the end of the first act, vowing never to write for the theatre again. On the second night there was a more sympathetic house, and the play went down well. By the time it came out of repertory in November it had become 'an esteemed play'.[4] Nevertheless Chekhov must have been surprised a few weeks later to receive a registered letter dated 11 December 1896 and written in English:

Dear Sir

I have read with great admiration several of your stories in Russian, and have translated one or two of these, and am trying to introduce your work to the English public. Short tales are not as a rule liked by the English reader, but we hope to find among the younger generation a certain number able to appreciate the psychological truth and delicate workmanship of yours.

But I hear that your play, the Sea-Gull, has made a great sensation in Petersburg. If you would care to entrust me with the translation of it, I would make every effort to bring it before the English public. I have some influence with the Independent Theatre and with several dramatic critics and have excellent connexions with publishers. I can confidently say your work would have better chances in my hands than in most.

I have already translated almost all Tourgeniev and my translations have been exceptionally well received. I am sending you my version of *Zapiski Okhotnika*

[*A Sportman's Sketches*] – in case you read English – that you may judge of the standard of my work.

May I ask you, if you are willing for me to try my luck with your play, to let me know how I may procure it. Is it printed? if not may I ask you to send me a lithographed copy?

My father in law, Dr Garnett (Keeper of Printed Books of the British Museum) wishes me to ask you for a complete list of your writings, that we may add them all to the Library of the Museum. Forgive me for troubling you in this way and believe me –

Very truly yours

Constance Garnett[5]

Chekhov replied that *The Seagull* would appear in the next issue of *Russkay a Mysl*[6] and he would send it to her. 'If only we could arouse the attention of the English public to its merits!'[7] Constance wrote to Dr Garnett. She had already translated 'a short peasant tale'[8] – probably 'Peasant Wives', but David Rice was having no success in placing it; and it was to be thirteen years before *The Seagull* appeared on a British stage, and then not in Constance's translation.

Her life was now centred on the Cearne. She no longer had rooms in London, and rarely went there. The Cearne provided a shelter for her natural shyness. She always enjoyed visits from congenial friends, but could safely withdraw from more general society. She went to Newnham for the annual commemoration in February, but when Dr Garnett tried to get her to attend a luncheon for women writers, or chair a conference on women as librarians, she declined. Such energy as she had left after running the house – and both Bert Hedgecock and Alice Martin left in the summer of 1897 – was devoted to working at her Russian and looking for worthwhile works to translate. Constance was still politically alert, but she had almost lost touch with the Fabians, and was becoming increasingly disillusioned with them. On 19 March 1897 the minutes of the Executive Committee noted: '16. *Resignation*. Mrs Garnett. Accepted, but Sec instructed to ask wherein she regards the Society as going on the wrong track.' If Constance answered this request her reply is not to be found among such of the society's correspondence as has been preserved among the Fabian papers at Nuffield College. David Garnett believed that her reason for abandoning Fabianism was that 'Constance and her eldest sister Clementina cordially detested the Potter sisters and particularly hated the brand of State Socialism which owed so much to the efforts of Mr and Mrs Sidney Webb.'[9] There is no doubt about her aversion to Beatrice Webb, who had joined the Fabians at exactly the same time as herself;[10] she had a sincere contempt for her 'worldliness, her insularity and her personal ambition',[11] qualities of which she herself was curiously free. But this only became apparent later; Beatrice Webb had not yet become the power in the society that she was later to be, and the Webbs' 'brand of State Socialism' would not come about for many years. But their vision of the future was already beginning to be adumbrated:

the Webbs concluded that superior societies could be built only by superior people. They had come increasingly to look for an elite which would play this role in Britain; by the end of the century they were sure that this task would be undertaken by the new class of salaried experts – scientists, social scientists, professional people of all kinds – whose skills could be devoted disinterestedly to the service of the community. They saw themselves in this light and they assumed that other specialists would work as loyally for public as for private enterprise. The civil servant was their modern counterpart to Plato's guardians and Comte's enlightened managers.[12]

Constance could well have been a candidate for that élite and was in some ways sympathetic to the Webbs' ideas. But she had learned from Stepniak that 'The enemy of Russian freedom was not the autocracy but the bureaucracy',[13] and what she had since seen and read of Russia had only confirmed it. The Webbs' élite was merely an idealisation of that bureaucracy which was such an intolerable denial of freedom.

She remained on friendly terms with Shaw and Ramsay MacDonald, and with the local Fabians, the Oliviers, Peases and Salts, who had first attracted the Garnetts to the site of the Cearne. Now the Cearne was beginning to attract its own circle of colonists and visitors. Fanny Stepniak had come to Crockham Hill. The Nazarbeks were at Holly Farm with a sinister entourage of Armenian bodyguards. Harry and Lucy Cowlishaw were now married and had bought Kiln Farm, near Edenbridge. By April 1897 Constance and Edward 'found them quite a picture in their old farmhouse, which they have transformed into a deliciously poetical abode'.[14] Dr and Mrs Garnett came down from time to time; Arthur was a frequent visitor; and Olive, back from Russia, was with them on 27 June, 'looking so happy and different'.[15] She was now engaged to Alfred Powell, who had told Edward and Constance the news two days earlier. 'It was what we had secretly hoped for, both of us, for some months, for Alfred's interest in Olive was too patent to escape the notice of a fairly observant child.'[16] Powell was an architect friend of Harry Cowlishaw's, a cultivated and sensitive man, but no match for the potent memory of the more masterful Stepniak; and the engagement was broken off before the year was out.

Another family visitor planned to have Harry build a cottage for her near by. When Grace Human was on her visit to England she had bought a site two fields to the west of the Cearne, on the same southern edge of the Chart woods. In August 1896 Harry and the builder had made a start by 'measuring out the land'[17] but it was not until October of the following year that the house began 'rising rapidly'.[18] The house that Harry built was in something of the same manner as the Cearne, solidly put together of the same lumpish stone, and with similar windows and hatted chimneys. But it turned out altogether odder. One end was deliberately left unfinished, for later extension, and its features seemed to have been dumped in the wrong places, so much so that a family legend grew up that Harry had made a wax model and sent it out to Colombo for approval. On the way back it melted in the Red Sea, and was wrongly reassembled by worried lascars and slavishly copied by ignorant workmen.

Before Grace's Cottage was completed another colonist arrived, at-tracted either by Edward or by Harold Frederic, an American novelist and European correspondent of the *New York Times*, who was living at Kenley, some eight miles from the Cearne. Frederic wrote to Stephen Crane: 'Mr. Edward Garnett would be an El Dorado to an American publisher of the superior class. He seems to be able to scent a new talent in fiction from a thousand miles, and as a critic he possesses both sincerity and distinction of manner.'[19] Crane was only twenty-five but was already an experienced journalist. He had made a name for himself with his astonishingly convincing novel of the American Civil War, *The Red Badge of Courage*, which Heinemann had put into his Pioneer Series in 1896, and he had been shipwrecked and had served as a war correspondent in Greece. In 1897 he came to England with Cora Taylor, whom he had met when she was running the Hotel de Dream, a house of assignation – if not quite of ill-fame – in Jacksonville, Florida. She was 'six or seven years older than Mr. Crane, with big blue eyes and reddish hair'[20] and they lived together as man and wife, but he could not marry her, as her husband, the younger son of an English baronet, refused to give her a divorce.

Edward was much struck by Crane's 'strange eyes, with their intensely concentrated gaze . . . those of a genius',[21] and in 1898 defined the genius of his particular artistic method: 'The rare thing about Mr.

Crane's art is that he keeps closer to the surface than any living writer, and, like the great portrait-painters, to a great extent makes the surface betray the depths.'[22]

In June 1897 the Cranes moved into Ravensbrook, a 'singularly hideous villa'[23] on the near side of Oxted. Edward recalled how on Crane's first visit to the Cearne, 'I was so struck by the exquisite symmetry of his brow and temples, that I failed to note, what a lady [?Constance] pointed out when he left, the looseness of his mouth. Yes, the intensity of his genius burned in his eyes, and his weak lips betrayed his unrestrained temperament.'[24]

But the Cranes did not settle at Oxted. In April 1898 Stephen went off to report the war in Cuba, and by the time he returned Cora had moved, as Edward recounts: 'one day, on my happening to describe to him an ancient Sussex house, noble and grey with the passage of five hundred years, nothing would satisfy him but that he must become the tenant of Brede Place'.[25] The Cranes lived in style for a while in the stately home, which belonged to Winston Churchill's aunt, but not for long. Crane was fatally ill with tuberculosis and died in a clinic in the Black Forest on 5 June 1900.

During his stay at Ravensbrook he had established a friendship not only with Edward, who remained a lifelong admirer, but also with Joseph Conrad, whom he met in London in 1897. Conrad and Crane at once took to one another. Edward described 'one of the few occasions' he saw them together. Conrad

was delightfully sunny, and bantered 'poor Steve' in the gentlest, most affection-ate style, while the latter sat silent, Indian-like, turning enquiring eyes under his chiselled brow, now and then jumping up suddenly and confiding some new project with intensely electric feeling.[26]

Conrad, of course, besides writing to Edward in terms of increasing affection – 'Dear Garnett, Dearest Edward, My *very* dear Edward, Best of Men' – was a regular visitor at the Cearne. He was forever anxious about his work, and needed continual reassurance from Edward, who was by no means always an acquiescent critic. 'For many many hours' Edward wrote, 'I sat with Conrad in those early years trying to assuage his doubts, fears and anxieties about his writing powers.'[27] When he visited the Cearne in March 1898, Constance wrote, 'poor man, he seems very nervous and exhausted'.[28] Edward described how a few months later on a warm night we sat long in the porch in the lamplight, smoking and arguing, while the moths fluttered into our glasses, and at length, after midnight, Conrad, exasperated, got to his feet, saying sarcastically, 'It's indecent! I shall not forgive you for letting me unburden myself like this. Why didn't you stop me!' We were worn out, I by his desperation, and he by my sympathy.[29]

It was during Conrad's March visit, as Constance wrote, 'Nellie Heath has been here painting his portrait.'[30] The painting, now in Leeds Art Gallery, shows something of Conrad's nervous exhaustion, as well as the 'sardonic brooding and disenchantment with life' though not 'the extraordinary soft warmth of Conrad's eyes'[31] remarked on by Edward, who wrote:

The painting was executed in a single sitting at the Cearne while I tasked myself to entertain him. One of my anecdotes drew from him the following: 'Yes, dear Edward. But have you ever had to keep an enraged negro armed with a razor from coming aboard, along a ten-inch plank, and drive him back to the wharf with only a short stick in your hand?'[32]

Yet when Edward described to Conrad 'a terrible family tragedy of which I had been an eye-witness' – it can only have been the death of Arthur Black – Conrad cried out: 'Nothing of the kind has ever come my way! I have spent half my life knocking about in ships, only getting ashore between voyages. I know nothing, nothing! except from the outside. I have to guess at everything.'[33]

It was probably on this memorable March visit that Conrad made friends with David, who described the scene:

There was a jolly wind, and it was washing-day. I was alone with Conrad, and suddenly he was making me a sailing boat. The sail was a clean sheet tied at the top corners to a clothes-prop and hoisted with some spare clothes-line over one of the clothes-posts. The sail was lashed at the foot, and I held the sheet fastened to the other corner in one hand while it bellied and pulled. The green grass heaved in waves, the sail filled and tugged, our speed was terrific. Alterations were made and the rig perfected and when, an hour later, Edward came looking for his guest, he found him sitting in our big clothes basket steering the boat and giving me orders to take in or let out the sail.[34]

Fanny Stepniak gave a very different account of the occasion:

Yesterday I went to the Cearne to see Mr Conrade . . . and I saw him. I am glad I went, but (or perhaps because?) I shall never repeat such an experiment again. Best of all I liked Nellie Heath – there is no nonsense about her. She is painting the hero and a very good bit of work it will be. Now let me describe the man. He is dark, dry, shapeless, with a cruel smile in his face. First of all he has nothing Polish neither in his appearance, nor in his manners. I took him for an Irishman at first glance. He is decidedly unsympathetic, his eyes have such a hard expression that you would never dream to see them veiled by a tear of tenderness or compassion. He has strong likes and dislikes, to be sure, judging by the few remarks he made on men of our time. I liked his book much better. The missus and the baby were absent, kept by some illness. The great man had tea with us in the big room and very soon disappeared in the study, where he was kept all the time in undisturbed quiet, only Edward having free access to the room. Edward himself is very nice, much better than his idol, he is a dear warmhearted boy, only too easily influenced by others. But in what he cannot be influenced is his literary, artistic judgement. I enjoyed very much reading the 'Narcissus'. Soon after six I left the house, the atmosphere of which was oppressing to me. Connie did not even put on her charming ways, I believe she was already exhausted by the hero worshipping exertions of the day before. And I breathed freely when I was out in the wood, bathed in soft moonlight, full of spring perfumes and the company of N. H. (who was going to the Oliviers to supper) only added to my enjoyment.[35]

Constance certainly did not find Conrad an easy visitor, though she never saw him with Fanny's jaundiced eye. When he visited the Cearne in September 1898 she wrote to Olive: 'Conrad is with us, and our minds . . . are chiefly occupied in providing a sufficiently refined and recherché menu every day for his artistic palate. He is rather nice and quiet though, and I like him better than I usually do.'[36]

Conrad, as a Pole, could not help being prejudiced against all Russians, whatever their political persuasions, for they represented the country that oppressed his own. He was distinctly conservative in his own politics – there is no place for democracy in the fo'c's'le of a sailing ship – and so he had little sympathy with Constance's Russian affiliations or her socialism, to say nothing of such conspicuously Russian friends as Fanny Stepniak. He admired Turgenev alone of the great Russian novelists, though he did not want to be thought of as a Slavic writer or a follower of Turgenev, or indeed of anybody else. Despite having been brought up partly in Russia he would not admit to knowing Russian – 'I don't even know the alphabet'.[37] As a boy he read *Smoke* in a Polish translation, and *A Nest of Gentlefolk* in French. It was not merely 'his Polish habit of paying everybody compliments'[38] when he wrote to Edward:

The truth of the matter is that it is *you* who have opened my eyes to the value and the quality of Turgeniev. . . . Turgeniev for me is Constance Garnett and Constance Garnett *is* Turgeniev. She has done that marvellous thing of placing the man's work inside English literature and it is there that I see it – or rather that I *feel* it.[39]

The Garnetts, for their part, could not help trying to place Conrad inside Slavonic literature. Constance had admired his writing, and particularly his use of language, ever since she had read the manuscript of *Almayer's Folly* in the summer of 1895. When she read *The Nigger of the Narcissus* serialised in the *New Review* she wrote to Conrad:

Two things have struck me particularly in it, – its extraordinary reality and the great beauty of your style. A letter of yours which Edward has shewed me lately has been the warmest and most appreciative praise I have received for my Turgenev and frankly I feel that praise from you who have such mastery of language is worth praise of forty English reviewers. For I feel, as I have always told Edward, that your brain does not think English thoughts, – as Turgenev's own, – it is more delicate, more subtle, richer and more varied than ours. Your use of adjectives – so chosen, fastidious, often ironical – reminds me again and again of Turgenev's manner. It is really you that ought to have had the task of translating him.[40]

Constance dedicated the fourteenth volume of Turgenev, *A Desperate Character*, 'To Joseph Conrad, whose art in essence often recalls the art and essence of Turgenev.' Edward inscribed several of the other volumes to Conrad, who replied by inscribing a copy of *The Nigger of the Narcissus* to Constance 'as the token of my admiration for your art and unswerving devotion which has, not so much interpreted – as absolutely re-created in English the works of the great Russian master'.[41] Nevertheless, as Glyn Turton has pointed out, the Garnetts did Conrad a disservice by 'making the Russian novel into a procrustean bed for a Pole, passionately committed to the English language'.[42] And nothing could have been more unwelcome to Conrad, and embarrassing to Constance, than the compliment that Robert Lynd was to pay her in 1908, when he implied that Conrad ought to have written his novels in Polish and left Constance to translate them into English.[43]

Constance's letter about Conrad's visit in March mentions some other important visitors who arrived on the day that Conrad left. These were Ford and Elsie Hueffer, who were to be tenants at Grace's Cottage, as Grace was not returning from Colombo: 'It will be very nice for us to have such pleasant neighbours so near. . . . It is a most beautiful little cottage and will just suit them.'[44]

Ford Madox Hueffer was only twenty-four, but he had already published six books, including the life of his grandfather, Ford Madox Brown. Madox Brown was a very old friend of the Garnetts, and for a while was their neighbour in St Edmund's Terrace. Ford Hueffer liked to say that his parents, Francis Hueffer, a German music critic working in London, and Catherine, daughter of Madox Brown, had done their courting in the Garnetts' drawing-room. Much of Ford's own courtship of Elsie Martindale took place under Garnett eyes and is recorded in Olive's diary. Ford and Elsie were both under age, and when Elsie's parents tried to make her a ward of court to prevent them marrying, they had run off, falsified their ages, and married at a register office in Gloucester with Chapple, the Garnetts' beloved old maid, as a witness. When the Martindales brought a court action, Robert Garnett represented the runaways.

Olive was attracted by Ford and his brother Oliver, but could not altogether approve of them or take them entirely seriously. Ford represented 'unreliability, inaccuracy and – genius'.[45] Olive felt that 'his lordly air is caviare to me, it delights me hugely, it is so absolutely unblushingly put on'.[46] David Garnett wrote:

The young Garnetts were inclined to regard the Hueffer boys as half egregious asses and half charlatans. The Hueffers, who originally respected the Garnetts, became more and more exasperated by their sceptical attitude and their strait-laced almost puritanical contempt for success and notoriety, which constituted the breath of romance for Ford and Oliver.[47]

David recalled Ford

at this period playing at being a farmer and an expert on agriculture, so he wore a smock frock and gaiters. The only sign of the farm was that he kept ducks. There was no pond for them, so Ford sank a hipbath in the ground and the ducks stood in a queue, waiting their turn to swim in it.[48]

Soon after Ford arrived at Grace's Cottage he was visited by Stephen Crane, who, seeing the unfinished end of the house with its ragged edge and fireplace open to the sky, thought it a 'bully baronial ruin'.[49] Ford did not take at once to Crane, but admitted that 'He could use a spade or an axe.'[50] Crane was not put out, and merely said, 'You must not mind Hueffer; that is his way. He patronises me, he patronises Mr. Conrad, he patronises Mr. James. When he goes to Heaven he will patronise God Almighty. But God Almighty will get used to it, for Hueffer is all right.'[51]

When Conrad was visiting the Cearne in September 1898, Edward took him over to Grace's Cottage to see the Hueffers. This was a more propitious meeting. Its immediate consequence was that the Conrads were able to leave Ivy Walls at Stanford-le-Hope in Essex, which Jessie had come to dislike, and move into Ford's farmhouse, Pent Farm at Stanford, near Hythe, which Ford now let to him, the previous tenant having been Walter Crane, the Fabian artist. The second consequence was that Ford and Conrad became literary collaborators. Both needed reassurance and support from one another, Ford more than he admitted and Conrad less than he pretended. They produced two books together, not altogether happily, and despite the doubts of H. G. Wells and Henry James, who told Olive Garnett and Elsie Hueffer that 'To me this is like a bad dream which one relates at breakfast! Their traditions and their gifts are so dissimilar. Collaboration between them is to me inconceivable.'[52]

The Hueffers stayed at Grace's Cottage for only a year, and left in March 1899. But it must have been during this time that Ford met David Soskice. Soskice was a Russian lawyer who had been a revolutionary since his student days and had spent three years in solitary confinement in the Peter-Paul fortress. He had come to Britain after a sojourn in France, bringing his wife and son, though his marriage was on the point of breaking up. Constance found him a cottage at Kent Hatch, but Madame Soskice and the boy soon returned to France. Constance liked him, and David described him as 'a squarely built man, with a curly black beard, a square forehead . . . and a literal mind and no imagination'.[53] He liked to collect facts, which Ford obligingly made up for him to put down in his notebook. Ford telling Soskice in his drawling voice that rye was England's largest crop, and that the most profitable was 'a very tall cabbage, the stalks of which supplied the walking-out canes for soldiers in the British Army'[54] became such an enduring Garnett legend that D. H. Lawrence would give hilarious imitations of it – though he did not meet Ford until more than ten years later.

Soskice's importance to Constance, however, was of a more practical kind. Three years after his encounter with Ford he met Ford's sister, Juliet. David described her when young as 'a ravishingly beautiful blonde, a good deal like an idealised child's doll',[55] intelligent and with 'a great capacity for enjoying life, and a rich sense of humour'.[56] They fell in love, and Soskice, having been divorced from his wife, married her. It was a surprisingly successful marriage, and it had the consequence that Juliet learned Russian, and in due course became one of Constance's more valuable collaborators. Constance found her 'a reassuring person. Her substantial rather crude good-heartedness gives one a feeling of a solid support in a tottering world.'[57]

Long before this Constance had found another helper in Sybil Rudall.

She it was who had helped Constance to provide food fine enough to satisfy Conrad. David described her as 'dark, with very black eyes and a gipsy look'. He confirmed that she was an inspired cook and added that 'In those days our food was usually rather plain and British and my father did not often drink wine, but there was always a decanter of whisky on the sideboard for men visitors.'[58] Edward, moreover 'was an extremely easy person to feed, as his natural contrariness led him to partake of whatever dish was unpopular. I think he also had a feeling of chivalry over dishes which were failures.'[59]

Edward had been in need of a real holiday ever since his illness in the spring and early summer of 1896. In that year they had had a rather unrestful holiday at the Huts, and in 1897 Constance had let the Cearne for part of August and September, and they had spent their holiday staying with the Nazarbeks, where Constance amused herself by learning the rudiments of Armenian. But the Nazarbeks' uncouth bodyguards, who casually helped themselves to their neighbours' fences for firewood, made themselves so unpopular that 'if Mr Stevens had not turned them out of the farmhouse, there might have been a massacre of Armenians in the weald of Kent'.[60]

In January 1898 Dr Garnett sent Constance a present of a watch and a cheque for ten pounds. She put the money by to pay for Edward to have a holiday in Italy: 'Edward does not speak of this plan with any certainty yet, as he has not addressed Mr Unwin on the subject – but I hope at least a fortnight may be managed. He has had no foreign trip before, and it would do so much for him.'[61] He eventually set out at the beginning of April. He went first to Paris, where he saw Nellie Heath and her painter friends, Auguste Bréal and Simon Bussy. In Italy he travelled constantly, and saw something of Genoa, Pisa, Rome, Perugia, Orvieto, Florence and Venice, appreciating the landscapes in the country even more than the art in the towns. He bathed on the deserted beach where Shelley's body had been found, and in Florence he stayed with the Steffens in 'a beautiful old-fashioned villa'.[62] He came home in much better health and better able to face his difficult employer.

Constance, too, was in need of a holiday abroad. Autumn and winter were bad times for her. Her sick headaches were more prevalent in autumn, and she had begun to have 'awful days . . . in January and February when day after day I have waked up low spirited and hopeless with rheumatism all over – not fit for anything but sitting over the fire'.[63] She was advised to try wintering abroad in a warm dry climate. She decided to go to Montpellier, taking David, who was then six-and-a-half years old. At first the plan was that Speedwell, aged eleven, should go with them, but 'the poor child's heart failed her at the last moment, and though Clementina urged her to go, she said she could not be away from her for so long'.[64]

Constance and David set out on the afternoon of 13 December for Paris, where they stayed with Madame Lavrov. David took to French food (a taste that he never lost) and Constance reported, 'He likes the cookery immensely and eats far more than at home.'[65] He enjoyed sailing a toy boat in the Jardins du Luxembourg, and with his few words of French went shopping and bought some sweets and a diary. On 19 December they took the train to Lyons, a journey of nearly twelve hours. It was Constance's birthday, and on the train David gave her the diary. 'The present was such a success,' he wrote, 'that I asked for the diary back and presented it again and again. Those who give presents often feel like this about them but usually have to employ more indirect methods in order to spin out the delights of generosity.'[66]

At Montpellier Constance found the architecture 'awfully depressing and the whole place has a sort of naked look, which makes one homesick for our creepers and green trees . . . there is no effort to make things beautiful.'[67] David, on the other hand, thought it a 'lovely town'.[68] But at least Constance found that the dry clear climate suited her, and while she was there had nothing to complain of but a couple of sick headaches. She quickly made friends with some Russian girls, students at the university. One of them knew Volkhovsky well, and another was a sister of a teacher in one of Sasha Shteven's schools. On 12 January, Russian New Year's Eve, she was invited to a soirée by the students, where a girl dressed in peasant dress sang and danced to a Little Russian song. 'It was one of the most charming things I have ever seen'.[69] Constance gave one of the girls English lessons, and met a Swedish professor, a friend of Gustaf Steffen, who taught her Swedish. She went to a performance of part of *Die Meistersinger* and was taken to the Carnival. It struck her as 'so ancient and so childish' and David was 'frightened by the grotesque masks'[70] at the battle of the flowers. However, she braved 'the dangers of being embraced by hideous figures in the street – to see the Grand Gosier, the Roi du Carnaval, tried at a mock trial in patois and condemned to be burnt',[71] but felt cheated when the effigy was trundled off to be used again next year and the bonfire lit without it.

They went on expeditions into the country, picking jonquils, enjoying the pink almond blossom and aromatic plants in the fields and admiring a river full of 'very beautiful and peculiar flowers imported from Madagascar'.[72]

She still found time to worry about David's health and to work at the final volumes of Turgenev's stories. But on 19 March, after nearly three months abroad, during which her own health had been excellent, it was time to return home. They stopped briefly in Paris to see Nellie Heath again, and reached London on the 22nd. There Constance was anxious not to stay at the residence in the British Museum, which she said 'has such associations for me – that settle down like a cloud at once upon me' – memories of working with Stepniak there perhaps? – 'What would be nicest would be to go straight to our own rooms . . . it would be nice to be by ourselves and all together . . . I love those rooms in Eversholt street – and I am so glad you have taken them.'[73]

They were not to be alone together in quite the same way for much longer. The pattern of Constance's life was about to be reshaped once and for all.

13

Fin-de-Siècle

On 23 March 1899 Olive wrote in her diary that she had heard from Elsie that the Hueffers were moving from Grace's Cottage to Aldington, near the Conrads in Kent.[1] A couple of days later, at two o'clock in the morning, Ford finished packing the piano and sent the furniture away from Grace's Cottage. Its new tenant was Nellie's father, Richard Heath. He was a widower of sixty-seven, a small man 'with silver hair and beard, blue eyes in which one was surprised to detect a twinkle of humour'.[2] Nellie came home from Paris to look after him.

Nellie Heath had been on affectionate terms with the Garnetts ever since her visit to Henhurst Cross in October 1892. She had occasionally joined in their London social life, and in September 1897 she had come to the Cearne to paint Constance's portrait.[3] And in the previous year Edward had gone to her rooms in Endsleigh Terrace to sit to her. She had been going through some kind of crisis in confidence in herself and her work, and while she painted him he talked to her and listened to her troubles. She in return read some of the incomplete manuscript of his impressionistic sketches of London and gave him unqualified, if somewhat incoherent, encouragement:

Edward do take plenty of time and don't get depressed, it is such a big conception, almost too gigantic – no it isn't a bit too gigantic but you must give yourself years of time, so to speak – It is wonderful that London part – I can't tell you how wonderful it seemed and how I enjoyed each word – because it is just the dreary mad old London I know and care about – and yet I am sure it is killing us – I mean this great crushing London is.[4]

At first he was a provider of brotherly sympathy. But then she found herself falling in love with him and he with her; and she was alarmed: 'you older and wiser people overwhelm me with your wills,' she wrote.[5] She ran away to Paris to stay with an aunt and work in the Louvre.

Edward visited her in Paris on his way to Italy, and for much of his time when he got there, he sat at café tables scribbling love letters and poems to her. She kept them all, as he did hers. There are five boxes packed with their correspondence. The letters hardly ever bear a date or an address and are the despair of the prying biographer. They are creased and tattered from having been kept in pockets or under pillows. The pencil is almost rubbed away, and Edward's scratchy ink even more illegible than usual. Whether their tone is exalted or – less frequently – depressed, they are generally expressed in abstract terms with little reference to the outside world. One seeks in vain for any consideration of how their relations with one another might affect Edward's with Constance. One learns far more from Constance's, reticent though they are, than from Nellie's or Edward's.

Late in life Nellie told a friend 'the possibility of a relationship was first mentioned by Constance herself, who said she would have no objection',[6] and she continued to encourage it. When Nellie paid a visit to London in the spring of 1899, Constance wrote to Edward from Montpellier, 'Why isn't silly little Nellie with you too? She ought not to stay in London on Sundays.'[7] The 'silly' was, of course, affectionate. Just before her return from France Constance wrote to Edward, 'After you and David, I think Nellie and Margaret [Nellie's sister] are dearer to me than all the world.'[8] She was anxious that Edward should not think that David was jealous of Nellie, and told him that the boy had spoken of her as 'a sweet little Puss' and said 'with great tenderness that we must stop in Paris for a few days in March if she is there'.[9] From now on Constance's letters to Edward become if anything more loving than before; and often they include an affectionate message for Nellie.

For Constance it was a variant of the old cliché: she had not lost a husband but gained a daughter. She was six years older than Edward, and Edward was four-and-a-half years older than Nellie. She had long loved Edward as a son rather than a husband. This might seem at times rather belittling. 'Poor boy', she would write, or 'Dear little Edward' – even David would begin his letters 'Dear little Dad' – though Edward was her equal in force of character and much more than equal in physical presence. But in reality it showed the depth of her love. Her maternal passion was far stronger than her conjugal affection, as she showed by her overwhelming love for David. She was genuinely fond of Nellie, and grew even fonder with the years.

Nellie was making an enormous sacrifice in becoming Edward's mistress. Edward and Constance were too bound together by David, by the Cearne and by their common literary vocation for there to be any question of official divorce. Nellie could have no admitted position. Their relationship was barely acknowledged by Edward's family, and certainly not approved of. Edward was in the habit of dining with his parents once a week. He never took Nellie, though she was welcome to visit the Garnetts on her own. There was no question of them having any children, nor, for many years, any kind of home together, though it is clear from the messages in Constance's letters that they managed to be alone from time to time in Edward's London rooms or at the Cearne when Constance was away. The affair and the marriage did not go on under the same roof. Constance might be free from convention in her ideas, but she observed the proprieties in her conduct.

Nellie therefore had to subsist on Edward's love and Constance's affection, and that of a few of their friends. She did not break up Constance's relationship with Edward. There was a long-standing intellectual intimacy between them which she could not enter. This was epitomised by an experience which, though it may have occurred only in a dream, was a painful indication of the reality. Nellie was walking down the beech-leaved path towards the Cearne. When she came to the little gate at the bottom she was halted by hearing the voices of Edward and Constance, talking with such easy intimacy that she could not bear to break in on them. Much distressed, she turned on her heel and went back to London.[10] Yet Edward himself felt that his relationship with Nellie was easier and more comfortable than with Constance. He told Nellie:

I have been taking a holiday to-day in this grey autumn weather and digging potatoes with Connie and Mrs Adams. After sleeping badly, physical exercise rests the nerves and tired brain. . . . I always find it easy to amuse people – a little wit goes a long way! By sketching lightly some ridiculous circumstance – such as my going to Sarah Grand or Mrs Humphrey Ward with my spiritual difficulties and laying myself humbly at the great woman's feet – I keep the women continually amused. But with you, my darling one, I never find it necessary to mountebank around.[11]

If Constance felt any jealousy, she was, as David wrote, 'able to conquer jealousy, or to ignore it, more than anyone I have known'[12] – though she had not been able to conquer it when Stepniak was making overmuch of Olive. From now on her relations with Edward were clouded by occasional storms. But they were no longer *about* their relationship; they had a clear external cause.

Constance need not have worried about having to stay at the British Museum on 22 March. Two days earlier Richard Garnett had officially retired from the Keepership of the Printed Books, and the Garnetts began moving out of the residence. He could have stayed on for another year, but Narney's health was failing and his eyesight had begun to deteriorate after long years of close reading. He had to leave the residence and go to 27 Tanza Road in Hampstead, 'a dark, narrow house of four storeys and a basement. There was a small garden behind, chiefly productive of saxifrage and cats.'[13]

Dr Garnett's presence in the British Museum had become a great Victorian institution, and his departure seemed to herald the end of that era, although the old Queen still had another two years to live. Confidence in England's greatness had ebbed from the 'high watermark' that Constance had witnessed at the Jubilee in June 1887, and it took an ugly knock in the summer of 1899.

One afternoon . . . [David Garnett wrote] Sydney Olivier arrived in a state of tremendous excitement. He was a senior Civil Servant in the Colonial Office, and he had just seen the draft of the ultimatum which Joseph Chamberlain, the Colonial Secretary, had persuaded the Government to send to the Transvaal Republic.[14]

Olivier and the Garnetts believed that war would certainly result.

Indeed, war in which the independent Boer republics were to be annexed was Chamberlain's object. Such a war was to the advantage of the shareholders of the Johannesburg gold mines and Kimberley diamond mines but were our soldiers' lives to be sacrificed for them? Sydney Olivier, accompanied by Edward and Constance, set off at once through the woods . . . to tell Richard Heath the news. I went with them, picking up scraps of information as I went. I remember Richard Heath standing short and resolute with blue eyes flashing as he heard the news and the sense of seething indignation in all the members of the little group.[15]

War did indeed break out on 11 October – though it was not quite so inevitable as they believed. Britain was immediately split into imperialists who supported Joseph Chamberlain's adventure, and pro-Boers who

saw it as a moral outrage, an attempt to crush a nation of small farmers and to bring their land – and the gold mines of the Rand – into a British South Africa; they believed that Chamberlain had throughout connived with Rhodes to this end and that Alfred Milner, Chamberlain's plenipotentiary in the long negotiations with the Boers, had manipulated Kruger into a hopeless fight.[16]

Edward naturally took the side of the underdog and had a detestation of imperialism. He hated to see the British Empire grow 'richer daily in patriotic fervour, in speeches, in cant . . .' and felt that 'in the midst of a general movement for Empire expansion, with talk of Federation, Jingoism, and with the doing of real work, the artists in literature are generally absent'. He therefore instituted the Over-Seas Library for Unwin. It opened in 1899 with *The Ipané*, an anonymous collection of stories by Cunninghame Graham, and each volume bore on its front endpaper a manifesto signed 'E.G.', which included the phrases quoted above and added: '"The Over-Seas Library" makes no pretence at Imperial drum-beating, or putting English before Colonial opinion. It aims, instead, at getting the atmosphere and outlook of the new peoples recorded. . . .'

The Limpsfield 'colonist' who had most experience of the 'atmosphere and outlook' in South Africa and was most bitterly opposed to the Boer War was J. A. Hobson. He and his wife had recently settled at Elmstead at Briar's Cross, a little over a mile from the Cearne, and his son Harold went to school with David and became a lifelong friend. Hobson was a radical economist who had blighted his career by propounding his 'oversaving heresy' that a wealthy minority by saving too much and spending too little caused unemployment and encouraged colonial expansion. As a result he was treated as 'unsound' by the economic establishment, but eventually recognised as an intellectual pioneer by Maynard Keynes. David remembered him well:

He was tall and very thin, with a moustache sprouting at odd angles, dark eyes behind glasses and nervous twitches, shakings and mannerisms. . . . He was brilliant in his comment and humour on every subject, but an unfailing stand-by was his wife. . . . She was a firmly-corseted, powdered American lady, affecting the Pompadour style, or the Marquise disguised as a Dresden Shepherdess, with very clear brown eyes and very regular features. She must have been a most beautiful girl. . . . When Mrs Hobson came out strong, as she often did, with some platitude, a glint would appear in J. A. Hobson's eye, his face would begin to twitch like a horse's skin when it unseats flies, and a premonitory gurgle would sound, followed very often by a silence, sometimes by a devastatingly innocent remark.[17]

The Garnetts found Mrs Hobson rather a trial, with her tantrums on the croquet lawn and her Vegetarian Play for which she vainly tried to enlist Edward's support. But Hobson himself was a valued friend for Constance. In him, as in Olivier, 'It was the excitement of new ideas, of intellectual discoveries or a vision of truth leading to a shared belief that she sought'[18] and they 'sought her out at longish intervals because she was the intellectual flint which could strike sparks from their steel'.[19]

Hobson had been investigating conditions in South Africa when the Boer War broke out. He had early divined the nefarious intentions of Rhodes and Beit, and he considered for a while serving as a war correspondent for the *Manchester Guardian* with the Boer forces. He then proposed that this job should be undertaken by S. C. Cronwright-Schreiner, a South African of British descent, who had married Olive Schreiner, the novelist, and added her name to his own, and who was also a passionate opponent of the war. In the end Hobson returned home and invited Cronwright-Schreiner to come and lecture in England and raised the money for him to do so. Cronwright-Schreiner arrived in January 1900 and went straight to Elmstead. He spent six months lecturing to gatherings of Liberally-minded local worthies in England and Scotland. The jingoists put up posters inviting the mob to riot and break up the meetings. Sometimes they succeeded, and Cronwright-Schreiner had to have a bodyguard to protect him. Edward was one of those who undertook this duty, and Cronwright-Schreiner visited the Cearne shortly before his return to South Africa.[20] When he came to write up these disagreeable experiences he gave his book the ironic title, *The Land of Free Speech*.

Constance wrote to Volkhovsky: 'We shall soon need a Society of Friends of English Freedom – we have practically no liberty of the Press or of speech just now. If one speaks one's opinions, one is called a traitor and enemy of the country and no one can get a hearing.'[21] The Fabians were far from providing such a society. They were bitterly split between those who opposed the war and those who felt that Joseph Chamberlain's imperialism was bringing to Darkest Africa a civilisation which, though by no means socialist, could be converted to Fabianism once it was established. An open split was avoided only by the dextrously Jesuitical arguments of Shaw, who nevertheless was unable to prevent the resignations of eighteen members, including Walter Crane, Emmeline Pankhurst, and Constance's friends, Henry Salt and Ramsay MacDonald. Olivier did not resign, but was so vociferous in his views that he became an embarrassment to the Colonial Office and was posted out to Jamaica to serve as Colonial Secretary.

His daughters, insolent in their natural pride and their force of numbers, burnt Joseph Chamberlain in effigy on Guy Fawkes Night, and got away with it. David and his friend Harold Hobson, innocent of any such aggressive action, were attacked by local boys who shouted 'Krujer!' and threw stones at them.

David 'gloried in Boer victories' and when he wanted to play soldiers he spent his time 'galloping an imaginary pony up the sides of the kopjes and ambushing and shooting down British soldiers'.[22] Afterwards he wrote:

I think this was a very bad and wicked thing and regret that my parents should have allowed it. . . . I should have been encouraged to love and honour England. Instead of which Constance entered into my games, and when we walked together through the woods she invented a game in which she was a Boer mother and I her son, escaping from our farm after it had been burned by General Roberts.[23]

But Constance no longer thought of herself bound to England – or Scotland. Through her work and her friendships with peripatetic exiles who had lived in many countries, she had come to see things from an international point of view. In this she was following Stepniak's example. She found British jingoism vulgar and hated the creed of 'my country right or wrong'. When she felt Britain was wrong she had no more qualms about pretending to kill British private soldiers than Stepniak had done in actually killing a Russian general.

The war brought strains within the Garnett family; and Edward and Constance had to refrain from discussing it with Robert and Richard, who took the imperialist line. Dr Garnett refused to sign a petition opposing the war and published a sonnet abusing President Kruger for his pride, presumption, guile and greed. But he still remained on very affectionate terms with Constance, who wrote to him on Boxing Day 1899:

I fear you must be feeling some anxiety on our account. I have felt for such a long while that it was impossible Edward should remain at Fisher Unwin's – the business seems to be going downhill in more ways than one. And it is so much better that such a crisis in our fortunes should come now when Edward is thirty than that he should have had to seek fresh openings a few years later, when he will be older – and when too our expenses for the boy's education must necessarily be considerable.[24]

Edward was finding it increasingly difficult to get on with Fisher Unwin, a cold humourless man, who liked to pose as 'the great and omniscient publisher, the patron of authors, who were exceptionally fortunate to be published by him'.[25] Edward duly left Unwin at the end of the year and began reading manuscripts for Heinemann. Constance added:

I do not myself feel apprehensive as to our future. I have complete confidence in Edward's energies and good sense. The only anxiety which troubles me is on the ground of his health. I doubt whether he is strong enough to stand a long strain of very hard work. His health is good as long as he leads a quiet life free from worry – but if he should be forced to depend on journalistic work to any great degree, I am afraid the necessity of working against time and the uncertainty of the work would tell upon him.[26]

Edward was indeed working very hard, and Constance had written to him at the beginning of the year from Montpellier: 'Poor boy! first I used to abuse him for being idle, and now for working! But it is time you did get to original work – not fritter your time over reviews for the sake of getting more money – or you will wake up in a few years to find the time has gone and nothing permanent done.'[27] This was to misapprehend the nature of Edward's gifts. His 'original work' was far less valuable than his critical writings and his nurturing of genius in others, of whom Conrad was only the first. Constance's own work was not 'original', but she did not feel that she had got nothing done. She had concluded her collected edition of Turgenev, as well as translating Ostrovsky's play, *The Storm*, for Duckworth. The fifteenth volume of Turgenev, *The Jew and Other Stories*, came out in January 1900, and she had translated all the novels and a generous selection of stories. (Two more volumes of stories were added when the edition was reprinted in 1922.) Stepniak had written two introductions and Edward seven – *A Sportsman's Sketches* and two of the volumes of tales had gone without them.

When Constance was on the point of finishing her twelfth volume of Turgenev, and did not then anticipate that Heinemann would take three more volumes of stories, she wrote to Volkhovsky:

It has been such a constant delight and engrossing interest for me for the last three or four years – and I hardly know what I shall do when it is quite done. I shall feel lost. All this work I owe in a way to you – for had I not met you, I should never have been interested in Russian, and should never have troubled myself to learn the language which opened quite another universe to me. Gratitude, I know, is not a Russian virtue, but still I think you may be glad to know that I remember with pleasure that it is to you I am indebted primarily for so much that I value.[28]

In the final volume Constance redressed Heinemann's slight with a dedication: 'To the memory of Stepniak, whose love of Turgenev suggested this translation.' And Edward used his introduction to mount a defence of the novel as an art-form, indeed to take the offensive and argue that 'the novel shares with poetry to-day the honour of being the supreme instrument of the great artist's literary skill', and that Turgenev was 'the greatest artist of our time'.[29]

Constance's achievement was celebrated in the columns of the *Academy* for 20 January 1900, which announced its 'Awards to Authors' for 1899, six prizes, each of twenty-five guineas, for works 'notable for promise, sincerity, and thoroughness in literary art'.[30] That for translation went to 'Mrs. Garnett for her translation of the novels of Turgenev'.[31] The other winners were Yeats for *The Wind among the Reeds*, Belloc for a biography of Danton, G. M. Trevelyan for *England in the Age of Wycliffe*, and two who are now largely forgotten, Gwendoline Keats and H. G. Graham. Naturally the accompanying review was full of praise: 'That Mrs. Garnett has conspicuously succeeded in a long and arduous task is beyond doubt. Her translation is faithful and correct. It is full of ingenuities unsuspected by the casual reader; and it has quiet and modest grace.'[32]

A later reviewer of Edward's book on Turgenev (1917) referred to 'Mrs. Garnett's never sufficiently to be praised version of the novels',[33] and generally the notices of the books as they had come out were very favourable. Mrs Humphry Ward, whose moral Christian novels Edward could not take entirely seriously, was so fulsome in her compliments that Constance was 'suffused with blushes'.[34] But she herself did not feel that she had succeeded. She knew that she was still learning her trade, and not only to understand Russian. 'I really only learnt to write English by writing it',[35] she said later.

She 'often regretted that she had begun her translation with Turgenev' – rather than, say, Tolstoy, who was so much more straightforward in style – 'and could never forgive herself for some early slipshod errors',[36] though by her own account she might not have improved on her first version if she had waited till she was more experienced. Once when she was translating *A Sportsman's Sketches* she gave the first draft of six of the stories to Stepniak to check. She had put, as she usually did, alternative words above the line wherever she was in doubt about the right one. But Stepniak failed to return the manuscript, insisting that he had already done so. Constance had to translate the six stories again, only for Stepniak to find the first translation among his papers. Constance compared the two to choose the best passages from each and was surprised to find that they were identical. 'I had hesitated in the same places, over the same words, and had written the same possible alternatives above the line in the same places. I concluded that though someone else might do a better version, it was clear that I could not myself. I had done the only version that I was capable of.'[37] But perhaps this merely shows that, without being aware of it, she shared the remarkable memory of her pupil Antonia Booth, who, after a week's lapse, could remember every word of the Caesar she had translated.

She had no illusions about the difficulty of the task. She wrote to Volkhovsky: 'Just now I am trying to translate a most beautiful, tragic fragment, *Davol'no* [*Enough*] – do you know it? It is almost impossible to do justice in English to the beauty and poetry of the original, but I cannot bear to leave it out of the volume.'[38]

And to her father-in-law:

I am struggling with 'A Lear of the Steppes' – a story I had meant to omit from my volumes, because I really felt unequal to it. But after all, my conscience was uneasy – and I am putting it in. I am trying to do nothing and think of nothing till it is finished. It is like a nightmare upon me – and I cannot feel quite myself till it is off – that will not be long, I hope, now.[39]

And when *The Torrents of Spring* had a slightly critical notice in *Literature*[40] she wrote: 'I quite agree with my reviewer – for the Torrents of Spring was translated with disgraceful haste – and I have a painful consciousness of its being inferior to the other volumes.'[41]

How good were Constance's translations? Views vary from the extravagant early praise (repeated after her death with some qualifications by Edward Crankshaw) to that of Vladimir Nabokov, whom Carolyn Heilbrun heard 'damn Constance Garnett's translations with a vehemence that could only have been justified had she violently abridged, or grossly distorted, the works'.[42]

An anonymous reviewer, praising *A House of Gentlefolk* in the *Athenaeum*,[43] wrote 'She is both literal and spirited' – an unusual combination. She saw it as her first duty to be faithful to her original, and having survived what must have been a frequent temptation to get on with *A Common Story* by abridging Goncharov's loquacious narrative, she likewise refused to 'improve' Tolstoy's arguments by presenting them in a way more acceptable to the English reader. 'Turgenev' she said, 'is much the most difficult of the Russians to translate because his style is the most beautiful.'[44] Just before her death she recalled: 'I was very much pleased because the Russian critic, Zhdanov, said it was impossible to translate Turgenev, and afterwards took the trouble to go through some of my translations carefully, and said he was amazed that it was possible for them to be so well done.'[45]

Glyn Turton, as part of his work on Turgenev in the context of English literature, made a thorough examination of Constance's translations of *Rudin* and three of the stories. He found that Constance did the difficult things well, failed at those that were nearly impossible, and occasionally slipped up on the easy ones. The difficulty in Turgenev was supposed to lie in his descriptive passages. Constance saw them as a challenge, and so took particular trouble over them. Turton found 'the accuracy and sensitivity of Garnett's handling of narrative and description' was 'rarely to be faulted'.[46] Others have gone farther. David thought that her versions of such stories as 'The Brigadier' and 'Byezhin Prairie' had an 'extraordinary quality'[47] that none of her other translations could match; and this was recognised by the publishers who issued her translation of the latter story as a textbook for teaching *English* literature to Japanese students.[48] Natalie Duddington, a native Russian and an experienced translator of Russian into English, thought that Constance had 'an extraordinary sensitivity to the nuances of meaning and the "flavour" of words'[49] and that her versions of the concluding passages of *Fathers and Children* and *A Nest of Gentlefolk* were 'pure poetry'.[50] She and David could not be called impartial witnesses. Edward Crankshaw, however, after quoting a passage from 'The Tryst', exclaimed:

That is the kind of thing before which, whether in the Russian of Turgenev or the English of Constance Garnett, you have to throw up your hands in acknowledgment of magic. There is no knowing how it is done, the translation no less than the original. And if that is not genius, then I don't know what is.[51]

Sir William Haley, exasperated at the 'grudging attitude to Constance Garnett' at the time when her reputation was at its lowest, wrote:

One can only say that, whatever may be their defects, there are whole episodes and passages in Constance Garnett's words which conjure up a scene or stir feelings in a way that other, quite possibly more correct, versions have not been able to accomplish. This is particularly true of the works of Turgenev.[52]

Constance said at the end of her life that 'The qualifications for a translator are to be in sympathy with the author he is translating, and most important of all to be in love with words and interested in all their meanings.'[53] By these criteria she was, despite her relative inexperience and incomplete knowledge of Russian, supremely well qualified to translate Turgenev, an author with whom she felt particular sympathy. As Conrad put it: 'She is in that work what a great musician is to a great composer – with something more, something greater. It is as if the Interpreter had looked into the very mind of the Master and had a share in his inspiration.'[54]

Constance always found dialogue more difficult than description, and Turton compares her translations unfavourably with those of Richard Freeborn for failing to make an adequate distinction between peasant and normal speech. He is probably right that her background made her feel that coarse rustic speech was unfitting for a writer so poetical as Turgenev. Her training in the classics made her prefer received English. On the other hand it has to be said that very few translators have succeeded in rendering foreign rustic speech into English, and that Freeborn's versions have a distinct whiff of Mummerset.

Turton found that she occasionally gave up the struggle to translate puns and faulty Russian, and while her omissions were few, there were – as she knew only too well – some careless and obvious slips.[55] Nevertheless, as Turton wrote: 'her errors, when they arise, are rendered more conspicuous by the very care and accuracy that is generally manifested in her translations'.[56]

She was not helped by her publisher. She went through a copy of the first edition of *A House of Gentlefolk*[57] and made a large number of corrections. They are mainly of slight misunderstandings, accidental omissions of repeated similar phrases, and so on, rather than gross errors. Only about a third of these have been corrected in the Illustrated Edition of 1906. The remaining errors have been allowed to stand, perhaps because she could not afford to pay Heinemann to make them – and yet this applies even when the book was reset and they would have cost nothing extra. She also recognised that she had made an error in adopting the title, *A House of Gentlefolk*, adding, 'The Russian means "A Nest of Gentlefolk", but I was afraid the public would think it too queer. Afterwards someone published a version called *A Nest of Hereditary Legislators*, and my title has now been changed to *A Nest of Gentlefolk*, quite rightly.'[58] But in fact it never was changed, perhaps for the same reason.

No doubt Constance was right to regret that she had tackled Turgenev so early in her career. But she could not have made a better choice with which to establish her reputation. This had little to do with the merits of her translation; it was because she – or rather Stepniak – happened to have chosen exactly the right moment. Turgenev's pessimism and stoicism (which would respectively have been congenial to Edward and to Constance) were well suited to *fin-de-siècle* disenchantment. The self-consciousness and introspection of Turgenev's characters matched that of the aesthetes of the nineties. Thanks partly to Shaw's advocacy of Ibsen and Heinemann's publications, English readers were taking a greater interest in foreign literature. For them there were only two great Russian novelists, Tolstoy and Turgenev (Dostoevsky was not yet taken seriously). Tolstoy's reputation had been the higher in the 1880s, but English prudery had baulked at *The Kreutzer Sonata*, and Tolstoy's polemics had gained him more notoriety than readers. Thus in the nineties Tolstoy was down, and so Turgenev was up. His success was even helped by commercial factors. The three-volume novel, which had been the staple of the Victorian circulating libraries, had ceased to be profitable to them, and they were on the look-out for shorter works. Short stories, which had been established in America and on the continent by Henry James, Maupassant and Turgenev, were at last becoming accepted in England.

Thanks to the critical writings of Henry James – and of Edward himself – the novel, with its power of combining science and poetry, was beginning to be recognised as a form of high art, and Turgenev's work 'served as a model for, and epitome of, that peculiar combinative power of the novel'.[59]

Edward's promotion of Turgenev as a model for practising writers began to have its effect. Conrad was far from being the disciple of Turgenev that the Garnetts would have liked to think he was. But there were others. Arnold Bennett, a versatile young man who had escaped from the Potteries and from being a London solicitor's clerk, had begun by making a living writing sensational fiction. Then he took himself in hand as a writer and became a deliberate highbrow and aesthete. On 14 February 1897 he wrote to Edward:

May I ask you to be so good as to give me further particulars of the book *Souvenirs sur Tourguéneff* mentioned in your introduction to *On the Eve*. . . . My excuse for thus troubling you must be that I am making a study of Turgenev as a constructive artist in fiction, and that I fully share your admiration for his work. . . . Strictly technical criticism (particularly on the point of construction) seems almost a minus quantity in both England and France. It is one of my ambitions to revive it – if indeed it was ever really alive.

I may mention that I have more than once had the pleasure of appreciating your edition of Turgenev in the columns of *Woman*, a little paper of which I am editor.[60]

Bennett duly wrote at length about Turgenev in the *Academy* on 4 November 1899. He became obsessed with Turgenev and for a while modelled his writing entirely upon him; but though he continued to admire Constance's other translations, they remained acquaintances rather than friends.

Another young writer, much influenced by Turgenev, did, however, become considerably more than an acquaintance. John Galsworthy had had a conventional English upbringing. He had been trained as a lawyer and called to the Bar, but was well enough off not to need to practise. Instead his father sent him on long voyages with the notion that they provided a practical education for a gentleman and might include a modicum of business on the way. At about the same time as Constance was travelling in Russia he went to Ekaterinoslav to inspect a factory and came back by way of the Crimea. A year earlier he had gone on a long sea voyage hoping to meet Robert Louis Stevenson in Samoa. Instead he found himself on the *Torrens*, where, as he wrote: 'The first mate is a Pole called Conrad and is a capital chap, though queer to look at. . . .'[61]

Galsworthy, on the other hand, looked as an Englishman should, with his high balding brow,

level steely blue eyes, firm compressed lips, always correctly dressed . . . a rimless eyeglass dangling from a thin black cord, or screwed firmly into his right eye. Galsworthy was a man who held himself very upright and was very upright. He had little humour but could be jolly. He was the reverse of subtle – though the two warring elements in his nature enabled him to see both sides of many questions. . . . he was incapable of believing that many serious matters are best treated frivolously.[62]

Though one would not have guessed it, he had a deep uneasiness about himself. He felt he was an outsider in the class to which he belonged, and he made himself one in 1895 by falling in love with his cousin Arthur Galsworthy's wife, Ada. Thereafter they lived together more or less secretly as man and wife. Ada reminded David Garnett of 'bumble bees seen among the velvety petals of dark wallflowers'.[63] She was musical and intelligent, and she translated Maupassant.

It was Ada who persuaded Galsworthy to start writing. His first book, *From the Four Winds*, was a collection of adventure stories published by Unwin under a pseudonym. His second, *Jocelyn*, was a novel on the theme of adultery; and by the time Conrad brought his old friend Jack Galsworthy to the Cearne in the summer of 1900 he was working on *Villa Rubein*, which was modelled 'on Turgenev's method'.[64] Although the Garnetts had not met him before, he had written 'to Constance, in the first instance, because he admired the works of Turgenev, which he had read in her translations'.[65] He considered Turgenev 'the finest natural poet who ever wrote novels' and one who had introduced the principle of selection into his fiction 'until there was that complete relation of part to whole which goes to the making of what we call a work of art'.[66]

Edward had also had earlier dealings with Galsworthy, but not so happily as Constance. Galsworthy had submitted his stories to Unwin with a letter written on paper from his London club, and Edward had reported:

The fact is the author is a man of action *and he is not artist enough* to score a high success in literature, we should judge. If however he wishes to appear as author and is willing to take all the risks, and we suppose as a Junior Carlton man he is pretty well off, we see no reason why he should not appeal to the public and get respectable press notices – on commission terms.[67]

Unwin took his advice and published the book on commission with Galsworthy paying the capital cost. When the manuscript of *Jocelyn* arrived, Edward was rather less dismissive, but proposed that the book be again published on commission. He reported:

Mr. Galsworthy is an excellent fellow, a good Briton and one neither stiff nor prejudiced. He visits foreign countries diligently and examines foreign manners intelligently, but he is always hopelessly *bored* and sees things always through the eyes of a Clubman who carries England with him wherever he goes.[68]

Unwin, with an ineptitude all too common among publishers, passed on to Galsworthy the gist of Edward's remarks about seeing life through the windows of a London club. It was perhaps a cheap gibe, but it had enough truth in it to rankle, and when Galsworthy was leaving at the end of his first visit to the Cearne he remarked to Edward with a gleam in his eye, 'I'm not such a fool as I seem.'[69] It went on rankling for ten years or more, even after they had become close friends and Jack and Ada and Edward and Nellie had spent many holidays together; and in rankling it provoked Galsworthy to become an artist.

Constance's relations with Galsworthy had no such unhappy beginnings. His idealism and seriousness appealed to her more than they did to Edward, who was apt to be sceptical of such things. And when he came to stay at the Cearne later in 1900 he endeared himself to her and greatly impressed David by his sangfroid in an emergency. The Peases were away and had asked the Garnetts to look after their half-wild cat that had newly kittened. Unfortunately the Garnetts, despite being cat-lovers, also had two dogs, one of which, Puppsie, was 'a collie of imbecile disposition afflicted with a spasmodic twitch of the left forepaw'.[70] Puppsie tried to attack the cat, and when David tried to drag him away,

the cat sprang at me and missing my eye, tore my eyebrow asunder. . . .

The incident had unhinged her, and she subsequently attacked everyone who entered the room. Jack Galsworthy was scratched but not so severely as I. At last she was trapped in a basket, and Jack and Constance carried the yowling animal and its kitten back to their home, where they liberated them in a woodshed, leaving enough provisions for a few days.[71]

Throughout all this Galsworthy remained calmly detached, as he did when 'the miscreant Puppsie' found something unspeakable, described by Edward as a dead rat, and by David variously as a bullock's or a sheep's head seething with maggots, and dragged it into the house. He calmly fetched a shovel and buried the horrible object at the bottom of the garden.

It should not be thought that Constance's appreciation of Galsworthy's sangfroid was because of any lack of it in her husband. A few months later Edward behaved with equal coolness in a far more alarming predicament. Bert Hedgecock, who had groomed Shagpat when first they moved into the Cearne, had been sacrificed as an economy measure soon after Edward had had typhoid. But Edward, out of a quixotic feeling for the underdog, took on his elder brother Bill. Bill had the reputation of not being able to get on with his mates, who thought him a 'funny' man, and of having a temper that got him into trouble. Constance was afraid of him, and annoyed with herself for being afraid and with Edward for having rushed her into agreeing to take him on.[72]

Then, on 6 February 1901, four days after Queen Victoria's funeral, Olive noted in her diary: 'Edward came to dinner and gave us a long account in the style of "Lord Jim" of his exciting adventures with poor Bill who went mad at the Cearne and had to be taken to the infirmary as a criminal lunatic. Connie and Bunny escaped to Fanny.'[73] Exactly what happened is hard to determine. At the time Constance said that it produced no effect on David but 'a kind of pleasurable excitement' –

'His comment was that it was almost as good as having robbers in the house!'[74] When he eventually came to tell the story it was in a novel, *Beany-Eye*, and though his narrative carries utter conviction, it is the conviction of art rather than history. 'It is, however, much to be doubted' as Iris Barry remarked while praising the book in the *New York Herald Tribune*,[75] 'if what actually happened all those years ago has much semblance to what is now recounted.' David omitted any details of the episode from his autobiography, because he said he had told the story already, yet he admitted that the fictional Beany-Eye incorporated features of another labourer besides Bill, and described many things in the book that he could have neither seen nor known.

Certainly the house and the woods are pictured in the book exactly as they were, and there is historical as well as artistic conviction in the fictional version of his mother. She is described as 'a very busy woman and for several hours a day the affairs of Vronsky, Levin and Dolly were perforce as real to her as those of her own household'.[76] Though she was exasperated with Edward for having taken on a maniac, she was nevertheless thrilled by the adventure of being besieged by him at night in her own home. This rings entirely true. So too does the portrait that emerges of Edward, whose growing feeling of responsibility for the man who had tried to murder him overcomes his momentary anger and fear. Whether Bill actually besieged the house armed with an axe and battered vainly on the doors that Harry Cowlishaw had built so solidly, or in the fury of his mania hurled both the wretched dogs sixteen feet in the air one cannot tell. But Bill's pitiful letters from the Brookwood Asylum still survive, and are exactly as David printed them. By the spring of 1904 the authorities deemed it safe to discharge Bill from the asylum. With some help from Edward he emigrated to Canada, where he seems to have kept out of trouble, and continued to write grateful letters to his benefactor for several years.

The copy of *Beany-Eye* that David gave Edward is inscribed 'with love and gratitude'. And Olive considered the book to be a finer tribute to Edward's courage and humanity than any of his more formal obituaries.[77]

14

Tolstoy by Candlelight

In *Beany-Eye*, the crisis of which took place in February 1901, Constance is described as working on *Anna Karenin*. She had wanted to translate the book ever since she first read it in Russian in September 1896. There were already at least two English translations. Vizetelly had been first off the mark in 1884, followed by Nathan Haskell Dole two years later. Constance had read one of these and thought it 'so exceptionally bad that it gives hardly any idea of the original'.[1] But Heinemann was reluctant to embark on a new translation of Tolstoy, having in all probability lost money on *The Kingdom of God is Within You*. Instead he continued to offer Constance translation from French, which she could not afford to refuse, but which to her relief once again came to nothing. She started work on *Anna Karenin* on her own initiative, and on 8 January 1900 Edward went to see Pawling of Heinemann, but failed to persuade him to take it on. She had plenty of other distractions. In March she struggled with the vegetable garden in the face of most unhelpful weather, feeling, as usual, that 'to be forced to call upon a greengrocer for supplies would be a novel and humiliating experience for me';[2] and in April she translated nothing at all, such was the pressure of visitors and housework.[3] But she remained confident that her translation would be 'of use sooner or later',[4] and at last, in early June, by which time she had got a third of the book done, Heinemann agreed to take it on,[5] paying her, it would seem, at the rate of twelve shillings per thousand words, better than for Turgenev, but with no royalty.[6]

The work went on through the autumn and winter. Fanny came three days a week. When Constance had done a batch she read the Russian aloud to Fanny, and then they both looked through the translation. Fanny was desperate for work, for she could hardly afford the price of coal. The translation of *Anna Karenin* was at last completed in May 1901, but Constance would not be paid for it until it was published in the autumn, and she had no further translation in prospect. She wrote to her father-in-law:

> I have been deferring this letter from day to day hoping to have some definite news of a reassuring kind about 'War and Peace' but it does not come. Edward doubtless told you that it seemed practically arranged that I should translate 'War and Peace' and I had begun upon it and completed 100 pages or so when unexpected 'developments' arose and now Heinemann – no doubt wisely – has decided not to undertake a new translation. It is still undecided whether he will purchase sheets of the new American translation – and whether if he does so, he will think it well to give me the work of revising it.[7]

The 'new' American translation was intended to supersede the one by Nathan Dole in the same series as Aline Delano's version of *The Kingdom of God is Within You*. It was edited, if not entirely translated by Leo Wiener, Assistant Professor of Slavic Languages at Harvard University, who had been brought up in Russia. His edition of Tolstoy was published in twenty-four volumes by Dana Estes of Boston from 1904 to 1905.

While Heinemann hesitated over *War and Peace*, Constance started work with Fanny on some of Tolstoy's stories. Their relations were happier now that the Garnetts were living as frugally as Fanny herself, who wrote to Olive: 'Connie looks so flourishing under the poor regime, that she is ashamed to complain. How nice it is to be poor, provided one has no debts!'[8]

Edward's relations with Heinemann were also at first much happier than they had been with Unwin. 'Mr Heinemann and Mr Unwin' Constance wrote, 'suggest the fable of the sun and the wind and the traveller's cloak. Mr Heinemann's amiability succeeds in getting an amount of work out of his employés that Mr Unwin's chilly and repellent methods never managed to do.'[9] As a result Edward did far too much and looked 'tired and overworked'.[10] Much of the work was uncongenial and could have been avoided.

> Heinemann has a most unfortunate system [Constance wrote – and, alas, the system is by no means extinct] of giving translation work to quite incompetent persons who don't know English – and then giving their unintelligible translations to be revised to Edward, who does not know the original languages. I feel for the poor authors almost as much as for the reviser! First it was a terribly tedious Universal History from the German which took us both some weeks of work – now it is a novel from the Italian, execrably translated. The result is of course after many hours of the most tedious work imaginable, anything but satisfactory.[11]

At the same time Edward could not refuse the more rewarding opportunities, usually offered with uncomfortably short deadlines, to write
critical articles. He had turned his attention to Tolstoy at much the same
time as Constance had done. He had already discussed Tolstoy and
Turgenev in the *Anglo-Saxon Review*[12] when, on 6 June 1900, he wrote
to Tolstoy that he and Constance had been asked to provide a joint
article about *Resurrection* for *Harper's* provided that Tolstoy would add
an address to the American people.[13] Edward suggested that Tolstoy
should use the occasion to attack Anglo-Saxon hypocrisy, but the old
man had more tact and replied on 21 June in English that he would like
to thank the American people

for the great help I have received from their writers who flourished about [the]
fifties. . . . I should like to ask the American people, why they do not pay
more attention to these voices . . . and continue the good work in which they
made such hopeful progress.

My kind regards to your wife, and I take [the] opportunity of once more
thanking her for her excellent translation of 'The Kingdom of God is within
you'.[14]

Edward and Constance duly wrote their article, but it must have been
thought too radical by the editors of *Harper's*, and it was taken by the
North American Review. The issue for April 1901 opened with a long
article by Tolstoy himself, 'The Root of the Evil' – which does not seem
to have been translated by Constance. He began by describing the 'evil'
in harrowing terms, the obscene contrast between the sufferings of
peasant and industrial poor and the indolent luxuries of the rich, and
then castigated the Church for having perverted Christ's teachings and
allowed these injustices to happen. His letter to Edward was appended,
with some minor amendments. Then followed Edward and Constance's
article about *Resurrection*, It is an apologia for Tolstoy, setting him in the
context of Russian history, and giving a broader relevance to his views
than was admitted by the critics who dismissed them as an aberration of
genius. One cannot tell how much each of them contributed, only that
the quotations from the book were not translated by Constance, but
taken from Louise Maude's edition, which Edward had reviewed the
previous year.[15]

Edward also wrote of 'Tolstoy's Place in European Literature' in
the *Bookman*[16] and worked hard that summer on his article, 'The
Contemporary Critic', in which he set out his credo of his function in
recognising and fostering living genius, and attacked the academic critics

for their obsession with the past and blindness to the merits of their contemporaries. *Blackwood's*, which had commissioned it, took fright and turned it down, but it eventually appeared in the *Monthly Review* in December 1901, and did more than anything else to establish Edward's reputation.

Heinemann, the sun in the fable, did not shine on Edward for long. On 2 July 1901 he wrote a letter to Edward, which beneath a cloud of courteous generalities was effectively giving him the sack. Edward forwarded it to his father with one of his own, which set out the situation more intelligibly:

to put the matter in a nutshell, I may say that as Pawling's protegé I have, from the first, been looked on by Heinemann with some jealousy, and he has now taken the opportunity of putting his own man in my place.

Had the present Publishing Season been a successful one Mr Pawling assures me that I should have heard nothing about the matter – but the fact that Trade in books for the last 18 months, and especially this Summer's season has been extremely flat and disappointing for nearly every Publisher has worked against my chances and position in every respect.

That my dismissal is certainly not due to lack of care on my side I can most certainly avow. I have worked extremely carefully and diligently at Heinemann's in the hope of building up a position, and I have worked too for the extremely small sum of 3£ to 3£ 10/ a week. . . .

Nowadays, however good and clever Fiction may be, if it is not carefully 'boomed' and manoeuvred beforehand, it stands but little chance, and of course the Reader cannot arrange to 'boom' a critique for the books he selects and helps into being.[17]

For Constance crises rarely came singly. Within three weeks of Edward receiving Heinemann's letter she suffered another blow. Her brother Robert was forty-one. Of recent years she had not seen so much of him as of Grace and Clementina, but as children they had been very close. Robert had remained a bachelor, devoting himself entirely to his work as House Surgeon at the Sussex County Hospital at Brighton. His one indulgence was to go, as his father had done, for strenuous walking holidays in the Alps. At the beginning of July he had gone with seven friends to stay at the Hôtel Mont-Cervin at Valtournanche on the Italian side of the Matterhorn. At four-thirty on the morning of 23 July five of the party set out with a guide and a porter to climb the Tête du Lion. They were all inexperienced climbers, but it was not too difficult an ascent. However, after they had set out they changed their plans and decided to tackle the climb to the Matterhorn hut, a much more difficult and dangerous proposition. They reached it safely enough, at about twelve o'clock; and on the way down all went well until they came to the snow traverse leading from the Col du Lion on to the Tête du Lion.

Mr. Mallam, Mr. Johnston, and the porter in that order on the first rope passed this place safely, and waited on the other side for the party on the second rope. Here the order had just been changed, and Dr. Black, who had been leading, changed places with the guide, who was last and who now led, the ladies being between them. They were getting well over when one of the ladies slipped and fell, dragging the others after her. The first party, after finding out from the porter that it was impossible to reach them, hurried down for assistance.[18]

A relief party 'found Miss Trew and the guide at 10.30 p.m., badly bruised but alive'. Robert and Miss Bell were both dead.

'Poor Connie bears it very well;' Edward wrote to his father on 26 July, 'in fact so well that I fear the blow is only accumulating in her mind.'[19] Not until 30 August did she feel able to thank her father-in-law for 'the deep sympathy I knew you were feeling for me'; and then she wrote:

For a time I felt so numbed, so stupefied by the suddenness and awfulness of it that I could not face it or realise it at all. Now I am thankful today I feel stronger and am getting back energy again. I am afraid Ernest and his wife and Clementina will feel the loss of Robert very deeply and very permanently. We had always reckoned on Clementina's settling finally with him later on. He would I know have liked to have her with him. Now I am afraid the future must seem lonely and desolate to her.[20]

It was a hard, sad summer. Constance had 'a rather sharp little attack of sciatica'.[21] They were even shorter of money than usual and subsisted on the produce of the vegetable garden and on bread which Constance made in the brick oven, supplemented by the mushrooms that Edward collected in the Chart Woods. Richard Garnett offered money and help, but Constance, with her Scottish frugality, asked for no more than a good reading lamp – they had only one good one, which Edward used to work by in the evenings, and otherwise they made do with candles – and the Russian volumes containing Tolstoy's short stories, the texts for which she had been obliged to borrow from the Russian Free Library and Reading-Room, which catered for Russian immigrants in Whitechapel.

The volumes of stories took a long time coming from Russia; and she was frustrated to find that other people were translating tales of Tolstoy's which she had hoped to do herself:

I rarely hear of a book of translations from the Russian without finding that it contains something of which I had been coveting the translation. Mrs Maude I hear is bringing out a volume of Tolstoy's War Stories, some of which I have lately been reading with an ardent desire to set about translating them myself.[22]

Her ambitions were by no means confined to Tolstoy:

I am looking forward with some trepidation to my first efforts to translate Gorki. He writes an extraordinary language – largely slang, which even Russians find difficulty in interpreting – and when one does succeed in arriving at his meaning, it is a task to discover suitable equivalents in English. But I have been wishing for a chance to try my hand at him, so I trust those American publishers will commission us to furnish them with a story.[23]

Gorky was born in 1868, 'the son of poor folk', and 'had tried his hand at many kinds of manual labour', as Edward wrote in the *Academy*,[24] 'Hence it is that his tone . . . has the freshness and conviction of an artist who is painting life and is not elaborating fictions.' He was 'the latest Russian writer to be received with enthusiasm by his countrymen' – and not only by them. At least three volumes of translations of his work appeared in America in 1901 and a further five in England in 1902. One of these, *Twenty-six Men and a Girl*, had an introduction by Edward and inaugurated a series of paperbacks at Duckworth. But though the translations were by a number of hands, including those of Vera Volkhovsky, Constance had no part in any of them.[25] When Gorky was featured in the *Monthly Review* in November 1901, the story, 'Makar Chudra' was translated by M. Mojaysky, and the accompanying article was by R. Nisbet Bain, who also pre-empted Constance with two volumes of Tolstoy's stories. Her one contribution was to provide Edward with material for his *Academy* article and to translate the opening of 'Malva', a passage of description somewhat in the manner of Turgenev, quoted in the article.

Dr Garnett also offered to provide money for David's schooling. This had been rather chequered. In the autumn of 1897, when he was only five, Constance had planned to send him to school at Limpsfield, but, as Olive reported:

The admirable schoolmistress at Limpsfield left to take up an appointment (more lucrative) in Australia the day before the Limpsfield parents were to entrust the flower of Limpsfield youth to her care for the Autumn. She had indeed written to the Cearne apropos of Bunny's coming, the third day previous. Consternation and indignation of the neighbourhood – especially on discovering that she had been in treaty for the better appointment since June last – and indefatigable efforts of Mrs Pease to procure immediately a successor with a higher moral standard resulted.[26]

Whether or not Mrs Pease was successful, David did not stay long at school before Constance reverted to teaching him herself. More recently she had been paying Nellie's brother Carl to come in every day and give him a lesson. Carl Heath was a teacher by profession and a pacifist and social reformer by vocation. He had taught slum children in the East End for three years until the work told on his health, when he came to Limpsfield to teach the Olivier and Hobson children as well as David. Eventually Constance might be glad of money to help pay for his schooling, but for the moment she decided to have his holidays 'begin at once and to let them last for three months. . . . By the end of that time I trust our position will be more definite. . . .'[27] She continued nevertheless to give David an hour's lesson every day, and he worked for an hour on his own. His enthusiasm at the moment was the *Local News*, which he edited. In January he had written to his grandfather, 'Will you send me a poem or article on Cats I believe you are a specialist on them', remarking to his mother that it would be a great thing to have as 'Grandpapa is quite well known in the literary world already'.[28] The old man duly obliged with a poem about one of the Tanza Road cats, which any editor would have been proud to publish:

Marigold

> She moved through the garden in glory, because
> She had very long claws at the end of her paws.
> Her back was arched, her tail was high,
> A green fire glared in her vivid eye;
> And all the Toms, though never so bold,
> Quailed at the martial Marigold.[29]

In October 1901 Heinemann finally committed himself to a 'new edition' of Tolstoy's novels 'uniform with the Edinburgh Edition of the Works of Robert Louis Stevenson'. The format, medium octavo, was larger and distinctly more handsome – and more expensive at fifteen shillings for the two volumes of *Anna Karenin* – than the Turgenev. The books were printed on good paper in a distinguished Scotch Roman with gilt tops and bound in dark green cloth.

But Constance had a bad autumn and let her Russian 'go'. At the end of the year she had translated only a third of *The Death of Ivan Ilyitch and Other Stories* when she received a peremptory summons from Heine-mann to finish it. She got it done by the beginning of February. Although Heinemann had agreed to the new edition, he was anxious about *War and Peace*, He did not want to put such a huge egg in so frail a basket, and entrust the translation of a novel of half a million words to an overworked woman, plagued with sick headaches and suffering from deteriorating eyesight, who had a house and a kitchen garden to run, a family and friends to feed and a son to educate. The echoes of the affair reached Olive's diary: 'Heinemann actually wants War and Peace to be done in a hurry by collaborators! Connie's indignant refusal.'[30] If the translation were not to be entirely her own work Constance would have nothing to do with it. Heinemann had to relent.

Meanwhile, also in October 1901, the Garnetts' position had become 'more definite'. Edward wrote to his father on the 4th:

You will be glad to hear that I have now concluded an arrangement with Duckworth by which I shall 'read' for them on the same terms as I had at Heinemann's.

I have also settled with them to start a certain series, which, if successful, will bring me some money, and also give literary work to several friends.[31]

Constance added, in a further letter:

I am very thankful, for Edward has been exerting himself in all sorts of ways to a point when there seemed to me a great danger of his breaking down. And of course it is great piece of luck, too. There are so few houses in which Edward could possibly be employed that one could hardly expect him to find a vacancy at once.[32]

Gerald Duckworth was two years younger than Edward. He had started his own publishing firm in Henrietta Street in 1898, apparently as an occupation suitable for a gentleman. He was Virginia Woolf's half-brother, though in character and inclination he belonged less to the world of books than to that of the London clubs – he was far more of a clubman than Galsworthy. Leonard Woolf found him a 'kindly, uncen-sorious man',[33] but Anthony Powell, who joined the firm of Duckworth twenty-five years later, believed that 'His interest in books, anyway as a medium for reading, was as slender as that of any man I have ever encountered'.[34] By then he was 'a big burly man, [with a] slight grey moustache, small rather baleful eyes behind steel spectacles, a vaguely dissatisfied air . . . he moved gloomily through the office, a haze of port-fumes and stale cigar-smoke in his wake. . . .'[35] Nevertheless he had published some worthwhile books even before Edward arrived. It was in his series of Modern Plays that Constance's translation of *The Storm* had appeared, along with *The Father* by Strindberg and *Love's Comedy* by Ibsen, and for which Constance's abortive translation of Stepniak's play was intended. In his first three years he had published books by Henry James, Galsworthy and his stepfather Leslie Stephen, and got himself a potential best-seller in the shape of Elinor Glyn.

On his last day at Heinemann Edward made an important new friend. W. H. Hudson was then sixty years old, and had been living in England for the past thirty-two years, surviving precariously by his writings. He sent the manuscript of *El Ombú* to Heinemann. Edward thought it a work of genius, but Heinemann havered and feared that it would not sell. At last Hudson came in to the office to get a decision. Edward told him that he had written a masterpiece:

Its grave beauty, its tragic sweetness, indeed, had swept me off my feet, as it does now when I read it. Hudson glared at me, astonished, as though he wished to annihilate me, and asked my name. I told him, adding, 'It's my last day here. Where can I meet you?' Suddenly his face changed and he said, 'Let's go and find a place to lunch.'[36]

That lunch at the Mont Blanc was the first of many. Heinemann turned the book down, but Edward made it the first title in the Greenback Library, a new series he inaugurated at Duckworth, and he continued to publish him. Some time early in 1902 Hudson came down to the Cearne and met Constance and David, who wrote:

He was tall, six foot three in height, but seemed less, as he usually stooped to listen to whomever he was talking to. He had grizzled dark hair with a curiously flat top to his head. His nose was twisted, it had been broken at some time, and he had deep-set eyes, brown with a touch of autumnal red in them, and grizzled well-trimmed beard. . . . His coat, made of a rough tweed, had tails with pockets in them and a waistcoat and trousers to match. He always wore a shirt with a stand-up starched white collar and starched linen cuffs, and he wore black lace-up boots. . . . He was a quiet and silent man whose emotions were kept hidden; only after getting to know him could one tell that there was an ember glowing within, which could sometimes be blown into flame.[37]

He soon made friends with Constance, and especially with David. When the boy reported having seen a strange frog, he had complete faith in the story; they trespassed together in the mud of a pond on the Trevereux estate, and Hudson found that it was indeed a rare natterjack toad. He made all three Garnetts hide under gorse bushes to listen to the nightjars' 'churring, vibrating rattle',[38] while he called to the birds in their own voice. He treated David as an equal, and with some justification, for the boy was an experienced naturalist by his tenth birthday.

Constance, however, required something more of her son by way of education besides natural history and woodcraft. She had long been concerned about where to send him to school and how they should pay for it. She liked the idea of Bedales, but did not want to send him away to a boarding school. She decided that when he was twelve she would have to let the Cearne and live for a few years near a good school 'so that I may be able to be with David and help to push him on in his school work'.[39] By the end of 1902 she thought it was 'high time he should be with other boys and under regular discipline. He has a particularly sweet and temperament. . . . what I rather dread is that . . . he may become too soft and tender.'[40] In Marjorie Pease's view she spoiled him dreadfully.

In the spring of 1903 she decided, as a temporary measure, to send him as a day-boy to Mr Chater's school at Westerham. The fees, twelve pounds a term, plus a further four guineas for lunches, were more than she and Edward could afford, but Dr Garnett with his usual generosity paid them in full. After a delay because of an outbreak of scarlatina, school opened on 5 May. David bicycled down and up Westerham hill to and from school on an antique Bantam, a diminutive version of the old penny-farthing, that had belonged to Arthur Garnett.

It had a front-wheel drive geared with a series of cog-wheels, a large front wheel and smaller back wheel. . . . There was a plunger-brake on the front wheel and, though the tyres were pneumatic, there was no inner tube and outer cover, they were of one thick tube, unmendable if punctured and irreplaceable when worn out. . . . Mounted on this museum specimen and wearing a French beret over my untidy mop of hair, I presented myself to the critical inspection of the other little boys and was at once christened 'Onions'.[41]

But the other boys were not unkind to him. The war had ended in June of the previous year, and he no longer had to run the gauntlet as a pro-Boer. Mr Chater was a good schoolmaster, but his assistant was an ignorant and disagreeable man who made life so unpleasant for David that he did not return to school after the summer holidays.

It was the age of the bicycle, and there were other cyclists in the family besides David. Arthur, of course, was indefatigable and cycled everywhere. He thought nothing of biking down from Kew, where he was now working in the Royal Botanic Gardens, to the Cearne for the weekend. The Chart was hardly good cycling country. The track from Kent Hatch, down which the masons had brought their tumbrils of stone, was far too steep, and the other paths were slippery with dead and rotting leaves and ridged with tree roots. Nevertheless Constance got herself a bicycle and 'biked with Fanny Stepniak'[42] most assiduously. Later Edward taught Olive to ride her bicycle.[43] Old Richard Heath took up cycling at this time. Tolstoy was a keen cyclist and rode for considerable distances on a solid machine with a single plunger-brake and no mudguards. Even Henry James rode a bicycle, and David, on a visit to Rye with his new camera, took a photograph of the Master in his cycling clothes, standing proudly beside his machine. The picture came out perfectly, but has since been lost.

Besides such relatives as Hugh and Grace Human on leave in the autumn of 1902, they had more exotic visitors. On 4 November of that year Fanny Stepniak brought Louise Michel to the Cearne. In 1871 she had been the *Vierge Rouge* in képi and man's uniform, a heroine of the Communard barricades in Paris. She had been exiled to the penal colony of Nouméa in the Pacific until 1880, when she was allowed to return to Paris, only to be imprisoned three more times for revolutionary activities before seeking the safety of England. She was now in her seventies, and Constance, who thought her the greatest orator of the age,[44] found her 'a wonderful old lady, still persists in being brisk and active, sat by the fire looking at a splendid new book on Hogarth'.[45]

Age, however, was catching up with another old lady. In June 1903 Narney went to stay with Harry and Lucy Cowlishaw who had moved from Kiln Farm to Four Elms Farm. On Friday the 19th Lucy wrote to Olive that her mother was in bed with a chill. On Monday Edward walked over from the Cearne to see her and thought she seemed better. On Tuesday morning Edward came to town as usual, and Narney was suddenly taken very much worse. Dr Maude, who was also Constance's doctor, was called, and when he saw Narney's condition, sent a telegram to her husband: 'Consider Mrs Garnett's state very grave, come this evening to Four Elms.'[46] Dr Garnett was out when it arrived, and Olive was just about to leave the house to visit Rebecca Mocatta. She dashed first to tell Narney's brother, Edward Singleton, only to find that he was at Lord's watching the MCC play an American touring team from Philadelphia, and then back to Tanza Road to pack a bag for her father, who was due home again at four for tea. He was able to catch the 5.15

from Charing Cross, and at eight in the evening Olive received a further telegram: 'Operation so far satisfactory.'[47] Her diary is no more specific about the nature of the illness and the emergency operation carried out in the farmhouse, but her niece and editor, Anne Lee Michell, believed that it was a strangulated hernia and that gangrene had already set in.

Edward came to Tanza Road expecting to dine there as usual, and unaware of the crisis. Early the following morning his father telegraphed again: 'Matters most serious. Come with Edward if you think well.'[48] Olive and Edward went down by train, arriving shortly before one o'clock. But their mother was already dead. Richard and Edward and the nurses went back to London. But Olive stayed; and so did Constance, for whom it must have been a painful echo of her own mother's death twenty-eight summers earlier. Olive wrote:

Connie sat with Lucy and me. Ida [nurse to the Cowlishaws' baby, Mark] and I went upstairs, and I held Ida's hand and kissed Mamma three times. She looked most lovely, like a queen. I never saw her look so handsome and calm in life. The birds were noisily flying in and out of their nests under the roof.[49]

Olive returned to London on Thursday. She had been in a depressed mood and had had violent neuralgia even before this latest shock. Now she 'Felt so shaken I sent for Dr Mallam and asked him to help me to go to the funeral and to take me in hand.' 'Eight years!'[50] she exclaimed cryptically, with her previous bereavement in mind. On Saturday:

Glorious weather. . . . Papa, May and Guy, Robert, I, Mr and Mrs Moir [friends of Edward Singleton's, with whom he lived] and Uncle Edward went down from Victoria . . . drove through the lovely lanes to the cottage, and found there Edward and Connie, Harry and Lucy, Arthur and Ida. I went upstairs. Mr Deadman was screwing down the coffin. We then all unpacked the wreaths and placed them in the hearse, and followed it to Hever, where we had a service in the church. . . . Ford walked into the churchyard just as all was done, and drove back to Edenbridge with us. . . . It was all a dream to me.[51]

Meanwhile Constance was making new friends. For nearly ten years the Cearne had had no nearer neighbour than Scearn Bank Farm, at the end of the meadow and just short of Grace's Cottage. To begin with it had been a farm labourer's cottage, then it had been taken by a colonist of a rather more dubious kind than Constance's Fabian friends. She was a lady, known to her disciples as 'Little Mother', 'who had done welfare work among the girls in the East End of London'.[52] She had gathered half a dozen of them to form the nucleus of an ideal community, sheltered from the wicked world, but not from her moral and menial exploitation.

From this unlikely source the Garnetts recruited one of their most stalwart helpers and friends. After a while under Little Mother's tyranny, Li Whale – Li was short for Elizabeth – 'the most intelligent and strong-minded of the flock',[53] ran away and came to live at the Cearne and to work for Constance. Then, when Little Mother moved on, Li lived at Scearn Bank Farm herself with her sisters and her old father. At first she just took in washing, but she soon became a regular feature of the Cearne, and could be relied to come over from her cottage and keep house for Edward when Constance was away, and to help when there were visitors.

Then, some time in the summer of 1903, the seclusion of the Cearne came to an end. David met two strange ladies in the wood:

one very tall, florid and large of limb; her companion stocky, with short hair and eyes that twinkled behind bifocal spectacles. They came, viewed, and measured the field lying next to the Cearne. Then to my parents' dismay, they bought it and proceeded to erect a . . . great ragstone barrack of a house, which looked like one arch of an embattled railway bridge. . . .[54]

The new house was to be called Scearn Bank, and the oddity of its design was partly due to the need to collect rain-water from the roof which had large flat catchment areas in unexpected places.

Amy Sheppard and Frances Ede were both qualified doctors, though Dr Ede never practised. Constance and Edward soon forgave them for invading their privacy, and they became friends. Edward teased both the 'lady doctors'. David shared many interests with Dr Ede, who shot rabbits with a rifle and played host to parties of suffragettes who came down to practise pistol shooting. Dr Sheppard was an ophthalmologist, later to become distinguished in her field.

Constance was soon glad to have expert advice about her eyes so near at hand, though she did not rely only on Dr Sheppard. She had always been extremely short-sighted even as a child. She had to hold the book up to her face and peer at it closely to distinguish the words, especially if they were in Cyrillic. It was not the first time she had had eyestrain when she wrote to her father-in-law on 2 May 1903:

Edward will have told you no doubt that my eyes have been troublesome. I went on Wednesday to see the oculist and am warned by him that I must take a long rest and be very careful in the future. It is rather depressing, but I still hope that with rest and precaution in avoiding strong light, I may be able to use them more freely again later.[55]

Constance later told a friend that she suffered from 'ulceration of the retina'.[56] This is one of the consequences of what is now called 'degenerative myopia'.[57] In ordinary myopia, or short sight, from which Constance had always suffered, the axial length of the eye is too great for the focal length of the lens, and glasses are needed to focus a clear image on the retina. Degenerative myopia seems to be due not, as Constance and her friends thought, to straining the eyes by working in poor light, but to a congenital weakness of the tissues supporting the retina. Under pressure from the vitreous humour inside the eye these tissues may stretch. This can cause the retina to split, sometimes also with haemorrhages impairing the vision, and in severe cases the eye bulges outward, increasing the axial length and making it even more myopic. Constance seems to have suffered lesions of the retina, perhaps with haemorrhages. With her vision deteriorating, her eyestrain became worse. She was 'strictly forbidden all reading and writing',[58] so she tried writing without looking at the paper, but the lines would stray and become entangled with one another. So she tried to teach herself to use a typewriter 'without looking at the letters'.[59]

Her typewritten letters to her father-in-law, with their faltering margins, their frequent mistakes and their envelopes addressed in David's childish hand are an eloquent testimony to her plight. Then after four months with little hope of ever being able to use her eyes again she wrote – still with the typewriter:

I cannot tell you how inspirited I feel at the hopes Mr Fleming gives me for the future. He tells me that he feels confident of my being able to use my eyes in time, not as freely as in the past but still to use them for reading without danger of injury. Meanwhile I must give them complete rest and wear blue spectacles for many months, perhaps for a year. I know how you will rejoice at this good report. I can hardly believe in it yet. I had so thoroughly schooled myself into resignation into the inevitable, as I suppose loss of sight, that I can scarcely credit my own happiness.[60]

Fortunately she had managed to complete *War and Peace* before her eyes broke down. Galsworthy sent her his 'warmest congratulations' on having done so at the beginning of April,[61] but the manuscript can hardly have been ready for press, for Heinemann, who had earlier been so impatient, did not bring it out for another eighteen months. For any revision she must have relied on Fanny's eyes. Checking the proofs was the worst problem. She could not read them herself, and the job was skimped.[62]

Nevertheless, when she came to look back on her work at the end of her life she said, 'I should like to be judged by my translation of Tolstoy's *War and Peace*'. She did not explain her choice, which was an unexpected one, since she added, 'Tolstoy's simple style goes straight into English without any trouble. There's no difficulty.'[63] She always maintained that Tolstoy was 'the easiest author going. I could translate him in my sleep.'[64] A Russian friend of hers has told how when reading Constance's translation of *Anna Karenin* 'once I had started I forgot which language I was reading it in, English or Russian'.[65]

When Constance's translation of *Anna Karenin* came out a reviewer in *Blackwood's* was disappointed to find the style of the translation so inferior to that of Turgenev. Upon which Constance commented that, while she had spent far longer over every page of Turgenev,

I could never feel that I had done justice to the original, while I really think the English version of Anna is clearer and more free from glaring defects of style than the Russian original. So at least Fanny Stepniak has often declared when we have been reading my translation together. Tolstoy makes no attempt to write good Russian – and more than that – he seems wilfully to go out of his way at times in not doing so. Though of course he does write here and there wonderful passages, especially in conversations, where one feels no word could be changed without loss.[66]

In view of these remarks it is interesting that Henry Gifford, who has made a detailed comparative study of the better translations of Tolstoy should commend her for 'her refusal to tamper with Tolstoy's syntax',[67] and because 'she would accept the angularities and not shrink from his repetitions. . . . She has reproduced his mannerism, and yet contrives to write an English that does not seem uncouth or defiant, as a literal translation without her modest harmonies probably would.' [68]

Constance's chief rivals were the Maudes, though contrary to her expectations they did not bring out their translation of *War and Peace* until 1922–3. Professor Gifford writes:

Aylmer Maude and his wife were qualified in everything except a creative sense of language to make the ideal translation. They had lived long in Russia (Louise Maude was born there); they knew Tolstoy intimately, and Aylmer Maude understood, and appraised with an independent mind, the ideas and aims of Tolstoy. Also, as he tells us, they kept each a vigilant eye on the other's performance. The result is a lucid and accurate version, at home with the peculiarities of Russian life, and written in the serviceable prosaic English of the kind we associate with Mark Rutherford or Gissing.[69]

They knew Russian better than Constance, who had never lived in the country, nor even learned to speak the language naturally or to write it with confidence. She was apt to make slips through ignorance, and now that she was having to rely upon other people's eyes, through mishearing or misreading. Aylmer Maude went through his copy of her translation of *War and Peace* noting all her errors, most of them very slight – some of which he listed in the appendix to his *Life of Tolstoy: First Fifty Years* (1930). But she had advantages to outweigh these faults. She had that sensitivity to the 'flavour' of words remarked on in her versions of Turgenev, as Professor Gifford shows in his comments on her translation of *Anna Karenin*:

The appeal of Constance Garnett consists in her sensibility. She can write with a delicacy of touch which the Maudes, for all their diligence and good sense, seldom achieve. This shows particularly when she hits on some phrase so apt as to seem definitive.[70]

He instances Princess Betsy Tverskoy's remark to Anna when she is making fun of Countess Lidia Ivanovna's coterie: '"When I am old and ugly I'll be the same", Betsy used to say, "but for a pretty young woman like you *it's early days for that house of charity*".'[71] Professor Gifford adds:

Again it seems right that the exclamation used by both Anna and Vronsky in the distress that follows the consummating of their love, *radi Boga*, should be rendered as 'for pity's sake' (II.11); and that (earlier) Anna on seeing her husband at the station in St Petersburg should have found herself saying: 'Oh, mercy! why do his ears look like that?' (I.30). Mrs Garnett muddles at least one of those utterances from Fyodor after the threshing scenes which matter so much to Levin (VIII.11); but his final remark comes over in her version with a naturalness not approached here by the Maudes. They put it stiffly: 'Take you, for instance, you won't injure anyone either. . . .' Constance Garnett overlooks the 'either' (*tozhe*); but she catches the rhythm of ordinary speech: 'Take you now, you wouldn't wrong a man. . . .' This translation comes alive because it is not cluttered with terms alien to a rustic vocabulary – 'for instance', 'injure' – and because there is the sanction of a traditional way of life expressed in that simple phrase 'wrong a man'. The emphasis on 'man' is correct. Fyodor several times uses the word *chelovek*. He expounds a morality in which the due relation with God ensures a proper regard for man. But the precept falls differently in the Maudes' version: it has not been realised, and the insensitivity to rhythm betrays that.[72]

A Russian scholar, T. Motyleva, who has studied the translations of *War and Peace*, similarly commends Constance for preserving Tolstoy's repetitions (Professor Gifford's 'angularities'), though she considers that she has tampered with Tolstoy's syntax more than the Maudes did. But on the whole she finds Constance's translation 'incomparably more thorough' than any that had gone before: 'She strives to translate the work of a Russian writer so that it sounds natural and fluent in English. . . .'[73]

Constance's translation should have been the definitive version of Tolstoy. But it came to an end with *War and Peace*. Heinemann's plans were disappointed and he lost money on this expensive and abortive library edition. But once he put *War and Peace* and *Anna Karenin* into a single-volume 'popular edition' in 1911 they became a profitable property, for which, of course, Constance got nothing, and they have remained almost uninterruptedly in print ever since. A new edition in the nineteen-seventies sold no less than a hundred thousand copies.[74] Nevertheless Heinemann always thought of 'his' Tolstoy translations as an unfortunate mistake, and having got the two most popular novels on his list, he was happy to relinquish the rest to his competitors.

Constance, for the moment, was in no condition to continue. It was some time before she resumed work; and she did not translate another book by Tolstoy for eighteen years. It was left to the Maudes to undertake a complete edition of his works in 1928–37. Constance's Tolstoy did not have the impact of her Turgenev, because Tolstoy had already made himself felt as one of the great writers of the world. But its influence lasted longer, and her *War and Peace* became a standard version, alongside the Maudes', where it still remains.

Tolstoy was the only one of her classic authors whom Constance had actually met, and when he died in November 1910 she remarked to Edward, 'I feel quite sad – as though some near friend were dead. There will be no one so big again in our time.'[75]

15

Russia in Summer

Having completed her work on *War and Peace* so far as her eyes would let her, Constance needed and deserved a holiday. Early in 1904 she decided that David, who would be twelve in March, was old enough to travel with her to Russia. She started teaching him Russian, which he 'learned extremely rapidly, but with little idea of grammar'.[1] They were planning to stay in Petersburg with Madame Lavrov, who had become an old friend since they first met at the Stepniaks', with Sasha Shteven, who was now married to a landowner called Yershov, and with the family of Aleksandr Ivanovich Ertel, whom they did not yet know, though he had visited England to see his friends the Kropotkins. It was Sophie Kropotkin who had arranged the invitation.

This was a very different journey from Constance's adventure as Stepniak's emissary ten years earlier. It was governed by two important promises: Constance had promised her father-in-law, 'I will be very careful that not a word of criticism shall be heard from David or me that could wound the most sensitively patriotic and orthodox ears in Russia'.[2]

This was especially necessary in time of war. Russia and Japan had for some time been engaged in a scramble to carve up what they could of China. The Emperor had been encouraged to go to war by V. K. Plehve, the Minister of the Interior – the nearest thing to a prime minister that was then possible under the Autocracy – who hoped that a victory on the other side of the globe might arouse the same kind of jingoism as the Boer War had done in Britain and so unite the people behind the Tsar and make them forget their grievances. On 4 February 1904 the Japanese, as is their wont, made a pre-emptive strike on Port Arthur, the Russian Pacific naval base, and proceeded to besiege it. The British were supporting Japan to the extent of being committed to coming in on the Japanese side if the French were to come in on the Russian.

Fortunately it did not come to that, but British travellers in Russia might well encounter some hostility.

Edward, mindful of having had typhoid, had other anxieties, and David had promised him that he would drink no water that had not been thoroughly boiled.

They travelled by sea on a Finnish ship, the *Polaris*, which was full of Finnish emigrants returning in steerage from America. She sailed from Hull on 11 May, and for the first twenty-four hours Constance and David were both too seasick even to undress. But, as soon as he was well enough to write, David, who took his duties as an ethnographer seriously, sent a letter to his father:

The sailors all have lovely Finnish knives. The sailors are almost all Finns and are a round headed type with hair like faded flax and are always trying to play practical jokes on one another.

The people of hull talk a different dialect, as if they had no teeth. They are a long headed type quite different from the Kentish people and have weasel eyes.[3]

The ship docked at Helsingfors, which was then in the Russian empire and subject to a policy of Russification. David bought himself a Finnish knife, and some oranges and apples, proudly doing his shopping in Russian from a Finn who knew less Russian than he did.

From Helsingfors they went on by train, where David nearly fainted from the fug, and reached St Petersburg on the 16th. David enjoyed himself there, and greatly appreciated the excellent Russian food. He saw 'a fashionable lady driving down the Nevsky Prospekt, in an open troika with an enormous bearded coachman on the box, while beside her on the seat of the carriage was a large bear cub, about half-grown'.[4] There was also a bear, or rather a bear's skin, on the floor at Madame Lavrov's, which so obsessed him that he stole one of its claws. But his chief impression was of soldiers in uniform.

The streets were thick with officers in white blouses, peaked caps and epaulettes, high boots of Russian leather, jingling spurs, sabres worn in the Russian manner, back to front, and rolled grey overcoats worn slung round the body like bandoliers. There were Cossacks, Circassians, Generals of enormous size, military of all arms and all ranks, and the saluting was incessant.[5]

Constance, however, wrote:

It is very pleasant to find none of those vulgar manifestations of Jingo feeling here, such as one saw all over London during the war. One can see there is patriotic feeling, and much gloom, but it does not take the offensive form it took with us. There is no doubt that all classes are very sad, so different from the strange indifference we saw in the British public at the time of our 'reverses'.[6]

The Russian 'reverses' consisted in the humiliation of having their great Pacific fleet sunk, scattered or bottled up in Port Arthur by an enemy they had hitherto despised, while on land the war had not produced significant victories on either side. Plehve's policy was not working.

Constance and David had hardly arrived in St Petersburg when all their plans were altered, as Constance wrote to Edward:

Alas! a letter was waiting for me at Zina's from Sasha! Her little girl has got typhus – she calls it. . . . Of course this upsets all our plans. . . . I could not go to Sasha while she is in such anxiety even if there were not a question of infection to consider. . . . What do you think? Should I arrange to go from Moscow to Madame Ertel as we are free to do? . . . Don't be anxious about us, my dear little Edward. If you knew how I feel the responsibility here every moment of the boy, you would not be afraid of my doing anything silly.[7]

Edward could not have been more anxious than Constance was herself. She wrote to him endlessly about the dangers to David's health, the exact nature of Sasha's daughter's disease and the need for boiled water. Fortunately there was almost always a samovar boiling on the table. 'Of course he must not touch raw fruit (such as strawberries) growing in the ground nor salad either. But there are always plenty of delicious little cucumbers which are quite safe when peeled.'[8]

In Moscow they were met by Madame Pogosky, who was planning to start a shop for Russian peasant industries in London, and by her son Leo. 'I think she is such a fine woman and doing such a splendid work. We can't judge how good a work it is in England, because it is so much more valuable and more difficult in Russia.'[9]

After a week in Moscow they took the slow train journey to Morshansk, half a day's drive from Khludovo, where the Ertels lived. The railways were encumbered with trains full of horses and hay and troops. David stared at the faces – gay, bored, friendly, sullen – of soldiers being shifted 'thousands of miles in cattle-trucks on a slow journey to the slaughterhouse'.[10]

Their host at Khludovo, Aleksandr Ivanovich Ertel, was 'a big man, rather aloof and Olympian in manner . . . with humorous eyes and a sparse beard, wearing a blue flannel suit with a chalk stripe, polished top boots and a broad brimmed hat'.[11] Ertel's grandfather, Constance wrote, was a German soldier of Napoleon's army – taken prisoner – and his father was almost, if not quite a peasant. It is wonderful how peasants rise in Russia – when once they get a start. I suppose it is his mixture of German blood that gives him his reputation of being such a first-rate administrator of the estates he manages.[12]

Ertel had worked with peasants on his father's farm, but his attempts to run one of his own had been a disaster, and he had nearly starved to death. He had become involved with 'advanced circles' and had, like Constance's other Russian friends, been imprisoned in the Peter-Paul fortress and suffered exile. He had corresponded with Chekhov and written a novel, *The Gardenin Family*, which Tolstoy had read at a sitting. But it was only when he took up estate managing that he was successful. Now he looked after an area as big as England scattered in a number of estates across Russia. Though he shared some of Tolstoy's views, he wrote: 'to distribute one's property among beggars is not the whole truth. It is also necessary to preserve all that is good in myself and in my children: knowledge, culture, a whole number of truly valuable habits, most of which require not theoretical but *hereditary* transmission.'[13]

The other members of his household were Marya Vasilievna, who had been living with him as his wife for the past nineteen years (they could not marry because of his earlier marriage) and their two daughters. Natalie (Natasha or Tata) was seventeen, and Elena (Lolya) had her fifteenth birthday while the Garnetts were at Khludovo. Constance thought Natalie was cleverer than any girl of her age that she had ever met, 'so clever that she has always been treated as though intellectually grown up since she was about ten years old'.[14] David wrote of her: 'She had a keen, indeed brilliant, intellect, rather sphinx-like features and a considerable sense of humour – a very remarkable young woman.'[15] Lolya 'was a warmhearted, impulsive and eager girl, but she was of softer material than Natasha'.[16]

Besides these two daughters they had living with them Elena Grigori-evna Goncharova (Lenochka), 'the most conventionally beautiful of the three, taller, with a willowy figure, and beautiful large grey eyes with dark eyebrows and lashes and dark hair'.[17] She was not above flirting with a boy of twelve. There was also a delightful old babushka, who was actually Ertel's aunt; then there were Miss Haslam, the English governess, and a young man, a foundling, named Kirik Levin after the character in *Anna Karenin*. He had come into the family in a strange way some twenty years previously. Ertel was driving a sledge one winter's night through freshly fallen snow. 'Suddenly they felt a bump and Alexandr Ivanitch called to his driver to stop. They got out and found the runner of the sledge had touched a bundle of clothes. He picked it up and found a baby boy, who turned out to be none the worse for the adventure.'[18] Ertel had him brought up by a village woman and sent to the village school, where he did so well that he was employed in the estate office and then sent to Moscow University, where he later became a lecturer in ancient history.

During their stay at Khludovo Constance and David were lodged happily in a little log house in the garden, with a large square 'raised platform', or rather a veranda, where Constance sat writing

in the midst of such an uproar of birds as I have never heard in my life. All of them are going to bed and the little singing birds seem to shrill their loudest that their sound may not be quite drowned in the tumult made by the multitudes of rooks. Now and then the shriek of the merlin is heard, and that makes all the others louder than ever.[19]

The food was always abundant and delicious at the Ertels', and Constance felt herself 'in danger of getting too fat and David of getting spoiled'.[20] He recalled a dinner party, at which

The soup was accompanied by little pies, always filled with delicious and unexpected delicacies – minced cockscombs, sweetbreads, mushrooms and sour cream. Then there was caviare in large dishes and hot toast; an enormous fish with wood mushrooms; a couple of roast sucking pigs, stuffed with buckwheat kasha, which drank up the fat; new peas, thin pancakes with sharp cranberry sauce and thick layers of sour cream, and lastly a vast ice pudding, stuffed with grated pistachio nuts and fragments of candied peel and angelica. . . .[21]

Every morning David had his lessons. He would write a Russian exercise for Marya Vasilievna and translate half a page of 'very simple'[22] Tolstoy for his mother, while she wrote a letter, did a little work or knitted beside him. In the afternoon Marya Vasilievna improved her English by reading *Vanity Fair* aloud to Constance, who was still under strict injunctions to rest her eyes, though she could not help 'thinking my eyes are really better',[23] but did not dare to reckon on it till she had seen the oculist again. She still abstained from reading and sewing, but wrote endless affectionate letters home, usually including a loving message for Nellie, and was able to use a sewing-machine to run up shirts for men at the front.

When David's lessons were over he was free, and in his element. Ertel gave orders that he should have a pony, and he was provided with

Moochen, a little wall-eyed bay, and a Russian saddle, 'a heavy affair with a wooden frame and a leather cushion behind and in front between wooden pommels. It is far easier to stick on a horse on a Russian saddle, because little balance is required.'[24] On wet days he spent his afternoons in the stables with the men. On fine days he went out on Moochen:

I very quickly learnt to ride [he wrote], and after a few days was allowed to venture out alone. I soon found there were large herds of horses a mile or two away, in [the] charge of boys of my own age. . . . For most of the day the herd-boys rode slowly round the grazing herds, but at midday one of them made a fire and cooked a meal. . . . When the meal was ready, the boy who had cooked it waved his arms and shouted, and the others rode up and slid off their bare-backed ponies. For only one or two had saddles; the others had long loops of cloth made like a roller towel, flung over the back of the horse, in the ends of which they thrust their bare feet. Thus they had stirrups without a saddle. The ponies were tied to willow trees near the fire, and then all the boys stood in a circle and crossed themselves and bowed their heads in prayer before they unfastened wooden spoons hanging from the string tied round the waist, and sat down to eat their meal. I immediately made friends with them, helped the cook to make the fire, stirred the pot, and then crossed myself before I sat down with them.

At first I was required to go back to the house for a late luncheon, but soon I obtained permission to join the peasant boys, and sometimes was able to take them some butter or oil to put in their kasha. But there was no begging on their part and no calculation that I should bring my share. Before the cruel mockery of Marxian Communism, there was religious communism among the peasants of Great Russia. Several times while we were eating, some passer-by came along and one of the boys would always get up and call out an invitation. . . .

They all wore a string with a cross hanging down round their necks under their Russian shirts. . . . The older ones wore lapti, shoes woven of willow bark, and fastened with cross-garterings of string or linen; the younger ones were barefoot. Most of them were bare-headed and had thick mops of hair, trimmed occasionally with a pudding basin. I picked up lice in my hair from them but learned something of primitive Christianity, a most moving and beautiful religion to see practised. I have never come across it since.[25]

David had other excitements: he was given a knout, 'a lovely thing. . . . All the people who take care of horses have them';[26] he made great friends with a groom called Nikita, whose wife embroidered him a red Russian shirt; and he had one alarming adventure: 'On Friday on his way home his horse shied at some rag fluttering at the crossroads and he was thrown off – luckily not hurt at all. The pony bolted home to the great alarm of the stable men – who came flying out on horseback to look for him. He lost a shoe, which has not yet been found.'[27]

While they were at Khludovo the proclamation of mobilisation arrived – an awful calamity for the village, as Constance explained:

The proclamation arrived at 3 o'clock in the night on Sunday and on Wednesday morning early 40 men from the village and 6 from the estate were marched off followed by the whole village, weeping and mourning as though at a funeral. . . .

Only a few men go from the estate, because most of them come from other districts, where mobilization has not been proclaimed; but among them is Ivan Ivanitch, the head machinist, who is loved by everyone and is one of the most valuable men. Ertel is much distressed at losing him. It seems a pity that the men are raised by districts, so that all the men available in certain places are taken and no men in other places. This leads to so much suffering – 5 families are left in the village with no labourer only women and children and old people. The Zemstvo makes them an allowance of flour, but this does not go far.

Horses too are commandeered both from the village and the estate, and 98 have been taken. This means a loss, for the price given is not what would have been got later from private purchase. David was delighted that his beloved little Moochen was at first refused, but alas! they found they had not got enough, and the poor little pony went off to Morshansk again last night to be reconsidered.

I wish the people who are urging compulsory military service at home could see what it means in practice.[28]

Fortunately for David his pony was reprieved at the last minute and he was able to go on riding with the herd-boys. Constance took him to a meeting of the Mir (the name, which also means 'world' and 'peace', for the village community):

The cases were chiefly family quarrels. A widow brought an action against her brother-in-law, who had taken her field, and the aggressor raised a laugh by exclaiming: 'Why does she want the field? She's got no cattle but a cat.' The village elders decided that the brother-in-law should continue in possession of the field, but must pay her a fixed sum in rent, or half the crop.

A more serious charge of malicious wounding was reported to the District Commissioner, with a request for the exile of the offender.[29]

Ertel had 'a knack of picking up the best and most capable men' all 'sober, honest and clever and good-tempered'.[30] He was liked and obeyed and would have 'no drinking or irregularity of any sort'.[31] But Constance thought that the other peasants in the Tambov province were 'an exceptionally degraded lot'.[32]

At a recent wedding three women drank themselves to death, and such deaths from drink are they say not uncommon. A poor peasant family will spend over £10 on a wedding – about half the money on vodka – getting into debt and starving for years afterwards. They tell me awful stories of the way the men treat their wives. The poor creatures are always coming to Madame Ertel for help – and now she is hated by the peasants because she has often succeeded in getting the women passports so that they could leave their husbands and go away. They regard beating their wives as a natural right and say they will soon have no women left, threaten to murder her for interfering.[33]

After nearly a month with the Ertels Constance thought it safe to go and stay with Sasha Yershov. They set out at two o'clock on the morning of 28 June. The drive to the station before dawn was glorious, but it took them all the rest of the day in third-class carriages to reach Volovo. Although Sasha's daughter had recovered, she was now smitten with a new crisis. Her mother-in-law, who lived in St Petersburg, had had two strokes, and was seriously ill. Yershov could not stay with her because his manager had been taken for the war, and he had to come back and look after the estate himself. David recalled him as 'a small fat man of yellow complexion, somewhat like a Mongol Napoleon in appearance. He never smiled, and his conversation consisted of statements which it was unwise to challenge.'[34] Sasha was 'most warm and sweet' and 'quite won David's heart',[35] but her husband could hardly have been more disagreeable. He was so reluctant to have guests that he would not at first send a carriage to meet them, and only later relented.

They were lodged in the schoolmistress's house, where they were kept awake by bedbugs and the lack of proper curtains until David managed to nail up some rugs. Constance 'felt uneasy and oppressed all these days from the sense of insecurity and the impossibility of getting to bed much before midnight, of getting enough boiled water for David who was always thirsty and kept his promise to you heroically'.[36] One day they got nothing to eat until nearly four o'clock except 'almost uneatable bread'.[37] The food was covered with flies, and when Yershov asked Constance whether they had as many flies in England she tactfully replied, 'No, but we have plagues of wasps.'[38]

Constance was impressed by the local peasants, who were much handsomer, cleaner and more prosperous than those in the Tambov province, and most beautifully dressed. She bought a dress from one of them. 'Every thread in it had been grown as hemp or flax, retted, spun, dyed and woven by the woman from whom she bought it. The only parts not home-grown were the buttons and the gold and silver thread used in embroidery.'[39]

But the peasants seemed to be afraid of Yershov, and Constance and David were glad when they could return to the 'peace, regularity and comfort'[40] of Khludovo, 'a quiet easy journey with a whole sofa each in [a] rather empty 2nd class carriage'.[41] It was the first time they had been so extravagant, but Constance considered the 'extra 8 or ten shillings fully worth it when we are both a little exhausted'.[42] David was weighed on his return and found to have lost five pounds.[43] It was, as Constance said, a great mercy that the original plan of spending two or three months with Sasha fell through.

Constance told Edward, 'There is so much to tell about our visit to Sasha and most of it I cannot write about.'[44] One of these proscribed subjects was probably Tolstoy. He had been excommunicated in 1901, and all mention of him in the press was forbidden. He further exasperated the authorities by issuing, in that summer of 1904, a manifesto in which he said that it was the duty of every Russian, soldier or civilian, to refuse to take part in the war.[45]

David later wrote that Constance had greatly hoped to visit the Tolstoys at Yasnaya Polyana, which was less than twenty miles from the Yershovs' estate, but 'Yershov could not endure Tolstoy's name to be mentioned and would not have allowed us a carriage to go there.'[46] Tolstoy was much on Constance's mind, but she was careful not to mention him by name in letters that might be opened. Although she had completed the translation of *War and Peace* before she set out for Russia, it had not yet come out and she was anxious about its reception. She wrote to Edward, '*Don't* for goodness' sake put in any note about the proofs not having been properly corrected',[47] and later,

I have found here a portrait of the 'capricious old toad' in middle age – a photograph quite new to me – and I think it very interesting – it is the carnal man as distinguished from the spiritual old man and the idealistic youth. . . . I think it might suit Heinemann to use it as frontispiece for 'War and Peace'.[48]

But *War and Peace* was published without a frontispiece, so the photograph cannot be identified.

Even in the peace and comfort of Khludovo they could not avoid the outside world. The Tsar had been dissuaded by his uncles from placing himself at the head of his armies in the East. 'Instead Nicholas toured military encampments, reviewing troops and passing out images of St. Seraphim to soldiers about to entrain for the Far East.'[49] In due course he arrived at Morshansk. On 7 July a 'smart official in a grand uniform' arrived at Khludovo 'to ask what carriages we could provide for the Tsar's suite'.[50]

Our coachman – a delightful man [Constance wrote] had gone already . . . with the best 'koliaska' and the three splendid black horses. From his face I imagine it is the proudest day of his life – his pleasure only perhaps a trifle dashed by a consciousness of one or two shabby places in the 'koliaska' and of his own cap not being quite new and up to the level of his red silk shirt and splendid metal belt and black velvet sleeveless jacket.

It was suggested to take David and Lyola to Morshansk to see the Tsar tomorrow, but it would have meant sleeping there two nights in a great crush and much fatigue – so I decided against the boy's going.[51]

It was perhaps as well that David did not go, for on the way home the coachman 'got drunk and . . . returned with two of the best horses lame and one of the carriages slightly damaged . . . there was a most frightful row and it went on for some days'.[52]

About a fortnight after their return to Khludovo, Constance fell ill, owing, she believed, to having drunk kvass made from unboiled water while she was with the Yershovs. It was not typhoid, but an infection variously described as gastric influenza or enteritis. She had violent diarrhoea, headache and fever and could take no solid food. Other women on the estate had been similarly afflicted, but not so seriously. 'They are certainly a tough people. The mosquitoes don't bite them, the stinging nettles don't sting them and the microbes haven't the same chance.'[53] David looked after his mother:

for 5 nights he has got up once in the night to warm up milk or broth for me. He seems very well and bright still and not a bit worn out. Only one day – last Friday – when I was so very ill and feverish and almost fainting with pain, he was rather frightened and touched me very much by the way he slaved away all day, fetching and carrying and never left the platform. But next day as soon as I was myself again he was quite reassured and happy in his gorgeous new shirt. He is a strange and happy mixture of childishness and wisdom and common sense.[54]

Edward sent a telegram which arrived as 'Don't dravel till well', and Constance delayed her departure. While she was recuperating 'a gentleman coming from Moscow on business to see Alexandr Ivanitch' brought some 'astounding news'.[55] As David described it:

One day when we were returning from a walk in the park with Alexandr Ivanitch, Maria Vassilievna, Natasha and Lenotchka, we were met by Lola, her face lit up with joyous excitement. Clapping her hands, she cried out: 'What do you think has happened! Plehve has been assassinated!' Wild excitement followed among all those present, who would have greeted the news of an overwhelming victory over the Japanese enemy with comparative indifference. But, though

217

steeped in revolutionary ideas, Constance was somewhat taken aback by the unquestioning delight with which a young girl announced the murder of the Prime Minister of her country.[56]

In writing to Edward she was scrupulously non-committal, and merely said that the assassination 'produced an immense sensation, as you can imagine'.[57] Edward Crankshaw wrote of Plehve's twenty-three years in office, 'It is hard to think of a single beneficent action performed by him.'[58] He was 'the second Minister of the Interior to be picked off in two years'.[59] The bomb which killed him was thrown by a Socialist Revolutionary student called Sazonov, but, such were the treacherous complexities of Russian politics, the organiser of the murder was none other than Yevno Azev, 'the police agent employed by Plehve himself to infiltrate the revolutionaries'.[60]

At Khludovo everyone was 'very sweet'[61] to Constance, persuading her to stay on a few days longer. Every day she felt a little stronger. Eventually they left on 6 August.

We felt so sad at parting from everyone yesterday. The boy shed a few tears when he said goodbye to the men and lads in the stables and one or two of them cried too he told me. But now with the journey and the excitement of a concertina one of them gave him and all the responsibility of getting hot water and food at the station he has quite recovered his spirits.[62]

All the same it was a tedious journey. The train was three hours late starting, and they had a further three hours to wait when they changed at Ryazhsk. Sybil Rudall, who had come to Russia, much as Olive had done, had to wait six hours for them at the station in Moscow.

From Moscow they paid a brief visit to Madame Linev, who lived nearby and whose collection of Russian folk songs Fanny and Constance had translated into English, so that they could work on proofs together.[63]

Before they could leave Russia their passports had to be stamped with an authorisation to do so. The dvornik who was supposed to arrange it got drunk instead. Constance had to go to the police station, where she was 'admonished for coming in person at the wrong hour instead of sending the dvornik – we should have waited till he was sober'.[64] But they got their permits.

They returned home overland. When they reached Warsaw on 12 April they had to drive across the city from one railway station to another. They found 'the whole town brilliantly illuminated and a prodigious firework display in progress along the banks of the Vistula. . . . Constance learned from a Russian guard at the railway station that a Tsarevitch had just been born, the heir to the Empire of all the Russias.'[65]

There was little else to celebrate. On the same day that Constance and David had set out from Moscow the Russian fleet attempted to break out of Port Arthur and engage the Japanese in a major action. It was soundly defeated. The land battles dragged on, consuming vast numbers of men and getting no nearer to relieving Port Arthur. The scale was enormous. At Mukden in February 1905 six hundred thousand men were engaged in a savage battle for a week. The Russians lost ninety thousand men and countless wounded. Their Pacific fleet was largely out of action. Their Black Sea fleet was disaffected and prohibited by treaty from passing out through the Dardanelles. In October 1904 the Baltic fleet set off half way round the world to teach the Japanese a lesson. It had reached no further than the North Sea when it mistook some British fishing boats for Japanese submarines and sank one and killed two sailors. For a moment it looked like war with Britain. In Madagascar the fleet stopped to refuel. There it received the news that Port Arthur had fallen. After much delay it sailed on, only to be blasted out of the water by the Japanese on 27 May 1905. The war was finally brought to an end in August.

It was fortunate that Constance had not chosen to travel to Russia in that turbulent year of 1905 which was afflicted with much else besides the war.

'What is going on in Petersburg to-day?' Olive asked in her diary on Sunday 22 January. She had reason to be anxious. A strike in the Putilov steel works had grown into an enormous, but loyal, demonstration of workers who planned to march on that day to the Winter Palace and present a petition of their grievances to their 'Little Father', the Tsar. Two hundred thousand people in five shambling columns headed for Palace Square, unarmed and singing hymns, holding up holy icons, banners and portraits of the Tsar. But before they could reach him they were mown down by the guns of his soldiery. Ninety-six people were killed and over three hundred wounded. As Crankshaw has caustically observed: 'A monarch cannot allow his personal guards to shoot down in droves in front of his own house an unarmed assembly of working-men, to say nothing of harmless onlookers, and continue to be revered as the source of all wisdom and kindness.'[66] But the Tsar did not see it like that. He refused to blame any of his soldiers. The Holy Synod went out of its way to exonerate the authorities. Ertel was disgusted. He felt that the government was deliberately trying to prevent any possibility of peaceful reform, and thus making certain that there would be a revolution as violent as France in the days of the guillotine. 'And it is being greatly assisted by the nasty, base, ignorant and stupid orthodox clergy . . . arousing hatred, sowing the seeds of suspicion, blatantly distorting the whole point and motives of the movement – wasn't it the very same thing that caused the red terror in 1792, and the white terror during the restoration?'[67]

Less than a month after Bloody Sunday the Tsar's uncle, Grand Duke Sergey, the much-hated commander-in-chief of the military district of Moscow, was assassinated. Once again this had been organised by the double-agent, Yevno Azev, who had been responsible for the death of Plehve; and the Ertels took the news in much the same way. Aleksandr Ivanovich wrote to Natalie: 'There cannot be many people who will feel any regret; he was a hard-hearted, stupid and ridiculous man.'[68] The Tsar, however, took it hard, and the court were alarmed. He could no longer show himself to his people, and was effectively imprisoned in Tsarskoe Selo and Peterhof, or on the royal yacht.

Throughout 1905 there were strikes and serious disorder. The railways, which Constance had come to know so well, were paralysed; and this grew to a general strike. Workers organised themselves for the first time into *soviets*, or councils. Soldiers and sailors mutinied. Universities were closed, and students preached revolution. Natalie, at St Petersburg, found her lectures 'blockaded'. Peasants seized land and withheld taxes, and sometimes rioted and attacked their landlords, more from personal grievance than for political rights. They set fire to Yershov's house, but left Ertel in peace.

On 30 October the Tsar was at last prevailed to accept a Duma, or constituent assembly. But he made sure that he still had the last word. Leon Trotsky, who, unlike Lenin and the other exiled revolutionaries, had returned to Russia to take part in the uprising, wrote:

Freedom of assembly is granted, but the assemblies are surrounded by the military. Freedom of speech is granted, but censorship exists as before. Freedom of knowledge is granted, but the universities are occupied by troops. Inviolability of the person is granted, but the prisons are overflowing. . . . A constitution is given, but the autocracy remains. Everything is given – and nothing is given.[69]

But the process of change had begun. It could only be delayed. It could no longer be stopped.

16

Bad Eyes and Good Friends

Constance and David returned to England on 13 August 1904. She had no translation to do, and her eyes were still not fit for her to do it on her own. The oculist told her:

the inflammation has practically subsided and the scars have healed; but he advises great care – in fact using my eyes as little as possible for the next two years – after which I may reckon on a steady improvement year by year, as the change towards greater length of sight that takes place about forty-five will be a continual gain to my eyes.[1]

Three months later her progress with reading was still slow.

She had planned to move to London so that David could go to a day school there and she could help 'push him on in his school work',[2] but she was in no hurry to do so. She took her time finding a flat and equipping it. Meanwhile she continued to teach David herself, and Pat Clayton, Kate's son, came to share in lessons. In the summer of 1905 David camped in the woods. Besides the Olivier girls, he had as companions Hermine and Michel, the children of Auguste and Louise Bréal, who had been living nearby from 1899 to 1902. The children imagined themselves Red Indians and had 'a most enjoyable month'[3] as they roamed the Chart Woods, built a hut, where they could cook and sleep, and plundered a gamekeeper's gibbets for their anatomical collections.

Just as her eyes were beginning to recover Constance suffered a relapse of her 'internal troubles'. In June 1905 she reported to Dr Garnett from the Cearne:

I am going on very well, but there is no idea of my getting out of my room this week. The nurse, who has had experience of several such cases of internal inflammation tells me several weeks of rest in a recumbent position are usually necessary to ensure a complete cure. . . . So I must be content to be patient. . . . I lie in a very pleasant room near the open window with the roses looking in, and enjoy the rest and freedom from pain. I can read and sew and give

David some of his lessons. Possibly next week if it is dry and warm I may be able to be on a couch in the garden for a little time.[4]

The summer of 1905 was a critical time in the Garnetts' relations with the Galsworthys. When Edward read the manuscript of *The Man of Property* in May he took exception to Bosinney's suicide. He did not think it credible that any man should kill himself because his beloved had been raped by the husband she hated. Edward was the more opposed to it, David believed, because Bosinney's character was based on his own. The argument rumbled on through June and July. Constance wrote to Galsworthy endorsing Edward's views, and he replied with characteristic generosity:

And first please think that we have both of us only increased affection and admiration for you both. I think it is one of the very hardest things to honestly criticize the work of those of whom we are fond; but it is what one expects and longs for from true friendship – and every time the courage is found makes the link stronger.[5]

When Constance read the book in its final form she wrote to him:

I have enjoyed it immensely – it gains much by being seen as a whole. The mass of detail seems to fall into harmony and relevance, and every point does its share in filling in the picture. I still think – as at first – that Irene is the finest piece of work in the book. I admire the self-restraint with which you treat her – you give her no single exceptional endowment, except a beautiful figure. I don't quite know *how* you make her so irresistibly charming. I feel a childish regret at not having more of Irene and Bosinney; it is like stepping out of a suffocating drawing-room into the sunlight, when one has a glimpse of them. The book ought to be a great success, but who can tell? We can only pray.[6]

It was indeed by far the most successful of Galsworthy's books to date, was well reviewed and sold five thousand copies.[7]

Constance and David migrated to London in the summer of 1905. She took a flat at 19 Grove Place in Hampstead, and by August she was well enough to spend her time with Olive's help cleaning and polishing their new home. On 18 September David started going to University College School in Gower Street. He was not happy there, and lived for the weekends at the Cearne. His nature notebook is full of observations of the life in the Chart Woods and the progress of his bees. As Edward wrote to Galsworthy, 'David . . . reminds me extraordinarily of what I was at 13. . . . He is interested in *everything*, and never *does* anything!'[8]

There was now no question of letting the Cearne. It was still the focus of the Garnetts 'social life, and where they had their friends to stay.

There they held an exhibition of thirty-five of Nellie's pictures, 'a most charming collection',[9] and there they entertained Madame Pogosky who had come over 'to open an exhibition for the sale of the production of the peasant industries' of Vologda.[10]

By October Constance was used to her new way of life and 'comfortably settled' in London with 'friends all round us'.[11] The Garnetts at Tanza Road were not far off. Ernest and Dollie Radford were at 1 Portland Villas in East Heath Road with their three children, Maitland, Hester and Margaret, in a small house with the rooms piled one above the other. It was

always overflowing with people. Dollie and Ernest had multitudes of friends and so had children. . . . it was seldom that the family sat down to a meal without laying one or two extra places for friends who had dropped in or had to stay on because they were in the middle of an aesthetic discussion which could not be interrupted.[12]

They could ill afford this hospitality. Dollie was 'hopelessly impractical in business matters'.[13] Ernest, after his breakdown, was now 'a heavy, tired man, rather corpulent, going bald and with a noble forehead',[14] still with a fine brain but 'only half awake'.[15] His occasional lectures cannot have earned much; the Radfords were always short of money and were forever being bailed out by Ernest's more businesslike brothers. Their financial straits were exacerbated by the cost of educating Maitland. He was a variously gifted young man. 'He could ride a horse, sail a boat, speak well in public and set the company in a roar of laughter. He might have been one of the young men to whom, in Lord Birkenhead's words, the world offered a host of glittering prizes.'[16] But he was set upon becoming a doctor, despite constantly failing his examinations. He was eight years older than David, who liked and admired him immensely. Margaret, who looked like 'a stained glass saint by Burne Jones',[17] was 'half an angel and half a changeling, and altogether a child',[18] and so less and less able to cope with the real world.

David – and less frequently Constance – went to the Radfords' for play-readings, the giving of papers and talks, and for conversation, such as David at sixteen described: 'all the family were very skittish as they sometimes are (the dears!) . . . Hester, Margaret and Maitland abusing each other finely. They also discussed a friend who I long to see as they left her no virtues or appearances from the kindest of motives.'[19] Constance had long ago expressed her dislike of this kind of talk. She and Dollie were good friends, who were always coming to one another's help in emergencies. But she was very much less sociable than Dollie. She preferred a quiet life, and when David ran a temperature she was apt to think it was due to over-excitement, and wrote: 'He must live very quietly, just as I must.'[20]

She made new London friends, such as Ernest Rhys, founder editor of Everyman's Library, and his wife, Grace, who also lived in Hampstead and offered the same kind of literary hospitality as the Radfords. But those that she saw most of at this time were Jack and Ada Galsworthy, whom she visited at least once a week although they were at the other end of the town at 14 Addison Road, Holland Park. 'Dear Galsworthy,' Constance exclaimed, 'I feel so warmly to him. I keep thinking of his face with that wonderful sort of radiance and tenderness in it.'[21]

On 7 March 1906 Constance wrote to her father-in-law with the routine news that she had been looking after Dollie Radford, who had been ill, and that Nellie Heath was staying with them at Grove Place. Richard Garnett was now seventy-one. His health was poor and his eyesight failing. During March Olive nursed him as he grew gradually weaker. On Good Friday, 13 April, she wrote, 'Papa passed away peacefully at 5.15 this morning in the presence of Edward and Nurse Wallis.'[22] Four days later he was buried at Highgate cemetery. Constance was there, with many of his family, and a host of representatives of the literary establishment.

Richard was of an affectionate nature, and had been as fond of Constance as of any of his own children. He had been continually generous, not only paying the twelve guineas a term for David's schooling, but also with well-chosen presents, especially of books, which he picked with great expertise. Although he was slow to share the Garnetts' enthusiasm for Russian literature, he kept a constant look-out for articles and other new publications that might be useful in Constance's work. She had a far happier relationship with the gentle and learned old man than ever she had had with her own father. She would miss him greatly as a friend and as a correspondent who encouraged her to write letters worthy of his literary taste. They provide an articulate record of seventeen important years of her life and prove that she was far from being unable to write well except when translating others. Her letters to Edward – at least when she was in England – were never written with such care, and being as a rule undated and with no need to be so explicit in their references, give nothing like such a clear account of her life.

Richard's death was a financial as well as a personal loss. He left no will. His estate amounted to £450 for each of his children, and Robert and Edward gave their share to Olive, who could no longer live in Tanza Road, but had to find a new home with Arthur in Kew. Constance would have to find the money for David's schooling elsewhere.

For Edward his father's death was not only a blow but also an embarrassment. During the last couple of years the old widower had become more and more attached to Violet Neale, who had come into his life through their shared love of Shelley. He had always been susceptible to intelligent young women. But Violet was not of the same calibre as Mathilde Blind or Clementina Black – or for that matter Constance herself. Edward, a prejudiced witness, thought her 'possessed of extraordinary tenacity of purpose, terrifying self-absorption, highly neurotic and hysterical, a girl of 31'.[23] Inspired by her Richard had published in 1905 an anonymous volume of 252 aphorisms on love. He called it *De Flagello Myrteo* after a sprig of myrtle from a bush planted by Shelley, which she had sent him with a letter that Edward thought showed 'extraordinary lack of delicacy . . . and almost incredible absence of taste',[24] but which touched the old man in his bereavement. The Garnetts were somewhat embarrassed by the book and jealous of Violet Neale, whose relationship with the family was not helped by Olive 'whose cold and critical manner' Constance wrote, 'would make anyone hostile and suspicious'.[25] They were alarmed by what Edward called 'VN's genuine and absorbing desire . . . to make her relationship with RG *immortal* and she will succeed probably in making him sufficiently ridiculous. She will no doubt publish RG's letters unless stopped by the law.'[26] Robert set about invoking the law, and Constance wrote to Edward: 'What a hateful nuisance it all is! Can't you make her feel by a straightforward appeal that all you desire is to save your father's memory from scandal? Surely she too must wish that?'[27] And eventually she did.

Now that Constance was settled in London it was much easier for her to indulge her passion for serious drama. The English theatre was on the verge of what William Archer called a period of 'almost miraculous renascence'.[28] During her earlier years in London Constance had seen plays by Ibsen, Shaw and Henry James. In the summer of 1905 she had come to town with David to see Eleanora Duse in *La Dame aux Camélias* performed in Italian. The effect that Duse made on David was overwhelming: 'For those wonderful hours nothing mattered but that supremely tragic woman, and it was happiness enough to have heard that wonderful voice.'[29] David goes on to tell how: 'Afterwards in a daze, Constance and I went round to the stage door and waited for her. Across the road was another theatre, the stage door of which was surrounded by a throng of exquisitely dressed young men, in shining top hats, morning coats, striped trousers and spats.'[30] They were waiting for Gertie Millar,[31] the star of *The Spring Chicken*; but 'There were scarcely half a dozen of us waiting for the plainly dressed and tired-looking Italian woman.'[32] Both actresses came out together, so that

the first thing that Duse saw was the heroine of *The Spring Chicken*, all frills and flounces, parasol and picture hat, being fêted by an adoring throng of gilded youths on the opposite side of the street. Then she looked round and saw us and burst out laughing, waved her hand and thanked us very prettily and graciously, but when she had got into her cab and was being driven away I could see her fall back against the cushions to laugh again.[33]

Constance saw Mrs Patrick Campbell as Hedda Gabler at the Court in March 1907; and almost certainly Lydia Yavorskaya (Princess Bariatinsky) in the same part on 7 December 1909, when she brought her own company from St Petersburg, and also played, rather more convincingly, the heroine of *La Dame aux Camélias*, all in Russian. She went several times and 'so have had quite a gay week'.[34] But it is only through chance references in letters and Olive's diary that we have any record of what she saw, and hardly ever what she thought of it.

She had no practical experience of the theatre. Edward, on the other hand, though not so assiduous a playgoer, had in some respects a natural gift for the theatrical. He wrote and produced two plays for David and the Olivier girls and their friends to act at the Cearne. The first was about Robin Hood and 'fairly close to *As You Like It* in its setting'.[35] David was 'a comic Friar Tuck' with 'a bald head and a big belly',[36] and Harold Hobson was a masked executioner. The second, performed on 6 and 7 January 1904, was more ambitious and was based on the story of Dermot and Grania. Edward was an excellent producer:

He knew exactly what he wanted [David wrote] and could storm at us in pretended rage, or tease, or coax, or flatter until he got it. I was at first puzzled and then suddenly got the idea and developed into a wonderfully ribald ham actor. The result was my first personal triumph: Bernard Shaw told my mother that I was a born actor and that it would be a crime if I were not trained for the theatre. . . .[37]

But just as Edward's great critical gifts seemed to desert him when he wrote his own fiction, so his theatrical sense tended to fail him in his more ambitious plays. The most serious of his four serious plays was *The Breaking Point*, a modern problem drama. It tells how a girl is destroyed by the conflict between her elderly father and her lover. She finds herself with child, but dare not tell her father, and finally drowns herself in the river. The theme is an indictment of male egoism, such as might have been a subject for Ibsen. But it is simple, savage and direct, with none of Ibsen's strange poetry. It was, as David remarked, as if Edward were trying to punish his audience, and if well acted it would have been more than they could bear. Conrad wrote very percipiently:

I don't think, my dear fellow, you have realised the firmness of mind necessary to an audience who would face your play. . . . the play is too concentrated. It hits one exactly like a bullet. You can see it coming – I admit – but that doesn't make it easier in the least. On the contrary, it prolongs the agony and brings on that feeling of *helplessness* which I think is fatal to the effect of the play. . . . The effect is nightmarish. . . . We are flung right into the middle of a situation that is already gone *too far*.[38]

Nevertheless the play was accepted by Frederick Harrison, Manager of the Haymarket Theatre. All plays then had to pass the scrutiny of the Examiner of Plays, a retired bank manager called G. A. Redford, who acted for the Lord Chamberlain. Redford preferred not to censor plays directly, and dealt only with managers, never with authors. He took offence at the heroine's unmarried pregnancy and wrote to Harrison suggesting that he withdraw the play rather than officially submit it for a licence. But Edward was a fighter, he counter-attacked the Examiner of Plays for his immorality and his hypocrisy in allowing 'improper' subjects only if they were treated as comedy. *Lysistrata* was allowed, but *Oedipus Tyrannus* refused a licence 'perhaps because incest in the royal family might set a bad example'.[39]

Granville-Barker's *Waste* had also been censored, and it was not difficult for Edward to stir up Galsworthy, who 'went to Barrie, and with Gilbert Murray we induced all the leading authors to sign a protest written by myself'.[40] For a while it was a full-scale public row. William Archer devised a demonstration to accompany a deputation to the Prime Minister, Campbell-Bannerman:

The Dramatic Authors of England are to assemble in Trafalgar Square. Barrie will address them from the base of the Nelson column, and the Savoy orchestra will play 'Britons never will be slaves'. The procession will then form, and will be headed by Pinero and Shaw walking arm in arm. Immediately behind them will come Garnett and Galsworthy, each bearing the pole of a red banner with the inscription 'Down with the Censor!'. An effigy of Redford, which is being prepared by the Savoy property-man, will be carried by Frederick Harrison and W. B. Yeats, and over its head will wave a banner, carried by Gilbert Murray, with the inscription 'Ecrasez l'Infâme!'. Arrived in Downing Street, Swinburne will declaim an 'Ode to C.B.', and the speakers will be Ford Madox Hueffer, Desmond MacCarthy, Maarten Maartens and Ernest Rhys – dramatists who cannot be suspected of interested motives, as they have never written any plays.[41]

But, alas for this fanciful apotheosis of the liberty of the stage, the Prime Minister fell seriously ill, and they had to be content with a far more modest deputation to Herbert Gladstone, the Home Secretary. As usual a committee was set up, and as usual nothing was done. Stage censorship was not abolished until 1968.

The Breaking Point could be shown only at 'private' performances, and these were eventually provided by the Incorporated Stage Society at the Haymarket on 5 and 6 April 1908, but with a very indifferent cast. On the first night Edward and Nellie, Constance, David and Olive were all in the author's box, with Bernard Shaw and his wife in the box opposite. Arthur Garnett was in the stalls, the Radfords and the Galsworthys were there, and John Masefield came up to the Garnetts' box in the interval. It should have been a grand occasion, but for David at least it was misery.

Conrad's cruel words proved exactly true. We could see it coming, but that did not make it any easier in the least. The play hit one exactly like a bullet, and the wretched audience flinched as the ridiculous travesty of Edward's play proceeded. The agony was prolonged and the effect was nightmarish.[42]

Olive, on the other hand, thought the acting was 'conscientious, but laboured and did not often grip the audience who were interested but not moved'.[43] And two days later she reported, 'Press notices of the play all say it was dull, not at all "shocking", well acted but somehow did not "come off"'.[44]

Galsworthy fared much better. Edward had first suggested, late in 1905, that he should write for the stage. Galsworthy set to and completed *The Silver Box* in six weeks and sent a copy to Edward and Constance for their comments. Constance told Edward, 'I have read Jack's play and like it very much – it does not aim of course at artistic perfection.'[45] And Edward, as usual, wrote with more detailed criticism.[46] By April the manuscript was with Granville-Barker and Shaw, who accepted it almost by return. It opened on Tuesday 25 September at the Court Theatre, and Constance went to the first night. Four days later she wrote that she was 'only today quite recovered from the excitement'.[47] The play was an immediate success; it ran for twenty-nine performances – a long run for the Court – and the Prince and Princess of Wales came to the last night.

Galsworthy's second play, *Joy*, which opened on 24 September 1907, was a setback. The public found it 'dilatory and shapeless',[48] and it had a poor press. 'I am afraid', Constance wrote, 'Ada is very low about "Joy". She has no resisting power somehow – she simply wants it taken off at once, instead of wanting to fight.'[49] As for Galsworthy himself, with his public school upbringing, he wrote, 'Quite a pleasant thing getting a bath of cold criticism.'[50] It ran for only eight matinees.

As a result of this failure, managements were wary of his next play, *Strife*, but eventually James Barrie persuaded Charles Frohmann to run it for six matinees at the Duke of York's. Edward and Nellie, Constance and David all went to the first performance, which happened to fall on David's seventeenth birthday, and Constance was a little fussed to find beds for them all in the flat. They met at Eustace Miles's vegetarian restaurant for lunch and then 'went in luxury to the stalls' while David was relegated to the gallery. On this score he was indignant. But he thought the play 'a great success and very well acted',[51] and so did the critics and public. 'Did Jack tell you' Constance wrote to Edward, 'that someone said of him "Galsworthy – why he's the most dangerous man in England!" quite seriously. There's greatness!'[52]

In London she also saw a good deal of H. G. Wells and his wife Jane. Wells had made a memorable appearance at the Cearne. David recalled him as

a small figure, bouncing along like a rubber ball between the tall figures of Edward and Sydney [Olivier], each a head taller than he was, like a boy walking between two men, and all three walking in quite different ways. Edward walked in a long, casual, lurching stride, H. G. positively bounced with ill-suppressed energy, and Olivier strode with aloof dignity, apparently unaware of his companions, to whom he was listening attentively.[53]

In January 1906 Wells began campaigning to reform the Fabian Society. His ambitions were nothing if not radical. 'He scorned the traditional habits of the Society, rejected the Basis – the Society's written constitution – and attacked the Old Gang, deriding the Webbs as petty-minded and complaining that Shaw's levity reduced "this high business of Socialism" to "an idiotic middle-class joke".'[54] His view of the Fabians was not so different from Constance's, but she recognised that what he was up to was not genuine politics but politicking, and she would have none of it. She did not rejoin the Society. Edward, on the other hand, who was no socialist, loved mischief, and not only joined the Society himself, purely in order to lend Wells his vote, but persuaded many of his friends to do so, and Constance was quite indignant with him.[55]

Wells failed in his attempt, and three years later he upset the Fabians again – and many other people besides. In October 1909 he published *Ann Veronica*, which caused a scandal not only because the heroine proposes to her college teacher that she should become his mistress, but also because it was based closely on Wells's own affair with Amber Reeves, the daughter of respected Fabians. When Amber found she was pregnant, Wells sold his house at Sandgate and installed her in a cottage at Woldingham in Surrey. He and Jane moved to 17 Church Row in Hampstead. To many people, such as the reviewer on the *Spectator*, who described *Ann Veronica* as 'a community of scuffling stoats and ferrets, unenlightened by a ray of duty or abnegation',[56] Wells was now an outcast. But not to Edward or to Constance, who liked him and appreciated his hospitality. Constance thought Wells's failings were 'all redeemed (he is a bit vulgar, you know) by his being so affectionate – really fond of his fellow-creatures'.[57] She made a point of going to Church Row, and ensuring that it was she and not Edward who invited them to the Cearne, because she feared that Jane Wells might be 'a little sensitive about only *men* coming to them and visiting them – few women have stuck by them'.[58] It was at one of the Wells's parties that she met Arnold Bennett and came back 'glowing with gratification'[59] at the compliments he had paid her on her translations of Turgenev 'to which, he declared, he owed much in learning the art of a writer'.[60] Wells also sometimes provided the sort of absurdity that she most enjoyed. A few years later he visited Russia, and Constance wrote to Edward:

Imagine what the Russian paper you have forwarded to me contains! An interview with Wells in Petersburg in which the indomitable little man (he's a regular Tartarin!) describes his travels through Africa, America, and Siberia – undertaken solely for the purpose of shooting rare animals! – so he is represented as saying!! 'Besides his literary pursuits, the English author enjoys a well-deserved reputation as a traveller and fearless hunter of big game!' observes the interviewer. After recording (or inventing) the most amazing statements by H.G. about his exploits, the interviewer adds finally: 'Wells makes on one the impression of an excessively modest man!' Well! well! it is a world.[61]

Constance continued to take an informed, if not particularly active, interest in politics. She was overjoyed when the Liberals ousted the Conservatives at the General Election in 1906, and this was also because she believed that a Liberal government would be more sympathetic to movements for liberty abroad. And so it turned out. On 23 July a conference met in London of representatives of all the twenty-two parliaments in Europe. The Russian Duma, which had been set up in May, and had survived ten weeks of stormy relations with the Tsar, was the youngest of them, and likewise sent its delegates. But on 22 July the Tsar suspended the Duma. Campbell-Bannerman, who was to make a speech of welcome in French, was undeterred. When it came to the turn of the Russians, he cried, 'La Douma est morte! Vive la Douma!' and the delegates rose to their feet and cheered.[62]

Constance tried to keep alive Stepniak's campaign against Russian autocracy. In September 1906 a young Polish Jew called Selig Zingar arrived at Grimsby and, thinking it would help his request for asylum, foolishly told the immigration authorities that he had 'thrown a bomb over a barracks wall at Warsaw, with fatal results'.[63] He was in due course arrested at the request of the Russian Government, though they admitted that he did not correspond with their description of the man responsible. To the magistrate he was a foolish young man who would not have been in trouble if he had kept his mouth shut; but to Constance he was part of an honourable revolutionary tradition. She wrote to the *Daily News*:

Russia is in a condition [of] civil war. The Russian Government has within the last twelve months admittedly massacred or put to death without trial thousands of men, women, and children, and is daily exiling hundreds of families to the Arctic circle without food or clothing. The unarmed people can only defend themselves and avenge their friends by such acts as that of which this lad is, rightly or wrongly, accused. To extradite him or any other Russian who has escaped to our shores is, in effect, to hand over to the enemy an escaped prisoner of war.

If in the past the law had been thus interpreted neither Stepniak nor Vera Zassulitch, both of whom lived many years honoured and respected among us, and whose names are reverenced throughout Russia, would have been safe from being handed over to the Russian executioner.[64]

The *Daily* News published a fierce leader: 'We are astonished that after yesterday's proceedings, in which the Russian prosecution practically abandoned its case against Zingar, the Bow-street magistrate should have remanded the accused in custody.'[65] And the following day he was released.

Constance no longer went to May Day rallies, but on 9 February 1907 in 'wet, dismal weather'[66] she shared a carriage with Dollie Radford in a great procession in aid of Women's Suffrage. Many of her friends were there too, Mrs Francis Hueffer and her daughter, Juliet Soskice, in 'a small motor',[67] and Clementina Black and Olive and Matty Garnett in carriages, but most of the women marched on foot through mud and slush. For Constance it was a relatively uneventful occasion. But poor Olive and Matty had 'a disreputable and incapable driver – a man!'[68] who arrived so late that they were left at the very tail of the procession. When they halted for a while at Hyde Park Corner Olive and Matty walked ahead to greet her friends, only to discover on their return that their driver had

departed into a public-house. . . while we were left helpless in the row with the procession disappearing in the distance! Eventually he returned, more fuddled, and the rest of the time we spent trying to keep up with the procession amid the jeers of an unfriendly populace and such remarks as 'Why didn't you stay at home and do the washing?' 'Yah! Boo! Get married and then we shall hear no more of it. ['] etc. etc. Hard on me who had done the washing, and Matty who vainly displayed her wedding ring. Passing through Clubland the men's faces were a study, and ran the gamut of dislike, scorn, contempt, amusement, pity irritation etc. The crowd yelled at us and was distinctly hostile and insulting.[69]

Constance had been kept informed about the continuing battle for intellectual supremacy within the Russian Social Democratic Labour Party exiled in Switzerland between the Maximalists and the Minimalists – as the Bolsheviks and Mensheviks were then more generally called by outsiders. Both parties were Marxist, but whereas the Mensheviks be-lieved that capitalism would decay and could be overthrown with the minimum of force, the Bolsheviks believed that it would be necessary utterly to destroy existing society. Vera Zasulich, with whom Constance had struck up a 'warm friendship'[70] during her stay in London in 1895 – 6, did not, despite the renown she had achieved by her attempt on General Trepov, believe in violence in general. She was a disciple of Plekhanov, the veteran Marxist and leader of the Mensheviks, and until she retired from politics in 1905 she regularly sent his writings to Constance, who declared they were 'the dullest in which man had put pen to paper'.[71] Zasulich was bitterly opposed to the man who came to dominate the Bolsheviks, as Peter Struve, a Marxist intellectual, wrote: 'Vera Zasulich, the cleverest and subtlest of all the women I have ever met in my life, felt an antipathy for Lenin verging on physical aversion – their subsequent political quarrel was due not only to theoretical or tactical differences, but to the profound dissimilarity of their natures.'[72]

In 1907 the Russian Social Democrats decided to hold the fifth of their occasional congresses in a last attempt to resolve the split in the party. At first it was planned to be at Viborg in Finland, but the advance delegates were driven out by order of the Russian police. They were equally unsuccessful in Stockholm. In Copenhagen their presence was taken to be a personal affront to the King, who was brother to the dowager Empress of Russia. So they had to move on to England, where Lenin had spent some time in 1902 and 1903, but had never felt at all at home.

The Congress eventually opened at the Brotherhood Church, a 'tin tabernacle' off Southgate Road, Islington. Outside it had a faintly churchy appearance. 'Inside there was no trace of anything ecclesiastical,' Gorky wrote. It was 'unadorned to the point of absurdity.'[73] Nothing could have been more unlike the golden interior of a Russian church. The three hundred-odd delegates were welcomed by a speech from Constance's old friend, Ramsay MacDonald, who happened to be a member of the congregation. Thereafter for more than three weeks the debate which was to determine the future of the party continued in Russian, interrupted only on Sundays and Wednesday evenings when the church was needed for its usual purposes.

After ten days the Economic Committee reported that they had run out of money, delegates had used up their funds while being harried from pillar to post, and unless more could be found the congress would have to be closed forthwith. Plekhanov had tried to borrow two thousand pounds from a 'well-to-do Englishman',[74] which would have been enough to wind up the congress and get the delegates home, but had been offered no more than three hundred. Supposed sympathisers in Birmingham were no more forthcoming. In England, the Russians learned, the usual way to raise money was to throw a dinner party, and Felix Moscheles offered to do so. Moscheles was an elderly painter with a musical background. His father had been a pupil of Beethoven, and he was a favourite godson of Mendelssohn. He was patron and honorary uncle to Mark Hambourg. He admired Mazzini and Stepniak and had painted them both, though Olive thought his portrait of her friend was 'horrid'.[75] He had a penchant for panaceas from Esperanto to hypnotism, and was 'the protagonist of every imaginable progressive movement'[76] and also fairly well to do.

On 26 May he invited a delegation of seven Russians, including Gorky (who was popular in Britain and had a reputation for being able to raise money), Plekhanov and Lenin, to meet English liberals who might be sympathetic to their plight. Constance was asked if she would attend and interpret the Russian speeches. She said that she was too ignorant of Marxist political terminology and proposed Fanny Stepniak. In the event both women went, but what other English guests were present seems not to have been recorded.

It was a thoroughly unhappy occasion for the Russians. They were expected to wear evening dress, which of course they did not have and could not afford to hire. Though they spruced themselves up as best they could they were thoroughly ill at ease surrounded by impeccably dressed English, who, being unable to converse, stared at them like 'wild beasts in a zoological garden'.[77] Lenin felt humiliated and was in a bad temper. He made a short, blunt and embarrassed speech, 'as though his presence patently belied his convictions',[78] while Fanny translated. Then Plekhanov spoke charmingly and wittily in French. But even as a money-raising venture the evening was a fiasco. Nothing was forthcoming and Lenin vowed he would never again beg from capitalists.

Constance may well have seen more of the delegates than was possible on this unfortunate evening. By David's account she was impressed by Lenin and thought him 'a man of tremendously strong character, intelligent and humane in his outlook'.[79] She had also heard good reports of Trotsky from Vera Zasulich, 'who had liked him and had befriended him',[80] but Fanny thought the other Bolsheviks 'a set of self-righteous crooks', [81] and Constance was equally dismayed by them. Among those at the congress was Josef Djugashvili, later known to the world as Stalin, who on his return to Russia only a few weeks later organised a bank-robbery in Tiflis in which three men were killed and more than a quarter of a million roubles stolen,[82] only to be lost to the cause because 'Lenin ordered that the money should be passed on by Dr Zhitomirsky, who was still acting as a police agent'.[83]

The delegates' immediate money worries could not be solved by such an expropriation, but they were eventually rescued by Joseph Fels, an American philanthropist who lived in England where he marketed his naphtha laundry soap. He agreed to lend seventeen hundred pounds, provided that it was repaid by the end of the year. Some two hundred and forty delegates signed a document pledging that they would do so. Lenin, though repeatedly urging others to sign, refrained from signing himself. The congress, having seen Lenin establish his friendship with Gorky and his hold over the Bolsheviks, was able to go home. The schism between Bolshevik and Menshevik was now irrevocable, and they did not meet again.

Despite constant demands the loan was not repaid for fifteen years. Fanny was quite unperturbed by this behaviour. Though she regarded the Bolsheviks with contempt, she 'felt that it was ridiculous for a capitalist to expect to be repaid for a loan contracted "on the honour of the party"'.[84] Constance, on the other hand, with her 'Scottish horror of financial crookedness',[85] was deeply shocked. She continued to put her faith in international socialism, and in many ways to give Lenin the benefit of the doubt, but David was not brought up as a Bolshevik.

His schooling at University College School, despite all Constance's efforts, was still unsatisfactory; he was unhappy there and did badly at English and mathematics. He was frequently unwell, sometimes quite seriously, though never so seriously as Constance feared. He had mumps, hotly followed by measles, but Constance's fear that he might be consumptive was a thoroughly false alarm. Eventually, in the autumn of 1907, she removed him from school and sent him to the London Tutorial College in Red Lion Square; and in December 1908 Dr Mallam removed his tonsils, which he noted in his diary with gruesome pride, were 'about the size of a sheep's kidney'.[86] These two operations made all the difference to his life.

But for Constance and Edward this was not a comfortable time. Through force of circumstances they found themselves each in the position the other would have preferred to occupy. Constance was always happier in the country, especially at the Cearne. It had been bought in her name and with her money. She claimed she cared 'at least 100 times as much'[87] as Edward did about the garden. Now that she visited it only on occasional weekends and in the holidays, she was no longer mistress there, and had to rely on Li Whale to keep an eye on the house. Edward, on the other hand, belonged more fittingly in London, with his social life centred on luncheons at the Mont Blanc, and was by nature a weekender in the country. Constance was frustrated by having found her vocation, and then being forced by her eyes and the apathy of publishers to pursue it in penny numbers. Edward was desperately overworked, and besides his reading for Duckworth was involved in the taxing business of reviewing, which, if it was to be done properly, entailed the threefold mental effort of reading and digesting, organising his ideas, and then finding the words in which to express them, a task that he never found easy.

Nellie wrote to her friend Louise Bréal at about this time: 'I think he is well, though he complains incessantly of feeling he has no brains which I think means he finds his work rather too exhausting and is always feeling unfit – but he is extraordinary his heart is never tired – and it has no hard places in it.'[88] He was as absent-minded as ever. Constance would write to him about accepting an invitation from the Gaylord Wilshires 'the American socialist who runs the paper or did' for 'Tues. night the 20th'.[89] Four days later she had to write in exasperation:

I do wish you would read my letters and make an effort to take in what I say.
    The Wilshires' invitation is for Tuesday the 20th as I wrote to you several times – that is *next* Tuesday. I can't put off answering any longer. For God's sake, let me know by return whether you will go.[90]

But to no avail. Edward did wire, but only to say: 'Certainly accept for the 28th.'[91] Constance knew when she was beaten, called him 'an incorrigible old darling'[92] and let it go at that.

There was a crisis in the summer of 1908. Constance was on holiday with David at St Servan on the outskirts of St Malo when she heard that Edward had invited Louise Bréal to stay with him alone at the Cearne. She must have been used to Nellie going there alone, indeed in 1898 she had urged Edward not to leave her behind in London. But to Louisette, as they called her, she took strong objection:

I have no *personal* feeling – I like Louisette and love the two children. But I should think it silly and undesirable for any young woman of our acquaintance . . . to come and stay with you alone at the Cearne . . . not only the quite conventional people, but even all the more or less unconventional people who know you, would almost all assume a special relation between you, if they heard (and of course people always *do* hear) that she had stayed alone with you. . . ..
What would confirm people . . . in any such idea, is that Auguste has so entirely dropped coming to Limpsfield – that must help to set people gossiping. . . .. if Auguste were to take it into his head . . . to divorce Louisette, the mere fact of her having stayed alone at the Cearne would be quite enough for any jury, French or English.[93]

This was not impossible, as the Bréals' marriage had more or less broken up, and Auguste was at that time living in Spain with a Spanish mistress.

But had he been looking for a co-respondent, he could have found a more plausible one than Edward. Louise had fallen in love with a Jewish doctor called Camille Wolf in 1906, and for sympathy and advice had gone to Edward, who had advised her not to expect too much from Wolf and suggested that she should spend a fortnight with him at the Cearne. What their relations were one cannot tell, but Edward was not deterred by Constance's outrage, and she was still angry:

the Cearne is all I have of my own in the world . . . and I hate to have the place 'spoilt' for me. If you use your imagination you must see that the sort of gossip I dread is more wounding for my dignity than for anyone's . . . you really don't care for Louisette – and though her passion for Wolf seems always to have the effect of flinging her upon you, I assume that she hasn't a life and death sort of feeling for you either. . . .. You are always so sweet about wanting one to be happy and thinking I don't have a good time enough. It is strange, for I am always feeling that you are destroying my good time! And it seems it would be so easy for you to be a little different – *not* to say and do things. . . ..

After all, there is no one living I care so much for, except David, and I know how much you care for my happiness. It seems such madness that with that we should let such a state of things grow up that I dread being with friends if you are there. If only you could feel anxious I should be able to be myself, to express myself – or even could simply realise that my dignity is part really of yours – that to put me out of countenance (to call me 'a boiled owl' for instance before the Lucases) is degrading us both. I want harmony – smoothness – I sometimes feel I would rather you hate me and treat me nicely and with respect – than be fond of me as you are and always be trying to wound me and make me ridiculous. It seems to make life so coarse – and that's the worst of all – much worse than real unhappiness.[94]

Constance's misgivings about scandal were not unjustified. A year later, by which time Louise was heavily pregnant by Wolf, she wrote:

Is Louisette staying at the Cearne? Mrs Rothenstein, whom I met dining at the Brailsfords', told me she is and seemed to derive much secret delight from meeting me at Hampstead, when Louisette had told the Bussys that she is 'staying with the Garnetts' at Limpsfield. . . .. Mrs Rothenstein did enjoy herself. She began 'isn't it perfectly *extraordinary* that she is going to have another baby – but (to me) I dare say *you* weren't surprised – you know all about it' – the underlying imputation seemed very patent and all this before the Brailsfords, who met her staying alone with you last summer.

I had to say I had seen her – when directly asked this later on – so now please let me know when and where I can see her, as it's horribly uncomfortable telling lies at random which people can so easily find out to be lies.

In the afternoon at Madame Henkel's concert Gertrude began 'Did *you* know about Madame Bréal? – isn't it extraordinary?'

Everyone seems for some reason to feel it *so* extraordinary and people who haven't heard of Wolf and know Bréal is always in Spain (this was remarked upon as a strange feature in the case) naturally are inquisitively scenting out a scandal and fixing it where it seems to fit.

It does make me sick. It would really be so much better if Louisette would bring Wolf with her. Practically by screening him she exposes you.[95]

In all this strange episode we have only Constance's side of the story. Nothing remains to show what Edward and Louise felt – let alone Nellie. What did she feel about Edward's behaviour? Why did Constance never suggest that she too might be upset, or think that she too might give grounds for scandal? Somehow Nellie managed to remain apparently untouched and curiously invisible, not only during this episode, but for all these years before the War.

17

Two Painful Episodes

During those first years at Grove Place Constance had no regular translation, and what little came her way was political rather than literary. She still had to rest her eyes. She would start on something and then have to lay it aside. 'It has rained incessantly. . . . I have done no translation, my eyes have ached and it has been so dark.'[1] At the end of 1905 there were plans for her to translate a new history of the Russian revolutionary movement to be written by Leo Deutsch, one of the Geneva exiles. But after the 1905 revolution there was an amnesty, and on 2 November 1905 Constance told Olive 'her translation is off'.[2] 'Deutsch . . . cannot think of the past at such a moment and is going back to Russia. He says he hopes we shall understand – the moment he has worked and longed for for 32 years has come. Perhaps it's as well in view of my eyes.'[3] But on 19 January 1906 Olive noted tersely, 'Deutsch arrested.'[4]

Nicholas Tchaykovsky, the founder of the 'Tchaykovsky Circle', who had spent more than twenty years of exile in Britain and America, made the same mistake of trusting in the amnesty and was 'banished to Siberia by administrative order',[5] despite the efforts of Constance and other English friends who collected money for his bail and defence.

In October 1906 Constance wrote to Edward, 'I have done two days at translating Sophie Perovskaia and so feel cheered. I had begun to feel I should never do any more work.'[6] Perovskaya had been involved in planning the assassination of Alexander II in 1881 and was the first woman to be executed in Russia for a political crime. The proceedings of her trial had just been published in Russian. But Constance's translation came to nothing.

Her next job was likewise political, a harrowing account by Madame S. A. Savinkov of her frantic attempts to rescue her imprisoned sons from a barbarous bureaucracy and shield her ageing husband from the knowledge of her agony. After much worry and work in cutting it to satisfy the editor, it appeared as 'A Russian Mother' in the *Albany Review* in April and May 1907.[7]

In the following summer she for once had a shot at translating poetry. It was a sonnet by Pushkin, urging the poet not to prize the people's love – a sentiment that Edward would have heartily endorsed – which, with some help from Clementina, she translated into vigorous blank verse. It appeared in the *Nation*,[8] the only time that she published any separate verse translation. Thereafter, even in translating verse quoted in novels, she generally preferred to leave the task to Juliet Soskice.

Juliet helped to take the strain off her eyes at this time, and probably had a hand in the first substantial commission she had since completing *War and Peace*. *The Revolt of the 'Potemkin'* is the classic account of the events in the summer of 1905 that were immortalised as legend in Eisenstein's film. The book is written with revolutionary fervour in the language of political propaganda. When David first read it he found it an exciting adventure, but later he wrote that the story 'was one of almost inconceivable incompetence and ignorance of ships and naval gunnery on the part of the mutineers. At one moment they wished to bombard the arsenal, but were persuaded by a petty officer that this was impossible without a large-scale map!'[9] The sailors were bamboozled because they were ill-educated and illiterate. 'Authority in Russia', Crankshaw wrote, 'was so unsure of itself that it dared not encourage literacy among the children of the poor.'[10] It was not surprising that the Russian navy was so soundly beaten by the Japanese, whose policy was exactly the opposite.

Soon after 'A Russian Mother' appeared Constance heard from Ford Madox Hueffer that he would like to have a story by Tolstoy from her for a new magazine, the *English Review*.[11] She chose a powerfully anti-militaristic sketch of war in the Caucasus, which she called 'The Raid' and worked at it on and off when not busy with *Potemkin*. She had got it only half done in November 1908, when Ford telegraphed that he must have the rest of it at once. With Juliet's help she polished off the remaining five thousand words in a single day.

The *English Review* was launched in December, and David, then sixteen, wrote pessimistically, 'I am afraid this magazine will not last more than a short time.'[12] But he went on, 'The first number is splendid. A poem by Hardy, and stories by Henry James, Conrad, Jack, and Tono-Bungay by Wells. I am longing for the next number.'[13] Meanwhile he read *Tono-Bungay* aloud to his mother.

On the day after his seventeenth birthday David brought home a new college friend, an Indian called Sukhasagan Dutt, and noted in his diary: 'He brought back the "Potemkin" which had much stirred him. He also brought an Indian Nationalist paper Swaraj.'[14] Like his mother, David was attracted by coloured peoples. Two months earlier he had re-read Robert Drury's journal of his captivity in Madagascar which he had been given by his grandfather some years before, and had copied out a passage that ended with the words: 'if an impartial Comparison was to be made of their Virtue, I think the Negroe Heathens will excel the white Christians'.[15] David had at first mistaken Dutt for a native of Madagascar, but in fact he was a Bengali. David 'took for granted, without investigation, that British rule in India must be bad, exactly as most British boys of my age took for granted that it was good',[16] so he was not surprised that Dutt opposed British rule in India. But, having been brought up to admire Stepniak and Zasulich, he was surprised to find that Dutt had no use for terrorism. His elder brother was in prison for having made a bomb which had been thrown at an English magistrate, leaving him unharmed but killing two Englishwomen who happened to be nearby. 'This affair had set Dutt profoundly against terrorists and terrorism at a time when the awakening nationalism of India was expressing itself in a spasmodic series of murders.'[17] Dutt introduced David to two other Hindus, Narajan Pal, the son of one of the minor Indian nationalist leaders, and Ashutosh Mitter, and soon Constance was writing to Edward, 'Give David a blank cheque. . . . He will want a little money – as he goes to the Cearne with two Hindoo boys.'[18]

At what is now 65 Cromwell Avenue, just across Hampstead Heath from Grove Place, was India House, which belonged to an old Mahratta called Krishnavarma, who from the security of Paris produced a 'seditious rag'[19] called *The Indian Sociologist*. The Indians all made merciless fun of him, but 'he was nevertheless regarded by the British authorities as the leader of a most dangerous, seditious movement'.[20]

David went to a meeting there and soon fell under the spell of Vinayak Damodar Savarkar. 'He was small, slight in build',[21] and David thought he had 'the most sensitive face in the room and yet the most powerful'.[22] Savarkar read aloud from his propagandist history of the Indian Mutiny with such a strange staccato delivery that David did not at first realise that he was speaking English. At that same meeting he became acquainted with a disagreeable Tamil called Aiyar and noticed a 'tall young man

with a most gloomy expression, who stood leaning against the door-post
... in a Byronic attitude'.[23]

David was at the Cearne on 2 July when he read in the *Daily* News

that Sir Curzon Wyllie had been assassinated at a soirée for Indian students at
the Imperial Institute by a young Indian called Dhingra. A Parsee doctor, who
had flung himself between the assassin and his victim, had also been killed.
Dhingra had been overpowered before he could commit suicide.[24]

David did not recognise the name Dhingra, and only later realised that
he was the Byronic young man. Could he have been so foolish as to
mistake Wyllie, a relatively minor official, for Lord Curzon, lately Viceroy
of India? David was worried that his friends might be implicated, and
his parents anxious lest he get involved with terrorists who had no excuse
of a Russian connection.

The press played down the political aspects of the murder, looking
for other possible causes – did Dhingra smoke *bhang*? had he not recently
failed his examinations? – and emphasising Wyllie's exemplary record in
India. A meeting was held at Caxton Hall at which loyal Indians were
encouraged to pass a resolution expressing their 'horror and indignation'
at 'the terrible crime'.[25] Savarkar tried to protest that it should not be
called a crime until Dhingra was found guilty of it, but before he could
do so he was beaten over the head and ejected bleeding from the hall.

Dhingra was, of course, convicted, and was hanged on 17 August. At
his trial he tried to read out a statement, but was prevented from doing
so. Shortly afterwards Savarkar gave a copy of this statement to David
and asked if he could get it published. This was not difficult. Robert
Lynd, literary critic on the *Daily News*, was a family friend. David took
it to him and next morning it was in print. From Dhingra's demeanour
in court it seemed far more articulate than anything he could have
written, and David was convinced that Savarkar was the author. He
began to see rather more of Savarkar 'and was more than ever struck by
his extraordinary personal magnetism. There was an intensity of faith in
the man and a curious single-minded recklessness which were deeply
attractive to me.'[26]

Despite the official suggestions that Wyllie's murder was a fanatical
act without political significance, the authorities were convinced that it
was the result of a plot and that Savarkar was the ring-leader. They had
some justification for this because before long he was involved in yet
another assassination, this time in his native city, Nasik. Some years

earlier his elder brother had been sentenced to six years' imprisonment for printing some seditious songs. The magistrate who had sentenced him had just been assassinated, and Savarkar was found to have sent some pistols to India and his younger brother caught concealing arms in the thatch of his house. Savarkar was persuaded to lie low in France until things had died down. He did not stay there long enough, and on 13 March 1910 when he returned to England he was immediately arrested, not for anything he had done while he was in Europe, but for sedition and inciting to murder in India.

Constance was distraught for David's sake. 'The fact is' she wrote to Edward, 'he loves him with that first rush of romantic devotion and adoration – it is the first time he has felt this. Remember how you felt once – and what it would have meant to you at 18, if this awful thing had happened to the person you adored.'[27]

The government did not want to charge Savarkar with being an accessory to the latest offence, because he had been in England at the time and would have been tried by English law and so received a relatively mild sentence. They wanted to extradite him to India where the laws on sedition were severe, and the punishment was exile to a living death on the Andaman Islands. So they 'dug up some speeches that Savarkar had delivered in India several years before, and for which they had had ample time to prosecute him at the time'.[28]

Constance set to work to counter this injustice, 'which comes practically to extending the repressive legislation in force in India to this country',[29] and was busy writing circular letters to her old Fabian friends and such likely sympathisers as Henry Nevinson and William Rothenstein. She managed to raise about fifty pounds, 'which was a substantial help towards expenses'.[30]

David took more radical action. He visited Savarkar in Brixton Gaol, where he was held on remand, and devised a plan to rescue him by overpowering the detectives who took him every week to Bow Street for the formalities of a remand. At first he thought he might be able to recruit some Sinn Feiners to do the heavy work and raised the matter with Mrs Dryhurst. Florence Dryhurst and her daughter Sylvia – who married Robert Lynd – were friends of Constance's. Mrs Dryhurst had known Shaw at the time Constance first met him, and helped Charlotte Wilson to edit her revolutionary journal, *Freedom*. Her drawing-room 'was often filled with Sinn Feiners, Egyptian Nationalists, Armenians, Georgians and Finns'.[31] Then he learned from one of Savarkar's friends that 'there were two men in Paris who would willingly go to gaol for long periods in order to rescue Savarkar. But if they were brought into England, they would be closely watched.'[32]

Without telling anyone else but Savarkar he made elaborate plans to drive him, disguised in woman's motoring gear, to the south coast and smuggle him to France. He told Mrs Dryhurst that he would not need any Sinn Feiners, and then slipped over to France to contact Aiyar and smuggle the Indian rescuers back to England. He was hardly out of Mrs Dryhurst's house before Mabel Hobson dropped in, and Mrs Dryhurst told her all she knew about his plans. Mabel told her parents, and they thought it wise to inform Constance.

At eight o'clock on Sunday evening, 29 May, Edward dashed off a note to Nellie:

I am on my way to Paris. D. is there, engaged in a wild romantic scheme – which may have most serious consequences. Luckily C. discovered it this (Sunday) morning, and I go by the night mail to find him and bring him back. I have all details – and the poor boy is living in pure romantic cloudland: swept off his feet by his affection for S., and perhaps the tool of others.

C is most ill. I left her absolutely a prey to nervous breakdown with fainting fits.[33]

Next day he wrote to her again: 'I think I have succeeded in the object of my mission, although I have not yet succeeded in getting hold of D.'[34] He had traced Aiyar, who had done nothing about getting a boat to smuggle the rescuers – nor had David succeeded in doing so – and who put him in touch with his son. Father and boy returned to England together, David aware that Aiyar had been thwarting the plot all along.

In his account of the affair David merely wrote: 'When we got back to the Cearne, Constance was still in bed. I went into her room, spoke to her, and went to bed immediately myself.'[35] Constance cared for David, and for his safety, more than anything else in the world, and this must have been one of the most agonising experiences of her life – too agonising ever to be spoken of or written about.

David realised that he had been a fool, risking his future for a cause in which he did not really believe. Savarkar did succeed in escaping, but only briefly, by soaping himself all over and squeezing out through a porthole while the ship that was taking him to India was anchored off Marseilles. He managed to reach the shore, but the French authorities made no attempt to prevent his British gaolers from seizing him and taking him back aboard, thus provoking further controversy and eventual

French demands for his return. Nevertheless he continued on his voyage to India and was sentenced to life imprisonment on the Andaman Islands. He was not finally released until 1937.

While engaged in this revolutionary activity David had, of course, been continuing his schooling. He had at last passed his matriculation examination in January 1910, and he was due to go to the Imperial College of Science in South Kensington to read Botany in the autumn. This was a great relief to Constance. Edward had had little formal education and did not value it. He thought that Constance was 'stern and indomitable'[36] about getting David through examinations. She knew that if she had not done so exceptionally well in her own school examinations she would never have gone to Newnham, and that without her training in the classics she would hardly have had the mental equipment to master Russian. She, on the other hand, thought Edward was expecting too much from David in other respects:

Parents almost always think their children selfish because they don't undertake duties in their homes – but I doubt if it's natural they should. You were the same in your father's house. I remember May declaring that you were utterly selfish. I know I hated having anything to do in my father's house – and took no interest in it whatever. That's nature – and parents must accept it and not make it worse and more defined by trying to resist and being bitter. The boy will be just as unselfish to *his* children as we have been to him.[37]

Constance was worried that they might not be able to pay for David's education. Edward earned fifteen pounds a month from Duckworth, and might make an extra five guineas from reviews in the *Nation* and perhaps a guinea from the *Daily News or Manchester Guardian*. Constance's royalties from Turgenev were then only about ten pounds a year, and her new work could not have brought in more than another twenty or thirty pounds. Edward had the only bank account, and Constance had to ask him for a blank cheque from time to time, but it was she who saw to his Income Tax Return, and worried how they were going to make ends meet and that Edward was working too hard trying to do so.

Running the Cearne and the flat in London was more than they could really afford. Constance thought again about letting the Cearne; for they could none of them bear the thought of selling it. David wrote to her about this time: 'Whatever we do you must never sell the Cearne – it is a great and peaceful place', adding with romantic optimism, 'Five hundred years from now when our bodies have nourished rose trees and our souls will lie forgotten, the Cearne will still gaze at the blue hills of the Weald opposite. They may run trains through it but it will never change.'[38]

Nevertheless Constance found her thoughts 'all turning towards Letchworth'.[39] The Garden City had become a centre of colonist friends to rival the Chart Woods. Harry and Lucy Cowlishaw were at Uplands Farm. Fanny Stepniak had moved in November 1908 from Crockham Hill to Norton, a village just outside the town, and Nellie's sister, Margaret, and her husband, Arthington Pease, lived in the Garden City where he was headmaster of the school.

On 23 January 1910 Olive recorded: 'Edward and Connie are thinking of letting the Cearne and going to Letchworth for a year',[40] though Constance was still anxious about those she would be leaving behind. Kate Clayton would be 'fearfully upset at our leaving the Cearne. The only holiday she ever gets is coming there'[41] and added to Edward, 'You ought to tell Li that we shall probably shut the Cearne up at the end of the month, so that she should be looking for other work – I'm afraid she must feel the break-up very much.'[42]

But the break-up proved unnecessary. The money was found without it; and the Cearne remained unlet. David did, however, go to Letchworth. He needed some further coaching in Chemistry, Physics and Mathematics, and Constance sent him off to stay with Lucy and Harry, and to be taught by a schoolmaster in Hitchin. He was not happy with the Cowlishaws. He was irked by Lucy insisting on saying grace both before and after every meal and on making her own bread 'which was brown, damp, and very heavy, besides that she put too much salt in it'.[43] Lucy was irked by his obvious unhappiness and told her friends that he was 'not of an affectionate nature'.[44]

He was glad to get away and to spend the spring of 1910 at the Cloisters, an eccentric building full of turrets and with beds that hung from the ceiling, which Harry had put up in Letchworth for Miss Lawrence. She was 'a remarkable lady with a battered brass ear-trumpet'[45] whom David described as 'one of those ladies, more numerous in the first decade of the twentieth century than today, who confidently expected to change the nature of the world by the expenditure of a few thousand pounds, which would enable the theories of philosophers to be put into practice'.[46]

In July, having escaped from the 'serious consequences' that he might have suffered as a result of the Savarkar affair, David was sent to Germany, to learn German and spend the rest of the summer at Boppard with a family whom Ford had found for him, and later to go walking with Ford and eventually alone in the Black Forest.

Constance thought it wise to draft a letter of warning for Edward to send him: 'Before you go to Germany I want to speak to you about a subject of the gravest importance. You have come to an age when new instincts and feelings may at any time put you in a position of the greatest temptation and danger.'[47]

Constance believed that her father's terminal illness was locomotor ataxia – by then known to be a consequence of syphilis – and was anxious lest David should do anything to cause himself 'the bitterest regret and misery for the rest of your life'.[48] She was also concerned, as she wrote in Edward's name, because 'you may within the next few years be led by real love into intimacy with some girl, as I was with your mother before our marriage' and that he should take proper precautions ('Malthusian sheaths') to avoid begetting an unwanted child.[49]

Meanwhile the money they needed to keep afloat had been found, though not without much anguish. Ernest Radford, who knew only too well what it was like to be constantly hard up, determined that something should be done for Constance. Civil List Pensions, which had been instituted in 1837, enabled the Prime Minister to award small annuities to impecunious and deserving authors and their relicts. In October 1909 Ernest sent a draft petition to Galsworthy, who gave his support 'with the utmost alacrity'.[50] As eventually drawn up it had some thirty signatories, academics (including the Professor of Russian at Oxford and the Principal of Newnham), politicians (Sydney Olivier and three Members of Parliament), a host of writers from Archer to Yeats, and some newspaper editors and book publishers.

Asquith was persuaded, and early in January Constance received a letter marked 'Private' informing her that 'the King has been pleased to award you a Civil List Pension of £70 per annum in consideration of the merits of your translations from the Russian'.[51]

Constance was delighted, but she was anxious about Edward's reaction:

I don't know how you will feel, but it seems to me that no one *can* say (as you said many people would) 'he's living on his wife's pension,' since £70 is less than one person could live on in our manner of living. At the same time it means security from want for me and if I should live to be very old, it may be the greatest boon. It ought to enable you to make a better provision in your will for Nelly. Meantime £70 is exactly what I had calculated David would cost us for the next three or four years at the College of Science. I can't help thinking that only rather mean and contemptible people *could* feel it a slight to you. Anyway it's a good precedent that a married woman should be taken on her own merits and I feel that while it's enough to be worth having, it's not enough to damage you, even if there were evil-minded people wanting to say ill-natured things.[52]

But Edward was outraged, not at being thought to live on his wife's pension, but because he considered it insulting to be offered any kind of help from any branch of the establishment that he so despised. He made a 'hideous scene'[53] with Dollie Radford, wrote a furious letter to Galsworthy, and hustled Constance into agreeing against her better judgement to decline the pension. She was wretched for Dollie's sake as much as for her own, and urged Edward to write and apologise to her.

I can't see her again without apologising for you – and that puts you in such a position – much worse than if you apologise genuinely yourself. As for your suspicions of her being actuated by jealous desire to injure you etc – that's mere frenzy – a morbid imagining. Her views of money are such that she would never imagine what we are feeling or how other people might feel. It's much more likely she felt, if anything, how splendid it would be for you to be more free to write immortal dramas![54]

And as to Galsworthy:

I feel greatly distressed about Jack and fear you have really wounded him. Nothing could be more ungracious. I wrote yesterday and beg you to write today to do your utmost to make it right. We have no right whatever in the heat of our surprise to throw any kind of blame on him for lack of delicacy etc. . . . It is silly to get so excited and to strike out right and left at our dearest friends.[55]

Galsworthy wrote Edward a sober rejoinder:

What I can't understand is why you should both be so insulted. I've always regarded a pension on the Civil List as an honour only conferred on people who have deserved well of the State for their services to the State; and although I quite understand that you would have refused to initiate a request for it, I don't see why you should be hurt if it were conferred without your knowledge or request.[56]

It was David who, at the age of seventeen, had, as Constance said, 'such a loving heart that it gives him a wisdom beyond his age',[57] and whose letter to his father healed the breach between his parents:

I feel that mother will be miserable unless she gets it. You must know her character [and] your own well enough to see that in the long run doing without it – the continual remembrance of the possibility of having had it – will cause her greater misery and more futile regret than the fact of [her] having it will cause you.

I love both my parents very tenderly but see them full of imperfections. In mother, I see a peasant's true valuation of things. She has all the time a sense of what she could do for Auntie Katie, etc, with it, in her mind. Also a sturdy independence.

You on the other hand are quick to anger and quick to form opinions. She does not know what she wants until she has brooded for some days. . . . What is to you and me a cause of anger for a few days – some trivial thing – to mother is a cause of lifelong regret – it grows slowly to be a rankling ulcer . . . I have written to you dear Dad because I feel it will not be so lasting to you as [to] mother. I love you so and you know I am more like you temperamentally.[58]

Edward recanted and now told Constance that he had a million times rather she accepted than regretted afterwards that she had not. 'I ought to have realised,' she remarked, 'after these 20 years that you are always unreasonable on impulse – and generous and clear-headed on second thoughts.'[59]

After further reflection she replied:

What I want most *is* to accept. Already by Wednesday morning I felt wretched at my weakness in having been rushed to a decision before I had discovered what I felt – and I think even then I knew that my scruples were fantastic and did not apply – and yours seemed to be superficial and in a sense paltry.

It's horrible to be acting in a way you hate. . . . But I feel I shall always regret it – that I have sacrificed something that would have been a source of greatest pride and happiness – perhaps for years – to a feeling . . . you must in your heart partly despise.

To me it's not only the money though of course that means far more than anything you can imagine – I'm so different from you – but the honour, the recognition of the work – the feeling that my work is still a source of profit to the family – it would make more difference than you understand.

The failure of my eyes has been such a bitter grief – more because it has made me useless than because of the boredom – and now this would come as such a compensation. It does seem awful that it can't be except at the cost of your feeling dishonoured – when I owe all the happiness of these 20 years to you and your goodness.

Darling, feel warm to me if you can. It's awful to think of my acting against your interests or strongest wishes. Bunny and you and Nellie are the three nearest to me in the world – and what I most dread is being an encumbrance on you.[60]

Edward wrote a 'warm sweet generous little letter'[61] that healed the ache in her heart, and she replied: 'Whatever comes of it now, I shan't have that sick feeling about it. We both have made mistakes – but I feel I can forget them and not have that poisonous feeling that corrodes my whole being so that I can't rest.'[62]

The whole drama has lasted no more than ten days. It took a little longer to sort things out with the Prime Minister's office. Not until 4 March did she hear that the pension had been reinstated, and she wrote and thanked Ernest Radford for the trouble they had put him to, adding 'I do feel proud of receiving this public recognition of my work and of being probably the first married woman (not a widow) and the first translator who has received it.'[63]

Meanwhile, when Constance was still in the middle of the Civil List crisis, she had the offer of a very substantial piece of work. 'Here's a complication!' she wrote to Edward on 14 January:

Williams and Norgate write the work in question is Tolstoi's Letters – 300,000 words – and they want it done by March 15 – but if I couldn't do all I could do part. . . .

Of course no one could do 300,000 in the time. But if Juliet can work with me, we could do 100,000 in 20 or 25 days work without my using my eyes (except on the proofs – perhaps not even on that) and it would mean £45 or £50 between us. I would love to do this.[64]

Later that day she telegraphed the publisher that she and Juliet would undertake a third of the work – a hundred thousand words – at ten shillings a thousand 'to be ready by March 15'.[65] The Russian text arrived on 20 January. Constance and Juliet set to work. But before the end of the month a telegram came from Williams and Norgate telling Constance and Juliet to 'suspend operations'. 'It seems there's a hitch and they may have to alter or omit some letters – so we are having a holiday – very welcome and opportune.'[66] Operations were not resumed. They were paid twelve pounds for the twenty-four thousand words they had completed in ten days.

There must have been other disappointed translators besides Constance and Juliet. 'How did Natasha get on with the Tolstoy letters with Mr Duddington?'[67] David wrote to his mother from Germany.

Natalie Ertel had come to England in the spring of 1906 to complete her education. She went to London University where she won a scholarship and took a First in Philosophy in 1909. She was at this time much attracted to Theosophy, and on her arrival in England went to stay with another Theosophist, the Rev. John Nightingale Duddington, who had recently been appointed Rector of Ayot St Lawrence, where he lived with his wife and daughter Iris, 'a very beautiful girl . . . who hopes to be an actress'.[68] Their house was the brand new, ugly Rectory, which they vacated almost at once for a smaller and more convenient building so that it could be let to Shaw and eventually become Shaw's Corner and a place of pilgrimage.

Natalie, who was twenty when she first arrived in England, was a spirited and intelligent young woman, of formidably strong character, very Russian, and ever hot for certainties, which she was able to find, first in Theosophy and later in the Russian Orthodox Church. A young woman friend wrote of her at this time: 'I have an unbounded admiration for Tata, and when she speaks to me her magnetic personality mesmerizes me into doing anything that she tells me to, and, what's more, into feeling an intense desire to do it.'[69] It may be going too far to say that Duddington was mesmerised, but there is no doubt that he fell in love with her, and by November 1907 Natalie was telling her father of their plans to live together. They were an oddly-matched couple, and the same young woman friend wrote to Constance:

I want to know your opinion about Mr Duddington. He seems to me a very worthy gentleman, and I should like him if he stood on his own merits and not as the future husband of Tata – but as a husband for Tata, oh how I disapprove of him. One evening Tata was talking to me about philosophy and I was listening, and had forgotten everything in the world but what she was saying, and suddenly Jack came in and we seemed to drop down to earth with such a thump, and as I looked at the two I thought how incongruous they were. . . . Perhaps I am wrong and it only seems so.[70]

There were others who were struck by him in the same way. Constance, however, always spoke of Jack Duddington affectionately, but it was with Natalie that she found real intellectual companionship and for her children that she showed real love.

Duddington, of course, had to give up his living at Ayot St Lawrence, and earn what he could elsewhere, among other things by helping Natalie translate Russian. As time went on he found more substantial jobs (ending up as Director of the Whitechapel Art Gallery), while Natalie gradually took over from Juliet Soskice as Constance's amanuensis. She has described how: 'I would read one sentence at a time aloud to her in Russian, she would translate it into English, and I would write down what she said. Working in this way was very tedious and exhausting for her, and I was always full of admiration for her patience and will-power.'[71]

Although they differed in their views on religion, on politics, indeed on almost everything except Russian literature, they became fast friends. A few years later Constance wrote to Natalie:

And do you know really how much I value your friendship. That sounds cold – but it means a lot – it means that besides the affection and warm feeling I have for you, I always recognize that you have something to give me – that different and in many ways opposed as we are in intellect and outlook our minds *meet* and your mind gives mine something to feed upon. After all you know it's precious few people I can say that of![72]

18

Chekhov Spurned, Dostoevsky Beatified

Constance had been trying to persuade someone to publish Chekhov's writings ever since she had first heard of his story, 'Ward No. 6' in 1893. She had not had much success. Nor had anybody else. Apart from a couple of selections of tales translated by R. E. C. Long, which had appeared in 1903 and 1908 and sunk virtually without trace, there was very little of his work to be had in English.

In January 1906, at Galsworthy's instigation, Constance had 'fished up' her 'imperfect version' of Chekhov's tale, *Peasant Wives*, and begun correcting it, though she was afraid he would find it 'too grim and ugly'.[1] It was probably the same tale that she had translated nine years before and David Rice had failed to place for the same reason; once again nothing came of it.

She did better with Ford. He took three tales, 'At a Country Cottage', 'That Hateful Boy' and 'A Gentleman Friend', for the *English Review*. But before they could appear he sold the review to Sir Alfred Mond, with Austin Harrison as editor, and Constance had a scare:

Have you heard what the beastly Academy is doing, threatening to bring an action against Ford for having used the name 'English Review', which they claimed belonged to them. It's simply blackmailing, they are beasts. And now Mond says if the copyright of the name can't be established, he won't buy the Review – so I hear. And poor Ford has no money.

I'm interested personally – it seems so likely I may not get a cheque for the Tchehov sketches![2]

But the takeover went ahead and the 'sketches' eventually appeared in February 1910. A few weeks earlier she had tried 'The Trousseau' and 'Boys' on the *Nation*, but to no avail. Then Mrs Grant Richards, editor of the *Englishwoman*, a serious journal promoting Women's Suffrage, asked her 'to forward her any short translations that might do for it – so I am getting several in order'.[3] Constance thought 'The Trousseau' might appeal to her, but instead she took 'Hush'. And that was all for another four years.

Meanwhile Constance had been even less successful with Chekhov's plays.

In January 1906 the Moscow Arts Theatre set out on its first foreign tour, playing in Warsaw, Prague, Vienna, Berlin and several other German cities. Constance heard rumours that there was 'a very exciting scheme for persuading the . . . company to come to London this summer',[4] and wrote to Edward, 'I am translating the 'Cherry Orchard' of Tchehov on spec – I want to do it before the holidays.'[5] The play had opened in Moscow on 17 January 1904 to great acclaim, though Stanislavsky was as usual at odds with the author about how it should be played; and Chekhov was a dying man with only six months to live. Constance finished her translation by April, but the Moscow company did not come to London, nor indeed was *The Cherry Orchard* in their touring repertory. With a view to getting the play put on in English, she sent her translation to Galsworthy, who was already interested in Chekhov. Galsworthy sent *The Cherry Orchard* on to Kate Clayton to be typed, and wrote to Constance:

I've only read two Acts, but they're very fine. I don't see an English audience standing it in its present form, it wants cutting. *Don't* have 'You're a never-come-off'; have my 'Ye've got no backbone.' Think – it's the last word of the play, and backbone is a fine thing. Moreover ten to one the audience will think Nevercomeoff. . . .[6]

The rest of the letter seems to be missing, but clearly Galsworthy was suggesting that Nevercomeoff sounded like some Russian proverbial character. Constance's final version ends with Firs saying 'Ech! I'm good for nothing.'

She tried it on the Stage Society. Shaw and Olivier were both on the Committee of Management. *You Never Can Tell* had been their first production in 1899, and Olivier's play, *Mrs Maxwell's Marriage*, which Olive had so disliked, had been their second. The Society said nothing, but in February 1907 she heard that there were paragraphs in the papers announcing that they were going to do it. 'I think they might have told me!' she exclaimed, 'I want to go to rehearsals – and shall also take Tatia Ertel [Natalie] who has seen it done beautifully in Moscow.'[7] But it was a false alarm, perhaps even a baseless rumour. Nothing happened. She likewise offered it to Laurence Irving, who was interested in all things

Russian, but with no more success. The typescript continued to languish in the drawer of the settle at the Cearne.

At last in 1911 the Stage Society decided to put it on. On 29 April Constance went to see them about it, and on the following day Natalie came and went through the text for a last revision. Constance was apprehensive: 'I'm afraid they'll make an awful hash of it! I can't conceive English actors taking it as anything but a screaming farce – and rather a stupid one! I should like to cut out a lot of the most incomprehensible stuff.'[8]

With or without her and Natalie's help, the Society proceeded with rehearsals. It was not the first Russian play they had put on. There had been translations of *The Lower Depths* by Gorky in 1903, *The Power of Darkness* by Tolstoy in 1904 and *The Inspector-General* by Gogol in 1906. And in 1908 they had done *The Bread of Others* by Turgenev, translated, at least nominally, by J. Nightingale Duddington, though Natalie must have had the larger hand in it.

Nor was it the first of Chekhov's plays to be acted in Britain. That honour belongs to George Calderon, who had directed the Glasgow Repertory Company in his own translation of *The Seagull* in November 1909. Calderon had studied in St Petersburg for two years, and he was sufficiently confident of his knowledge of the theatre to have written a play, *The Fountain*, which had been put on earlier that year by the Stage Society. For *The Seagull* he managed to elicit a considerable degree of ensemble playing from his cast, and, having lectured the critics beforehand with his views on Chekhov, received a surprisingly good press.

The Stage Society was not so well favoured. Although Mary Jerrold (Varya), Lola Duncan (Charlotta) and Percival Clarke (Station Master), had all appeared in *The Seagull* in Glasgow, their director, Kenelm Foss, had nothing like so clear an idea of the play as Calderon had. Constance's misgivings were well justified.

The Cherry Orchard opened on Sunday 28 May for two performances at the Aldwych Theatre. The members of the Stage Society were supposed to be the elite of London's intellectuals. Henry James was there, sitting with Somerset Maugham and Mrs W. K. Clifford. Maugham described how

Henry James was perplexed by *The Cherry Orchard* . . . and in the second interval he set out to explain to us how antagonistic to his French sympathies was this Russian incoherence. Lumbering through his tortuous phrases, he hesitated now and again in search of the exact word to express his dismay; but Mrs.

Clifford had a quick and agile mind; she knew the word he was looking for and every time he paused immediately supplied it. This was the last thing he wanted. He was too well-mannered to protest, but an almost imperceptible expression on his face betrayed his irritation and, obstinately refusing the word she offered, he laboriously sought another, and again Mrs. Clifford suggested it only to have it again turned down. It was a scene of high comedy.[9]

Alas, Foss's production was not high comedy, nor high anything else. A correspondent of the Russian journal *Teatr i Iskusstvo* found it 'unutterably sad to witness this charade' and thought the play was staged, as Constance had feared, as a farce, the costumes were a travesty, while Playfair shamelessly hammed as Pishtchik.[10] Most of the audience were as perplexed as Henry James, but not so well-mannered, and they 'hooted in amazement'.[11] By the end of the second interval nearly half of them had left.

Olive Garnett went to the second performance, a matinee on the 29th. In her diary she merely noted: 'The play and the audience; Russia and Ireland. Zangwill, the Wellses, Rhys, the Bariatinskys, Connie, Radfords.'[12] She does not, alas, tell us what she thought of the play, but from this cryptic reference it seems she may have been one of the first to mention the similarity between the decaying societies of Russian landowners and the Anglo-Irish 'Ascendancy', which has occasionally been exploited in subsequent productions of Chekhov.

For Constance it must all have been an exasperating and painful experience. The press was on the whole hostile or politely bewildered, finding *The Cherry Orchard* 'queer, outlandish, even silly',[13] and blaming the author rather than the translator or the production. But as John Palmer, dramatic critic on the *Saturday Review* later wrote:

I well remember the amazement with which I read these notices on the morrow of my own burning conviction that I had seen the first great and original comedy produced since the beginning of my critical career upon this REVIEW. I have carefully preserved these criticisms, and I mean to re-read them whenever I find myself beginning to believe in the dignity and usefulness of my profession.[14]

And there were other exceptions. Arnold Bennett, though he did not think it a 'great play' but 'an intensely original and interesting play', stoutly defended 'Tchekhov's dramatic masterpiece. . . . Its naturalism is positively daring. The author never hesitates to make his personages as ridiculous as in life they would be.'[15] He put the blame for its reception on the audience: 'The managing committee of the Society is a very enlightened body; but the mass of the members are just as stupid as any other mass.'[16]

Frank Swinnerton found himself 'sitting entranced, surrounded by empty seats',[17] and at once sought out Long's translations of the stories and declared himself a 'Tchekhovian'.

The Cherry Orchard was the first of Constance's translations of a play to be performed (*The Storm* had still not reached the London stage), and though the critics did not blame the translation for the fiasco, the Stage Society began to question whether they should not have used a translator more familiar with the theatre. A week after the performances were over Constance wrote to Edward:

Something rather unpleasant has happened. Dr [C. E.] Wheeler sent me a message through Margaret [Radford] that Calderon had been overheard telling Whelen [Chairman of the Council of Management] that he could form no idea of the play (the C. O) because mine was such a wretched translation – and that now no-one would be willing to take up a Tchehov play anywhere as this poor translation would set the public against it. Dr Wheeler told me this because he thought the translation might be again discussed (I gather it has been!) at the Committee and perhaps I could vouch for its being correct. I told him Natasha had compared it word for word – and that she would vouch for it (except for the billiard phrases which we cut a good deal – or translated ad lib.)

But this makes me feel that I should like to publish my Cherry Orchard at once and shall not for a moment consider Calderon's feelings. . . .

Would you write to Sidgwick for me . . . or should I write to Heinemann first and offer it to him?[18]

It cannot have been the accuracy of the translation that was being impugned, but its suitability as stage dialogue. In this respect Calderon's was probably better. Yet producers have neglected his version, and preferred to use hers, adapting it (with or without acknowledgement) to their own theatrical needs, and sometimes thereby providing productions as good as any that have been put on in English. But for the moment neither Sidgwick nor Heinemann would publish Constance's *Cherry Orchard*. Grant Richards did, however, publish Calderon's versions of *The Cherry Orchard* and *The Seagull* in the following year.

According to Herbert Farjeon, Bernard Shaw, who seems not to have been in the audience, 'characterised the production to Mrs. Edward Garnett (the translatress) as the most important in England since that of *A Doll's House.*'[19] Shaw began to champion Chekhov as he had done Ibsen. But Chekhov's influence was much slower to be felt than Ibsen's.

It was not, for instance, until 1916 that Shaw attempted to emulate Chekhov with *Heartbreak House,* and seven years later he still could not persuade William Archer, once the apostle of the New Drama, to accept Chekhov. Archer complained that Shaw was offering him a jellyfish and calling it a cat: '"Nonsense!" you say, "Your natural history is mid-Victorian. It may have been called a jellyfish about 1870; but Tchekhov has changed all that, and we now call it a cat. . . ."'[20] Shaw replied:

The alternatives are not a cat and a jellyfish, but a clockwork cat and a live cat. The clockwork cat is very ingenious and very amusing (for five minutes); but the organisation of the live cat beats the construction of the mechanical one all to nothing; and it amuses you not for an age but for all time.[21]

Constance meanwhile had begun tackling another Russian writer who was to have a much more immediate impact.

Dostoevsky had been dead for nearly thirty years, and many Russians thought him their greatest novelist. But he was still little known to English readers. Vizetelly had issued translations of several of the novels by Frederick Whishaw in the 1880s, and two of them had gone into a third edition. But by the time Edward came to write about Dostoevsky in 1906 they were unprocurable and Dostoevsky almost forgotten. 'No doubt', Edward wrote, 'the reason for our neglect of the great Russian author lies in the Englishman's fear of morbidity',[22] and he proceeded to defend Dostoevsky, mainly by attacking the fear rather than denying the morbidity. Constance could not be expected to be sympathetic to Dostoevsky's irrationalism, religiosity and reverence for the Tsar, but in fact she admired him, and thought he had been much maligned.

In the *Academy* Edward could hardly campaign explicitly for a new translation by his wife. Arnold Bennett had no such inhibitions. In 1909 he first read *The Brothers Karamazov* in French and 'thought it contained some of the greatest scenes that I have ever encountered in fiction. . . . When I mentioned it to friends I was told that I had gone daft about it, and that it was not a major work.'[23] Then he met Constance, probably at the Wellses' on 23 December 1909[24] and he 'made inquiries from her about it, and she said: "It is his masterpiece."'[25] 'And now, Mr. Heinemann,' he concluded, 'when are we going to have a complete Dostoievsky in English?'[26] But Heinemann did nothing, and a year later Bennett returned to the charge:

I do not suggest that there would be a great deal of money in Dostoievski. But I do suggest that, in collaboration with a publisher in the United States, it might be done without loss, and that it ought to be done; and that it is the duty of one or other of our publishers to commission Mrs. Constance Garnett to do it.[27]

Within the next two or three weeks Heinemann took the hint.

Natalie Duddington had also been campaigning for Dostoevsky. On 18 December 1908, the day that David had his tonsils out, he 'came back to dinner and just got a glimpse of Natasha who is translating "An honest Thief with mother'.[28] It was published six months later in the *Living Age*.[29] Natalie was likewise quick to defend Dostoevsky's reputation. In November 1910 Laurence Irving put on his adaptation of *Crime and Punishment* at the Garrick Theatre, entitling it *The Unwritten Law* and playing Raskolnikov himself. When E. A. Baughan, whom Max Beerbohm described as 'quite the dreariest of all dramatic critics – the most arid and pettifogging and theatre-detesting',[30] wrote that the play had retained the central idea of the novel 'that homicide may be justified, and that, indeed, it is practised in the public affairs of life'.[31] Natalie was incensed. She wrote at once to Constance (for who else could the 'young Russian graduate' be?):

For Heaven's sake, stand up for Dostoevski, write for me that the critic has evidently not read the novel, the 'central idea' of which is that homicide is never justifiable. . . . The impudence of it! Poor Dostoevski must have turned in his grave at hearing his ideas so distorted. And the muddle that is made of 'Crime and Punishment' in this play! Really, people ought not to murder masterpieces like that. Let them write their own stuff and leave the great dead in peace![32]

Constance merely added: 'I think all readers of Dostoevski will share this feeling.' and sent it on to the *Daily News*, where it appeared on 19 November. By this time she may well have started translating Dostoevsky. She wrote to Edward, 'Natasha is very enthusiastic over the idea of translating Dostoevsky – she would like it to be the Brothers Karamazov – her favourite book. Would there be a chance for this?'[33]

Heinemann accepted the proposal early in 1911, but he did not want to make any public announcement until the autumn, adding: 'Please bind Mr. Arnold Bennett to secrecy at present and tell him how much we shall welcome his aid on behalf of the series when the time comes.'[34] He must have been anxious about the cost of producing such long books (*The Brothers Karamazov* is about five times as long as *Fathers and Children*) which might not sell, and he did not offer such good terms as for Turgenev and Tolstoy: only nine shillings a thousand words and no royalty. Edward, however, remained convinced that the sales of Dostoevsky would not be enough to earn any royalties anyway. And so she agreed.

By March 1911 *Crime and Punishment* was finished. Heinemann did not wait before announcing the new edition, and Arnold Bennett was cock-a-hoop:

I feel like a social reformer who has actually got something done. . . . Mr. Heinemann is about to publish the principal novels of Dostoievsky in a translation by Mrs. Constance Garnett. . . . I do not claim any merit on account of my agitation. I am prepared to hear from Mr. Heinemann that he was entirely unaware of my agitation. I don't care. I can swallow any coincidences. This thing is coming to pass. And those English novelists who cannot read Russian and are too idle or too insular to read either French or German, will at last have an opportunity of studying the greatest scenes in fiction ever written by anybody. . . .[35]

Despite all that Bennett and Natalie could say, Constance still shared Edward's view of Dostoevsky's likely reception by the British public. She was deferring *Crime and Punishment* not because Dent had taken the occasion of Laurence Irving's play to push out an old translation, which she found 'omits passages and makes a good many croppers',[36] but because she thought it would not attract British readers.

By September 1911 the translation of *The Brothers Karamazov* was delivered to Heinemann, who proceeded to brood on it. A 'distinguished Russian'[37] had told him that there were passages in it that were 'appallingly shocking', and he was alarmed for his reputation. Constance could not imagine what they could possibly be. Fanny Stepniak suggested 'the jeering at the orthodox superstitions. . . as there is nothing else which could shock a Russian in it'.[38] Heinemann would not get around to reading it, and when chivvied by Constance, wrote that he was 'putting the book in hand, leaving it to you to tone down such passages as might be thought offensive in this country'.[39]

During 1911 Constance had much on her mind besides translation. She was more than usually unwell. With surprising docility she and Edward let David go off on his own to Russia at Easter. He fancied himself in love with Ursula Cox, a cousin of the Oliviers, who was staying with the Ertels in a large flat in Moscow. He pursued her there, but even before he arrived his feelings for Ursula had evaporated, and he had an enjoyable holiday, uncomplicated by any painful emotions, going to the Easter Service at night in St Basil's Cathedral, and picknicking on the Sparrow Hills.

But for the less fortunate people in Russia it was not an auspicious year. Much of the harvest failed. In some areas virtually the entire crop did not ripen, and once again there was the threat of famine. At first the authorities refused to recognise the gravity of the situation. Eventually, in November, 'under the pressure of the Duma and the Press'[40] they admitted that eight million people were in need of relief. By that time 'most of the peasants had already parted with their cattle and horses, and had exhausted all their personal means'.[41] Private relief was prohibited, 'for the Government feared that such organizations would become centres of opposition propaganda'.[42] The Imperial Free Economical Society in St Petersburg, however, was exempt from this ban, and so enabled a Russian Famine Relief Fund at last to be set up in London in May 1912, with Ralph Vaughan Williams, already an established composer at thirty-nine, as the treasurer. But it received little notice in the press. There was more conspicuous, though far less serious and widespread, distress nearer at home as a result of a coal strike and the sinking of the *Titanic* on 14–15 April.

With such important distractions Constance found it 'very difficult to gain any support . . . everything has been against it'.[43] She wrote to *The Times* a temperate letter, explaining what was being done for the starving in Russia, and that 'early summer till the next harvest' was the worst time.

Many years ago I stayed in a Russian province where there had been famine the winter before, and what I saw then haunts me still – the white, weak faces of men and women, the dreadful absence of children. The babies all die, for the starved mothers have no milk, and the children quickly succumb to dysentery, &c., from eating the famine bread, made from straw, bark, and refuse. One woman said to me, 'I had ten children. They are all dead.'[44]

Another vivid evocation of the famine was to be found in a collection of photographs among her papers. They were taken in the Samara district in March 1912 by a superb professional photographer. The pained and patient children's faces, and the nearly naked babies in the snow, provide images of hunger and cold that are impossible to forget.

Constance spent her weekends in town writing for subscriptions from her friends. Most sent shillings, but a few of the more generous or well-to-do gave guineas. She preserved some of Vaughan Williams's receipts, and there may well have been others. They show that she raised thirty-five pounds, eleven shillings and fourpence, a sum which does not seem quite so pitifully small when it is seen as Edward's salary from

Duckworth for ten weeks – or sufficient to keep two hundred peasants alive for about a month. By 18 May Vaughan Williams was able to report that more than eight hundred pounds had been raised, of which six hundred had already been sent to Russia. And by the middle of June she noted that the sum had risen to seventeen hundred pounds – less than one-hundredth of the amount that the Lord Mayor's Fund raised for the victims and survivors of the *Titanic*.

The Russian authorities continued to be hostile to outsiders and to discourage foreign help. Bernard Pares wrote to *The Times*[45] to discount the view that 'help for the starving peasants sent from England is unacceptable', only for the same newspaper to carry a 'semi-official statement' on the following day: 'it is learned in competent quarters here that foreign contributions have hitherto been very few and of small value. Moreover the authorities now have the situation in hand, and, owing to the good crop prospects, further contributions are not considered necessary.'[46] Fanny Stepniak was outraged by this curmudgeonly complacency: 'Nothing but dynamite', she exclaimed, 'will cure Russia of the pest eating the heart of the Nation. It's much worse than the Famine.'[47] The Free Economical Society was more gracious and passed a resolution specifically thanking Constance for her part in collecting funds for famine relief.

On the same day that half a column of the *Daily News* was occupied by the appeal for the Russian Famine Fund, a full column was taken up by Robert Lynd's review of *The Brothers Karamazov*. 'It is possible' Lynd began, 'that the greatest literary event of the year in this country will be the appearance of the first volume . . . of Mrs Garnett's translation of the novels of Dostoevsky.'[48] And he concluded his enthusiastic exposition of the book: 'in the end his genius simply overwhelms us . . . like some mighty upheaval of nature'.[49]

Lytton Strachey, writing anonymously in the *Spectator*, was less overwhelmed but no less eulogistic. He made an even stronger case for the greatness of Dostoevsky, with whom he was clearly familiar from having read him in French; and he refused to be carried away by notions of morbidity, or to see Dostoevsky as a monster:

Paradoxical as it may seem, it is yet certainly true that Dostoievsky, with all his fondness for the abnormal and the extraordinary, is a profoundly sane and human writer. In this respect, indeed, he is the exact opposite of Tolstoy, who conceals a neurotic temperament under the cloak of a strict and elaborate adherence to the commonplace.[50]

And he concluded by comparing Dostoevsky to *King Lear* and the Elizabethan and Jacobean dramatists: 'The art which wove out of the ravings of three madmen in a thunderstorm the noblest and profoundest symphony that human hearts have ever listened to is, in its essence, the same art that went into the making of *The Idiot* and *The Possessed*.'[51]

Many of the reviewers treated the publication of *The Brothers Kara-mazov* as an important literary event, rather than the appearance of a new version, albeit for the first time complete, of a classic with which they should already have been familiar. Several remarked on the cheap price (3s. 6d.) and on the unattractively economical format: a single volume of 838 pages crammed with type between measly margins, unlike the far more spacious and elegant volumes of Turgenev and Tolstoy.

Edward sent copies to his old friends. Conrad did not like the book at all – 'he is too Russian for me'[52] – but was his usual courteous self about the translation. Galsworthy reserved his main comment until two years later:

I'm reading *The Brothers Karamazov* a second time; and just after *War and Peace* I'm bound to say it doesn't wash. Amazing in places, of course; but my God! – what incoherence and what verbiage, and what starting of monsters out of holes to make you shudder. It's a mark of these cubistic, blood-bespattered-poster times that Dostoievsky should rule the roost. Tolstoy is far greater, and Turgenev too.[53]

The younger generation found Dostoevsky more congenial. Bennett, of course, was enthusiastic. Hugh Walpole took the book with him on holiday in Cornwall and 'was so overwhelmed with excitement at his new discovery that, without pause to consider, he dashed off a letter about it to Henry James',[54] who replied at length on 19 May:

At least when you ask me if I don't feel Dostoieffsky's 'mad jumble, that flings things down in a heap,' nearer truth and beauty than the picking and composing that you instance in Stevenson, I reply with emphasis that I feel nothing of the sort, and that the older I grow and the more I *go* the more sacred to me do picking and composing become. . ..[55]

But these uncomprehending elders were in a minority. Among younger and more fashionable readers, as Frank Swinnerton put it, 'we heard on all sides . . . roars of ecstatic discovery. How pale Turgenev seemed! How material and common in grain our realistic writers! How drab the life of restrained feelings!'[56]

Dostoevsky was 'beatified, canonized, sainted,' wrote Thomas

Seccombe, one of those with whom Edward used regularly to lunch at the Mont Blanc, 'The floodgates of the Russian temperament are being opened. . .. We welcome the oncoming flood.'[57] Diaghilev's Ballets Russes had been greeted with similar enthusiasm the year before when they astounded London and danced in a Coronation Gala, and they were due to return to London in six weeks' time. The cult was given a further fillip when Roger Fry's second Post-Impressionist Exhibition opened on 5 October 1912 with its avowed intention of showing the new movement 'in its contemporary development not only in France, its native place, but in England where it is of very recent growth, and in Russia where it has liberated and revived the old native tradition'.[58] With the latter and with the advent of Freud, Dostoevsky contributed to a larger movement of artistic liberation in what Galsworthy described with such distaste as 'these cubistic, blood-bespattered-poster times'. Of all his literary judgements, Edward's notion that the British public would never take to Dostoevsky was the most mistaken.

Constance still did not believe that English readers would ever find *Crime and Punishment* palatable, and was incensed when her publisher seemed to be trying to steal a march on her:

That silly Heinemann has just sent proofs of 'Crime and Punishment'. When last I heard, he definitely arranged for the 'Idiot' to be the next vol. and I consider it will be a great mistake to put 'C and P' so early in the series. I have written to him about it. If people have been attracted by the first 3 or 4 vols, they may buy 'C and P' to complete their set. Otherwise it's hardly likely to sell. . . .[59]

Heinemann's judgement of the market was far sounder than hers. But he did not press the point and merely told her that he was printing it 'only in order to take advantage of the cheap rates in the summer'.[60]

Constance seemed unaware of all the fuss she had caused, and quietly got on with translating *The Idiot*. Besides Juliet and Natalie, she had recently acquired another helper to read Russian aloud to her. Sybil Rudall, after several adventurous years in Russia, had returned to England. Constance noted with some surprise: 'Sybil really *is* going to marry her Professor [Charles Wilson of University College, London, then in his sixties], who seems a good old fellow in some ways and a great Persian scholar, though somewhat crazy – we must hope his craziness will continue to take its present harmless form.'[61] They were duly married and took over Grace's Cottage, Richard Heath having died on 10 February. The professor proved harmless enough, a 'faun-like and Victorian . . . shy elderly figure carrying an umbrella whom one met under the beech trees'.[62] Sybil was available to read aloud to Constance, and did much of this work, but she was apt to lead Constance into errors when her imperfect knowledge of Russian led her to mispronounce unfamiliar words, and she could not resolve 'difficulties' as Natalie could. Grace sometimes helped her with revisions and proofs; and the typing was still done by Kate, or Kate dictating to her son Douglas. 'They do work hard for their £3, poor dears,' Constance remarked, 'but in a way Katie enjoys it and says it is a rest from housework.'[63] *The Idiot* was finished in August 1912, but Constance was not paid for it until May 1913, when she received £118 from Heinemann. After she had paid her various friends for their help she was left with £60. The next volume was, as she wished, *The Possessed*. *Crime and Punishment* came out as volume four in 1914, and thereafter she brought one or two volumes a year until all twelve volumes were completed in 1920, some two-and-a-half million words in all.

As Constance began to realise that Heinemann had a series of potential best-sellers on his hands, she came to regret that she had been persuaded to ask for a flat fee, and to have a genuine grievance against her publisher:

I have been translating for you for twenty years and my work has been uniformly praised by all the critics both English and Russian and has in fact gained me a reputation rather unusual for a translator.

Yet I am actually being paid less for what I am doing for you now than for the work I did when I had no name and no experience.[64]

She was, moreover, having now to pay a substantial amount of her earnings to Sybil and Natalie. But Heinemann insisted that the Dostoevskys were not yet in profit, and he could not forget his 'unfortunate Tolstoy translations'[65] – he was never the most tactful of men. At last 'after a prolonged and bitter correspondence'[66] he agreed to improve the terms for the last five volumes, increasing the initial fee by three shillings per thousand words and paying a five per cent royalty after three thousand copies had been sold.

Helen Muchnic, writing on Dostoevsky's English reputation (1881–1936), maintained that Constance's

was the first adequate translation in English and remains the most honest, close, and natural one. It reproduces better than other translations the special quality of Dostoevsky's style, an eminently 'plain' style, of a plainness that is the product of two qualities: a sharp intelligence which strikes through to the ultimate simplicity of what it observes, and a democratic temper which expresses itself most easily in colloquial rather than 'literary' idiom. A good translation should convey his effect of bare simplicity.[67]

She made a detailed comparison of a passage from *The House of the Dead* in five different translations (one of them in French), noting that

Even Constance Garnett, who is the most successful in approximating to the original, must use 286 words to Dostoevsky's 193. But her additions are either necessitated by linguistic differences – Russian, for example, has no article either definite or indefinite, and being an inflected language, may often omit pronouns – or they are made for the sake of clarity.[68]

For Constance herself, translating Dostoevsky was not so much a feat of skill, as of endurance and self-discipline, especially as so much of it had to be read aloud and taken down by someone else. At the end of her life she told David: 'Dostoevsky is so obscure and so careless a writer that one can scarcely help clarifying him – sometimes it needs some penetration to see what he is trying to say.'[69] And David later recalled that 'One of her greatest difficulties in translating Dostoevsky . . . was to make the English as vague, imprecise in meaning and rambling as the original. She was always having to stop herself from giving way to the temptation of putting what he was trying to say more clearly than he had succeeded in doing.'[70] This is a long way from Muchnic's 'plain style', but it is how Dostoevsky strikes many readers, for instance Ernest Hemingway, who asked Evan Shipman:

'How can a man write so badly, so unbelievably badly, and make you feel so deeply?'

'It can't be the translation,' Evan said. 'She makes the Tolstoy come out well written.'

'I know. I remember how many times I tried to read *War and Peace* until I got the Constance Garnett translation.'[71]

Some scholars have now shown, at least to their own satisfaction, that Dostoevsky's 'loose construction' and 'unbelievably bad' writing were the considered results of his artistic intention. If this is so, all the more credit to Constance for her restraint and care in trying not to 'improve' him.

It was not, however, as a stylist that Dostoevsky was revered. He was seen as a great creative force and a penetrating psychologist, and though some might still consider him a monster erupting into the House of Fiction he remained a formidable influence on twentieth-century literature. Long before Constance had completed her last volume of his works she had made Dostoevsky's name a household word – and he had done the same for her.

19

D. H. Lawrence: 'Little Demon of Perversity'

D. H. Lawrence was well acquainted with the Garnetts long before Constance got to know him. In the miner's cottage where he was brought up they 'regarded with a reverence amounting to awe'[1] a set of Richard Garnett's most imposing legacy to posterity, the twenty-volume *International Library of Famous Literature* (1899). Lawrence read widely in it and gained a good knowledge of the world's literature, though it was curiously weak in translations from the Russian, and when he first heard of Edward in September 1911 he mistook him for its editor. He was by then twenty-six years old, a qualified teacher in a school in Croydon. He had literary ambitions and had been reading the *English Review* since it first began. His friend Jessie Chambers sent the editor some of his poems, Hueffer accepted them, and this set him off on his literary career, or, as he put it:

Ford Madox Hueffer discovered I was a genius – don't be alarmed, Hueffer would discover *anything* if he wanted to – published me some verse and a story or two, sent me to Wm. Heinemann with *The White Peacock*, and left me to paddle my own canoe. I very nearly wrecked it and did for myself. Edward Garnett, like a good angel, fished me out.[2]

Ford tried to make a similar discovery of David: 'Send him to me for a few years, Connie, and I will teach him to write like Flaubert.' 'The offer' David added, 'was not considered seriously and I missed the opportunity of becoming a feather in Ford's cap.'[3]

Lawrence, however, was such a feather. Ford published some of his poems in the third issue of the *English Review*, and all but one of the following eight issues included a contribution of some kind from him. But Ford's editorship lasted only a year, until December 1909, when he sold the *Review* and handed over the editing to Austin Harrison. And though Constance thought Harrison 'a nauseous little creature',[4] he printed what Ford had taken on, and the *English Review* continued to publish Lawrence from time to time.

In the summer of 1911 Edward was appointed English representative of the American Century Company and was on the look-out for good short stories, and it was for this reason that he got in touch with Lawrence. They met on 4 October, and Edward was immediately attracted by the 'loveableness, cheekiness, intensity and pride' of a young man who was already 'roguishly aware of himself'.[5] He invited Lawrence for the first of several week-ends at the Cearne. Lawrence felt very much at home there and found the place 'exactly like the 15th century . . . all in perfect taste'.[6] Constance and David remained in London, leaving Li Whale to come over from her cottage and keep house and Edward free to apply his judicious mixture of general flattery and particular criticism without interruption. As Lawrence wrote:

We discussed books most furiously, sitting drinking wine in the ingle nook, cosy and snug in the big, long room. We had a fine time, only he and I. He thinks my work is quite extra. So do I, of course. But Garnett rather flatters me. He praises me for my sensuous feeling in my writing.[7]

Later, in November, R. A. Scott-James, the literary editor of the *Daily News*, was also there to meet Lawrence, and they sat by the fire while Edward expounded the nature of his genius, and

just how, with that background, it lent itself to that fearless exposure of body and soul which was the reality of creative art. And Lawrence, at first shyly, but with growing confidence, began to see himself through Garnett's eyes and to relish the *rôle* of the distinctive 'genius' allotted to him.[8]

But in that cold season Lawrence stood out of doors too long talking to Edward as he chopped wood, and he caught a chill which worsened into pneumonia. He very nearly died and was long recovering. 'An illness changes me a good deal –' he wrote, 'like winter on the face of the earth.'[9] His doctor told him he 'mustn't go to school again or I shall be consumptive'.[10] Thereafter he escaped from teaching, but not from consumption.

One day in the spring of 1912, probably 17 March, he went to lunch in Nottingham with Professor Ernest Weekley, who had taught him French when he had been a student at University College, and he immediately impressed the professor's unlikely wife. Frieda was a German aristocrat, the daughter of a baron, with a 'Freifräulein' and a 'von' to her name. Ivy Low thought she was 'very beautiful, very central

European, but not elegant in the way London and New York women are elegant. She was picturesque in her fair way, and a bit sloppy and arty. Embroidered Rumanian blouses were right up her alley.'[11] She was six years older than Lawrence. She had been married for twelve years and had three children, the eldest of them a boy of eleven. She was bored by her life as a professor's wife, and much attracted by Lawrence.

On 17 April he wrote to Edward about her: 'She is ripping – she's the finest woman I've ever met – you must above all things meet her. . . . I'll bet you've never met anybody like her, by a long chalk. You *must* see her next week. I wonder if she'd come to the Cearne, if you asked us. Oh, but she is the woman of a lifetime.'[12] He duly brought her down to the Cearne, for Edward was already 'the only man in England who would be a refuge'[13] and the Cearne 'the nearest place to home that I've got'.[14] It was spring, the apple-trees were in blossom, and the place could not have been more hospitable to lovers. Lawrence was inspired to celebrate the Cearne in a poem which is almost as much a tribute to the beauty of the Weald as seen from the seat at the foot of the orchard as a declaration of love to Frieda sitting on that seat while he lay on the grass beside her.[15]

Then Frieda went to London to bid farewell to her children, and on 3 May she and Lawrence left for Germany.

Edward continued to act as mentor, confidant and unpaid editor and literary agent, doing his best to place Lawrence's work and put it into publishable shape. He persuaded Lawrence to make a drastic revision of his third novel, *Paul Morel*, and then went through *Sons and Lovers*, as it had now become, and cut it by about a tenth. 'You did the pruning jolly well,' Lawrence wrote, 'and I am grateful. I hope you'll live a long time, to barber up my novels for me before they're published. I wish I weren't so profuse – or prolix, or whatever it is.'[16]

Later in that summer of 1912 David decided to spend part of his vacation in Munich. As Lawrence and Frieda were staying at Icking, only a dozen miles away up the Isar, it was natural that Edward should suggest they should meet. Lawrence wrote with instructions, and added: 'I look fearfully English, and so I guess do you, so there is no need for either of us to carry the Union Jack for recognition.'[17] He was right, as David wrote:

He did look fearfully English. The bare-headed, slight figure moved towards me; I noticed a scrubby little moustache, and I was looking into the most beautiful lively, blue eyes. . . . Lawrence was slight in build, with a weak, narrow chest and shoulders, but he was a fair height and very light in his movements. This lightness gave him a sort of grace. His hair was of a colour, and grew in a particular way, which I have never seen except in English working men. It was bright mud-colour, with a streak of red in it, a thick mat, parted on one side. Somehow it was incredibly plebeian, mongrel and underbred. His forehead was broad, but not high, his nose too short and lumpy, his face colourless, like a red-haired man's, his chin (he had not then grown a beard) altogether too large, and round like a hairpin – rather a Philip IV sort of chin – and the lower lip, rather red and moist, under the scrubby toothbrush moustache. He looked like a mongrel terrier among a crowd of Pomeranians and Alsatians, English to the bone. He was the type of the plumber's mate who goes back to fetch the tools. He was the weedy runt you find in every gang of workmen: the one who keeps the other men laughing all the time; . . . and is always cheeky, cocky, and in trouble. He was the type who provokes the most violent class-hatred in this country: the impotent hatred of the upper classes for the lower. Certainly Lawrence had no need to carry the Union Jack.

He was all this, but once you looked into his eyes you were completely charmed, they were so beautiful and alive, dancing with gaiety. His smile lit up all his face as he looked at you, asking you silently: 'Come on . . . let's have some fun', and the invitation of this look was irresistible, at least to me. I could no more hold out against it than a well-behaved spaniel can resist the mongrel terrier's invitation to slip off poaching.[18]

And as for Frieda:

At first sight, she might have been a handsome sister of the sweating German mother in the train: she had the same sturdy body, as strong as a horse, the same magnificent shoulders, but her head and the expression of her eyes were very different. Her head and the whole carriage of her body were noble. Her eyes were green, with a lot of tawny yellow in them, the nose straight. She looked one dead in the eyes, fearlessly judging one and, at that moment, she was extraordinarily like a lioness: eyes and colouring, and the swift power of her lazy leap from the hammock where she had been lying.[19]

Such was the description David was later to write of his new friends. Constance was curious to know what they thought of him, and when a letter arrived at the Cearne from Lawrence for Edward she could not resist opening it to find out. She was not disappointed:

He's awfully like you, in a thousand ways – his walk, his touch of mischief and wickedness, and nice things besides. But he hasn't got your appetite for tragedy with the bleeding brow. . . . You should see him swim in the Isar, that is effervescent and pale green, where the current is fearfully strong. He simply smashes his way through the water, while F. sits on the bank bursting with admiration, and I am green with envy. By Jove, I reckon his parents have done joyously well for that young man.[20]

David was completely charmed by them. As he later remarked, 'I have always been particularly attracted by happy lovers.'[21] But, as he soon realised, they were far from being happy lovers. Ernest Weekley was distraught and threatened them 'alternately with murder and with suicide (the latter his own)' Lawrence wrote to David. 'I always expect a streak of greased lightning to fly out when we open an envelope from him.'[22] There was always 'this drawn sword of the children'[23] between them. There were enormous differences of class and temperament. 'I am common . . .' Lawrence wrote, 'But Frieda is a lady, and I hate her when she talks to the common people. She is not a bit stuck-up, really more humble than I am, but she makes the *de haut en bas* of class distinction felt – even with my sister.'[24] She did not know how to cook or do the housework. She 'did not have to do anything – it was all right for her just to "be"'.[25] Lawrence, on the other hand, found it a relief to make marmalade when he 'got the blues thinking of the future. . . . It's amazing how it cheers one up to shred oranges or scrub the floor.'[26] Whereas much of Lawrence's sex was in his head, Frieda's was voraciously physical. She 'always loved a new man'[27] and had had several affairs before Lawrence came on the scene. In August 1912, less than four months after she had first taken up with Lawrence, she seduced David's handsome young friend, Harold Hobson, and she would have happily done the same to him had he not, with unusual prudence, resisted the temptation.

Lawrence and Frieda played host to another of the Garnetts 'friends besides Harold Hobson. Antonia Almgren was a niece of Constance's old friend, Lina Eckenstein. She was an artist, married to a Swede and with a small daughter, Gisela. She made a speciality of embroidered pictures. Her grim view of Stonehenge in purples and greens, with mammoths marching across Salisbury Plain under a lowering sky, hung for many years over Constance's bedroom mantelpiece. She thought it was 'magnificent – much the best thing she has done'.[28] Antonia, or Tony as they all called her, stayed a while at the Cearne in 1911 and David recalled her 'huge dark eyes which seemed to grow bigger as she responded to my father's teasing, or when my uncle Arthur made her the object of one of his crushing sarcasms, which were quite incapable of crushing her, for she was full of spirit'.[29] It was she who taught David 'something about physical love, but the lesson that a liaison is not satisfactory for more than a few weeks, unless one is in love, was not in the least what I had expected, or what I wanted to know at nineteen'.[30]

In the summer of 1912 her husband, who Constance thought was 'very mad, poor dear'[31] pursued her across England. Constance and Sybil Rudall scoured the countryside for a cottage where she might hide; and Constance also wrote to Edward in June, 'If you come across a nice cheap lodging (*not* one where you stay yourself with Nellie) that would do for Tony and Gis [e] la for a fortnight from June 15 to 29 – do note name and address – to board in a farm might do – but it must be cheap. It's rather urgent.'[32] They eventually found her a lodging at Chelwood Gate. Then in February 1913 Tony decided she wanted to go abroad. Robert Garnett advised 'if T. decides to go abroad she had better go *as soon as possible*'.[33] In March Constance wished her willy-nilly on to Lawrence and Frieda, 'I don't think T. had better defer going till an answer comes from the Ls? If they can't take her, couldn't a room be found for her there? in the neighbourhood?'[34] By that time they were in Italy, by Lake Garda. Lawrence welcomed someone to help him with the housework, and wrote that she was 'just prodding the cauliflower with a fountain pen, to see if it's done. It explains the whole situation.'[35]

Lawrence had thus been much involved with the Garnetts, a close friend of Edward's for nearly two years, and of David's for half as long, before Constance got to know him. If she had met him in England it was only briefly, but she must have heard a great deal about him. She read his letters and his books, and in March 1913 she wrote: 'David has been reading me "The White Peacock". I agree with him that it's a better book than "The Trespasser". Something in it recalls Jefferies all the while, and I believe I should have guessed him consumptive, if I had known nothing of him.'[36]

She had certainly not met Frieda and was eager to do so. She thought 'she must be cute, for she sizes Tony up at once',[37] Frieda having written to David, 'I like Tony for many things; she is chasing greatness as if it were a rabbit and she wants to put salt on its tail!',[38] 'which' Constance commented, 'is what I've always had an inkling of – and is so rare in women that one can't help prizing it when one suspects its presence in the smallest degree – also her independence – but "she's cold to give one shivers"'.[39]

Then on Monday 7 April Constance wrote to Edward in some alarm: 'The Lawrences are coming after all! David has had a letter saying they would turn up on the 10th or 12th!! Thursday or Sat. next.'[40] This was going to cause some problems: 'We shall be a big housefull – as I can't turn Margaret [?Radford] out till I go back to town on Monday. If Nelly would care to come, (which I should love) there would be a room free at Li's cottage. Or I could go over there and give her my room.'[41] (Nellie never shared a room with Edward – at least when Constance or company were present; nor is there any evidence that Lawrence was aware of her relationship with Edward, though he later took quite an interest in her paintings.) Edward would have to put off the guest he had already invited for the week-end.

Frieda will probably prefer *not* to meet people. I gather from Tony's letters that she's at rather a crisis, poor darling. . . . People so often don't mix. . . . Harold [Hobson] came on Saturday and left early this morning. He threatens to come next week-end, d— n him! I told him we couldn't ask him, as we should be full up, but he said he'd sleep in the wood. I wish he could be choked off so that we could enjoy the Ls in peace – but I am powerless against the massive impenetrability of his egoism.[42]

After all this pother Lawrence and Frieda did not turn up. They kept 'chopping and changing'.[43] They had been coming so that Frieda could 'see the children by hook or crook – chiefly by crook',[44] though Lawrence had a horror of her 'stopping her son as he comes from school, and seeing him so'.[45] Now they had a wild notion that Frieda's mother 'shall ask Prof. W – with whom she still corresponds amicably – to send the children to Baden Baden, perhaps for Whitsuntide, so that Frieda may see them there'.[46] But nothing came of this plan, as Weekley grew more and more hostile, so they decided to come to England after all.

In June Constance learnt that Lawrence and Frieda had arrived and were bent on staying at the Cearne, even though Edward would not be there. Li Whale, moreover, was away, so Constance would have to go down and cope with the housekeeping herself. Once again she had to rearrange everything to suit her guests.

Bless those Lawrences! I had fixed up my programme so tight – clearing off the revision with N [atalie] till Friday, then Katie and I were going down . . . for a week or 10 days to clear off 'the Possessed'.
   Well – I'm writing round to fix up as best I can . . . for they can't go down to find everything locked, no food and no one to do anything. It's a pity they are coming just before the boy's exam, which is next week.[47]

But once they had arrived she was charmed by Lawrence, as Edward and David had been, for, as David wrote:

Lawrence had a special gift for entering immediately on deeply intimate relations with everyone he met: he had shoals of human relationships, for he could charm every human creature who attracted or interested him and at first meeting almost every fresh separate person did attract him. . . . He couldn't buy a stamp without starting some intimate contact.[48]

Lawrence shared with Constance a great love of flowers – he had got a Distinction in Botany in his Teacher's Certificate – and both found relaxation in working in the garden. Lawrence was happy to spend a morning 'netting the raspberries'.[49] He marvelled at the ease and fluency with which she turned out her pile of translations of Dostoevsky at her feet. He liked to tease her and call her Constanza Davidovna. David's sympathies, however, were firmly with Frieda:

there was a streak of cruelty in Lawrence; he was jealous of the children and angry with Frieda, because she could not forget them. Now that she had come back to England, she was longing to see them, and the spiteful, ill-conditioned, ungenerous side of Lawrence's character was constantly breaking out in different ways.[50]

David 'spent several afternoons in London with her, hanging round St Paul's School in the hope that she could intercept her son and see him for a moment or two'.[51] But after Lawrence had agreed to join Frieda in one of these meetings Constance wrote to Edward: 'There has been a blessed calm here the last few days – varied only by Frieda's insisting on expecting Prof. W. to come down here and shoot Lawrence.'[52] Although she loathed interfering in other people's affairs, she liked rows even less, and she bravely told Lawrence:

I didn't believe their relations could survive these conflicts and as a sensible man he ought to see it and part before he makes things too hard for her. Well, he says I don't understand – that his love is of the permanent sort – and that it's all that F. only *half* loves him – but he'll *make* her love him altogether – (This apparently involves her forgetting the past!) I think the talk has had a good effect in making him behave a bit better – but F. is very tactless and her denseness in some directions makes him almost scream with anguish – and I'm afraid it's a bit beyond her to change effectually. . . . Bunny is being very sweet and I don't think we need be afraid in future of F. and L. having too much influence on him. He is always trying to calm them.[53]

The precarious calm continued: 'L. and F. are in a peaceful and cheerful mood for the minute,' she warned Edward, 'so don't upset them by talking of their mutual relations or they'll be at hammer and tongs again.'[54] And on 7 July, when the visit was drawing to a close, she wrote again:

L and F stay till Wed. when they propose going to Margate. I don't think L. will come to town today. . . . We have had a peaceful time – Lawrence very sweet – he is a nice person in the house – and F. rather trying – she won't let things drop. L. has been helping me by thinning the carrots. The rain has made me eager to do a little in the garden – everything is thriving except for the rabbits.[55]

Lawrence offered to snare the rabbits, but Constance did not trust him to do so successfully, and was punished for her lack of faith when they 'nearly cleared off the carrots which Lawrence thinned so nicely for me'.[56]

Lawrence wrote to Constance soon after he had left:

I wish I was at the Cearne. It is the sort of place I fit into – something so solid and unmovable about it, something unexpected and individualised: that bare workmanlike study, that farm-house hall, that burst into country houseism and culture in the big room, with the lapse into disgraceful, almost brutal roughness – nearly like Squire Western – under the fire-place: the common place kitchen and the dejected scullery – oh Lord, I could live for ages at the Cearne, and be happy.[57]

The Garnetts did not provide him only with a refuge and literary advice and management. They acted for a while as a sort of general agency. Kate Clayton and her son, Douglas, undertook to type his manuscripts. Constance and David, as well as Edward, were kept busy sending his stories to likely editors and forwarding the resulting cheques to the author. David made the selection for his *Love Poems* in the spring of 1913; and for a while Constance even provided a banking service, keeping his money in her own account and forwarding it as required.

Sons and Lovers had been published in May 1913, just before Lawrence and Frieda came to the Cearne, and had had excellent reviews. Lawrence was beginning to be a celebrity. He made new literary friends: Middleton Murry and Katherine Mansfield, Edward Marsh and W. H. Davies; and others not so literary: Herbert and Cynthia Asquith, Philip and Lady Ottoline Morrell.

From time to time Lawrence would be taken over by what David called 'the black fiend from the revival meeting' and then 'he would storm and rage and sit nursing his devil as though it were a fire of green wood. Not for anything would he let his flame of wrath splutter out.'[58] His relations with the Garnetts became more equivocal. At one moment he would write to Edward, 'Thank Mrs Garnett for her letter – she's awfully good to us'[59] and five days later to Frieda's sister, 'Garnett was awfully nice, but I don't like Mrs G. and I hated her cold blooded sister from Ceylon.'[60] Eleven days later he was asking Constance out to stay with him in Italy.

He had a disconcerting habit of taking against those he had formerly liked or admired. When Constance first got to know him at the Cearne he had a fairly unqualified admiration for the Russian writers she had translated, most of whom he had read in earlier versions. But within a year he found them 'dull, old, dead',[61] and before long Dostoevsky was 'like the rat, slithering along in hate'[62] and Turgenev 'a sort of male old maid' given to 'journalistic bludgeonings'.[63]

Nevertheless he continued to send friendly messages to Constance, and she to feel goodwill towards him.

On 20 October she read in the *Daily News* that Weekley had been granted 'a decree nisi with costs and custody of the children' on the ground 'of the misc onduct of his wife with the co-respondent, Mr. B. H. Lawrence [*sic*], described as an author',[64] and she commented: 'I hope the costs are not very heavy. I'm afraid he'll be in straits, unless Frieda's people are prepared to help. They really ought to, for it's quite as much her responsibility.'[65]

By that time the guilty couple were in Italy. On arriving at Lerici, where he stayed at the Albergo delle Palme, Lawrence wrote to Edward:

I am so happy with the place we have at last discovered, I must write smack off to tell you. It is perfect. There is a little tiny bay half shut in by rocks, and smothered by olive woods that slope down swiftly. Then there is one pink, flat, fisherman's house. Then there is the villino of Ettore Gambrosier, a four-roomed pink cottage among vine gardens, just over the water and under the olive woods. There, D.V., is my next home. . . . Now you will come and see us – and so will Constanza Davidovna – she promised – she would be so happy.[66]

Constance loved to spend the worst of the winter abroad – it did wonders for her sciatica. Li urged her to go, and she accepted the invitation. She took, not Edward, but Vera Volkhovsky, both for companionship and to read Russian aloud to her, for she hoped to translate some more Dostoevsky. At first Frieda was 'horrified'[67] because she thought Constance's companion might be Tony Almgren, whom she had taken against. Fortunately they liked Vera, who remained a friend.

Lerici lies in the grandly named Gulf of Spezia, a small arm of the sea no more than ten miles long and five miles across. La Spezia, a large port and naval base, shelters at the head of the bay behind a long breakwater. The port of Lerici is a cove on the north-eastern side, just outside the breakwater, with mountains behind, and the town of San Terenzo at the nearer and Lerici at the further end. Beyond Lerici the mountainous coastline is broken into a jagged series of rocky coves, in the fourth of which is Fiascherino, where Lawrence had found his villino.

Constance and Vera spent the night of 24 January 1914 in the Grand Hôtel d'Italie at La Spezia, and the next day they were met by Lawrence, who took them on the vaporino to Lerici past grand scenery and under blue Italian skies. The sun seemed to have done him good – 'at least he seems better – his voice much stronger and he doesn't cough – but he looks holloweyed and thin, of course. Frieda blooms like a rose.'[68]

In Lerici they stayed, as Lawrence had done, at the Albergo delle Palme. Constance was enchanted with it:

Delightful to wake up this morning and throw open my shutters and windows. One might be in a ship – from the window one sees nothing but the water which comes up to the wall of the road below – and you hear the lapping of it all the time. I can't see the sunrise but we get the full sunset, and this morning it was very beautiful seeing the mountains all bathed in pink light as the sun rose. There's a flagstaff out of my window which makes it seem all the more like a ship. . . . I went down feeling it might be too early and very gauche and English on my part to expect breakfast so soon, but Francesco's angelic smile removed all uneasiness. They all smile at one as only little children are smiled at in England.[69]

Vera was equally delighted:

She says she hasn't felt as lighthearted for years. I don't believe we shall do any work unless the weather changes. It would be madness to work while the sky is so blue. Lawrence says they had a snowfall here about a fortnight ago and a lot of olive trees were broken by the snow – the people being too lazy to knock the snow off – instead of doing that all the women went to pray to the Madonna to take away the snow – while the men stood about swearing and shouting their grief. The snow all melted next day.[70]

Constance had never been in Italy and knew not a word of the language: 'I do wish I had brought some sort of grammar or word-book. I could soon have picked up a little Italian – and I feel so silly not even able to say "please".'[71]

Lerici was hallowed ground to Richard Garnett, who had written an introduction to the journal of Edward Ellerker Williams, with whom Shelley had spent the last few months of his life at Casa Magni, an almost derelict former boathouse on the shore, some two hundred yards from San Terenzo. Shelley enjoyed sailing the *Don Juan* with Williams, but Mary was miserable and had a miscarriage, and Claire Clairmont was distraught at the death of Allegra, her daughter by Byron. 'Nature is here as vivid and joyous,' Shelley wrote, 'as we are dismal.'[72] Shelley was hastening home to Lerici from a visit to Byron and Leigh Hunt when the *Don Juan* sank and he was drowned.

But the tourists had not yet started to come. Lerici was still an industrial town, and living was cheap. 'You see no middle-class people at all – all look like factory hands or peasants – except a large sprinkling of very uninviting-looking young women. Lawrence says the sailors bring a lot of shady characters in their train.'[73] Constance was reminded of the 'little grubby back lanes'[74] of Montpellier:

Steep houses with just slits of windows in them – and little bare turnings in between like ravines between precipices – very dark and chilly. Nowhere a trace of care or of decoration – or regard for appearances – dirty half-washed clothes hanging out of windows – nowhere a curtain or a flower in the window – stucco peeling off everywhere – and stains on all the walls – with heaps of filth and refuse in every gutter and every corner – and overhead a glorious deep blue sky and sunshine and at every turn a lovely view of blue sea and pinky gray mountains.[75]

At eleven on their first morning Lawrence came in a boat to row them over to his house at Fiascherino. 'From all accounts it is a terrible walk – perhaps beyond my powers – almost mountain climbing – so I don't think we shall see such a great lot of them.'[76] But in fact they were invigorated by Italy and walked as they never would have done at home.

On the 30th they walked to San Terenzo, 'a very squalid little port – and oh my dear, the smells!'[77] They watched the fishermen 'draw in a net and take out the little silver fishes that flashed about like quicksilver in the sun'.[78] She saw the fishermen at work and described them in much the same terms as Lawrence might have done:

It's nice to watch the Italians doing anything – they are so concentrated – the sort of concentration you see in a cat watching a mousehole – and it seems as though all their actions come easily by instinct – so they are never clumsy or awkward. You see old women carrying tremendous great loads balanced on their heads, stepping down the steep mountain paths which are like stairs made of loose cobbles – and they never hesitate or stumble. They all seem to have a perfection of balance naturally that English people could only get by training.[79]

Lawrence brought them their letters, and while the beautiful weather lasted took them on walks up the mountains. They went shopping with him, chugging into La Spezia on the little vaporino, and having tea with the British consul, Thomas Dunlop, whom Lawrence had already enrolled to type his new novel. Lawrence invited them to his house to meet some of the English residents:

They see a great deal of all the respectable English people here – none of whom know that they are not legally married – and they are very popular – naturally. They must be a real godsend to the English villa people – for no people in the world are so dull as communities of English living abroad. . . . I should have thought they'd have found all these English residents rather a bore – I mean they strike me as having nothing in common with them – ladies who read Merriman and confess to liking 'The Rosary' and who say to Lawrence archly 'Now do confess, Paul Morel is meant for yourself, isn't he?' after reading 'Sons and Lovers'. But you know what a social creature he is and besides I believe it flatters him to feel that even with these people he can be a success.[80]

Constance and Vera continued to spend much of their time walking: 'It's extraordinary how well filled our days are and yet we never read or work. We are practically always out from soon after breakfast till sunset only coming in for lunch.'[81] On 3 February they

had a wonderful walk . . . it was up, up, up, through little stone-paved paths and gullies in the hill-side – almost always between olive-trees, which are very beautiful here, quite unlike the fat cabbage-shaped trees in the South of France. At last we got to La Serra – the queerest of villages – or rather a little town. There's not a level square foot in the place – every little street or lane is really a staircase – very narrow between tall houses – often with arches from house to house – extraordinarily picturesque. The brilliant blue sky and the patches of glaring light peeping in here and there in these little dark ways between the houses give an extraordinary effect. . . .
  Then we clambered up higher still till we got quite to the top of one of the lower mountains – (or hills) and there we lay in a tiny little terrace with two olive-trees in it. I never saw so much stone – everywhere stone ways – stone walls – stone cottages – stone enough to build all the cities of the world. It *was* a lovely place – such a view of the sea below us and to the rear the snow tops of the Carrara mountains.[82]

And in the eve ning Lawrence and Frieda came to dinner at the Albergo delle Palme and 'stayed talking and arguing till eleven'.[83] On the following afternoon they 'clambered up another gully with Frieda to tea with a Mrs Huntington, a remarkably nice woman who has a villa here and has lived all her life in Italy'.[84] Mrs Huntington was an exception.

She knew that Lawrence and Frieda were not married, and 'as a good Roman Catholic strongly disapproved of their conduct, but her humanity triumphed and she showed herself a kind friend to them'.[85] And she took Vera out walking when Constance was unwell for the day.

Amid all this social round Lawrence as usual found time to write. Before Constance's arrival he had sent Edward the beginnings of a new novel, then entitled *The Sisters*. Edward as usual told him he must rewrite it. Constance reported back: 'Lawrence has begun writing his novel again with great spirit. He told me of your letter and said you were quite right. He didn't seem downcast, at all, but I fancy full of confidence that he could get it right. He has plenty of pluck and is very industrious.'[86] And a few days later:

Lawrence has put a good face on the blow about his novel, but he has looked very white and pinched the last few days. He says he agrees with you entirely. Frieda and he seem to have been having a set-to yesterday and the day before – and both looked as if they had been crying – but today they are both happier again. Lawrence is a queer little changeling – there's a sort of little demon of perversity in him, and yet he is so full of bonhomie and genuine friendliness and kindness. Frieda shows to much greater advantage in her own house.[87]

Later Constance tackled him about the new book herself:

I spoke to Lawrence about the first draft of 'The Sisters'. He said he had begun it again because it was so 'boshy, don't you know' and suggested I should read it. Well, having now read most of it, I agree with him that it *is* awfully poor stuff. The characters aren't living at all, one doesn't believe in them, or take them at the author's apparent valuation. They seem simply invented to hang the pages of description of sexual experiences and emotions on to, and the theories about those emotions. And I felt all the time that all the love part is ladled out so disproportionately that it isn't effective. It palls really because there's no light and shade – it all seems cheap intensity and violence at the same hysterical pitch all through. It seems to me much below The White Peacock and The Trespasser and I'm glad he realises it isn't up to much. Of course there are very good bits in it – and the underlying notion is good and strong – but it's so incredibly shapeless and inartistic – so sloppy in its presentation. I feel uneasy about his future if he can go off like that. But the new beginning he has made is very promising (though of course he sets off at the top note of intensity with the father of the heroines and one doesn't see how the interest can rise after that quite).[88]

The manuscript of *The Sisters* that Constance read was in fact the second draft, not the first. Only a few pages survive. The new beginning, which was for a while entitled *The Wedding Ring*, eventually became *The Rainbow*, but there were many further rewritings to be done before Lawrence arrived at the final version.

Constance was also worried about him being so far from home: 'I'm afraid as time goes on his work may suffer from his being cut off his natural environment. He'll exhaust the material he has gathered from his early surroundings and the life he is leading now doesn't seem likely to provide fresh stuff for him.'[89] In this she was mistaken. Lawrence was already writing perceptively about Italy, and was to draw inspiration from his travels for the rest of his life.

Constance, who, David said, 'could be very tactless' but 'was never intentionally rude to anyone',[90] must have been painfully outspoken to Lawrence, for he afterwards wrote to Edward, 'Mrs Garnett says I have no true nobility – with all my cleverness and charm. But that is not true. It is there, in spite of all the littlenesses and commonnesses'.[91] On the other hand she provided a convenient ear for Frieda to 'go to her and pour out my Lawrence woes to her and she listens patiently and feelingly',[92] an experience that she cannot have enjoyed.

After a couple of weeks the weather broke: 'To-day we have a really hopeless day – the first – sky and sea are leaden grey and rain is falling fast. Vera is wisely putting in the time in bed – and there's nothing for me to do but write letters and think of home.'[93] She worried about work to be done in the garden at the Cearne, and was anxious that Li Whale should get on with the spring cleaning while she was away. Ten days later the weather was even worse: 'There has been a regular storm raging in the bay for the last three days – we could hardly sleep at all last night. . . . If it should be as bad on Wednesday as last night I should not care to cross the bay in one of the poor little vaporinos. . . .'[94] But she crossed the bay safely and was home by 27 February.

Lawrence and Frieda returned to England on 24 June. They paid one more visit to the Cearne. On 4 July Constance wrote to Edward about a new servant girl:

I have been having a slow time. Emily's sister is one of those oppressive country girls who says 'oh, yes' to everything in a tone so monotonous and devoid of all human feeling that it makes me want to howl with depression. But the Lawrences will liven me up. Poor dears, I'm afraid they'll be disappointed to find neither you nor David here – but they'll have each other to quarrel with.[95]

A few months later Constance wrote:

Don't ask the Lawrences down, as you may be tempted to when you see them – I don't feel that I could stand his fervid intensity over his personal emotions and Frieda's trivial second-hand generalizations just now (though you know I am fond of them both really).[96]

She did not have another opportunity, and Lawrence was moving on. He had just appointed J. B. Pinker as his professional literary agent, and he felt he did not need Edward's help as he once had done. On 13 July he and Frieda were married, and he was no longer in such need of a refuge – and within the month he met S. S. Koteliansky, with whom he was to work on Russian translations, and who in his very different way was to take Constance's place for him.

In the following year Lawrence wrote a furious letter about David's new friends, Francis Birrell, Duncan Grant and Maynard Keynes. He told David that they made him dream of black-beetles. He was repelled by their homosexuality, but also because they had 'no reverence, not a crumb or grain of reverence'.[97] Indeed they believed in the positive value of irreverence, and that nothing should be sacred from intellectual inquiry. This was one of the things that David found so exciting about them, and he refused to give them up.

At the beginning of 1913 Lawrence had admitted to Ernest Collings, 'I am a great bosher'[98] and then in the same letter stated prophetically, 'My great religion is a belief in the blood, the flesh, as being wiser than the intellect.' For Constance, who could not accept any religion, least of all one which denied the supremacy of the intellect, this was, despite the warmth of her affections, bosh. And however much Lawrence might dress it up as a philosophy it remained so for her and the rest of the Garnetts. As David remarked, Lawrence used up 'his human attachments rather fast, demanding too great an allegiance of some, and giving others too little, while others he drove off by preaching at them or explaining them to themselves'.[99] But the Garnetts did not abandon him. Edward upheld him against the disparagement of Galsworthy, Hudson and Robert Lynd and wrote a defence of Lawrence against the 'moralists'. And, like David's friends, they rallied to his support when *The Rainbow* was suppressed.

David's mature judgement of Lawrence was that he was 'a whole hive of genius',[100] but he also made a comparison with Tolstoy, with which Constance would fully have agreed:

Indeed both in their gifts, and in the limitations they seem wantonly to have put to their intelligences and their art, there is a curious resemblance between

Tolstoy and Lawrence. In their vitality, their astonishing understanding of women, their attitude toward science and toward the greatest works of art and toward other artists, in their desire to change the world spiritually by founding small communities, in their hatred of their disciples, . . . in all these and many other ways there is a curious parallelism between them. And if Tolstoy was a great artist spoiled by ideas, by religious impulses, so was Lawrence, only spoiled much more.[101]

Whatever David felt about the 'spoiled' Lawrence, he considered that he 'had very great virtues which are rare in men: every kind of courage, also hatred of every sort of mess'.[102] David was always proud of having known him, and retained a great affection for the man he knew, and an admiration for his unique art.

Lawrence, too, retained an affection for the Garnetts. In the same letter in which he castigated David's friends and invoked his dreams of black-beetles he wrote: 'I love your father and I love your mother. I think your father has been shamefully treated at the hands of life. Though I don't see him, I do love him in my soul – more even than I love your mother.'[103] And he wrote sympathetically of Constance: 'She seems like an old fighter, and her cause is lost. The cause is lost, God knows. But then, the fight itself is worth it, I suppose –'[104]

Her cause at that moment was that of international decency and sanity, which did indeed seem to Constance to be lost when the Great Powers went to war in August 1914.

20

Lost Causes

Constance spent the summer of 1914 at the Cearne, putting up innumerable visitors, working in the garden and translating Dostoevsky. Natalie had taken Jack Duddington and her infant daughter Anna to Russia to see her family, but Sybil Wilson was still at Grace's Cottage to read aloud *The House of the Dead* to her. She later moved into a wooden hut, known as 'The Datcha', nearby. This was to be the nucleus of a collection of shacks, which Edward nicknamed 'Dostoevsky Corner' on account of the eccentricity of its inhabitants.

Grace herself was in Ceylon, where she was leading an increasingly separate life from Hugh, pursuing with that degree of fanaticism which had so alarmed Dr Garnett, and with the aid of a news-sheet especially devoted to the purpose, the twin aims of abolishing prostitution and prohibiting the sale of alcoholic liquor as a beverage. Having no children of her own – she had had a miscarriage while on a visit to the Cearne with Hugh – she had adopted a tea-planter's daughter, Ruby, whom Constance had described in 1910 as a 'little alien child – so noisy and hard and unlike any children who have been here before'.[1] Ruby was now fourteen years old and at school in England, where she was yet one more of Constance's responsibilities. Li Whale had left Scearn Bank Farm and moved to Letchworth, where she looked after 'heaps of children'[2] and carried on, in a more unselfish fashion, the good work that 'Little Mother' had begun. In her place Constance now had Emily King, 'an attractive woman of about thirty, full of adventurous spirit, with a passion for gardening and outdoor life',[3] who had worked for Louisette Bréal for a dozen years and been the nurse of her youngest child. She loved Constance, who found her 'a great comfort to me in every way'.[4] She was exactly suited to life at the Cearne. 'A tent, or a gun,' David wrote, 'a new variety of lily, or a new breed of domestic fowl brought a sparkle to her eye and a flush to her cheek.'[5]

In September 1912 the Garnetts had for some reason left the flat in Grove Place and taken lodgings at 4 Downshire Hill, a 'nice little old house – very democratic – *very quiet* . . . humble yet a good address',[6] but after a year and much hectic flat-hunting had moved to 19 Pond Place in Chelsea so that David could be nearer to Imperial College. But there was nobody at the flat in July 1914. Edward and Nellie were on holiday in the west of Ireland, and David was camping with Noel Olivier and other friends in Cornwall, having left no very definite address.

When Constance wrote to Edward at the end of July with hasty news of books for him to review, of prospective visitors, work in the garden clearing away old gooseberries and currants and emptying the cesspit, she added, 'There seems a great European crisis going on – and there has been fighting in Dublin.'[7] And on the very eve of war:

The war news is much more than exciting – it's awful, beyond all conception – I'm afraid there is very little doubt we shall join in . . . You see Germany is now at war with Russia, and France with Germany – Russia has forced this on the rest of Europe – and we are probably secretly backing her. You see the financial news. The one hope is that the rise of prices and collapse of credit may quickly force the governments to their senses, before there has been an awful slaughter. . . . All the old gang – the regular lost-causers are getting up protests, anti-war demonstrations etc – but only the old gang – Hobson, Cunningham Grahame [*sic*] etc.[8]

One of the old gang was finally lost to the cause: Felix Volkhovsky died on 2 August at the age of sixty-nine. But there was one eloquent voice of protest which Constance said 'says for me all I have been feeling',[9] that of the veteran pacifist Goldsworthy Lowes Dickinson, who wrote an article on 'The Holy War' in the *Nation*. This was not the war in which 'some fifteen millions of men in Europe, the physically best, those who should be fathers of the next generations' would be obliged against their will to destroy 'all that has laboriously built up during a quarter of a century of European peace', but the struggle of the 'friends of reason' for 'the real things, for good instead of evil, for truth instead of lies, for love instead of hate. . . . That is our war – those of us who believe in reason – our eternal and holy war. In this dark hour of our defeat, let us not forget it.'[10]

Constance had always been a dedicated 'friend of reason', and her reason and her emotions were fully engaged over what she saw as the consequences of this appalling folly. Her experiences in Russia had given her an understanding of the realities of hardship, which few British people shared, and as usual she saw things from an international point of view.

We must all think of all now – not even of England only but of all Europe. If we don't starve, think of France – no hands for the harvest or the vintage – Russia with only women and children for the harvest – and poor Germany – drawn into all this by a brutal military clique who have got the upper hand of all the good and fine people in the country.[11]

She saw all kinds of hardship ahead. She feared that Charles Clayton, already a none too successful architect, would be out of work. Kate had told Constance, 'that if the war with Germany did come, she did not think Charlie would live another 18 months. . . . Now all their sources of income have been dried up – all the firms he was employed by are collapsing – or simply ceasing all work for the time.'[12]

Edward cut short his holiday in Ireland and came home to find that his job with Duckworth was still safe, but, as Constance wrote to David,

The New Weekly is done for by the war; the next number will be the last.
There will be a slump in books, no publishing, no reviewing going on – Duckworth says he shall publish nothing for 3 months for certain – and has already dismissed two of his employés. Dad's income will therefore be cut down to the £15 he gets each month from Duckworth – with no certainty of that continuing, unless the war is soon over – and with a satisfactory result. . . . Of course there'll be no Dostoevsky vols – or Tchehov either – for the next few months – so I shall not get anything but my pension.[13]

The demise of the *New Weekly*, an enterprising literary journal, started only in March with Scott-James as editor, represented another loss of income. In its short life it had published thirteen reviews by Edward, and three of Constance's translations of stories by Chekhov. Her Civil List Pension and the Marshall Scholarship that David had just won were the only income that seemed to her quite secure.

It was a time for the strictest economies. Constance had given up coffee, 'a fearful sacrifice',[14] 'and we have porridge and tea instead of bacon etc.'[15] She thought David ought to give up tobacco. 'We must cut off everything we can, absolutely – I mean, all amusements, luxuries, fares etc – for we cannot let people round us starve.'[16] 'No one with any patriotic or humane feeling would want to be spending any money on anything but helping now.'[17] 'When Pat tried to buy us 7 lbs of oatmeal, they would only sell him 3½ at Oxted – very public spirited of the shop I think.'[18] Constance wished she had planted potatoes – their price had shot up to sixpence a pound in Paris – and she worked hard in the garden: 'every corner of ground ought to be worked and sown quickly – it will be too late soon,' she told David. 'If you were here, I would dig up some of the grass ground – and sow roots. . . . and then I should get a goat from Sybil.'[19]

Most of all she was concerned for David, and thought he should train for ambulance work: 'if we get a naval disaster, we are certain to get conscription at once – and it would be better to risk your life doing good than fighting our German friends'.[20] 'They say the ambulance work is quite as dangerous, so you need not feel you are shirking.'[21]

Besides such acquaintances as David made during his visits to Germany, he had one friend, a Hungarian, and thus a citizen of Austria-Hungary, who was soon to become an enemy. This was Ferenc Békássy, a shy and gentle poet a year younger than himself, who had been at school with Noel Olivier at Bedales and made friends with Maynard Keynes at Cambridge. Less than a month before war broke out he wrote to Constance urging her to translate *The Keys of Happiness*, a novel by Anastasia Verbitsky, which had been coming out in parts in Russian.

Constance replied that she had her hands too full to consider anything else. By this time Békássy was back in Hungary. When war threatened between his country and Serbia he had been in England. Keynes had tried to persuade him not to go back, but when he failed he raised the money for Békássy to do so. Back in Hungary Békássy wrote to Constance on 29 July – only a fortnight before Britain declared war on Austria-Hungary: 'Of course half our relations are soldiers and have gone, or may go – you can imagine the state we are all in, anxiety, turmoil; and enthusiasm. . . .'[22] His letter did not reach Constance until after the war was over, and Békássy had long been dead, having been killed on 25 June 1915, within four days of arriving at the Russian Front.

The 'friends of reason' had lost their cause, and with one exception Constance's prognostications proved correct – they merely took longer to come into effect than she had feared. Publishers were cautious, but in fact did not do badly during the war, indeed they had something of a boom in their cheaper popular editions. Heinemann continued to bring out Dostoevsky as fast as Constance could translate him.

When she had tried to interest Heinemann in publishing Chekhov's tales in book form in June 1914, he had asked for more details and pointed out very reasonably that she still had a great deal of work to do on Dostoevsky, with only four out of twelve volumes yet published and one nearly ready for press. Though Constance must have been irritated by Heinemann remarking 'it never occurred to me that you would be interested in publishing Tchekof',[23] she told Edward, as negotiations slowly petered out over the next year, to 'avoid quarrelling with him – for that would put an end to any chance of my getting anything out of him over the later vols of Dostoevsky'.[24] Heinemann eventually shelved the idea of Chekhov for 'the duration' and continued for the moment to resist demands for more money for Dostoevsky.

Despite her forebodings Constance found before long that they were not doing too badly, 'though of course we shall have to be thrifty to the utmost extreme. . . . We certainly ought to be able to manage like that. It's after *1917* I am uneasy about!'[25]

Constance was well suited to her peasant life at the Cearne, battling for self-sufficiency in the hen-run and the vegetable garden. In her early days at the Cearne she had found autumn the sickliest season, when she was most liable to headaches. But in these war years when there was an autumnal feeling in the air and 'the mornings have that delicious bracing freshness':

I feel rising up that irrational rush of nervous energy that always comes in the autumn. It seems proof against the disillusionment of years and reason and experience. It must be just a physical heritage from the time when the women had to bestir themselves to harvest and store and work ten times as hard as at any other season in order to escape famine in the winter. Whatever it comes from, it is cheering.[26]

And when David came down to see her in January 1915 she seemed 'such a rosy healthy little darling'.[27]

Her concern was all for others. David, once Edward had dissuaded him from his first quixotic impulse to enlist, was safe for the time being. Edward was in a state of 'crushing gloom',[28] and at odds with his family, for Robert took a much more conventional view of things, as he had done at the time of the Boer War. Nellie was busy working for a Quaker committee to aid innocent 'alien enemies' in Great Britain made destitute by the war.

Louisette Bréal, with whom Nellie was now on terms of almost passionate friendship, wrote to them with such graphic descriptions of the distress in a French hospital, where Camille Wolf was *médecin en chef*, that Constance sent money to help and Edward and Nellie thought they should 'come and see if we can be of any service'.[29] After some hesitation whether they would be in the way and whether Constance should not send Emily back to Louisette to help, they went in November and December 1914. Much of what they saw there was harrowing: One gets absorbed in whether 43 has had ventouses sêches or not etc etc,' Nellie wrote, 'but nothing will make me forget the horror the men feel of the war and their longing for their homes'.[30] Nevertheless they came back heartened from seeing Louisette and sharing in her experiences.

Just before Christmas 1914 Nellie told Louisette: 'I think I have definitely decided to go and live at Pond Place and shall be moving there shortly. I wish I need not, but at such a time it seems absurd to be thinking of one's feelings of that kind. I feel to be with Edward as much as possible is the most important thing and that will be good.'[31] In January, and in this diffident and doubtful fashion after having been Edward's lover for nearly seventeen years, she moved in and for the first time shared a home of sorts with him. She was now forty-two, Edward forty-seven and Constance fifty-three. In February Nellie wrote to Louisette:

Edward is absorbed in work now. He is quite different from what he was at the beginning of the war. He spends 3 days and nights in London and 4 at the Cearne. It is not a *perfect* arrangement but it is the best we can manage and exceedingly nice in some ways. He is pretty well. David too and I find it very easy to live with them both.[32]

David, who had finished his fourth year at College before war broke out, and had been 'beginning to apply for jobs',[33] had been enabled by the Marshall Scholarship to do research. He had no lack of free time and spent it with none of the self-abnegation that Constance had demanded at the beginning of the war, but in a round of emotional and intellectual pleasures – neither of them without their corresponding agonies – going to parties and play-readings and on excursions with his friends in Bloomsbury. One of the most important at this time was Francis Birrell, son of the Chief Secretary for Ireland and one of those whom Lawrence had taken such violent exception to. 'Everyone else who ever knew him,' David wrote, 'of whatever age or sex, nationality or class, was charmed and delighted by him. The quality which made his friends love him was, above all, his innocence. . . . the innocence of Mr Pickwick which revealed itself as an incapacity for selfish calculation.'[34]

Birrell, who was unfit for military service, persuaded David to join him and go and work with the Friends' War Victims Relief Mission to France building temporary wooden houses for people whose homes had been destroyed by shellfire. Before David left England his father gave him lunch in a Soho restaurant, and a characteristic send-off:

'Dear Boy, you are going abroad alone. . . .' He paused and cocked a solemn eye at me and the thought flashed through my mind that he was going to touch on the moral dangers to which I might be exposed. . . . The pause lengthened interminably while he searched through several of his pockets without success. I had time to wonder what he was trying to find. Could it conceivably be some specific . . . against venereal disease? . . . At length he discovered what he was looking for.

'You will be all alone. . . the Quakers probably won't have one. . . I think you may find this useful in France,' and his big, exquisitely shaped hand, with its tapered fingers, opened. On his palm was lying a pocket corkscrew.[35]

Edward himself left England a couple of months later. Italy had come into the war on the Allied side only on 23 May 1915, and almost at once had been engaged in bitter fighting around Gorizia and on the River Isonzo in the north-eastern tip of the country north of Trieste. The British Red Cross Society organised an ambulance unit under the command of G. M. Trevelyan, and in August Edward set out 'motoring through France to Italy . . . with about 50 or 60 men and 26 ambulances'.[36] The ambulance unit established itself well behind and above the Isonzo in the Villa Trento, where Edward watched the endless convoys 'of vehicles and men and beasts . . . all journeying in travelling dust clouds'.[37]

At other times the beautiful mountain landscape looked empty and almost unaffected by war: 'A few miles off are the trenches and the boom of big guns sounds continually from the hills. But for that and for two or three observation balloons the country seems infinitely peaceful. All the futility and pathetic stupidity of war seem to be emphasized by the smiling landscape.'[38] At first Edward found himself only looking after suspected typhoid cases. Then the wounded started arriving, and he was busy as a dresser. Once when out in an ambulance he was caught in shellfire himself and remarked that 'Tolstoy's "The Wood Felling" gives a very accurate idea of the impressions and sensations when exposed to artillery fire'.[39]

Constance, as usual, was more anxious about David: 'This terrible stupid war brings anguish to all the mothers in Europe. . . . I have three nephews now in the army – two of them under 20, and such fine boys – of such good intelligence and gentle character – who have never caused their parents a day's anxiety till now. What mad waste it is!'[40] Her particular concern was that David thought his work would come to an end when they had rehoused the people at Sommeille and that the Quakers would not be allowed to undertake housing in other areas. He therefore wanted to train as an ambulance driver and to go and join his father in Italy. At the beginning of the war Constance had reassured him that ambulance work was as dangerous as fighting so he need not feel he was shirking. But love makes as many cowards as ever conscience did, and now she began to panic about those dangers. It was bad enough that Edward should be in those 'cruel wicked mountains'.[41] It was even worse to think of David, an inexperienced driver, negotiating those Alpine roads in an ambulance. She wrote t o Louisette and to Edward as well as to the boy himself – until David set her mind at rest with an impatient postcard: 'For Goodness sake don't worry about Italy and the dangerous roads in the marshes of the Isonzo. The work here will probably drag on.'[42]

Edward, however, did not stay long in Italy. Whether because of his own ill-health – ever since he had typhoid in 1896 he had suffered badly from varicose veins, which sometimes developed ulcers – or for some other reason, he was back in England by November. There he found that his job with Duckworth was no longer open. He tried to find some kind of government work but without success, and so had to subsist on literary journalism and reporting on occasional manuscripts for other publishers.

David came home on leave in October. At the Cearne he had long talks with Constance. Her attitude to the war was clear. She abominated all war and the present one in particular; she was an anti-militarist rather than a pacifist in Tolstoy's sense. She did not think it her duty to 'resist not evil'. On the contrary she thought the war evil, and had there been any effectual means of resisting it she would have done so. David at first had no such clear notions, and for a while he shared the view of some of his friends that they should enlist in order to help get the war over quickly. It was now clear that there was no prospect of a quick end and that the only hope was a negotiated peace.

David returned to France to go not to Sommeille but to the Institut Pasteur in Paris where he hoped to be able to do medical research. He took with him his friend, the painter Duncan Grant, who had been asked by Jacques Copeau to design costumes for a production of *Pelléas et Mélisande*. Duncan was five years older than David, handsome and proud but unworldly, with an air of childlike innocence, which, Frances

Partridge thought, 'wouldn't take in anyone, nor does it take in Duncan himself'.[43] David considered him almost totally uneducated. His friends used to say that he had not even learned the multiplication table.

But he could add and subtract so fast in his head that he would diffidently suggest that seven eights were fifty-six after a pause of only five or six seconds. To stupid people this may suggest that he is slightly half-witted, but the intelligent soon discover that Duncan is a genius who can only do things in his own way, or not at all. . . . If one appreciates originality, he is a continual source of delight. . . . Duncan is a pure artist and nothing else.[44]

David, who was in uniform and wearing a Service de Santé brassard, had no difficulty in getting into France. But Duncan's air of innocence aroused the suspicions of the authorities, who deported him as a dangerous 'pacifist anarchist'.

For Constance, who wrote at once to Duncan to sympathise, this was yet another piece of evidence that she was living in a 'gigantic lunatic asylum'.[45] When, on top of this, David learned that Lawrence's new novel, *The Rainbow*, had been suppressed, all his fury and despair at the evil stupidity of authority broke out, and for a day or two he was 'almost raving'.[46] Fortunately Lytton Strachey – who provided a fund of kindness at this time – had written to Constance's old idol, Jane Harrison, who happened to be living in the same Paris hotel, and asked her to be kind to her son. She took him to lectures on the Russian language – now her prime interest – and her 'rough warmth of manner and her intellectual enthusiasms, always brimming over',[47] won David's heart and came as a 'moral restorative'.[48] He decided that he could not become a soldier not simply because he could not support the war but because it would be wrong to delegate the responsibility for his own acts.

The job at the Institut Pasteur came to nothing. David went back to the Quakers for a while, and spent Christmas at a maternity hospital at Châlons, but he did not stay any longer. He wanted to be with Duncan, and Duncan, whom the French still considered an undesirable, could not come to France. David returned to England in January 1916, and on 3 February the Military Service Act brought in conscription. For a while he worked in the office of the National Council of Civil Liberties, helping to organise the fruitless opposition to conscription and trying to look after the interests of conscientious objectors. Before long he would have to declare himself one, and his own case would come up. Maynard Keynes persuaded him and Duncan that their chances of exemption would be better if they were already doing work of national importance, such as working on the land.

A cousin of Duncan's mother, a Miss Florence Ewebank, had just died; her house, gardens and orchard were empty and neglected. . . . It was soon arranged that Duncan should rent Wissett Lodge, that he and I should set up as fruit-farmers, and that Vanessa [Bell] should come down for the summer and keep house for us, bringing Julian, Quentin [her sons aged eight and five] and Blanche, the tall housemaid.[49]

David sent a stream of his letters to his mother, who told Edward: 'I get one every other day or so now that his interests are so much the same as mine,'[50] for, as she said, 'My letters are charmingly simple – they might be published in the Smallholder.'[51] She was 'much occupied with the potato question',[52] and such comfortably manageable crises as a rat in the hen-run or voles attacking the eight bushels of potatoes stored in the attic. She enjoyed getting an overhanging hedge cut back so that 'my vegetables all look as though they were drawing deep breaths of satisfaction as the light and air come in'.[53] There were exasperations, as when the hunt in full cry went over the garden 'smashing down my chicken run. . .. Insolent brutes!'[54] There were excitements when 'Naughty Emily killed a pheasant',[55] and emboldened in her poaching, which kept the Cearne in meat for two days, went on to shoot a peacock in mistake for one – with equally happy results. There were the small but real achievements of fruit picked and bottled and vegetables dug and stored for the winter, and the satisfaction of being able to provide supplies and comfort for Kate, worried sick over Douglas's fits and Charles's depression, and Grace, now home from Ceylon and out of touch with Hugh, except for alarming reports that he was ill. 'Dear little Gracie . . . she is rather like a little shadowy ghost in the house – so thin and so gentle – she always wrings my heart in a way no one else ever has or can.'[56]

Meanwhile at Wissett, 'I began to work very hard . . .' David wrote, 'I was young and strong and this was my first falling in love with working on the land.'[57] And all the time the Tribunal loomed. Constance worried about it and whether she and Edward should attend and give evidence. David told his parents that he hoped they would not be present 'as it would make him nervous'.[58] He was due to appear before the Halesworth Tribunal on 4 May and he thought it would be 'a dull show and unpleasant'.[59] Adrian Stephen, who presented their cases, mentioned that Constance was a lifelong pacifist, who had visited Tolstoy in Russia.

But the local farmers who constituted the Tribunal were not impressed. The Chairman, who did not realise that Tolstoy was a person and not a place, dismissed the case. They were, however, allowed to appeal.

David tried to persuade his parents to take the matter with a lightness which perhaps he did not really feel: 'reconcile yourselves to the appeal failing, and . . . my going to Prison for a short time. It is a nuisance as regards the farm . . . but I think there is little doubt I shall be a free man by the time the apple picking comes on.'[60] When the appeal was heard at Ipswich on 19 May, Maynard Keynes took efficient charge. They were both granted 'non-combatant service' – in other words they would be conscripted but would not actually fight, whereas what they were asking for was 'work of national importance' – to go on working on the land.

Although they still had the Central Tribunal to get past, it was a vast relief. 'It is such a blessing,' Vanessa wrote, 'not to have to fear the immediate arrival of the police.'[61] Edward turned up for the Ipswich hearing, and Constance arrived later in the day, after it was over. On the following day Vanessa wrote to Lady Ottoline Morrell:

We have Mrs Garnett here now – She is just what you would imagine and talks away steadily and continuously and sensibly exactly like one of her own translations if it weren't a translation – So she's not very exciting but very nice and full of valuable hints about fowls and vegetables.[62]

In mid-July their final appeal was granted, and they were allowed to work on the land. But they were unpopular with the Suffolk authorities, and it was a proviso that they should not be self-employed, so they had to leave Wissett and find work elsewhere. Vanessa's sister, Virginia Woolf, found Charleston, a farmhouse not far from where she lived at Asheham in Sussex. 'It lies at the foot of Firle Beacon,' David wrote, 'protected by trees from the west winds, facing east. There is a pond – a beautiful large sheet of water – in front of and considerably below the house. There is a walled in garden with pear trees all round the walls. . . . The house is a *great deal* larger than Wissett.'[63] After some initial hesitation, Vanessa took it, and was introduced on market day to 'a brisk young farmer'[64] called Hecks, who agreed to take on Duncan and David as farm labourers. 'I hope you are not too much disappointed' David wrote to his mother, 'at my not coming to work at Limpsfield',[65] adding in a later letter, 'I shall be able to come over quite easily to see you at the Cearne with infinitely less expense than at present.'[66] As it turned out, he was not so often able to get away from his employer, Mr Hecks. But Constance went to stay a few days at Charleston, and wrote to Edward:

This is a very jolly house – and I am enjoying it. Yesterday I spent pruning the plums and pears on the walls of the garden – such jolly flint-walls – it makes me regret that we did not have stone walls instead of beech hedges – a walled garden is delicious. Yesterday it was so hot and jolly. Today is stormy and I greatly fear I may not be able to be out gardening. Nessa went to town yesterday morning and will be back Saturday afternoon. We live in a very big kitchen – a jolly room – where the central table is always laid for a meal and never cleared – and there are books and writing materials on another table – and washing up at a sink goes on in another corner – and there is yet no . . . feeling of squalor but space for everything and everyone – 3 huge armchairs and a big dresser don't seem a bit in the way. . . .

An old woman and her granddaughter come very early and get the fire and breakfast – wash up etc. leaving just after dinner – so we have only to get tea and supper – and as everything is in one room there is wonderfully little work in getting meals. David looks a perfect picture of a young farmer – in his velveteen coat and his gaiters and his mild sunburnt face – but Duncan looks very white. David says that D. is better, though, and has begun to eat and sleep well.[67]

The word 'jolly' may not then have had the ring of false heartiness it has since acquired, but four in six sentences seems to be protesting too much, for whatever life at Charleston was then it was not often jolly. David wrote a poem at about this time:

> What is the matter with this house
> Where my poor heart would live at ease and sleep?
> The spider weaves at peace, the silent mouse
> Almost forgets his fears to play bo-peep
> Behind the kitchen chairs. We are not thus,
> We eat nor sleep, nor scarcely even live.
> What is the matter with this house – or us?
> What is there wanting? What offering must I give? . . .[68]

The matter was that David's relations with Duncan were not only 'unnatural' in conventional terms, but also unnatural in fact. Late in life he was asked if he had ever had 'homosexual leanings', to which he aptly replied, 'I was more leant against than leaning.'[69] This was the time when he was most heavily leant against. When he had first got to know them Vanessa had told David: 'She was in love with Duncan but couldn't feel jealous of a man. Duncan had always been in love with a man – Adrian for a long time, Maynard at one time. . .'[70] and now of course with David. But he, as Vanessa remarked, was a womaniser. He was very fond of Duncan, but it was easier for him to respond to Duncan's physical than to his emotional demands, which he found, as he remarked on one occasion, 'fearfully annoying. He made me furious by never getting off the emotional plane – tears in his eyes all the time.'[71] And he could not help fuelling Duncan's jealousy by escaping whenever he could for hectic affairs with various young women.

Meanwhile the work on the farm, for which they were paid twelve shillings and sixpence a week with fivepence an hour for overtime, was physically exhausting, and neither of them was good for much when the day was over. When Lytton Strachey came and read *Eminent Victorians* aloud to them David told Constance, 'I had to keep pinching Duncan to prevent his snoring too loudly'.[72] David, too, was more impressed by the book in print than when read aloud, and promised to send his mother the copy that Duncan had given him. He was particularly close to Constance at this time. He had long talks with her when he came to the Cearne. One cannot tell how much he told her and how much she guessed about his relations with Duncan, but it is clear that she herself was fond of him. Unfortunately she never wrote the chapter of her memoir listed in her contents as 'The War – Duncan Grant etc'.

David wrote to her at least twice a week, mainly about his concerns in farm and garden, and often including phrases in Russian. He tried his own hand at translating Dostoevsky. It was beyond his powers, but Duncan painted him while he did so, and the result can be seen in the Ulster Museum.

Natalie had returned to England after about a year in Russia, but at first things did not go well when she came down to the Cearne, as Constance told Edward:

I feel that I shall have to make some different plan about my work with Natasha. . . . It knocks me up too much – working all day and then not being able to sleep or being waked at night. N's nocturnal habits are very unfortunate. When she has been here alone with me, she goes to bed when I do, but when you are here, I – being already over-tired and nervy – can't get to sleep – or am waked up and lie awake from hearing you moving about or opening the study door etc.

Possibly it will be better for me to arrange to come up to town once a month to work with Natasha – or I might get her to come in the middle of the week when you won't be here.[73]

Natalie came in mid-week, and Constance came no nearer to expressing any jealousy of Edward's increasing intimacy with her. Constance was indeed very over-tired and nervy and much in need of rest and a holiday.

'I can't talk about anything I care about without wanting to cry.'[74] And her relations with Natalie were exacerbated by the exciting events of the spring of 1917. From the banner headlines and Arthur Ransome's dispatches in the *Daily News* she learned how the Tsar, still refusing to take any measures to gain popular support for an unpopular war, and unable to command the loyalty of troops to put down a workers' insurrection in Petrograd, had abdicated on 16 March. A provisional government was formed, mainly from members of the Duma, numb though it was from ten years of impotence in its dealings with the Tsar. It committed itself to continuing the war, it procrastinated over elections to a constituent assembly and it did little to appease the peasants' hunger for land, but within two months it had instituted a host of other reforms:

It had introduced the eight-hour day (partially at least) and carried through a political amnesty; it had abolished capital punishment and exile, instituted trial by jury for all offences, put an end to all discrimination based on religious, class or national criteria, created an independent judiciary, introduced the full liberty of conscience, the press, worship and association, separated church and state, revised the military code so as to give civilian rights to the soldier, and introduced industrial arbitration and rural self-government.[75]

Even Lenin had had to admit, when he went back to Russia that it was 'the freest country in the world'.[76] Constance's revolutionary friends returned in something like triumph. On 7 April at a concert at the Mariinsky Theatre in aid of the victims of the revolution, Vera Zasulich was honoured with some thirty other revolutionary heroes, and Vera Figner, who had been an accomplice in the assassination of Alexander II and acquaintance of Constance's, brought tears to the eyes of the audience merely by reciting the names of those who had suffered Tsarist prison, exile and execution.[77] David Soskice, who had spent some time in Russia after the amnesty of 1905, returned once more after the revolution to act simultaneously as a member of Kerensky's secretariat and a correspondent for the *Manchester Guardian*.

For Constance the spring revolution was a consummation for which she had been longing for a quarter of a century. But Natalie, now a devout Orthodox, and with her family at risk in Russia, took a very different view, and there was an inevitable explosion. It seems that the *Atlantic Monthly* wrote to Constance and asked if she could send anything that would throw light on the revolution. In reply Edward sent them Natalie's translation of an article which Constance thought would damage the revolution with serious readers and give them a distorted idea of it, and calmly wrote: 'My wife has been too busy to translate it but it has been done by a friend of hers.'[78] Edward even sent a copy of it to the *Contemporary Review* with his own prefatory note.

Constance was furious, not only at their underhand behaviour, but also because 'there is nothing – outside personal life – I have ever cared for so much'[79] as the Russian revolution. She felt that she would never feel the same about Natalie again. 'I shall always be on my guard against something sly being done which I should dislike.'[80] But before long, by reminding herself of 'all the kind, good, noble things'[81] Edward had done, she softened her resentment. Edward seems to have withdrawn the article from publication, and as usual David helped to make peace between his parents. Within three weeks Constance was writing to Natalie, perhaps with a touch of irony:

> Don't you think your Government is doing finely? . . . How awfully proud you must feel of them and how I envy you to be able to feel proud of them. One is always feeling so ashamed of the part England is playing now. I feel as though we were all being dragged into the mud by a vile crew of liquor lords and armament mongers with Lloyd George as the quickchange showman to do the vulgar patter for the mob. It is sickening.[82]

When Constance learned that Lenin had returned to Russia she wrote to David: 'I feel certain Lenin will capture power. I wish we knew what he will do with it.'[83] And when, sure enough, he did so in November, she wrote to Natalie:

> I am afraid you must be feeling very anxious about your people in this unsettled state. They are not in the country any of them, I hope? It is all very heartbreaking – and I don't want to talk to you about it – No! I had always hoped something from the Bolsheviks because it seemed to me (I am very conscious of my ignorance, of course) that they were more thorough-going International Socialists than perhaps any others in Europe – and as you know, I care more for International Socialism than anything else, so it breaks my heart that by the weakness or inexperience or lack of principle (whatever it is) of its representatives, it should be discredited to all the world. To me it has for twenty years or more seemed the hope of the world.
>
> But I know that having been bored by these people from a girl up and caring nothing about Socialism or anything political, you will not be able to help being exultant at their disgracing themselves. So it is better we should not talk about it. It makes me too sad. And anything like jeering at what is after all my religion makes me feel as cold as ice – and utterly un-Christian. And I certainly don't want to feel like that to you, dear Natasha. At least we are one in praying that the present chaos may not end in pure reaction. What I dread is a forcible

(veiled force of course) restoration of monarchy by arrangement with the Japanese. That is being plotted even now – and may be easily realised any day. Our Government has never disguised its desire for the restoration of the old regime.[84]

Not all accounts of the Bolsheviks described them as disgracing themselves, especially in those early heady days of the revolution. David had been brushing up his Russian not only in order to translate Dostoevsky. He was tempted to go to Russia with the Quakers, who were sending a relief mission to Buzuluk in Samara, where there had been only one light shower of rain in the whole season, and the crops had once again failed. This was one of the places that had been worst hit in the famine of 1912, which Constance had tried so hard to relieve. But when David realised that Mr Hecks would be unlikely to keep Duncan on by himself if he left, he felt he could not abandon him.

So David did not go to Russia, though he heard encouraging accounts from Robert Tatlock, a single-minded and enterprising Scottish Quaker, who had just returned from travelling over much of Russia, and was furious at the way the revolution was being misrepresented in Britain by all the press except Ransome, and even he was 'censored by our press bureau'.[85] The reports, for instance, in the *Times* and the *Daily Telegraph* that the Kremlin had been largely destroyed were quite untrue. Tatlock had been 'all over the Kremlin when it was over and couldn't see a bullet mark – not one'.[86] Whereas the British press was reporting that at Rostov-on-Don the Red Guards 'maltreated and often killed the children' as they came out of school,[87] Tatlock was much impressed by these irregulars, as David wrote:

They are rough, *honest, honest, honest* Russian workmen or peasants who have a complete belief in Social Revolution, Internationalism, and government by the proletariat, no capitalism and communistic organisation and effort and local autonomy. . . . Owing to robberies becoming a nuisance the Red Guards formed and if anything unpleasant happens you go and tell the Red Guards who send a man to protect your warehouse or house or whatever it is. He has a rifle and he refuses payment for his services but asks for coffee. . . and though Tatlock didn't say so I've no doubt he makes an awful mess of sunflower seeds. When they catch a man robbing they shoot him at once.[88]

Tatlock thought Lenin had come to stay:

Lenin is the kind of man whom nothing will alter or affect in any way, the only thing his enemies can do is to shoot him, nothing else will affect him in the least. He thinks Trotsky most frightfully clever. . . . You have the whole time a bewildered feeling that everything is just like London – or prewar Petersburg and the next moment you feel it is chaos.[89]

There was hardly any food to be got, but the ballet companies were still performing as usual, and one had no difficulty in getting a cab.

Another Quaker who brought encouraging reports from Russia to David and Constance was Reynolds Ball, who had actually been working at Buzuluk and looked like one of the victims of famine himself; he was lean and haggard, and had somehow lost most of his teeth. His 'indifference to his own welfare, his emaciation and his saintliness'[90] greatly distressed Constance. David has described a touching scene, when, with something like heroism, she refrained from disputing his account of the gift for telepathy that he had seen among the Russians and concentrated only on trying to get him to take some food. 'If she let him talk, he might be induced to eat another sweet biscuit.'[91]

Soon afterwards Ball died of typhus, contracted while working among famine-stricken children in Poland. 'Constance grieved for him more than any of his friends and never forgot him.'[92]

By the autumn of 1917 Britain was beginning to feel a taste of the hardships that were so widespread in Eastern Europe. The shortages that Constance had anticipated in the summer of 1914 were becoming a reality. Coal and oil were hard to come by. 'Matches we can get only at the rate of one box a week! We must be thankful we have wood.'[93] But in the end she managed somehow, which was just as well, for the Cearne was snowed up, with ice on the bedroom jugs, and 'the snow makes my eyes so bad (and my chilblains!)'.[94]

In the late summer of 1918 she was at last able to get away on holiday – she had failed to do so in 1917 – with David and Edward and Nellie at Welcombe near Bude in Devon. She thought it the most beautiful place she had seen in England, and, susceptible as ever to the beauty of her surroundings, she felt her courage coming back, 'and only pray that it may last'.[95]

Then in November the hateful war came to end at last. Emma's son, Felix Mahomed, had been killed in the Royal Flying Corps, and Nellie's beloved sister, Margaret, had died, and so had Ernest Black, all within a few months in 1917. But Edward and David had survived, as well as her other two nephews in uniform, Patrick Clayton and Kenneth Black. 'Isn't it glorious? And isn't it difficult to take it all in?'[96] she wrote to Natalie. But she was disgusted that British and French troops should have landed in Russia on 2 August to take up arms against the Bolsheviks, with Stepniak's old colleague, Nicholas Tchaykovsky, allowing himself to be a figurehead for their intervention:

it does seem even more awful that we should be at war with Russia now that we are at peace with the rest of the world. And you know it frightens me – and it has from the first – this intervention of the allies in Russia – not so much for what they may do, though that's bad enough. But when one party in a country calls in foreign soldiers to support them it is so likely to lead to awful outbreaks of violence on the part of the populace. It would be so in any other country. I feel so afraid there will be some horrible massacre of all the middle and upper class people. And it is so much more likely to happen when the 'people' feel helpless before foreign armies.[97]

For Constance the failure of the spring revolution was the great lost cause of her life. But she continued to oppose outside interference with the Soviet Union, despite all its faults. Long after she had turned against communism, she retained some sympathy for 'poor Lenin' – 'If only most people weren't scoundrels' he was 'reputed to have said'.[98]

21

Chekhov: 'A Perfect Flower'

During the war Constance came to resemble the figure who reminded H. E. Bates of his great-grandmother: 'She looked exactly like a country-woman who had spent her entire life feeding inexhaustible generations of chickens: than which no impression could have been more misleading. . . .'[1] It could not indeed, for at no time in her life had she worked harder at her translation. Between 1914 and 1918 she had published seven fat volumes of Dostoevsky. His cult was then at its height, for, as Gilbert Phelps observed,

it was the war itself, coming so soon after the publication of *The Brothers Karamazov*, that threw all the various intellectual and emotional currents of the period into violent agitation, and turned enthusiasm for Dostoyevsky into hysteria. The most extravagant symptoms of the Dostoyevsky craze belong to the war years. Some of them, no doubt, sprang from the contortions which apologists for the alliance with the traditional bogey man of Europe were called upon to perform.[2]

One of the more remarkable manifestations of this was the fervent tribute to the literary culture of their Russian brothers-in-arms, signed by thirty-four men and women of letters which was published in the *Times* just before Christmas 1914. Its tone was far too emotionally patriotic for Garnett tastes. But both Edward and Constance signed it, as did many of their friends – Archer, Bennett, Galsworthy, Jane Harrison, Henry James and H. G. Wells – as well as such diverse figures as Barrie, Hardy, Masefield and Newbolt. Its account of the discovery of Russian literature by English readers might have been written specifi-cally as a tribute to Constance's work:

It was a strange world that opened before us, a world full of foreign names which we could neither pronounce nor remember, of foreign customs and articles of daily life which we could not understand. Yet beneath all the strangeness there was a deep sense of having discovered a new home, of meeting our unknown kindred, of finding expressed great burdens of thought which had lain unspoken and half-realized at the depths of our own minds.[3]

David wrote his mother a fan-letter that well expresses the intensity of this Russian cult:

My darling – you are an amazing little creature. I wonder if you sometimes rest for a moment in your translation to realise the tremendously momentous thing you are engaged on? You have probably had more effect on the minds of everybody under thirty in England than any three living men. On their attitude, their morals, their sympathies. You probably only have a faint idea of what you have done. But upon my word letting rabbits loose in Australia is nothing to it. . . .

I think the publication of The Idiot has probably done more to alter the morals of my generation than the war or anything that happens to them in the war.

I speak of the educated class – who number thousands and thousands.[4]

He thought that even Constance herself had experienced these moral benefits: 'I think that Dostoevsky must have done you a lot of good (I know you think you're good enough without his help – and perhaps you are) but I mean he must have stretched your sympathies and emotions and worked on them a good deal.'[5] It was all the more important that she should complete her task: 'Be very careful of your eyes, and work slowly, and don't save money at the expense of comfort. It is silly. The material difficulties of life always seem huge but one floats over wave after wave without noticing them.'[6] Constance tried to use her eyes only for proofs. At this period Sybil did most of the reading aloud and taking down dictation. Natalie helped with revises and proofs and with occasional 'difficulties', but she was emphatic that she should not be given the credit for 'Mrs Garnett's amazing understanding of the subtleties of the Russian language. . . . I could sometimes help her work out a grammatically intricate sentence',[7] but that was all.

It was during the war that Constance at last found a publisher for Chekhov. Frank Swinnerton has told how he was at a party given by Scott-James when Edward came upon him doing up the fly-buttons that he had heedlessly left undone.[8] Caught at a disadvantage, and known to be working at Chatto and Windus and to have been a self-proclaimed Chekhovian ever since he had seen *The Cherry Orchard*, he could hardly refuse to publish Constance's translation of Chekhov's *Tales*. She had her plans well prepared:

The edition to be of 8 volumes, to be extended to 10, if liked later on, and to contain all the best stories – all there is that could be intelligible and interesting to English readers except a few early and quite inferior journalistic sketches.

One volume is ready.[9]

Chatto would commit themselves only to two volumes in the first instance, because of the uncertainties of war. But terms were agreed. Constance was to be paid twelve shillings a thousand words with an additional royalty of five per cent after fifteen hundred copies had been sold. Whereas she had never got a penny for the American sales of any of her books with Heinemann, Chatto let her keep the American rights for herself, and they were now looked after by J. B. Pinker, along with dramatic and other subsidiary rights.

The arrangement of the stories was not to be chronological or thematic, but designed so that each volume should contain an interesting selection, good in itself. The books were to be small crown in format – neat little volumes that would slip nicely into a pocket for a railway journey – like Heinemann's later reprints of Turgenev. They were to be fifty to sixty thousand words in length, interpreted as a rule as an even working of 320 pages. This often entailed shuffling a story or two from one volume to the next, which Constance was happy to do. Chatto and Windus, in the persons of Percy Spalding, Harold Raymond, Frank Swinnerton and Charles Prentice, were invariably prompt, efficient and courteous in their dealings, besides being literate and enterprising. Constance ate out of their hands for the rest of her life, while she became increasingly distrustful of Heinemann, with whom she was still heavily engaged on Dostoevsky.

The first two volumes of Chekhov, *The Darling* and *The Duel* – each of course supplemented by *and Other Stories* – came out on 21 October 1916. The first of them had a very brief introduction by Edward and included 'Tolstoy's criticism of "The Darling"'.

Robert Lynd was no less eulogistic about them in the *New Statesman* than he had been about Dostoevsky in the *Daily News*. Constance, who had explained that it was not to be a complete edition and had asked Chatto not to advertise it as such, must have been irritated when he wrote: 'We are now apparently to have a complete edition of the tales of Tchehov in English from Mrs. Garnett.' But then he went on:

It will deserve a place, both for the author's and the translator's sake, beside her Turgenev and Dostoevsky. In lifelikeness and graciousness her work as a translator seems to me to reach a high level. Her first two little volumes confirm one in the opinion that Tchehov is, for his variety, abundance, tenderness and knowledge of the heart of the Capacious and unclean animal' called man, the greatest short-story writer who has yet appeared on the planet.[10]

Otherwise the new edition did not receive much attention in the press. The wartime newspapers and journals were ghosts of their former selves, being short of paper, and that paper grey and brittle. Far fewer books were reviewed. Chekhov did not make the same impact as Dostoevsky but was carried along as much by the Russian craze as by his own merits, yet sales were good enough for Chatto to decide almost at once to proceed with the series.

Chatto had been interested in Constance translating a selection of Chekhov's letters ever since they had successfully published a volume of Dostoevsky's correspondence translated by Ethel Colburn Mayne in 1914, but the idea had lapsed, and it was not until late in 1917 that they took it up again. Constance was too busy with Dostoevsky and with the *Tales* to proceed with it until March 1919, when Spalding wrote:

I propose that the volume of Letters should be similar in size to the 'Letters of Dostoevsky' (a copy of which I believe you have) say for issue at 10/6 net, your translation consisting of about 100,000 words. The terms that we are prepared to offer are a royalty at the rate of 15% on the publishing price of all copies sold, with an advance on the day of publication of £60, you reserving the United States rights.[11]

These were far better terms than any Constance had yet been offered. Besides selecting and translating the letters from a Russian text borrowed from the London Library – it was impossible to get books out of Russia at this time – she also agreed to provide a Biographical Sketch of twelve thousand words, based on a memoir by Chekhov's brother, Mikhail. Translating the Russian text of this, which was longer than needed, made her feel very close to Chekhov.

The more one knows of Tchehov the more one loves him and sees what a sweet-natured delightful man he was – what a rare combination his brightness and wit and gaiety with such deep goodness and unselfishness – and such delicacy and artistic sensitiveness, together with such common sense and wisdom. I don't think there can ever have been a more lovable creature – and to think of his dying like that – going on for years with the symptoms of consumption and not bothering to cure it! But it seems to make all the turmoil and degradation and misery of human life worth while – that mankind can produce now and again such a perfect flower.[12]

But she was not so happy about trying to edit her text down to the required length. David has written that Constance 'found it an agony to

Constance at Montpellier   Lolya, Natalie, Lenochka, at Khludovo, 1904

Khludovo, 1904, Constance in the left of the doorway, David in a beret in the carriage

The Cloisters, Letchworth,
Cowlishaw's most eccentric building

Edward by the study fire
at the Cearne
Note the heavy stone corbels

Arthur Garnett at the Huts

write anything original'.[13] Enough of her original writings, none of which shows signs of hesitancy in composition, have already been quoted in this narrative to show that this cannot have been uniformly true. She was, however, always loath to write about Russian literature, and when, for instance, in September 1914 the *Field* asked her to review *Reminiscences of Tolstoy* by his son, Ilya, she passed the commission on to Edward, remarking to Nellie that he would 'certainly say that he will write it but I must sign it'.[14] In the event the sporting journal carried an unsigned review that was far too cosy to have been written by either of them. And when she needed translator's notes she seemed to suffer the same kind of block that prevents some otherwise fluent authors from being able to write their own blurbs. So she turned to David to edit the Biographical Sketch.

With the advent of peace David had given up any idea of a scientific career and started a bookshop in partnership with Francis Birrell. Constance was convinced that he should be a writer, though all he had done so far was competent hack-work, a little treatise on the kitchen garden, much reduced and adapted from a French manual, and a novel published under a pseudonym. *Dope-Darling* was written for money and intended to follow the formula of the romantic 'shocker' of the day. 'I enjoyed,' David wrote, 'putting in every cliché that I could remember',[15] but nothing in the book is as absurd as its sensational cover. He made a good job of the Biographical Sketch and Constance was 'delighted by the vigour and freshness' he put into it.[16]

Letters of Anton Tchehov to his Family and Friends, which came out on 5 February 1920, was an attractive book, the more so because Constance had insisted on including photographs, but its sales were modest, and she saw little of her fifteen per cent royalty beyond the sixty-pound advance. Chatto, however, were undeterred, and agreed to extend the *Tales* first to ten volumes and then to thirteen.

After that there only remained the two volumes of plays. For these she asked to be paid forty-five pounds a volume rather than per thousand words.

The *number* of *words* in a play is so much smaller than in a story covering the same number of pages – and the translation is at the same time so much more difficult. I know from experience (I have already translated 'The Cherry Orchard' for a performance) that a volume of plays will take me twice as long as a volume of stories.[17]

There had in fact been several performances of *The Cherry Orchard*, the two that the Stage Society put on at the Aldwych in 1911, and a further two by Madame Donnet's Art Theatre at the St Martin's Theatre on 11 and 12 July 1920. Madame Donnet was a Russian émigrée who was familiar with the productions of the Moscow Arts Theatre, and whose company had already put on *The Seagull* in 1919. She adapted Marian Fell's translation, which was 'stiff and often wildly wrong'.[18] Although she was Russian, her company was thoroughly British, so much so that Virginia Woolf remarked on 'the consciousness which hung about them of being well-trained English men and women ill at ease in an absurd situation, but determined to make the best of a bad business'.[19] Despite this, and the ponderous solemnity with which it was presented, she thought that by the end something of the play she had envisaged on reading it had begun to come through.

Constance wrote to Natalie:

I wish you could have seen the Cherry Orchard – but I expect you would have hated it too much. It was *better* acted than the Stage Society's – but too intense and kind of hard – none of the warmth and fluidity of the real thing – Lopahin [Joseph A. Dodd] especially was very well done and a real figure.[20]

While the dramatic critic of the *Times* still thought Chekhov was a passing fad, others, such as Frank Swinnerton, took occasion to praise the play; and Katherine Mansfield was completely overwhelmed. A friend recorded her 'mute and shaken delight'[21] at One of the most wonderful plays ever written'.[22] She even went so far as to assume that the play was as well known to her readers as *Hamlet*, though few of them could have seen it on the stage or read either of the two translations that had so far been published. Chekhov had yet to be made acceptable to an English audience.

The *Tales*, however, were becoming popular at last, just as the cult of Dostoevsky began to wane. Middleton Murry, whose critical study of Dostoevsky had come out in 1916 and was considered by Constance to be 'very good',[23] now turned his attention to Chekhov. Edward appreciated his praise of Chekhov's 'candour of soul' and 'pureness of heart', but took him gently to task for his ignorance of Russian literary history and social conditions.[24] Murry's praise of Constance's achievement was lengthy and fulsome. In reviewing the eleventh and twelfth volumes of Chekhov's *Tales* he compared her work to 'the epoch-making translations of the past – to North's Plutarch in the Elizabethan days, to Schlegel's translation from Shakespeare at the latter end of the German *Aufklärung*' concluding his two paragraphs of eulogy: 'It was no good giving us the nineteenth-century

Russians piecemeal; we needed the whole of them. To give us the whole was the work of a lifetime, to be surrendered with but the smallest hope of a commensurate reward. Mrs Garnett made the sacrifice.'[25]

The views of Katherine Mansfield, who had at last married Murry on 3 May 1918 after a long liaison, were more complex. She had written to Koteliansky, probably in July 1919, about Chekhov's letters to his family and friends: 'In Heavens name why do we not prepare the book immediately and race Mrs G? . . . here is this treasure – at the wharf only not unloaded.'[26] But Koteliansky, who translated other Russian works – and eventually some of Chekhov's stories – by his usual method, turning the Russian into his own idiosyncratic English, and trusting to such writers as D. H. Lawrence and Virginia Woolf to convert it into something more literary, did not win this race. A month or so later Katherine Mansfield wrote to him again complaining that 'Mrs G. . . seems to take the nerve out of Tchekhov before she starts working on him, like the dentist takes the nerve from a tooth'.[27] But within eighteen months she felt impelled to write to Constance in much the same terms as Murry:

As I laid down my copy of War and Peace tonight I felt I could no longer refrain from thanking you for the whole other world that you have revealed to us through those marvellous translations from the Russian. Your beautiful industry ends Madam in making us almost ungrateful. We are almost inclined to take for granted the fact that the new book is translated by Mrs Constance Garnett. Yet my generation (I am 32) and the younger generation owe you more than we ourselves are able to realise. The books have changed our lives, no less. What could it be like to be without them!

I am only one voice among so many who appreciate the greatness of your task, the marvel of your achievement. I beg you to accept my admiration and deepest gratitude.[28]

Constance duly replied on 19 February:

Your letter has given me the greatest pleasure.

The translator has many hours of despondency in which the struggle to adjust the conflicting claims of two languages is seen clearly in all its hopelessness and the resulting compromise seems something too poor and imperfect to be worth the labour. What has given me courage to persevere all these years in face of the always increasing sense of the difficulty – the impossibility – of successful achievement, has been the hope that contact with the work of the great Russians – even at second hand – must have its influence on the best of the younger generation – that it *could* not leave them unchanged. That has been my dream all these years.

Now you – representative as you are of the most talented and intellectual among the young people – tell me that I have achieved my aim![29]

But when, probably at the end of April 1922, Edward threatened to bring Katherine and her husband down to the Cearne, she replied:

I feel terrified at the thought of the Murrys coming! Don't you think it's best not to destroy the illusion but to remain a shrouded mysterious figure living in seclusion?

At the same time I should like to see them. You must decide when you see *her*. I should fancy her rather a difficult person, very what used to be called *fin-de-siècle* and decadent. If you do ask them, you would arrange to come with them wouldn't you? and it would be a weekday – and you would send me a wire as soon as you know that they are coming – so that we may have something edible for them. And you would ask them for a certain day, so that they could escape coming easily.[30]

Constance had reason to panic, she was hardly recovered from a serious illness, and the other people then in the house were too shy and inarticulate to provide much entertainment. 'Murry is dumb too. . . and I'm no great talker. I expect Katherine Mansfield and you would feel as though you had great bales of wet blankets to lift.'[31] But Katherine, who was dying of tuberculosis and had little more than six months to live, did not come, and the plan 'dwindled to a *tête-à-tête* luncheon in London'[32] with Edward.

This may well have been a relief to Katherine too. She was a little put out when Desmond MacCarthy, reviewing her collection of stories, *Bliss*, in 1921, wrote, 'Miss Mansfield's master in the art of fiction is Tchekov.'[33] The very first of her stories had appeared in the *New Age* in February 1910. She called it The Child-Who-Was-Tired', and it was an unacknowledged retelling of the tale of Chekhov's that Constance entitled 'Sleepy'. It had been included in R. E. C. Long's first collection, *The Black Monk*, but Claire Tomalin has persuasively argued that Katherine Mansfield was shown it in a German translation by her lover Floryan Sobienowski, a Polish adventurer and translator, and that he later blackmailed her about the plagiarism. She refused to allow a reprint of her first collection, *In a German Pension*, in which it had appeared, and she must have watched anxiously as eleven volumes of Constance's translations came out at the rate of two a year, and not until the twelfth, *The Cook's Wedding*, did the fatal story appear. Murry must have noticed the resemblance when he was sent the book to review, but whereas 'Other reviewers commented on the particularly striking plot of "Sleepy"',[34] he stuck to more general praise of Chekhov and the tribute to Constance already quoted.

What did other less engaged critics think of the quality of the translation? This of course depends on whom you ask. William Gerhardi, who wrote the first English work on Chekhov in 1923, preferred to use Constance's translations, though he was thoroughly capable of making his own. He thought that it was impossible to bridge the gap between the two languages: 'Translations from the Russian will never quite succeed in being natural. But Mrs. Garnett has contrived to make the best of what needs must remain a bad job.'[35]

The Russian scholar, Augusta Tovey, who published a study of translations of Chekhov in 1963, was surprised on looking into Constance's version of 'The Steppe' to find her making a few unexpected blunders, mistaking *cherep* (skull) for *cherepok* (potsherd), and suchlike confusions between similar words, errors that may have been due to ignorance, but could just as well have arisen because she misheard a word or Sybil misread it. Given the way they worked, it is perhaps surprising there are not more such errors. Tovey, on the other hand, considered Constance's

translation as a whole excellently conveys the idioms, the subtlest shades of meaning of words with all their emotional connotations, the expressions from various layers of the language. The translator has reproduced all the lyricism, music, colour and imagery of Chekhov's story. . . . Among the translators, pride of place belongs by right to Constance Garnett.[36]

This was not the general view in Britain and America at the time Tovey was writing. Constance's reputation was at its lowest, and Ernest Simmons even described Constance's version of Chekhov as 'a kind of Victorian death-rattle'.[37] Subsequent scholars have been far less dismissive, and Lauren G. Leighton, who has made a very thorough study of Chekhov in English – too long and detailed to be quoted here – writes that whereas Long's and Koteliansky's translations now seem outdated:

Mrs. Garnett has often been cited as an example of an outdated translator, but the fact is that her work has survived extraordinarily well. . . . No matter how persistently some modern critics try to dismiss her work as hopelessly 'Victorian,' she remains an icon. . . . Perhaps we have been conditioned to 'hear' Russian writers in Mrs. Garnett's popular translations, so that we are too receptive to her style, but analysis indicates that her work is superior to that of her contemporaries and that she developed principles of translation far ahead of others.[38]

Since then there have been new translators, particularly Ronald Hingley, and Patrick Miles and Harvey Pitcher working together. Miles has told me that when he and Pitcher began they vowed that they would look at no other translations first. He thought it unlikely that they would refer to Constance's because he had a poor opinion of the dialogue in her versions of the plays. But as a last resort when they 'were uncertain of a period English term or were stumped for meaning and had exhausted everything else' they consulted her translation. 'Almost invariably we were filled with respect for her solution.'[39]

In 1933 Edward edited for Cape a collection of fifty-three short stories by twenty-four writers published by that firm in the previous twelve years.[40] The book is a reminder not only that Chekhov had been what Galsworthy called 'the most potent magnet to young writers'[41] of short stories – to such contributors as Bates, Coppard and Malachi Whitaker (the 'Bradford Chekhov') – but also of the way in which the appreciation of earlier stories in this collection – such as 'The Dead' by James Joyce – had been modified by the immense popularity of Constance's little green volumes.

22

Dear Granny

'Do you know' Constance wrote to Natalie in the spring of 1921, 'David is going to get married on April 1st. It all seems very nice – and I am glad about it – but . . . "your son's your son till he gets him a wife!" The girl's name is Rachel Marshall. I have only seen her once.'[1] They were being rather impetuous, but at least they were prudent enough to change the date from All Fools' Day to 30 March.

Rachel, or Ray as she was always called, was some ten months older than David and was working as an assistant to Robert Tatlock, who had recently become editor of the *Burlington Magazine*. Her younger sister Frances wrote of her: 'Her hazel-brown eyes, set very wide apart beneath a broad and misleadingly tranquil brow, seemed to gaze out at the world with an expression suggesting that it was very different from what she would have liked it to be, but that she had her private consolations.'[2]

David told his mother: 'She is rather a peculiar girl; sometimes very shy but never covered with confusion as a result of it and the chief thing is that she is sensitive to everything round about her; she is badly educated but intelligent. . . . She has periodical outbursts of very high spirits.'[3] Above all, and this was something that always attracted David, she had an original mind and revealed to Frances 'such intoxicating possibilities as that nearly all ideas that people took for granted could be questioned'.[4]

Ray had been trained as an illustrator at the Central School of Arts and Crafts by Noel Rooke, but even before that her first published works had been some chastely drawn political cartoons for the front cover of *The Common Cause*, a suffragist journal, in 1910. The Marshalls, though never outsiders like the Garnetts, were strong supporters of progressive causes, and Ray's brother Tom, the one most like her in character, was 'setting up as a Labour candidate'.[5] He did not, however, become a politician, though David thought 'He is rather a good sort of man for it

I should say. Maynard and Sheppard always said he had brains.'[6] Her father, William Cecil Marshall, had had a serious stroke some time before and died on 24 January 1921 without David ever meeting him. He was fifteen years older than his wife, a successful architect, and in his youth had been a notable athlete, runner-up at the very first tennis tournament at Wimbledon in 1877 and amateur figure-skating champion. His heroes were Darwin, Ruskin, Tennyson and Leslie Stephen, all of whom he had known. He built himself a substantial house at Hindhead and called it Tweenways. It was full of good craftsmanship and well made furniture, with occasional decorations as ghastly as its name. David described a 'jolly' visit there, when he met Ray's mother, always known to the family by her initials as Mam, 'a particularly charming and sensible sort of character',[7] who had brought up six children, nursing them very professionally through their childhood illnesses, as well as having a busy social life and many interesting friends, including, for instance, Jane Harrison.

Tweenways was about to be sold, and Mrs Marshall, David told his mother, 'has practically offered us anything we like in the way of furniture'.[8] She also wrote to Constance:

As it seems likely that our two families are to be connected by marriage very soon, I hope you won't mind my writing to you, and saying what I think and feel about an event that must be equally interesting to us both. I don't feel as if we were quite strangers. Your brother taught me mathematics at Brighton, I have often seen your sister Clementina Black, and my sister Alice Dew-Smith (Alice Lloyd) knew you [at Newnham].[9]

David met Aunt Alice at Tweenways and found her 'an absolute dear, rather prim to look at and bubbling out unexpectedly with some joke'.[10] Mam's letter continued:

I have seen your son several times, and he has met all my family, and we all feel his charm and attraction, and believe that he and Rachel really suit each other. She is my third child, the two elder ones being already married, and I have a very great respect for her character and her abilities. Her friends are devoted to her, and are inclined to think so highly of her that it is rather difficult for her to live up to their expectations! About her feeling for your son there can be no doubt – she is genuinely in love, I believe for the first time in her life.[11]

She went on to discuss practical matters of money – Ray had a little income of her own – and where they should live, concluding: 'I shall be glad to hear from you. David has been warmly welcomed into this family, and I hope you feel that you can welcome Rachel.'[12]

Constance would have preferred someone she already knew and loved, but Ray 'very soon won Constance's regard, then her affection and then her love'.[13] Edward, however, welcomed the marriage wholeheartedly and from the start. He 'was intuitively aware that Ray could not stand up for herself and he never teased her. She, on her side, became devoted to him.'[14] Ray did not care for the rustic interiors of the Cearne, and would have liked to take a pneumatic drill to Cowlishaw's obtrusive stone corbels, but she was very much at home in the Chart Woods. She shared with David and Constance the experience of having been to Russia. She had a friend, 'a large ungainly Russian girl with huge eyes and a mobile charming face',[15] known always as Kunze from her surname of Kunzevitch, who had invited her to stay in the Caucasus. In 1913 they travelled across Europe in third class railway carriages – 'so airless – so full of spitting – so flea-y – so filthy'[16] – only to find at Warsaw that Kunze had forgotten the name of their destination. But somehow they reached Kunze's uncle's estate at Oshanetsky, and went on to stay with the Kunzevitches near Kislovodsk, where Ray spent her time riding through the mountains of the Caucasus, eating delicious plums and apricots and listening to crowds playing the balalaika. She brought back gramophone records of Russian songs, and when she played them 'her usual self-contained manner would suddenly explode into wild excitement, dancing and singing. "Ray has gone mad," someone would say, but not unkindly.[17] She also brought back sketches in notebooks, and a few more finished drawings, of Russian peasant life. When David met her she had already illustrated three books for Chatto and Windus, one of which, *A Ride on a Rocking-Horse*, she had written herself. Her illustrations, often using the flat colours of multiple wood-engravings, were both cool and tender. She had a particular sympathy with animals and children, which she drew with a total absence of sentimentality. She very much wanted to have a child of her own, and so it was with a sense of impending tragedy that Constance wrote to Natalie shortly before the child was due: 'Something so dreadful has happened that I can think of nothing else. Poor Rachel has lost her child. . . . Poor darling little Ray. I'm afraid she must be heartbroken, she has been living in a blissful dream for months – but I need not tell you – you will know what it means.'[18] Natalie, who was likewise pregnant was, however, safely delivered of a son, Sasha, a few weeks later.

Earlier that year Percy Spalding had written to Constance, suggesting that as the half-yearly Chekhov volumes would soon come to an end 'perhaps you would care to discuss another project. A good translation of Gogol is badly wanted. Would you be interested in doing it? . . . Presumably one would start with "Dead Souls".'[19]

She replied:

How curious that you should write about translating 'Dead Souls'! Or have you perhaps chanced to meet my husband and discussed the matter with him? I have for some time considered translating Gogol (when I have finished Tchehov's stories) and have been intending to write and ask whether you would undertake it. Certainly it would be best to begin with 'Dead Souls' and then see how that goes.[20]

It went well for Constance. Before long she was writing, 'I am getting quite fond of Gogol after all and begin to find him delightfully easy'[21] – though Mirsky describes his prose as 'hopelessly untranslatable – more untranslatable than any other prose'.[22]

Otherwise it was an autumn with little to rejoice over. She found herself involved with other people's problems – something which always worried her and prevented her from sleeping. Vera Volkhovsky was deeply depressed when Bertrand Russell married Dora Black. She had been in love with him and was persuaded that the cure for her depression was to marry Montague Fordham. He was a widower, a friend of the Garnetts' of twenty years' standing, an expert on agriculture, whose practical good sense Constance much appreciated. His daughter, Thea had been in love with David while still in her teens. His marriage to Vera proved to be no solution, and they were in despair. They both thought that Constance could somehow save the situation. Montague wanted to get Vera down to the Cearne and 'talk it out' with her in front of Constance. 'And this is the last thing I desire! And I don't believe *talking* will do any good at all.'[23] Eventually Montague and Vera went their separate ways, she to do relief work in Russia, where she was allowed, as her father's daughter, to adopt and bring back to England two orphans of the civil war. On her return Constance found her 'a changed being – hardships and having to disregard herself entirely and look after two babies have transformed her. Her nerves and emotions calmed, her real intelligence and vitality have a chance.'[24]

In that same disagreeable autumn of 1921 Constance had a relapse of her internal troubles. For some reason she was unable to go on using the 'support' that she had worn in the past and hardly been aware of. She did not go into further medical details in her letters, but told Natalie: 'I am not to dig, nor to do anything tiring at all – nor stoop from the waist to the ground (i.e. must not weed or pick things up, like picking up apples or potatoes). It comes to this: that I must give up the garden – and you know how I love it! The plants are like live things to me.'[25] She consulted Dr Annjuta Cyriax, Tony Almgren's sister-in-law, a Swedish specialist in massage, but the treatment she prescribed caused such discomfort that she could bear it only on alternate days, and then she had to lie down – 'while the whole object of the business is to enable me to take exercise'.[26]

She recovered from this affliction only to be much more seriously ill in the following spring. On 6 May she woke up with an 'awful pain in my left foot'.[27] The doctor told her that her heart was not working properly and that it was 'rheumatic gout'. She put Natalie off from coming to the Cearne, saying that she had 'to do nothing at all and lie down for a week'. Although she made light of it, adding 'Keep next week free as I hope by then to be all right',[28] her optimism is belied by her shaky hand. On the 24th, when she wrote urgently to David to come and deal with a swarm of bees, she claimed to be improving daily, but her hand was still as shaky as ever. For many weeks she was under doctor's orders, but at least in the summer she was able to lie out of doors sleeping or resting or getting on with her knitting and, it would seem, some translation. Ray, who was by now pregnant again, came to help, and so did Marta Pavlovna Theakstone, a tough middle-aged Russian who was happy to spend a day bailing sludge out of the septic tank, or to hold a conversation in croaks with a frog, but was lost in a city catching trains. She had a son, a bright boy named Leo, about whose schooling Constance was much concerned. Clementina came with a nurse in July, and by September Constance was able to go out every day for a short walk, but found it 'rather a struggle to keep up the habit, for my legs are so rheumaticky or sciaticky – especially my left foot and heel'.[29]

It was in the middle of this illness that Edward had proposed the abortive visit of the Murrys.

When Constance looked back on 1922 she thought of it as the year of 'my illness',[30] from which one might suppose that it was an unproductive time. But, perhaps just because there was little she could do *except* translate, she published more books in that year than in any other.

The last two volumes of Chekhov's *Tales*, *The Cook's* Wedding and *Love*, came out in February and November. Heinemann were publishing a new edition of Turgenev and agreed to add two further volumes of stories, *The Two Friends* and *Knock, Knock, Knock,* and to pay unusually generous terms for them, fifteen shillings a thousand words with a five per cent royalty on all copies sold. These came out in February and July. At the beginning of the previous year Edward had joined Jonathan Cape's new firm, where he remained for the rest of his life, and it was no doubt he who persuaded them to publish Constance's translation of *Christianity and Patriotism*, a short polemic against militarism and nationalism that Tolstoy had written in 1894. She had also undertaken to translate for Heinemann *The Last Days of Tolstoy*, an account by his disciple Vladimir Tchertkoff of the great man's scandalous end, when he ran away from his wife and family and died on Astapovo railway station. She took it on unread, but was so disgusted by its hypocritical and malicious moralising that she 'simply could not carry on with it'.[31]

But [as Natalie wrote] the contract had to be fulfilled, so she asked me to finish the translation and put my name to it. . . . Like a coward I agreed, although my feelings about the book were exactly the same as hers. To salve my conscience I asked Bertrand Russell . . . to tear Tchertkoff apart in his review, which he did, but in my opinion not strongly enough.[32]

And then there were the two volumes of *Dead Souls*, which came out at the beginning of November. In all they amounted to just short of half a million words.

The reviewer in the *Times Literary Supplement* wrote that 'Even in English "Dead Souls" is a masterpiece.'[33] and in the *New Statesman* D. M. (?Desmond MacCarthy) remarked: 'His style, now popular, now eloquent, is always direct. Mrs Garnett's translation is far the best we possess. It succeeds in rendering what we divine to be the lyric rush of such passages as Gogol's famous apostrophe to the Troïka; we catch in her version the silvery jingle of Gogol's bells.'[34]

Tovey has compared four versions of one sentence in this passage:

Chúdnym zvónom zaliuáetsya kolokól'chik
Garnett: The rínging of the béll mélts into músic.
Nabokov: The míddle béll trílls oút in a dréam its líquid solíloquy.
Guerney: With a wóndrous ríng does the jíngle béll tríll.
Reavey: The bélls are tínkling and fílling the aír with their wónderful peáling.

Constance's version is the only one that approximates to the rhythm and simplicity of the original. The elaboration of the others, Tovey says, is quite unjustified, for Gogol does not use alliteration or sound imitation.

It could be added that Guerney, while closest in sense, sounds like doggerel; Nabokov, on the other hand, in pursuit of an irrelevant sound effect, introduces quite extraneous meanings.[35]

Constance always tried to translate her authors into the language of the period in which they wrote, and looking back on her work she remarked: 'It would show grotesque insensibility to produce a translation of Gogol's *Dead Souls*, written at the same time as *Pickwick*, in the language of today's newspapers. I am particularly proud of having translated *Dead Souls* into English of the period in which it was written.'[36] This has not prevented an American publisher from employing a professor of comparative literature to go through Constance's translations of Gogol's stories removing the 'Victorianisms', a project which proved as inept in performance as it was misguided in conception.[37] Moreover, as Simon Karlinsky has pointed out, the reviser has not even succeeded in correcting some of her more obvious errors.

But despite her mistakes, she had a greater affinity for Gogol's style and treated his stylistic peculiarities with more sympathy and respect than the more recent translators of his works into English have. There is a striking contrast between Garnett's translations of Gogol and David Magarshack's versions. . . . Magarshack's understanding of the language is superior to Garnett's. Readers and critics who are not familiar with Gogol's originals often prefer Magarshack's translations as being more 'readable'. They do not realize that this 'readability' is achieved at the cost of systematically flattening and trivializing Gogol's texts, toning down or eliminating his surrealistic imagery, and converting his wild humor into something cute and coy.[38]

Constance's seven volumes of translations in 1922 did not constitute the whole of the Garnetts' output in that remarkable *annus mirabilis* of their literary fortunes. In the spring Cape published *Friday Nights*, a collection of Edward's most valuable work, his critical writings, and in the autumn David's first acknowledged novel came out.

Lady into Fox had been conceived at the Cearne and the first few pages were written only a few yards from the spot celebrated by D. H. Lawrence in his poem. Constance was entranced with it, and with Ray's illustrations 'which go so far to give the book its charm. I don't believe it would have had half its success without them.'[39] She wrote to Edward:

How delightful 'Lady into Fox' is! Just lately I have been reading Virginia Woolf's new book [*Jacob's Room*]. It is wonderful in technique and in the effect of the fragmentary scattered aimlessness of individual lives – and the shifting kaleidoscope of London – and the picture of the people is all fearfully true. But what people! all as dead as corpses – no feeling, no capacity for it and even consciousness of its existence in them. It makes one feel so oppressed. After that the tenderness and warmth of David's little story is very striking.[40]

She asked David to send a copy to Clementina, who congratulated him on 'that excellent, plain classic English which nobody, nobody writes nowadays, and which I have never succeeded in writing myself'.[41] The book became a bestseller, won the Hawthornden and James Tait Black prizes and has been in print ever since.

As Constance's health improved in the autumn of 1922, so did her creature comforts. The old kitchen range was laborious to use, and the oven, if not unusable, was even worse. David made her a present of a Valor Perfection stove. With its two easily-lit paraffin wicks, it seemed a luxury, and Constance went on using it for many years until the blue flames burnt so faintly behind their mica windows that the heat would barely scramble an egg. With a tin oven placed on top it provided the first baked food she had had for two years.

She also found herself a more permanent companion than Marta Pavlovna, who planned to go to Russia to do relief work either for Save the Children or for the Friends, as there was now worse famine than there had ever been before, and Lenin had had to call in outside aid.

Janet Hodge had first visited the Cearne at the end of the previous year at a time when Constance felt 'starved after seeing no one with much brains for weeks together. It isn't that one wants "intellectual" talk all the time – but whatever nonsense sensible people talk it's interesting.'[42] Janet was a factory girl from Glasgow, 'she has brains – real good Scotch brains – and also good spirits – and that realism in her whole attitude to life that comes from a childhood in contact with hard realities. She is really refreshing.'[43] She could not read Russian, but she could take dictation, and undertake almost every other kind of job. Although she did not get on with Natalie – Constance was amused to see them 'eye each other out of the corner of their eyes – awfully like two cats'[44] – she became a trusted friend.

David persuaded Constance to resume her old practice of wintering abroad. This she would not do until the 'great event' was over. Ray's child was due in the New Year, and on 8 January at her mother's London house her son was born, alive and well and named Richard after a long line of earlier Garnetts. David, who had been obliged to sit it out on the stairs reading *Tristram Shandy* while 'operations' were going on, was wildly euphoric. 'I have never been so pleased with anything as this creature', he wrote to his mother on the following day. At the same time he described the family resemblances in the smallest features of the 'terrible little Garnett' and even claimed for his son that 'His voice is rather musical.'[45] Constance likewise doted on her grandchild, as she had on her son. The most immediate result of his birth was that he provided Constance with a continuing bond with Ray almost as strong as she already had with David. The little object was a common focus for their love and concern, someone for whom she could make plans, devise presents and knit. Ray, who had hitherto written to her, just as Constance had done to her own mother-in-law, as 'Dear Mrs Garnett', could now begin her letters 'Dear Granny'.

Constance went to see her grandson and was shocked to notice that he had no eyelashes – 'suppose he never grows any?'[46] – and then she headed south, taking Janet with her, to Juan-les-Pins. 'This is a quiet little bay with a sandy beach on which invalid children lie having the sun-cure – I am hoping the sun will cure my sciatica and indeed I think I am already better.'[47] Her bodily comforts were better looked after than at the Cearne. 'Above all, there's central heating!. . . Central heating at the moment seems to me a much more hopeful solution of all our miseries than Communism!'[48] But she did not care for the other inmates. They did nothing but eat and sit about 'as though they had feasted with Circe. . .. They make me wish I had been born a cat.'[49] The women did not read or walk, they did not even knit or sew. 'I think it's worse,' she remarked to Natalie, 'for middle-class women, who happen to have no brains, to get old than it is for the working-class. Working women have to be active, if their hearts are bad, they die pretty soon, and if not they go on trotting about till they are ninety.'[50]

Constance and Janet managed to be reasonably active, though they had nothing to read but the *Times*, some knitting patterns and the second volume of Herzen's memoirs in Russian. She was now deep in translating them. In the middle of the previous summer, when her illness was at its worst, Spalding had suggested that she undertake them 'in order that Gogol might not be left to come out alone'.[51] This was particularly opportune as four volumes of a new edition of *My Past and Thoughts*, as Herzen called his memoirs, had just been published in Berlin, and a fifth was in the press. Constance read them and replied: 'I find it most interesting and should like nothing better than to translate it.'[52]

Alexander Herzen was the illegitimate son of a Russian aristocrat. His memoirs begin with his old nurse telling him of the family's adventures during Napoleon's occupation of Moscow. He grew up to be a rebel, with a reverence for the Decembrists who had plotted unsuccessfully against Nicholas I. He suffered internal exile and eventually went abroad to France, where he witnessed the uprisings of 1848, and to Switzerland and England. His life is a record of the politics of the time, especially of the interminable dispute between the Slavophils and the Westernisers, as well as of his personal life and his own unhappy marriage. Constance found his kind of intelligence most sympathetic. 'Herzen occupies my mind a lot. . . . How I should like to have a few good talks with him – not about his private affairs – but about modern developments.'[53] He is a most attractive writer, with a style as lively and free-ranging as the best kind of talk. Constance was tempted to cut a few of his digressions, but Spalding wisely insisted that she leave them in. Some of his descriptive passages are brilliant and still sparkle in Constance's translation. Mirsky says Herzen is 'easily translatable',[54] but she found him 'so difficult – often hard to understand – and almost always hard to translate';[55] and there were problems because 'he is so geological in his metaphors'.[56] Not only does he often use new words borrowed from French and German, but there are also many allusions to people and places outside Russia which have to be identified before they can be transliterated into their original languages – a task for Natalie at the British Museum – and some of these need further explanation in footnotes. These Constance had to provide, with no help from David, and she was often perplexed where to draw the line:

I try the names on young friends and find that such as Regulus, Mazeppa, Diderot awaken no echoes in their minds! Two quite decently educated girls (of university education) thought Mazeppa was a name you see engraved on rings (Mizpah!!) and the third vaguely connected it with circuses. I confine myself, however, to explaining references which I think might not be familiar to fairly well-read persons of my own generation.[57]

To which Spalding replied: 'If people don't know who were Diderot, Mazeppa and Regulus I am afraid they won't read Herzen any way, and if they do I don't think their ignorance will trouble them much.'[58]

All this had to be undertaken under some pressure, for Spalding had discovered, when he offered the book to Knopf, that Yale University Press had a rival translation by J. D. Duff already in hand. Chatto were keen to have Constance's out first and to undercut the other edition in price. Spalding therefore proposed that instead of being demy octavo like the Chekhov *Letters* and priced at ten shillings and sixpence a volume, it should be the same small crown octavo as the Chekhov *Tales* and sell at seven and sixpence a volume. This would not affect Constance's initial fee, but would reduce the royalty proportionately. She accepted at once.

Meanwhile she had also been having trouble with the two volumes of Chekhov's plays. She always found stage dialogue particularly difficult, and was least successful with it. She was not happy with the results. 'I don't know how it is, but I get more and more dissatisfied with my work – not with the having to do it but with doing it so badly.'[59] And there were technical problems. She had carelessly sent off *The Cherry Orchard* without revising her old translation to make the names conform to the system of transliteration she was now using; and the printers had had the usual headache with the stage directions because she had been inconsistent in her treatment of them.

The first volume came out in the spring of 1923 and the second in the autumn. In November of that year Spalding sent her a set of all fifteen little volumes of Chekhov bound in red leather. She told him how proud she was at having completed the translation and delighted with the way Chatto had handled it, adding: 'I should hardly have cared to do it at all if it could not have been published in cheap form accessible to the young people who cannot spend a great deal on books. And I believe the little volumes have been widely read and appreciated by just the class of readers I had hoped to reach.'[60] But she was not finished with Chekhov. First she had intended to translate Ivan Bunin's memoirs of his friend, and Chatto had gone so far as to draw up a contract when they found that Koteliansky and the Woolfs had anticipated them. Then on 28 May 1924 she wrote to Spalding:

A Russian friend writes to me that Tchehov's Letters to his Wife have just been published and that they are very interesting.

I should very much like to have the translating of them. . . . Translating Tchehov (except the agonisingly difficult Plays!) has given me more pleasure than any other work I have done, and I should be delighted to have yet a little more of it.[61]

Chatto agreed. But then Constance, who had noticed that the last volume of the *Tales*, entitled *Love*, had sold more copies in America than any of the others, suggested that the binding should be labelled 'Tchehov's Love-Letters', and Spalding was clearly a little shocked – 'perturbed' was the word he used – at such unwonted vulgarity. *The Letters of Anton*

Pavlovitch Tchehov to Olga Leonardovna Knipper eventually came out on 28 January 1926.

By this time Chekhov was at last established on the English stage, thanks mainly to Theodore Komisarjevsky, an unprepossessing but persuasive little Russian, of impeccable credentials. He had worked in the Russian theatre for thirteen years, and liked not only to direct but also to design the costumes and scenery. His sister, Vera, had been the one success, as Nina, in the first production of *The Seagull* in 1896; Chekhov himself told how 'at one of the rehearsals she acted marvellously, so that people sitting in the stalls wept with bowed heads'.[62] Komisarjevsky had a winning way with actors and especially with actresses, but in order to make quite certain that nobody was bored by the play he would take odd liberties with the text, especially when he found what he could get away with.

In 1921, two years after his arrival in England, the Stage Society put on his production of *Uncle Vanya*, but for only two performances on 27 and 28 October, in the middle of a run of Shaw's essay in Chekhovian drama, *Heartbreak House*, at the Royal Court. Komisarjevsky's production had for the first time some unity – '*one* atmosphere'[63] – but it was a long way from being a commercial success.

In January 1925 J. B. Fagan directed the Oxford Players in an indifferent production of Calderon's translation of *The Cherry Orchard*; and Nigel Playfair, who had acted Pishchik in 1911, and who was running an enterprising season at the Lyric, Hammersmith, transferred it from Oxford on 25 May. Most of the critics damned it, but Lady Cunard and Francis Birrell (David's partner in the bookshop) sprang to the defence of the play, if not of the production, and so did James Agate, the most influential critic of the time. Chekhov suddenly became the vogue, and on 22 June *The Cherry Orchard* transferred to the Royalty. Chekhov had reached the commercial West End stage at last.

Three weeks later Constance wrote to David:

A man called Ridgeway has written to me from the Barnes Theatre wanting to do The 'Sea-Gull'. I suppose he thinks 'The Cherry Orchard' was so good!! Pinker is conducting negotiations but I don't know whether anything will come of it. A fine hash English actors would make of 'The Sea-Gull'! and you know it isn't a *Sea*-Gull – but a *Lake* Gull – and what ought it to be called? The names of water birds sound very unromantic – puffin, for instance. You can't have a heroine drawing tears from the audience by saying 'I am a *Puffin*! No, that's wrong etc etc' *Sea-Gull's* bad enough. *Gull* alone is impossible. Imagine a girl saying 'I am a *Gull* etc' Do advise me.[64]

Philip Ridgeway was taking a considerable risk in putting on Russian plays on the tiny stage of the Barnes Theatre, even further from the West End than the Lyric, Hammersmith. He presented an adaptation of Dostoevsky's *The Idiot* in August, and *The Seagull* opened on 19 October 1925. Valerie Taylor and John Gielgud were excellent as Nina and Treplev, and one of the most successful scenes between them seems to have been largely directed by Gielgud himself. But the actual director, A. E. Filmer, was out of his depth with what Komisarjevsky insisted was a 'simple play'.[65]

Ridgeway then invited Komisarjevsky, who had just directed two successful performances of another of Chekhov's plays, *Ivanov*, in Marian Fell's translation,[66] to come to Barnes and take charge of *Uncle Vanya* and *Three Sisters* (once again in Constance's translation). He did wonders with the small stage, devising ingenious scenery for it, and the Daily *Herald* thought *Uncle Venya* a 'Wonderful play, wonderful acting, *made wonderful by the producer*.'[67] Not all were so enthusiastic, but it ran for a month at Barnes, and for another at the Duke of York's. In *Three Sisters*, which opened at Barnes on 16 February 1926, Komisarjevsky began to show his eccentricities. 'He dressed the play twenty years earlier than the author intended',[68] he cut all the references to Baron Tusenbach being an ugly man – the reason Irina cannot love him – and made Gielgud 'play the part in a juvenile make-up, with a smart uniform and side-whiskers, looking as handsome as possible'.[69] He persisted in this bizarre reinterpretation in every revival of the play, and apart from Desmond MacCarthy and one other reviewer 'not one of the critics, who went into ecstasies over the beauty of the production, noticed this very marked divergence from the express stage-directions and dialogue of the author'.[70]

Three Sisters 'played twice daily to excellent houses for six weeks'[71] but it was not transferred to the West End. It was however, revived at the Fortune three years later. But Constance was not happy with it, nor with Ridgeway's final production at Barnes of *The Cherry Orchard* on 28 September 1926, which Komisarjevsky virtually turned into farce. When she heard at the beginning of 1927 that Chekhov's sister, Mariya Pavlovna, was opening his house in Yalta as a museum, she sent her a set of her translations. Although she had been translating from Russian for more than thirty years, she was still not confident about composing a letter in that language herself and asked Natalie to do so. In it she remarked that Chekhov's works 'are much prized by our young people

– and that Komisarjevsky's productions of his plays – though to my mind quite inadequate – have been greatly praised by the critics and enthusiastically received by the public'.[72] It was to be many years before she saw a production of Chekhov that really satisfied her.

1926 was the year of the General Strike. Constance's sympathies were firmly with the strikers, particularly with the miners, whose wages the mineowners insisted upon cutting because of a slump in the coal trade. Baldwin bought a few weeks' peace with a massive subsidy while a Royal Commission sat, but without extracting any concessions out of the owners that might have averted a General Strike:

What a feeble person the Prime Minister seems to be [Constance exclaimed] – one would have thought that before presenting 24 millions to the mineowners he would have wrung out of them a guarantee for the future that would have prevented this disaster. A strong man would have made them understand that the only alternative to peaceable management was confiscation and nationalisation. And now – one doesn't see how it *can* end except in starving the unions into submission – and that's too awful to think of– for the working people will lose all faith in peaceful methods – and lots of them will be driven to desperation – and to building all their hopes for the future on revolution. I can't see how anybody can gain except the worst sort of communists and anarchists.[73]

As in 1914, she expected a long and painful siege, but the General Strike was only a nine days 'wonder. All the same, it was not a good time for the arts. Ridgeway eventually went bankrupt, and despite Chatto's and Pinker's efforts she got little out of him for her translations. Chatto were anxious about the future of her editions of Gogol and Herzen. She was 'awfully alarmed'[74] when Spalding wrote to her a few weeks after the strike was over to tell her that the latest volume of Gogol, *Evenings on a Farm near Dikanka*, had subscribed no more than 256 copies and only a further 66 had been sold since its publication on 22 April; they could not afford to go on losing money – 'all very nicely and kindly said'.[75]

Well, [she wrote to David] I felt like 'Lord now lettest Thou Thy servant depart in peace' as you may imagine. . . . But they really are angels – and bound to come to ruin. They wrote that they would not drop *any* of the three vols arranged for but would only space them out – the Gogol plays this autumn – and the next vol a year later and so on. This is a relief – but of course *one* vol a year instead of 3 means that I must somehow live on £200 (or less!) instead of from £300 to £400. I shall have to give up improving the garden and giving presents (my only two luxuries) and that won't nearly do it.[76]

There were in fact only two more volumes to come, one of Herzen in 1927 and one of Gogol in 1928, so that unless she undertook some further translation her income from new work could only dry up. By the end of 1928 she would be sixty-seven, and quite ready, as she put it, to 'depart in peace'. But her concern about her income was a false alarm. In 1927 Chatto thought it worth while to issue a *Selected Tales* of Chekhov. Her earlier translations continued to do well, and had become a useful literary property. Chatto and Pinker defended it valiantly, ensuring that she was properly paid when stories were printed in magazines or plays performed. And when Geoffrey Bles published a volume of Chekhov's *Letters on Literature* using her translations without permission they battled long and hard to get her a small royalty.

The BBC was also beginning to take an interest. In 1924 it had broadcast her translation of Chekhov's *An Unwilling Martyr*,[77] and from then onwards they showed a welcome preference for her translations over others. She received frequent fees for broadcasts of stories and plays by Turgenev and Chekhov, until by the end of her life hardly a month went by without a formal letter of request from the BBC.

23

The Empty Years Ahead

'Keep a warm heart to me,' Constance once wrote to Edward. 'My "independence" doesn't go very far – you know – your affection and the boy's I can't do without – and if you are both warm and loving I feel so rich that I can dare look forward to the empty years ahead.'[1]

Despite occasional exasperations on both sides, Edward kept a warm heart – to the end of his life he addressed his letters to her as 'Dear little Puss'. Perhaps because she had suffered so much infirmity throughout her life she was not taken unaware by old age, unlike Minnie Black, of whom she wrote, 'So many people seem *surprised* at being old – just as though it had never happened before and did not happen to everybody. It is curious.'[2] And now that she had reached those years she found that they were far from empty. At the Cearne there were frequent visitors, Edward and Nellie at weekends, Natalie in mid-week, but not so often now that she was no longer needed to help Constance; indeed it was now Constance who was helping Natalie with her own translations, checking proofs and trying to solve 'difficulties'. David and Ray came from time to time, and there were many others.

She enjoyed congenial company, particularly if it stretched her mind. As David's second wife, Angelica, wrote:

Her mind was agile: she seized on an idea as a cat might catch a bird on the wing, pulling off its feathers so as to expose the frailty of its substance. But there was no cruelty in Connie; she simply believed wholeheartedly in rationality, the triumph of objectivity, and in always trying to do one's best.[3]

But now she missed the sort of good talk she used to have with J. A. Hobson. 'What one longs for – and never has, even for half an hour a year – is talk with someone who is thinking along the same lines, but with a very much better and more original mind and more power of expression.'[4] She could still have a good talk with David, she told him, 'and you know I love both talking and being talked to. I used to talk a lot – and listen a lot – to your father at one time, but now he is usually exasperated by what he says as well as by what is said to him – and so one is always a bit on one's guard.'[5]

It was much easier with Natalie. Their minds met, even though Natalie would keep 'playing at sorcery – and philosophy. And all that is meaningless – and unattractive – to me.'[6]

After every bout of social life she felt a great need for solitude. It was almost a relief when she could find no one to help with the housework: 'the idea of a noisy, hilarious and vulgar, or sulky and ill-humoured servant always on the premises grows more and more distasteful! (I find myself rejoicing in its being apparently impossible to obtain a suitable one!)'[7] She could not understand why Natalie should think it morally wrong for her to like being alone:

Of course it would be silly to be *proud* of liking solitude – though on reflection I'm not sure that it is not an indication of a rather richer mind to be able to bear solitude well. . . . I am not ashamed of liking to be alone – it's a singularly inoffensive and harmless quality in the old – who are usually such a fearful bore and burden to everybody. I think I'm very lucky that I stand solitude so well. . . . [8]

Her friends' concern was natural enough. She was frail. Rheumatism and sciatica prevented her from hobbling very far. Though her eyesight had not deteriorated much in the last twenty years, her gardening had mostly to be done kneeling on a pad, so that she could see and reach the tiny alpines in her extensive rockeries. She could barely see her way about the house, and this sometimes had alarming results.

One day she had just gone into the lavatory when something quite noiselessly fell from the seat to the floor. 'In my blindness I thought it was a very large piece of whitey-brown paper.'[9] She stooped to pick it up, when it uttered a squeak and dashed out over her feet. She went to see why the hens were keeping up such a strange clatter and found one of them killed. Back in the house she came upon the same hateful creature running round the kitchen. It was a polecat.[10] She thought she had got rid of it – 'Sybil poked about everywhere with a stick – and was sure the beast had gone.'[11] But then in the study:

I saw something whitish on the floor in a corner and stooped to pick it up – it moved!!! – it shot across the room!! There was the same horror again! And do you know I uttered a shriek such as I didn't know I had in me! It was like a hideous bad dream. Sybil's black cat flew up on to a table in terror. Sybil – the brave and intrepid . . . flew after the brute with a poker and an awful scene of carnage followed – Sybil whacking and flying after it – and the brute snarling and shrieking – till at last she killed it . . . just think of the horror of a beast like that – indoors! – alone in the room with one – as you know I don't mind mice – but a beast as big as a cat that shows its teeth and snarls at one – and would kill a baby – or any helpless creature. I believe it has been about the house for a day or two. . . . I never thought I could be so terrified by a thing like that – I've fought with rats and killed them years ago – it's the horror of being so blind that one can't feel sure whether the thing's there or not – and it seemed so uncanny! – like being haunted by something. I feel thankful it's dead.[12]

She had a similar, if less alarming, experience some years later with 'an invisible cat'.[13] She never saw it, and no one else could find it. 'However when the house is quiet and I'm alone it mews – and I put down milk and in the morning it has gone. Queer!'[14]

Nevertheless she continued to prefer to live alone, arguing 'there is always Arthur – he'd come any minute if I needed help'.[15] But on 12 August 1927 he was drowned while bathing off Bridport. Constance was particularly shocked to lose him. 'Edward and I have often trembled over Bunny's safety – and I over Edward's – but somehow Arthur seemed sure and safe. Dozens of people must be grieving for him – he was a good friend to so many.'[16]

Later that month Edward made her a present of sixty pounds to buy an Austin Seven. 'It cannot go faster than 25 miles an hour. . . . Compared with Bunny's car [a Ford tourer] it is an old lady's donkey chaise to a stage coach'.[17] There was no question of her driving it herself, so this was 'by way of a bribe to induce me to have someone living here to drive it'.[18] She was obliged to engage various chauffeuses to live at the Cearne and perform this duty. Janet Hodge was well suited to the job. So was Joey Hitchcock, 'a big girl with round red cheeks, black eyebrows and fine great muscular calves – breezy – efficient and good-humoured – just a little pervading I'm afraid. She is doing great things in the garden.'[19] But Constance must have found it rather a trial to live with Mrs Riley, who was 'kind and good and efficient in the house'[20] but had been bored for ten years – 'It is awful to see anybody getting so little out of life.'[21]

With the car, which was housed in a barn for a shilling a week, it was now much easier for her to pay visits to her sisters. Clementina, staunch and sensible to the last, had died without warning on Constance's sixty-first birthday. Kate still lived in Croydon. Grace, who had long been effectively separated from Hugh and lacked Constance's talent for solitude, had gone to join the Mahomeds. Keriman was by then seventy-two, and Grace thought he had mellowed in old age. 'If we can keep together and be of any comfort to each other for the remaining years,' she wrote, 'I rejoice . . . we all three in our different ways do try to follow Christ,'[22] But three years later Emma had a stroke, and Constance found her

like a little white ghost – but I am thankful to say that her mind is quite clear, though her articulation is imperfect – and her hands are almost useless. We sat in the garden in the sun – most mercifully it was fine – and for all the sadness of it, it was a most beautiful day – like some sad lovely music. There is something so noble in her spirit.[23]

She lingered on, longing to die, for another four years.

More happily, Constance could visit David and Ray at Hilton Hall. In September 1924 David wrote to a friend:

It's – not a person but a – no, not an animal – but a house that I have fallen in love with this time. And I feel as I did when I was twenty, that it was irretrievable, irrevocable . . . that if I cannot live in that house I shall never live in any other . . . that if I am lucky I shall never be unfaithful even in thought to its bedrooms, though all the hotels in Europe shamelessly solicit me. . . .[24]

Hilton Hall, despite its name, was not at all grand – 'except in the way a grandmother is grand'.[25] It had been built in the early seventeenth century, and used for much of the nineteenth as a working farmhouse. On the advertisement put out by Knight, Frank and Rutley, which promised hunting with the Fitzwilliam and Cambridgeshire Packs, David underlined the words 'Septic tank drainage' and wrote in the margin 'Cesspool?' Constance, who had had much trouble with the drains at the Cearne, offered advice from an unlikely source: 'do consider the plan Tchehov always adopted wherever he went'.[26] This was to pump sewage from a cesspool into trenches between the fruit bushes in the vegetable garden: 'you would get grand crops of fruit.'[27] This mephitic system was not adopted, though David alleged, 'We drink our sewage – boiled. It sparkles like crystal.'[28]

In those days the house was cold, damp and draughty, and before Constance dared visit it she insisted that her bed should be 'tremendously baked – I am in such terror of bad rheumatism'.[29] Despite the success of *Lady into Fox*, David had overreached himself in buying Hilton Hall, albeit with Ray's capital, and was often short of money. Constance, who continued to live thriftily, was now beginning to benefit from royalties from her past work. She was able to renounce her pension and give or lend David money from time to time. A cheque for fifty pounds made it possible for Ray to have her second child at home, 'which is ever so much better'.[30] William was born on Easter Sunday 1925, the doctor, who had erroneously forecast twins, having to be hauled out of church to officiate. Ray now had twice as much news of grandchildren for Constance, who was eager for all of it.

She could also afford to be helpful outside the family, though not all her benevolence had happy results. For instance she was asked by an acquaintance to send money to a young man in Brussels to enable him to publish his writings:

from a weak fear of being thought mean I sent £2 to the young man – and now behold! 12 copies of his stories! – which it would be a compliment to call piffle, for they simply 'don't begin to exist.' *And* the enclosed criticism of Akhmatova in English!! – and what English! *And* a letter asking for my criticism of his work – and permission to send me two *stories in English,* which – if I understand him right – he wants to dedicate to me! Isn't it too horrible? What can I say to him? It was a sin to help him to publish his rot – they are not worth the paper wasted on them. And how can I tell him to take to grinding a barrel-organ – or some other honest calling? How terribly one almost always regrets kind actions! One's sins hardly ever lead to trouble, but any little act of generosity or humanity is visited upon one's luckless head and followed by acute remorse.[31]

There was something about Constance and the Cearne that attracted the dotty and deranged. None of those whom she had to deal with was half so mad or dangerous as poor Bill Hedgecock, but she did not have Edward's sangfroid and was 'constitutionally incapable of standing the sort of strain that interviews with and talks with deranged people entails'.[32] She was upset by the way 'the *character,* the whole *disposition* . . . deteriorates with the decay of the mind'.[33] She was caused immeasurable anguish by a whole family of near-lunatics in one of the shacks at Dostoevsky Corner, and was made really ill by the malice – in no way directed at herself – of a nephew's wife. She felt more kindly to Miss Ballam, an odd little body, never vouchsafed a Christian name, who was a devoted supporter of the Bolsheviks. She used to come to the Cearne to run up curtains and Constance's unambitious dresses, until she developed persecution mania and had to be confined for some time in an asylum. When she emerged she told Constance pathetically, 'I felt all the while if only they will let me get to the Cearne, I shall be able to get well'.[34] Margaret Radford, once 'a sweet unselfish dear child – now a spiteful, quarrelsome, deceitful woman'[35] was no less attracted to the Cearne. Constance went to great lengths to limit her visits, but continued to put up with her. Tony Almgren was almost as bad, because she infected Constance with her own paranoia about her husband. Once in Mallorca Constance was in a state of real terror lest Almgren – who merely wanted to see his daughter Gisela – should find out that Tony was staying nearby.

These troublesome women were the exception. For the most part her young friends were a source of pride and pleasure. She was fond of her nephews and nieces – though she did not always get on well with their spouses. Patrick Clayton, who had begun a distinguished career mapping the Egyptian deserts, was her hero. She loved Natalie's two children and more or less adopted others.

During her work for enemy aliens during the war, Nellie had taken pity on some of their children and brought them down to the Cearne, which they reduced to 'something between a pigsty and a Sunday school treat'.[36] Eddie Murray seems to have been one of Nellie's cases. He was an attractive little boy and Constance was much impressed by his intelligence and the workmanlike way he planted shallots. She took him on as an unofficially adopted son and paid some fifty or sixty pounds a year – roughly equal to her chauffeuse's wages – for his education and for him to be looked after in a cottage near Kent Hatch. He grew up to be a successful wireless engineer and a friend for life. And there were to be others, Eric Ritter and Tom Clarkson, whom she helped in various ways and who were more briefly part of her life. Perhaps the most important of these protégés, if only because he published a record of their relationship, was the latest of Edward's authors.

In December 1925 Edward reported for Cape on a novel, *The Two Sisters*, which showed a remarkably sensitive delineation of the female characters, and by a natural mistake a letter was dispatched to 'Miss Bates' offering to publish it. H. E. Bates – the initials stood for Herbert Ernest, but he preferred to be called Richard – was then 'a slightly-built young man with fair hair, blue eyes and a rosebud complexion. Suitably dressed, he could have impersonated a pretty and talented Miss Bates anywhere. Actually he was a keen soccer player and cricketer.'[37] Bates received much the same treatment from the Garnetts as Lawrence had done fourteen years earlier. They all admired his talent but were concerned at his facility, and both Edward and David could be quite fierce when they felt he was letting his 'facile demon' run away with him.

Edward 'exercised the most cunning combination of bullying, sweet intuition and sane advice',[38] and his magisterial letters, kindly meant though they were, could 'produce a sort of fainting fit'[39] in Bates. Being much in awe of Edward, it was with some trepidation that he went down to the Cearne to meet Constance:

No one could have been less like Edward. If Edward was the bear, Constance was the Jenny Wren, frail, bright-eyed, friendly, gay, enchanting. I took to her at once and she was in that moment, and remained ever afterwards, a person after my own heart. . . . The day, too, was one of those days that have about them something rare and auspicious. The Cearne was a stout stone-and-oak house standing half down a hill-slope with vast views into Kent and all about it now was a great blaze of scarlet-orange poppies, blue aquilegias, aubrietias, pinks, violas, lupins, all wonderful in the evening sun. And there began at once one of those excited conversations about flowers that Constance and I were often to repeat, so often to Edward's sly amusement, full of such horticultural fandangle as *Zauschneria californica mexicana*, over and over again, as the years went on, with my every visit there – every visit ending with prodigious exchanges of cuttings, seeds, plants, advice and on her side wondering admiration for my green fingers.[40]

Constance had not met a young man who cared so much for flowers since D. H. Lawrence: 'it is a joy to talk to someone who really is as much a maniac on the subject as oneself. . . . If literature does not keep him, he might set up a little business in rare rock-plants.'[41] She was worried that he would try to get on too fast: 'I think he is a very nice boy. It will be a pity if he takes to writing for a living – he seems to realise that himself.' He should 'get a light job in an office . . . and work at writing in his leisure – and give himself time to develop slowly and naturally'.[42] To this end Edward found him a job in Bumpus's bookshop. He placed Bates's stories in the journals, and wrote an introduction to *The Two Sisters*; while Constance tried without success to arrange a Dutch translation of his collection of stories, *Day's End*, and encouraged him to bear up to Edward's criticism.

Many years later, after Edward and Constance were both dead, Bates wrote an affectionate memoir of Edward. It offended Nellie and Natalie, who felt that the man they loved had been portrayed as an old monster. There is indeed something of caricature in Bates's first impression of Edward:

there came into the restaurant a semi-patriarchal, semi-diabolical figure in a floppy cloak-like overcoat, a grey scarf wound round his neck like a python, and a preposterously small felt hat. He had grey hair, grey jowl-like cheeks that quivered ponderously like the gills of an ancient turkey, and he appeared to have lost himself completely. He appeared also to be a most extraordinarily clumsy person; he was something over six feet tall and big-boned in proportion, but he was in fact extraordinarily agile . . . for so large a man. His thick-lensed glasses gave him an appearance that was in that moment, and for a long time afterwards, quite frightening. He staggered about for some moments like a great bear unable to recall the steps of a dance he had just begun, and then hung up his coat, hat, scarf and walking-stick on the hat-stand. He then smoothed his hair with his hands, gave several painful snorts of breath through his mouth as if the whole procedure had winded him completely, and advanced towards us.

I stood up, hypnotized and terrified by this enormous and grizzly figure, and as I shook hands there was in the air a faint smell of herbal cigarettes and a weird glint of myopic eyes.

'Mr. Edward Garnett,' someone said, and I could have fainted.[43]

I have to admit that this is very much the grandfather I remember. He *was* alarming in the flesh. At a distance he was lovable, and I could see that Ray was very fond of him, and he of her. He had a genius for choosing presents, for giving exactly the right book at the right moment. White's *Selborne* and Waterton's *Wanderings in South America*, and many others, came to me just when I was ready to appreciate them. When he turned up at Hilton or the Cearne he brought a welcome breath of fun and fantasy that Constance was unable to provide. But, affectionate though he was, some imp drove him to mischief. At the Cearne he once told us such blood-curdling tales of man-eating tigers, drawn no doubt from Lieutenant William Rice's classic work, that it was all William and I could do to convince ourselves there was not a monstrous tiger in the attic only waiting for the lights to go out to spring down upon us. He suited his teasing to our different characters. To William, who tended to be shy and silent in his presence, he would tell exciting stories at meal-times of the escapades of a notorious French thief known only as Le Voleur. And at each crucial point of the adventure, while William was gazing at him in expectation, his fork would steal across and purloin another sausage from the poor boy's plate. For me, who was apt to be too clever by half, encouraged by Constance's eagerness for any signs of intelligence, he would procure Mexican jumping beans, and lead me on to provide the most elaborate and fanciful explanations – magnetism, static electricity, and goodness knows what else – of why they rocked about on a heated tray. (Actually, of course, they had small grubs inside, which flinched when toasted.)

335

Our relations were much easier – if less exciting – with Constance. We felt that she belonged to us alone – unlike our other grandmother whom we had to share with nine cousins. She was not physically affectionate, and was not much given to cuddles and kisses, but she was always interested to know what we were doing and thinking. She was not so inspired a giver of presents as Edward, but she was a most satisfactory person to give things to. Anything we made for her, be it a crude little calendar or a sewing case with her initials worked in cross-stitch, was greeted with genuine delight.

I was deeply impressed when on my seventh birthday she gave me the first volume of Arthur Mee's *Children's Encyclopedia*, with the remaining volumes to come at subsequent birthdays and Christmases, accompanied by a letter telling me, 'You have now reached the age of reason.' I was very proud, if not particularly rationally so, of this achievement. I enjoyed *The Children's Encyclopedia*, which, though it was a recent impression, had not been updated for many years, and still carried a fanciful feature on 'Possible Flying Machines of the Future', strange contraptions of canvas on wooden poles, not unlike the 'Shakespeare' cot in which William had until recently been sleeping. As a gesture to modernity there was a small supplement explaining the workings of the motor car. To make it comprehensible to infant minds – though even at that age we were far better able to understand machines than ever Constance was – the engine had been much simplified, and had but one single cylinder the size of a dustbin under the bonnet.

After Christmas Constance would leave the Cearne and seek the sun for a month or six weeks, sometimes at Alcudia in Mallorca, sometimes at Pardigon, 'an old chateau transformed into an hotel standing in a park which leads down to the sea'[44] halfway between St Tropez and Le Lavandou. The mere relief at getting away was enough to make her feel better at once. She had come for the sun, but took it only in minute doses, sitting on the beach fully dressed and with her hat perched on the top of her walking stick to act as a tiny parasol. She was firmly convinced of the perils of sunstroke, and in summer was constantly urging David to make sure the boys' heads, and even their spines, were kept covered. She liked to take someone, such as Minnie Black or her daughter Helen, to keep her company and mitigate the rigours of the journey. When Helen Black served as her holiday companion, she was still translating and needed someone to take dictation; with her sister, Marion, who had recently taken a degree in classics, she read Euripides and played chess. This routine continued until 1930. By then the Cearne had central heating and she was better able to withstand the rigours of an English winter.

On one of these journeys to France she planned to stop in Paris and visit Jane Harrison, whom she had so admired so long ago at Newnham, but the distinguished old scholar was out of town, and Constance had to be content with receiving a fan-letter from her:

I did so want to see you. You are really a heroine of mine. I envy you the work you have done. I owe you a great debt, the debt all England owes – but it was not till after I learnt Russian that I realized the full extent of the debt – for only one who has compared your translations line by line with the original knows their extraordinary fidelity.[45]

The last volume of Gogol came out in 1928, and in July of that year Constance wrote to Olive 'I have given up translation for good now',[46] and so indeed she supposed.

But eighteen months later David had a visit at Hilton from his friends Stephen Tomlin and his wife Julia. They were both artists of great sensitivity, Tomlin as a sculptor chiefly of portraits, and Julia – in due course – as a novelist. Julia persuaded them to go and see 'a play by her favourite author'[47] at the Festival Theatre, Cambridge. It was Turgenew's *A Month in the Country* in a translation by M. S. Mandell and a production by Tyrone Guthrie. The play was written in the late 1840s, but it was not acted in Russian until 1879; nor in English until 1926. This was only the second English production. David wrote to his mother in some excitement:

you made a very great mistake in not translating Turgenev's plays and you must rectify it. A month in the country is one of the finest plays I've seen – of modern plays that is. It is as good as Tchehov and it is extraordinarily like Tchehov in its dramatic method. It is marvellous on the stage and well acted: but the translation is vile. Fortunately they left out some of the bad bits in acting. . . . You have always translated Turgenev better than any Russian author (except Tolstoy). . . .

These plays will be your crowning achievement if you don't hurry them, but translate a page at a time – walk about with a single speech in Russian in your head and translate it when you are satisfied. . . . You would be as enthusiastic as I am if you had seen this wonderful play last night: so tragic so indescribably comic and so bitter with an aloof almost God-like bitterness. . . . It really is your *duty* to translate these plays. . . .[48]

Constance was easily persuaded. She took her time, if only because her eyes were troublesome and she had the usual distractions of visiting grandsons and a garden 'so tempting that it seems a sort of insanity to attempt to do anything but sow and plant and weed'.[49] When she had finished *A Month in the Country* David read it and sent her his suggestions – 'No doubt many of them will annoy or offend – but remember a play has to be *spoken* and has to be made natural'[50] – and by the spring of the following year she was ready to offer it to publishers. Heinemann, who had published her earlier Turgenevs, had done the Mandell translation, and both he and Pawling were dead, so she had no qualms about sending it to Chatto. Prentice reported curtly to his partners: 'I found an entire, almost a devastating lack of interest in it, and had not the slightest desire to read on.'[51] To Constance he expressed a 'deep interest . . . It does seem an outrage to decline anything by Turgenev, especially when it has had the advantage of having been translated by yourself',[52] and was generally so courteous that Constance felt almost apologetic for having troubled him with it.

Eventually it was published, with her translations of two other plays by Turgenev, by Cassell in 1934. But David's hopes for royalties from productions were disappointed. Constance's translation of *A Month in the Country* was not given the production that it deserved until after she was dead.

Three Plays by Turgenev was her seventy-first volume, and after that she really did give up translation for good. She started to write a private memoir. 'Only persons of inviolable discretion' she told David, 'should know these things during the lifetime of the persons concerned. I think I must have a special appendix for family scandals and secrets and even so I shall not record quite all of them.'[53] The memoir, alas, was not completed, and it has no appendix.

She continued to be much concerned about the world's affairs. She was still inclined to socialism, but increasingly disillusioned by the stupidity of particular socialists. After the Conservatives comfortably won the election of October 1931 she wrote to David:

Why on earth did the Labour Party try so hard *not* to get votes? The cowards were so afraid they *might* get in, that they actually put socialising the banks and repealing the Economy Bill as the two first items in their manifesto – just when our credit abroad is threatened! Then went on to say they *would* balance the Budget without cuts – terrifying every Income-Tax payer in the country! . . . better to live 5 years under the Conservatives than hand ourselves over to these irresponsible imbeciles!

And now they affect to be surprised that they have scared off all ordinary people! . . .

Ray Garnett

Edward and David,
with the author up,
at Hilton Hall

Professor Charles and Sybil Wilson

Constance on the beach,
sketch by Helen Black

Constance knitting in the garden at the Cearne

Angelica Garnett

Constance in old age

Alas! if only I could live to see some good old-fashioned Liberals back! If Lloyd George had only gone off under his operation, there might be a hope![54]

She never regretted the passing of the old regime in Russia, but she was too close to witnesses of the new tyranny to have any of the illusions about the Great Socialist Experiment that prevailed among left-wing intellectuals outside Russia. Sasha Yershov, once the happily indefatigable and philanthropic Sasha Shteven, had written to her in 1923 an abjectly apathetic letter describing how she was living in penury on her son's meagre earnings and only praying that God would take her and spare her further sufferings.[55] Natalie's parents were both dead, her father before the revolution, her mother of typhus in 1919. Lolya survived typhus at the same time, and did not reach England until the beginning of 1927, when Constance was very active in getting her a residence permit, enlisting the help of the Oliviers and writing to the Home Secretary, Joynson-Hicks[56] – the same 'Jix' who was shortly to lead a crusade against Lawrence for his obscenity.

In 1933 Natalie translated Tatiana Tchernavin's *Escape from the Soviets*. Madame Tchernavin worked for the Soviet museums service, and her husband was an ichthyologist in the State Fisheries. They had both been supporters of the revolution at first, and were the sort of educated people who could have been most useful to the economy, but they suffered persecution and imprisonment as bourgeois intellectuals before they were able to escape by trekking with their small son to the Finnish border. Their tale of what it was like to be the victims of a brutal bureaucracy was extraordinarily reminiscent of Madame Savinkov's sufferings at the hands of the Tsarist police that Constance had translated twenty-six years earlier, but things were now vastly worse in scale and ruthlessness.

Madame Tchernavin came down to the Cearne, and Constance quite lost her heart to her: 'She is one of those splendid Russians of the type who were an inspiration to me when I was young – who set my whole life in the way it has gone – the right way for which I was fitted – though I should not have found it without them.'[57] But she did wish that her new friend would not talk Russian quite so fast and that she would take off her hat and coat indoors, 'she looks so much nicer without them . . . so young and fresh with her nice skin and abundant hair and lively intelligent face'.[58]

On 11 November 1933, shortly after *Escape from the Soviets* was published, Leonard Woolf reviewed in the *New Statesman* a book by

Allan Monkhouse, one of the Metro-Vickers engineers who was put on trial by the Russians in April of that year. Woolf maintained that he tried to make it a rule 'to believe absolutely nothing he hears about Russia, unless it be something extremely bad from a friendly or extremely good from a hostile critic'.[59] He was thus able to conclude his review: 'Reading this book one understands why those who hate Socialism and so passionately adore the existing system of profits, wars, and doles are so angry with (and so frightened by) Soviet Russia.'[60] Constance was provoked into writing him her political testament:

I know a good deal about you from Bunny. I have heard you on the wireless and always look out eagerly for your signature in the rare and happy expectation of finding intellectual sincerity.

In your review in the Statesman of Monkhouse's book (which I haven't read) I am for the first time out of sympathy with what you write. I do not hate Socialism nor 'passionately adore the existing system of profits, wars and doles'. But I do hate what is being done in Russia and I do dread the success and spread of 'Communism'. Yet it would not be fair to put me down as a 'hostile critic'. During the last forty years I have had many Russian friends, all sympathetic with the Revolution, many active revolutionaries. I rejoiced in 1917. Only very slowly and reluctantly, step by step, I have been driven by the desire to face the facts into my present position. You remember 'He who never changes his opinions loves himself better than he loves truth.' I am sending you Madame Tchernavin's book. Please read it. It throws light on the strange (to the English) habit of the accused in G.P.U. trials confessing their guilt even when innocent. But of course on your principle you will try not to believe it, for she is certainly a 'hostile critic'. Do you try not to believe anything bad about the Nazis told you by Jews who have escaped from Germany? If everybody tried to be fair in your particular way the victims of persecution would never get a hearing anywhere. Surely the character of the witness should affect the credibility of the story. I am continually astounded by the disingenuous attitude of progressive English people about the Soviets. They write 'Their ideal is a society in which inequalities of wealth and privileges of birth and rank have been abolished.' They never add the obvious fact that after sixteen years of Communist rule the disqualifications due to birth and education and the inequalities of rights (even down to the right to a food card) are far more oppressive than ever in the past (since 1861 anyway).

They seem unable to grasp that Russians are living people like ourselves. I spoke the other day to an advanced and very benevolent woman [Miss Ballam][61] (disgusted by the cruelty of the Means Test) of the 'liquidation' of the educated class in Russia, she responded with a sweet smile 'Oh, you mean the bourgeois!' as though [if] it were only a matter of the ruin and misery of a lot of shopkeepers there's no need to worry about it. And the same really goodhearted woman is genuinely indignant at the treatment by the Nazis of the Jews (surely for the most part 'bourgeois' too). Imagine the horror if somebody suggested the 'liquidation' of the three millions of English unemployed. Such cruelty is still unthinkable here, though it would be a real solution of the unemployment problem and much less [harmful] to the country than the destruction of the intellectuals and the million families of the kulacks (i.e. the most intelligent and successful peasants) in Russia.

You write (as though it were praise!) 'a government of devoted fanatics' – well – when you remember the privileges enjoyed by Government officials and 'Party men', their unquestioned authority and power, it is hardly credible that there should not be many whose professions of devotion to the Party are due to the immense advantages of belonging to it. Not that that should be a matter of regret. Those who think more of their comfort than their convictions are not often so cruel and mischievous as 'devoted fanatics'. Communism is a fanatical religion. Is anything more to be dreaded by all lovers of free thought and culture? Its theories make a strong appeal to the idealists, and its practice to the brutal, envious and ignorant. It is spreading rapidly. And how much of the 'noble ideal' is left in the Communism of the Mongols? About as much as of the Sermon on the Mount in the Christianity of the Crusaders.

Your review gives the impression that you think the material achievements of the Soviet Government so immense as to outweigh the spiritual degradation and mental distortion that accompany its terrorism. But you can't really think it. What do you care most for? Freedom, justice, respect for human life and dignity, equality of rights, reasonableness, culture, tolerance. Then surely you must dread a fanatical religion that despises all that 'bourgeois ideology' and rejects with contempt the precious gains won so hardly in the past.[62]

This remained Constance's view of Soviet Russia for the rest of her life. If Natalie had not kept a copy the letter might not have survived. It was not published in the *New Statesman*. There was always a sharp division between the political 'front pages', which included the correspondence and were in the hands of the editor, Kingsley Martin, who shared Woolf's views, and the literary 'back pages', which since the beginning of 1933 had been edited by David Garnett. He had had doubts whether he should take the job on – as had Constance – for he feared it might leave him no time to write. Moreover he thought Kingsley Martin was a barbarian, and 'The political tone is one which I *execrate*: the superior nose out of joint air as of someone saying: "I know you won't listen."'[63] But it was hard to earn a regular living as a novelist, and the New *Statesman* brought him five hundred pounds a year. He did a good job there, especially in his own weekly reviews, and he could at least see that Tatiana Tchernavin was not scorned as a 'hostile witness'. He sent the book to his brother-in-law Tom Marshall, by now a lecturer in sociology at the London School of Economics; and he gave it a fair and sympathetic review.[64]

While Constance had been obliged to modify some of her political opinions by the force of circumstance and disillusion of experience, her views on religion remained unchanged. When a hopeful new vicar called and quoted scripture to support his arguments, she retorted that she did not think that the Gospels 'which were written by ignorant men in Aramaic and translated two centuries later into bad Greek'[65] were a suitable subject on which to dogmatise. But she respected Christian ethics, and was much attracted by the Sermon on the Mount.

Altogether it is the most touching thing in literature. . . . The whole impression [is] of a rare and tortured spirit – whose sayings have been recorded by ignorant and obtuse followers, – and translated into exquisite English.

And then to think of the distortion of all that – into the old pagan sacrifice of eating the body and blood of your god – as in Egypt – and all over the East! Isn't it extraordinary! And apparently rational beings like Natasha maintaining at great length that the Bread and Wine she takes in Church occasionally both *is* and *is not* (as far as I can understand) the Body and Blood of Christ (who both *is* and *is not* identical with Jesus of Nazareth!)

It seems as though religion is a sort of contagious insanity.

But the Gospels are lovely. . . . Of course it is much more beautiful in English than in Greek.[66]

Her faith was in humanity. Despite all her own infirmities and all that was then going on in the world, 'I firmly believe', she said, 'that the vast majority of mankind are good and far more happy than miserable and I am naturally so cheerful that I don't need another life to make this one tolerable.'[67]

24

The Last Adventure

In 1937 I went to a school in Wimbledon, and William joined me soon afterwards. The school encouraged weekly boarding; we did not have to go away at weekends, but we liked to do so when we could. To reach our parents at Hilton we had to cross to the other side of London and then take the train sixty miles to Huntingdon. And for some of this time Ray was unwell with cancer. But the Cearne could easily be reached by taking a quick train from Wimbledon to South Croydon and then a Green Line bus, which dropped us off on the road between the Chart and Kent Hatch. It was a busy road, and in winter darkness Constance insisted that we tuck our handkerchiefs into the backs of our knapsacks so that they would show up in car headlights. After walking through the woods and slithering through steep drifts of beech leaves to the little gate, we emerged at the bottom of the garden looking up at the Cearne perched on its heaps of rockeries and standing even prouder than at first because the ground below it had been trampled down or washed away so that a fourth step was needed at the entry.

The heavy embattled door was never locked and opened almost soundlessly to reveal the characteristic resinous and smoky smell of the Cearne. Constance would be in the study, a small figure in a large easy chair, sitting, often in half-light or near darkness, listening to the big wireless that had been given to her by Eddie Murray.

'Just tweak on the light, please,' she would say, for electricity had come to the house in 1929, and she liked to choose the apt word for such innovations and to stick to it. The light revealed the appurtenances of her life: the wall of bookshelves, where, as boys, we were attracted by Knopf's borzois bounding along on the foot of the spines rather than the titles at the top; and opposite it on an oak table were her papers, letters to be answered and literary magazines, the *New Statesman* with David's 'page' – a leading review under the rubric of 'Books in General'

– the *Listener* and others. And somewhere in a corner of the room there was a pile of obscurer journals devoted to causes that ought to have been won long ago: *The Anti-Slavery Reporter and the Aborigines' Friend* and the publications of the Rationalist Press Association.

Constance was dressed mainly in her own knitting, comfortably shapeless garments of brown or peacock blue, sometimes with a plaid of some appropriate greenish tartan round her shoulders and with thick brown stockings and slippers below. Her eyes were protected by small thick steel-rimmed spectacles, and though she seemed to us to be purblind, she could in fact see better than she had done for years, thanks to new spectacles that she had been prescribed in 1935. I even seem to remember that she had a special pair for very long distances with which she was able to see the marks on the moon for the first time in her life. Her mouth, though spoilt by manifestly false teeth, was still 'capable of expressing considerable determination'.[1] She still had the same fair skin drawn tightly over conspicuous small cheekbones, and a tall smooth brow. Her fine hair had thinned and faded but not gone completely white, and clung to her skull, which seemed as frail as an egg.

Her face lit up on our arrival, she would get to her feet and make her way with one arthritic hand outstretched to pick up half-seen landmarks and obstructions, round to the kitchen, where some sort of supper awaited us on the Valor Perfection. There were no such needless luxuries as electric cooker or refrigerator. The milk from the cottage at the bottom of the hill came straight from the cow and was boiled at once to keep it from going sour. The skin was skimmed off and put in tiny brown casseroles to be used as cream. There was also something called 'Metchnikoff sour milk' after the Russian scientist who prescribed it for longevity, for it was not yet marketed in the English-speaking world as yoghourt, and had to be fermented at home from test-tubes of clear culture obtained from one of the London hospitals. The food was basic and the cooking poor, but the materials were good. Once a week she received from Natalie a round loaf of Russian bread. It was as yellow as a brioche, being made with the same well-egged dough as Natalie used for the rolls she offered up on the altar for the good of her friend's soul. Constance was much amused when she found this out and teased Natalie for believing in a God so venal that He could be bribed with little cakes.

The kitchen garden was still in excellent shape and so were the fruit bushes. There were regular campaigns of bottling and stores of apples in the attic, but I remember once finding slivers of something like grey cardboard in the stewed apples. It was cheese, intended for the macaroni, which in her blindness she had tipped into the wrong saucepan.

Constance herself ate little and reduced her needs to a minimum. At first she drank weak China tea with lemon. The tea became weaker and weaker until she omitted it altogether. In due course she left out the lemon, and by the end of her life she was drinking plain hot water. On the same principle, when she could no longer turn her mattress to air it she slept on a set of three army 'biscuits', as spartan a couch as one could well wish for.

She was always interested in our doings, but there did not seem to be much for us to do. At Hilton something was always being made or built or repaired. We had helped build our own swimming-pool, and other 'great works' were afoot. We could go birds' nesting – not then a mortal sin – poach rabbits or shoot rats with an airgun. At the Cearne there was plenty to read, and even a popular science journal, *Discovery*, for our special entertainment and instruction. There were some ancient games, 'Reversi', bezique and chess, but few means of undertaking new works. The saw in the settle drawer was blunt, and the one hammer had its head held on by a bent nail.

In the summer the garden was a joy – except in August, when we were rarely there. But the copse in one of the fields below the house, which had once been no more than a threshold of leafage below the extensive view, had grown up into a tall grove blotting much of it out.

We explored the woods. We enjoyed hunting for wood mushrooms with Natalie, who once, on hearing that I was interested in mathematics, vainly tried to convince me of some savant's theory that beauty could be reduced to formulae. Best of all we liked to go on walks with Nellie, whose gentle concern seemed to draw out one's confidences better than Constance's more eager interest. We saw a little of the elderly inhabitants of Dostoevsky Corner. Sybil now seemed like a benign old witch; and we were happier with Annjuta Cyriax, whom I remember as an angelic little bundle of furs who gave us jellied Siberian crab-apples and slices of smoked reindeer and demonstrated in her sixties how to toboggan down a snowy field on a tea-tray.

Because the people round the Cearne were all elderly, and new ventures were not afoot, the whole milieu seemed to us boys to belong to the past, not that Constance talked much about it. We did not realise that Conrad and Galsworthy and Lawrence had already consigned the house to a place in history. Not so the pilgrims who sometimes made their way to see Constance in her house by the woods.

This afternoon an American poet and his wife are coming to tea. It's rather awful. They've such a reverence for Conrad and D. H. Lawrence that they regard this house – because those heroes have slept in it – as a sacred shrine – and I have to play the priestess. It does make me feel a fool![2]

E. S. Bates (no relation of H. E.) was a more welcome admirer. He had praised her achievement in his little book, *Modern Translation*, and as a result he and his Danish wife came to the Cearne and became friends. He was in his sixties, much travelled, and his knowledge of Spanish and the classics made him appreciate the translator's art and value its cultural importance. Constance welcomed his scholarship, wide reading and international point of view.

She herself was always as much interested in events abroad as at home, and during the nineteen-thirties she was horrified by the rise of Fascism and dismayed by the Spanish Civil War. She felt that Britain and France were spineless in letting Mussolini get away with Abyssinia. She was certain that war was coming and dreaded what it might do to her family. But cheerfulness would keep breaking in:

Well, it's a wonder really that I'm not gloomy. I've nothing to look forward to but increasing feebleness of mind and body. I'm useless (not that that worries me in the least!) and can't expect anything thrilling to happen.

But the fact is that I'm usually lighthearted – and when the sun shines, or when I read something I like or hear Beethoven's Concerto in D on the wireless or look out at the sky in the evening and hear the owl, I feel happy. And you know, though I shan't live to see it I'm ridiculously interested in the future – and always speculating about it.[3]

Her favourite sister, Grace, had died in 1934. 'Though we have no ideas in common hardly,' she wrote, 'I love her more than any of my family – and nobody in the world wrings my heart as she does.'[4] And three years later she lost Edward. Early on the morning of 19 February 1937 he came into the kitchen at 19 Pond Place and said to Nellie, 'I feel ill, get the thermometer.' Nellie told him to go back to bed. But when she came to him a moment later he said he had a pain through his heart. 'It suddenly became unbearable and he threw himself over and died.'[5] He was sixty-nine and had high blood pressure and hardening of the arteries. His health had never fully recovered from typhoid in 1896.

He was cremated at Golders Green. His earliest and greatest literary friends were all dead. Neither Constance nor Nellie felt up to attending. So, as H. E. Bates wrote, 'it was a following of very young men who stood to pay homage to him that day – H. A. Manhood, Geraint Goodwin, Arthur Calder-Marshall, Rupert Hart-Davis, Hamish Miles and myself'.[6] He had, as Bates put it, 'a singular genius which could only be exercised by great unselfishness'.[7] And they, and many other writers of both sexes, loved him for it. So too had Constance, despite all the difficulties of their marriage.

A death, even of someone younger than oneself, inevitably recalls the past; and among those who wrote Constance letters of condolence were such ancient friends as May Morris and Labour's lost leader, Ramsay MacDonald, who spoke sadly of his memory of 'old times which I cherish, and which often return to me when sitting quietly keeping company with myself'.[8]

With Edward gone, Constance became closer still to David, who had long been the most important person in her life. Nellie moved into a small flat in 'a household of women all struggling to live'[9] in north London, and continued her work teaching crafts to the women in Holloway Gaol. They became her friends, for, as she used to say, 'all the nice people seemed to be inside and the nasty ones out'.[10] She drew closer to the remaining Garnetts, especially to Constance, and became an extra grandmother to William and me.

At the end of that year or early in 1938 Constance heard that John Gielgud's company was to put on her translation of *Three Sisters*. During the nineteen-thirties there had been a number of successful productions of Chekhov on the London stage. Not all were in her translation, but there were enough for her to benefit comfortably from the royalties. Yet none that she had seen could compare with the performances in Russian by a group from the Moscow Arts Theatre which had come to London in 1928 and 1931. She had better hopes of Gielgud, despite his having been so badly misdirected by Komisarjevsky as Tusenbach, and rather less so as Trigorin. She accordingly sent a letter of advice to Gielgud, who passed it on to the director, Michel St-Denis. St-Denis was a nephew and disciple of Jacques Copeau, for whose production of *Pelléas et Mélisande* Duncan Grant had hoped to design sets and costumes in 1915, and he had established a fine reputation of his own with his Compagnie des Quinze in Paris. She urged 'a few points':

Irina's unhappiness is due to the fact that, while she dreams of an ideal lover, 'my real one', of her only two actual suitors one, Solyony, who poses (to himself as well as to others) as a 'man of destiny', and plumes himself on being a duellist, scents his hands because 'they smell of corpse' etc, is simply a stupid brute who disgusts and frightens her, and the other, Baron Tusenbach, gentle, intelligent, sympathetic, and good, is so physically unattractive that the poor girl can't bear to look at him. When this part is played, as I have seen it, by a particularly good-looking young man (wasn't it your brother?), Irina's part is ruined – it makes her seem almost abnormal.[11]

It was, of course, Gielgud himself. She also urged that the sisters 'clothes should not be 'smart or showy' and that he should not think he had to stick literally to the text: 'I tried, as a faithful translator, to avoid using a word not in common use when the play was written but there is no need for such preciseness on the stage.'[12]

St-Denis accepted her points, and the play opened on 28 January 1938 at the Queen's Theatre and ran for three months. It was a 'landmark'[13] in the history of Chekhov on the English stage. The ensemble was universally praised. Constance was in raptures and told St-Denis:

You are surely a magician. Here you have set a whole group of good British citizens dancing, shrieking, skipping about, laughing and crying and saying just what comes into their heads as naturally as though they were Russians. . . . How wonderfully you have got the feeling of the Russian spring in the first act. 'It comes so suddenly – it makes us all hysterical' a Russian girl said of the spring.

By some miracle you – and the actors – all good – have succeeded in conveying that combination of ruthless realism with the feeling of sweet absurdity, the beauty – the 'music' of life, which is the very essence of Tchehov.[14]

She hoped that he might one day produce *The Cherry Orchard*, 'Tchehov's masterpiece – it's hard to imagine that he could have excelled it, had he lived'.[15] To Gielgud she wrote:

Ever since I began translating Tchehov . . . I've hoped and longed to see his plays adequately produced in England. Well, I had given up hoping for it. There have been conscientious, painstaking efforts (as at the Old Vic) but it seemed impossible for solid English actors to enter into the liquid temperament of Russians.

You have achieved it and I want to thank you for the great pleasure of seeing my dreams fulfilled.

No doubt you get hundreds of letters in praise of your success. But few of the writers know Tchehov as I do who spent years pondering and struggling – never satisfied – to find the right phrases for his exquisite sentences.[16]

Gielgud replied:

Much as I admire Komisarjevsky's work, I have to admit that the Frenchman is a far more brilliant student of Tchehov and seems to have entered with uncanny perseverance and meticulous exactitude into the whole subtlety of this play. I am very lucky in my company and in having been able to give seven weeks to rehearsing this production – which is impossible economically except with a repertory company. However, I owe Komis a great debt for the enormously interesting time I had with him in four or five productions – two of them (Three Sisters and Seagull) by Tchehov – and I think there is no doubt that, despite his rather perverse and capricious sense of humour and his poor opinion of the English public – his romanticised productions prepared the way during these last ten years for the success of this production, for actors and public alike have been led gradually to love acting in and seeing the plays – which, after all, are very difficult to play and to appreciate without the help either of a Russian or a fine producer who understands the Russian character.[17]

In replying to Constance, St-Denis wrote: 'I think that I will do the Cherry Orchard. It has been my ambition for years. But the fact that I have seen Stanislavsky's production in Paris in 1922 stopped me doing it myself. I don't like imitation.'[18] He had the play in rehearsal at the Queen's Theatre with Edith Evans and Ronald Squire when it was halted by the outbreak of war. He returned to Russian drama ten years later with the first stage production of Constance's translation of *A Month in the Country*, It was as notable as his *Three Sisters*, but by that time Constance was dead.

On 14 September 1938 it was announced that Neville Chamberlain was to fly to Munich on the following day to make his first visit to Hitler to resolve the crisis over the Sudeten Germans in Czechoslovakia. In fact the Czech government 'for the first time had the internal situation . . . in hand',[19] but as Churchill afterwards observed 'the last thing the Germans wanted was a satisfactory bargain between the Sudeten leaders and the Czech Government'.[20] Unfortunately Chamberlain believed that he could trust Hitler to keep his word and that he could solve the crisis himself. Unlike Natalie, and much of the British public, Constance did not share those illusions:

When I heard the news on the wireless I almost fainted with horror – and I've hardly slept all night. . . . Now we shall hear how nice and reasonable Hitler was. . .. Always playing into the bully's hands – just as in Spain. It may stave off war for a year or two – but then it will come just right for Richard and Sasha when they are 18. . . . If C. would take a revolver in his pocket and do for Hitler first and himself afterwards, the visit would be of some use – not otherwise.[21]

On 3 October, by which time Britain and France had effectively abandoned Czechoslovakia to Hitler, a letter appeared tucked away on page 19 of the *Times* behind all the accounts of the Day of Thanksgiving for 'peace for our time'. It was signed by a number of distinguished people and spoke of 'our lasting dishonour', adding: 'Had our policy this last six or seven years been different, this choice between war or submission to evil would never have arisen; and we could have preserved peace together with the effective defence of free and Christian civilization.'[22] The signatories recorded their protest 'and our determination to stand in future for a policy which will not expose this country either to dishonour or disaster'.[23]

Constance wrote to Sir Malcolm Robertson, who headed the list of signatories, and to her old friend H. G. Wells, who was also one of them, asking:

what measures are being taken to carry out the 'determination' in the last sentence.

Do you contemplate forming an organisation of all who would support that statement? If so isn't it of the first importance that such a movement should not appear to be sponsored solely – or even chiefly – by the Left? Its object should be to capture the many honest Conservatives, that's the only hope. For the mass of the British public would not entrust our foreign policy to the Labour party (they might to Eden and Duff Cooper).[24]

Neither Eden nor Duff Cooper, who had both resigned from the government in protest against its foreign policy, had signed the letter to the *Times* – nor, for that matter, had Churchill.

Constance also suggested that a fund be raised to publish an unauthorised translation of *Mein Kampf*, so that everyone should know Hitler's intentions, as he had 'allowed only the apparently innocent chapters to be translated'.[25] Wells replied despairingly that better education was the only answer. Constance agreed:

But meanwhile the senile group [she herself was seventy-six] who are in control of our destinies – and are consciously or unconsciously *pro*-fascist – are handing over our honour and our security to Hitler and Mussolini – and the better educated next generation may find themselves dominated by savages with whom the destruction of all real science and culture is an article of faith.[26]

Wells also sent her a circular letter expressing shame and apology addressed to ex-President Beneš of Czechoslovakia, which she and Vera Fordham signed, though she felt that it was too mildly worded. It was a gesture, no more.

Constance's feelings, therefore, when war broke out were quite different from what they had been in 1914. She greeted it not with outrage but relief: 'At least there is now some hope of freedom and decent civilization surviving. If it costs half the population of the world, that's less terrible than centuries of brutal despotism and slavery.'[27] Her practical preparations, however, were much the same as for the previous war. Eric Ritter came and dug up a patch of grass for extra potatoes. She installed some geese, though she found it hard to find food for them, and they were threatened by a vixen and her cubs in the wood. David brought bees, and was kept busy by them on his visits. And the vegetables again took priority over the flowers.

Remembering the meagre supplies of greasy margarine and the shortage of flour in the previous war, she filled the cupboard on the landing with gallon cans of cheap olive oil from Palestine and packets of ship's biscuits. These were thick and square, shaped exactly like the 'biscuits' on her bed, and so indestructible that a discontented sailor once wrote a letter of protest upon the back of one, stuck a stamp on it and posted it to the *Daily Mirror*, where it arrived unbroken. Most of these supplies survived to be eaten in the first austere days of peace.

Her friends saw the Cearne as a refuge. On the eve of war Margaret Radford threatened to come and bring her cat 'for the duration'. 'We are going to padlock the summerhouse which is bespoken',[28] Constance wrote to Natalie, and was relieved to be able to limit the visit to a day or two. Nellie, who moved from London to a sort of Dostoevsky Corner of black wooden shacks in woods near Bordon in Hampshire, was a frequent visitor. Constance was glad to be able to see that she was decently fed. Miss Ballam came too, and when Nellie was invited to Anna Duddington's wedding, she smartened up her 'last year's rigout for the occasion – and it is comic and pathetic to see the interplay of Nellie's fear that Miss B. will make her *too* terribly smart, and Miss B's regret that Nellie will persist in being oldfashioned and dowdy!'[29]

David, who was forty-seven at the outbreak of war, joined the RAF to work in the Air Ministry – a somewhat frustrating post where he liked to say that his only achievement was to have H. E. Bates commissioned as a 'war writer' comparable to the war artist Duncan Grant might have been. Some fine stories by 'Flying Officer X' were the result. But by now Ray was very seriously ill, and David took leave to look after her. She died on Easter Sunday, 24 March 1940, having spent the last weeks of her life bringing her photograph albums up to date.

Just over a fortnight later the war started in earnest. Constance 'felt sick with terror'[30] over her nephew, Kenneth Black, who was with the Canadian army in France when that country fell. Then on [31] May she had a telegram from Ruby, 'Ken back in England'. 'It made me idiotically weep with joy and relief – for I had somehow almost given up hope of his being alive.'[31] On the following day Dicky Garnett rang up with a similar message. He was Robert's son, but had inherited more of his uncle Arthur's simple tastes and engaging character. On his next visit to the Cearne he told Constance in detail of his 'terrific experience'[32] at Dunkirk, during which he had had no sleep for two nights 'and can't sleep properly now'.[33] He rarely spoke of it afterwards.

Southern England was now in the front line and Constance got 'in a slight fanteeg about the conspicuousness of the Cearne'[34] to enemy bombers and had the white window frames painted a dull shade of grey. But she refused to be alarmed by the threat of parachutists:

I'm not scared of *absent* terrors (a real burglar might alarm me – but the possibility of one would never affect me). As for parachutists – well, it has not occurred to me to think of them as a danger to *me* – only as a danger to aerodromes . . . the railway station or the waterworks.[35]

Gertie Camber, the tough countrywoman who came in every day to do the more essential housework before turning to the real business of the garden, brought news of 'Great excitement in Edenbridge – main street lined with Canadians – Churchill with Eden strolling down on foot talking to the men . . . now we feel as though we were at the centre of things.'[36] They were indeed. The Cearne was only six miles south of Biggin Hill airfield, the centre of fighter operations, and less than two miles from Churchill's house at Chartwell. Constance had not lost her sense of adventure at seventy-eight. As David wrote, 'Constance had the virtues which are particularly valuable during a war. She was clear-headed, never gave way to panic fears and was ready to put up with any shortages or hardships which came her way. Nor did she dread dying a violent death.'[37]

On 6 September, at the height of the Battle of Britain, she wrote to David:

There's a terrific battle going on as I write – a great spatter of machine guns – and planes whirling round – at a tremendous rate . . . There was a raid going on all last night – I gather – but I was only disturbed by it when there was a loud bang at 3.45 – and that was followed by something like a dozen bombs, not near enough to be alarming, though shaking the windows. At a quarter to five I heard the 'all-clear' signal. On the whole I had a good night and spent the whole of it in bed. . . . It is a pity people are so silly about the raids. Instead of trying to sleep through them, they seem to try to make the most of them by sitting up all night.[38]

Sybil Wilson, for instance, had taken in Fanny Stepniak and her sister, Sasha, to escape from the dangers of London. Now they cowered in one squalid room with sixteen cats and retreated terrified into a cupboard during air raids. No wonder poor Sybil fainted with exhaustion in the morning.

Constance was frustrated. There was work to be done in the garden, the sky was raining metal, and she could no longer move fast enough to take refuge in the house when she heard enemy aircraft approaching. So she asked David to buy her a helmet. The shopman advised him to have a steel one, as used by Air Raid Wardens, which would give much better protection than the lighter model made of black composition. But David chose the composition, for he 'felt sure that the weight of a steel helmet would give her a headache, which seemed to me a more immediately important consideration than whether she would survive a direct hit from a shell splinter or machine gun bullet'.[39] It was a great success. She happily went on weeding the garden during the battle, although the rest of her body was quite unprotected.

The big wireless enabled her to follow the war every inch of the way. She listened to the commentaries of Raymond Gram Swing and Philip Joubert. Churchill, who had been a villain at the time of the intervention in Russia, and a 'brute'[40] during the General Strike, had now become a hero. She was fascinated by such talks as Sir Charles Darwin on the invention of the electron microscope, though she felt the Children's Hour had become disgustingly pious. And she had a particular treat on 12 January 1941 when the BBC broadcast *A Month in the Country* in her translation, with Peggy Ashcroft as Natalya and Alec Guinness as Rakitin, the nearest thing to a full production that she was to hear. Variety she could not abide, though she sometimes got much amusement from popular songs. There was one that went, 'You're as pretty as a picture, a beautiful exhibition of art. . . .' 'Imagine, if you please,' she would exclaim, 'a young man praising his girl for wearing so much make-up!' She abominated the relentless cheeriness of Tommy Handley, whose 'Itma' was supposed to be such a vital prop to the nation's morale, and 'would say in tones of gentle piety, "I wish he had been strangled at the hour of his birth."'[41]

David, who left the RAF to write a history of the war in the air, was at Hilton that autumn, living with Angelica Bell, the daughter of Duncan and Vanessa. He had known her ever since her birth at Charleston on Christmas Day 1918. 'It is a queer little creature, very lovely and full of character and independent life. . . . It weighed 7½ lbs being put in a card [board] box on the kitchen scales.'[42] She was now the 'delightful and gifted creature',[43] trained as an actress, and an artist by inclination, whom Ray's sister Frances described: 'Her face is strikingly lovely, with great grey eyes and bistre-coloured skin, and her figure beautiful and distinguished.'[44] She sang to Frances's accompaniment, and the 'delicate combinations of pattern and colour' in her patchwork quilt put Frances's to shame.

William and I were also at Hilton for the holidays with a houseful of family friends, and at the height of the Battle of Britain David wrote to Constance urging her to join us, where she would be 'a *useful* visitor, as you will give a gloss of propriety to the ménage'.[45] Constance was reluctant to leave the Cearne. She liked Angelica and had long ago learned to accept David's affairs, which 'were in any case peripheral to her passionate need for him: he was a law unto himself, and as long as he did not exclude her from his life, all was well'.[46] But she found the war 'so fascinating to watch at close quarters'[47] that she did not at first want to come to the relative peace of Huntingdonshire. On 30 September, however, David went to fetch her in the car, passing Duncan and Vanessa's burnt-out studio on the way, and seeing the damage to Westminster Abbey and an air raid over Camden Town when they returned on the following day. She was quickly won by Angelica, completely accepted her, and 'treated her as though her youth and inexperience was no barrier between them'.[48] Angelica was touched by her 'open and guileless'[49] attitude, which soon became deep affection. After David and Angelica were married in May 1942 'she took it for granted,' as Angelica wrote, 'with what I now see as an ingenuous generosity, that I would make a good stepmother for Richard and William: I think it hardly occurred to her that there was no more than five years' distance between myself and them'.[50]

Meanwhile Hilton Hall was let, and they set up house in Sussex, a few miles from Charleston, until late in 1941 David was offered a job in the Political Warfare Executive, and he needed to have a London flat. But he tried to get down to the Cearne at least once a fortnight, to look after bees, shoot rabbits and squirrels, hack at invading brambles and above all to give comfort to his mother. 'It rejuvenates me to see you'[51] she told him, and Angelica has described how:

Her joy at seeing Bunny was rather like the unbridled pleasure of a puppy on the return of its master. Although Connie, over seventy at the time, did not bound or bark, her face shone with pride and pleasure, and the excitement perceptible in her rather high voice was an unmistakable sign that, for her, Bunny was the one thing in life that really mattered.[52]

Next, I suppose, came William and myself, and in wartime she was of course anxious what would happen to us. As early as 1936 David had toyed with the idea of sending us to America, and there were vague plans to evacuate William's school to Jamaica. But in the end we stayed put. After an abortive year of reading mathematics at Cambridge, I joined the marine section of the RAF in the autumn of 1941, and William volunteered to work in the mines two years later. Constance wrote to us regularly, and was as eager to hear news of us from David as she had been from Ray when we were children – 'she followed the career of each member of the family with the vibrant interest of those addicted to a serial'.[53] She was immensely proud of her nephew, Patrick Clayton, who had joined the Long Range Desert Corps, and even before Wavell had made his first advance against the Italians had won a DSO for capturing a fort hundreds of miles behind the enemy lines. After a few more such exploits he was captured by the Italians, only to escape from his prison camp and live for some months on the run in Italy. When sent back to Germany he became the camp's chief forger, and for much of the war Constance waited anxiously for news of him.

Her mind was as keen as ever, but on 6 November 1941, just before she was going to bed, she started trying to tell David about the Burma-China railway that she had read about in the *Times*, and the words came out as gibberish. She did not at first realise what was happening, and by the time he had got her to bed 'she suddenly recovered her speech and broke out in indignation, saying that really if she was to lose the faculty of speech as well as sight and strength it was a bit too much'.[54] It was a very nasty scare, and she had a few more such attacks, but they did not last more than a minute or two.

David had an extremely taxing job in Political Warfare. He was proud of being one of the few who were allowed to see the full invasion plan beforehand – and it has to be said that he was not naturally good at keeping secrets. Whenever he could, he and Angelica took their relaxation in the Pennines. In June 1927 he and Ray had driven up to Wharfedale to see the eclipse of the sun. He thought the eclipse a disgusting obscenity, but fell in love with his ancestral hills. He and Ray began taking walking holidays in the Dales, camping out and staying at small pubs. When they could no longer leave William and me behind, they took a shepherd's cottage called Duke Mary's in Swaledale for eight pounds a year. In April 1942, when the war news was far from promising (Singapore had fallen, Rommel had not yet been halted), David cashed in some shares which had nearly trebled in value since he had bought them on Maynard Keynes's advice, and bought a hill farm on the North Tyne, three hundred and thirty-eight acres of 'moor and crag, wild wood and river, fields and farmhouse'[55] for two thousand two hundred pounds. He thought of it as a memorial to Ray, who had loved such wild country, and it was also an effective demonstration of his faith in Britain.

He went straight up there with Angelica the day after they were married, and it later became a refuge and a resource for William, who got away from his Durham mine whenever he could and shot welcome supplies of grouse, pheasant and hare.

Angelica's first child, Amaryllis, was born on 17 October 1943, and gave Constance a new lease of grandmotherhood. She was able to indulge it more fully when David, wishing to be able to keep a closer eye on his mother, rented Scearn Bank, where the 'lady doctors' had lived.

Angelica moved down with the baby in the following March, and wrote:

Every day or two I used to take Amaryllis round to see Connie for an hour or so. The baby sat at her feet, while Connie fantasised about her nascent intelligence, remarking with pleasure on her likeness to Bunny. She was accepted as a fresh personality in Connie's life, reminding her of how delightful it was to be young.[56]

She continued to work in the garden, helped only by Gertie Camber, and it was there that Bates last saw her

groping with spectacles close to the ground in a bed of the vivid blue *Gentiana sino-ornata* she grew so well – to my great envy – with a glimpse of old brown bloomers from beneath her skirt, trying long after it was necessary or wise to scratch that rather impoverished hillside into flower.[57]

It had never, of course, been necessary or wise to have a flower garden – that applied only to the vegetables. The flowers were a matter of pure pleasure and an end in themselves. When Angelica wanted to pick a few to liven up Scearn Bank, 'she did not much like it, saying they looked more natural outside, although she made an exception for roses, as in their case picking amounted to pruning'.[58] There were never any cut flowers indoors at the Cearne, where Angelica, who had been brought up in the colour and aesthetic freedom of Charleston, found the 'clutter and disregard for visual harmony' painful, and the 'lack of light and colour'[59] oppressive.

For the most part Constance worked in the garden alone, accompanied only by her cat, Topsy. Harriet, her cat at the time of the adventure with the polecat, had a distressing habit of hiding live – or worse still, dead – kittens in obscure corners of the house. So Topsy was spayed and not allowed further indoors than Chopper's stable, the shed under the sitting-room floor, and lived mainly on mice and rabbits with only occasional household scraps and saucers of milk. Yet in a strange way she was devoted to Constance, as David remarked:

Whenever my mother went out into the garden Topsy would appear and settle down a few yards away to watch her intently, often for hours at a time. Constance would sometimes address a remark to her, such as: 'You are looking very well today, Topsy,' or 'You always choose a sunny corner, out of the wind'. But she never stroked her, nor did being stroked enter into the philosophy of the female eunuch.[60]

Meanwhile Topsy watched Constance as if she were a mousehole:

It was as though the cat were expecting something wildly exciting to happen at any moment, for one cannot believe that a cat should have been interested in the weeding of a rockery, or the pricking out of gentians or rock-roses. She was expecting something – but what did she expect so eagerly, without ever showing a sign of disappointment?

Topsy cared for nobody else. Nellie, who tried to pamper her and would have invited her into the house, she positively scorned.[61]

Constance rarely emerged from her garden. She had long since withdrawn from any sort of public life, unlike her neighbour and contemporary, Marjorie Pease, whom she much liked and respected, and who continued to be active in local affairs. One of Mrs Pease's protégés at this time was a German boy, a refugee from Hitler. When Constance found that he had begun learning Russian before he left Germany, she encouraged him to go on. He became fond of the bird-like little old lady in the woods, whom he saw as a benign governess, and used to call at the Cearne to see her, rarely leaving without a present of fruit or vegetables for the Peases.[62]

Marjorie Pease did not let many days go by without having a tea-party for some good cause. She had not been so disillusioned about the Soviet Union as Constance, and when Russia became our ally she helped raise money for the Russian Red Cross. Like Constance, she had been much attracted by Stepniak and remained on good terms with his widow. Stepniak, having died before the revolution, had had no opportunity to fall foul of the Bolsheviks and was still regarded as a hero in Russia. So Mrs Pease had no difficulty in persuading the Russian Ambassador to support her plan to put a carved wooden plaque in Stepniak's honour on the north wall of the cottage in Pasten's Road where he had lived in 1895. On Saturday 29 April 1944 'the memorial ceremony went off well . . . about 50 people – the cottage looked gay with bunting and 3 Soviet flags. . . . M. Zonoff from [the] Russian Embassy made quite a good speech.'[63] Neither Fanny nor Constance felt up to attending, but Constance wrote a tribute to Stepniak for the occasion (some of which has been quoted on page 81).

On that same weekend Frances Partridge came over to Scearn Bank with her husband and son, and described the inhabitants of Dostoevsky Corner and Constance herself: 'a colony of intensely lively old ladies. . .. They spend their time gardening away besottedly, tottering round to see each other, peering out of beady inquisitive eyes at any stranger, keeping a lot of cats.'[64] David took his visitors to see where a stick of incendiary bombs had fallen nearby in the woods and failed to ignite:

there were two or three great yawning chasms lined with raw, yellow earth. Nature, in the form of moschatels, anemones and primroses, came right to the edge of the ugly gashes man's ingenuity had made and filled with tortured masses of twisted metal, crumpled like balls of paper in a giant's hand, and tubular pieces of aluminium. Great clods of clay had been hurled far and wide among the spring flowers and trees.[65]

The Cearne was soon in the front line again. Scearn Bank had considerable areas of flat roof, designed originally to catch rain water. The nights were hot that June, and David and Angelica took their bed up on to the roof. There they had a grandstand view of the flying bombs. David used to write to me once a week, for I was then serving in West Africa – I think Constance was rather disappointed that I did not bring back an African bride, for she approved of miscegenation – and within a week he sent me a detailed description of them.

During these new raids Constance slept as soundly as she could, and when disturbed by a doodle-bug exploding she rejoiced that at least it had not reached London. David was anxious about her continuing to work in the garden when shrapnel was flying.

'I'm all right,' she insisted. 'I've got on my helmet. I wish you would wear one.'[66] She was more worried about them being at risk from flying glass from the windows next door.

I returned from Africa in August 1944 to find my father at the London flat, where he was lying in bed incapacitated from the waist down. He had been on holiday at Duke Mary's with Angelica and Amaryllis, when he had suffered a serious slipped disc. For Constance it must all have been horribly reminiscent of her own father's plight. But by the time I arrived he had just been told that he would not have to spend the rest of his life in a wheelchair after all – he could be operated on. It was a difficult operation, and the surgeon, already seriously overworked, collapsed with nervous exhaustion immediately afterwards. It took a month or two for David to recover the strength in his legs, and it was a great relief for his mother when he could take the bus from Oxted and walk through the woods to the Cearne.

The end of the war in Europe was celebrated on 8 May 1945. All Constance's immediate family had survived, and a week later it was increased, when Angelica's second child, Henrietta, was born. But Constance saw little of her, for David returned to Hilton in July, deftly persuading his tenant there to swap Hilton Hall for Scearn Bank.

Constance was by now very weak and frail. She lived only on the ground floor, with her bed tucked into the fireplace recess in the study, with the result – much to David's concern – that she had to do without a fire. She now considered it a triumph if she could get upstairs to the bathroom. David was horrified to find her in the small hours of one icy morning having a cold bath in the scullery, using no doubt the same old hip-bath which for many years had borne Galsworthy's footprint where he had stepped into it before the paint was dry.

David, Nellie and Natalie were all worried about her living alone. Only her doctor sympathised with her need for peace and solitude. 'I'm very thankful,' she told Natalie curtly, 'that I have a doctor who understands better what I need than many of my kind friends who prescribe what they would want in my circumstances.'[67]

She depended more and more on the wireless. She thought the BBC had done 'such splendid work in awakening the musical taste of the people'[68] and that it Ought to do the same for the English language, the richest and most beautiful in the world, by awakening the people to the beauty of the language and avoiding the debased jargon that is spreading everywhere'.[69] She welcomed the advent of the Third Programme, and listening to it was one of her 'chief pleasures',[70] so much so that she complained to the BBC that she was 'cruelly disappointed'[71] because a 'tedious Magellan story' was repeated in place of the published programme that she had hoped to hear. Six weeks later, on 20 November 1946, George Barnes, Director of the Third Programme, wrote to David to ask if Constance was well enough to take part in a proposed series of programmes about translation.[72]

By then she was seriously ill, suffering frightening attacks of breathlessness, especially at night, and David, Nellie and Emily took it in turns to come to the Cearne to look after her. He replied to Barnes:

She is now really a cripple, moves about on crutches and her heart is extremely dicky. Her mind is as active as ever though old age has tended to make her simplify the difficulties of the world and she is inclined to drastic remedies.

She will be much interested in the suggested programme on Translation. I will talk to her and see if I can draw her out.[73]

It was easy to do so. She was delighted to discuss the qualities of the writers she had worked on and the problems of translating them. He made rapid notes of what she said, which he put together into the only general statement about her work that she ever made. Much of it has been quoted here in earlier chapters.

She did not live to hear it broadcast, for she was now plainly dying. She was quite ready to die, for she had no fear of death, but her old adversary, her body, though primed with drugs to ease the pain, would not let her go. She died at last at three o'clock in the morning of 17 December, two days before her eighty-fifth birthday, having long outlived all her healthier brothers and sisters.

The doctor who came to sign the death certificate told David that, at rest in death, she had the body of a young girl.

Ten years earlier E. S. Bates had provided her epitaph: 'It would be hard indeed', he wrote, 'to find any record of a full life yielding fuller value.'[74]

Translations by Constance Garnett

Ivan Gontcharoff: A Common Story, Heinemann, 1894.

Leo Tolstoy: *The Kingdom of God is Within You*, 2 vols, Heinemann, 1894.

Turgenev: *The Novels*, Heinemann: i, *Rudin*, 1894; ii, *A House of Gentlefolk*, 1894; iii, *On the Eve*, 1895; iv, *Fathers and Children*, 1895; v, *Smoke*, 1895; vi, vii, *Virgin Soil*, 1896; viii, ix, *A Sportsman's Sketches*,1895 [sic]; x, *Dream Tales and Prose Poems*, 1897; xi, *The Torrents of Spring*, 1897; xii, *A Lear of the Steppes and Other Stories*, 1898; xiii, *The Diary of a Superfluous Man and Other Stories*, 1899; xiv, *A Desperate Character and Other Stories*, 1899; xv, *The Jew and Other Stories*, 1899 [1900]; xvi, *The Two Friends and Other Stories*, 1922; xvii, *Knock, Knock, Knock and Other Stories*, 1922.

Ostrovsky: *The Storm*, Duckworth, 1899.

Leo Tolstoy: *The Novels*, Heinemann: i, ii, *Anna Karenin*, 1901; iii, *The Death of Ivan Ilyitch and Other Stories*, 1902; iv, v, vi, *War and Peace*, 1904.

Constantine Feldmann: *The Revolt of the 'Potemkin'*, Heinemann, 1908.

Fyodor Dostoevsky: *The Novels*, Heinemann: i, *The Brothers Karamazov*, 1912; ii, *The Idiot*, 1913; iii, *The Possessed*, 1913; iv, *Crime and Punishment*, 1914; v, *The House of the Dead*, 1915; vi, *The Insulted and Injured*, 1915; vii, *A Raw Youth*, 1916; viii, *The Eternal Husband and Other Stories*, 1917; ix, *The Gambler and Other Stories*, 1917; x, *White Nights and Other Stories*, 1918; xi, *An Honest Thief and Other Stories*, 1919; xii, *The Friend of the Family and Other Stories*, 1920.

Anton Tchehov: *The Tales*, Chatto and Windus: i, *The Darling and Other Stories*, 1916; ii, *The Duel and Other Stories*, 1916; iii, *The Lady with the Dog and Other Stories*, 1917; iv, *The Party and Other Stories*, 1917; v, *The Wife and Other Stories*, 1918; vi, *The Witch and Other Stories*, 1918; vii, *The Bishop and Other Stories*, 1919; viii, *The Chorus Girl and Other Stories*, 1920; ix, *The Schoolmistress and Other Stories*, 1920; x, *The Horse Stealers and Other Stories*, 1921; xi, *The Schoolmaster and Other Stories*, 1921; xii, *The Cook's Wedding and Other Stories*, 1922; xiii, *Love and Other Stories*, 1922.

Anton Tchehov: *Letters . . . to his Family and Friends*, Chatto and Windus, 1920.

L. N. Tolstoy: *Christianity and Patriotism*, Cape, 1922.

Anton Tchehov: *The Plays*, Chatto and Windus: i, *The Cherry Orchard and Other Plays*, 1923; ii, *Three Sisters and Other Plays*, 1923.

Nikolay Gogol: *The Work*, Chatto and Windus: i, ii, *Dead Souls*, 1922; iii, *The Overcoat and Other Stories*, 1923; iv, *Evenings on a Farm Near Dikanka*, 1926; v, *Mirgorod . . .*, 1928; vi, *The Government Inspector and Other Plays*, 1926 [*sic*].

Alexander Herzen: *My Past and Thoughts*, Chatto and Windus: i, ii, iii, 1924; iv, 1925; v, 1926; vi, 1927.

Anton Tchehov: *The Letters of Anton Pavlovitch Tchehov to Olga Leonardovna Knipper*, Chatto and Windus, 1926.

Ivan Turgenev: *Three Plays*, Cassell, 1934.

Bibliography

Albert, Prince Consort: *Letters, 1831–1861,* ed Kurt Jagow, trs E. T. S. Dugdale (1938)

Archer, William: *The Old Drama and the New* (1923)

Bates, E. S.: *Modern Translation* (1936)

Bates, H. E.: *Edward Garnett* (1950)

Bell, Susan George: 'The Green Lawns of Newnham', *University Publishing,* spring 1981, 15, 24

Beer, Thomas: *Stephen Crane: A Study in American Letters* (1960)

Bennett, Arnold: *Journals,* ed Newman Flower (1932)

——: *Letters,* ed James Hepburn, 2 vols (1968)

Bergman, Jay: *Vera Zasulich, A Biography* (Stanford, 1983)

Besant, Walter: *All Sorts and Conditions of Men,* 3 vols (1882)

Booth, Charles (ed): *Labour and Life of the People: ii. London continued* (1891) [vol. i was entitled *Life and Labour of the People*]

Brading, Peter M.: *A Brief History of the People's Palace Library,* MA Study, University of Sheffield

Bunin, Ivan: *Memories and Portraits,* trs Vera Traill and Robin Chancellor (1959)

Clark, Ronald W.: *Lenin: The Man Behind the Mask* (1988)

Clyman, Toby W. ed: *A Chekhov Companion* (Westport, Connecticut, 1985)

Comtet, Maurice: *Vladimir Galaktionovič Korolenko (1853–1921): L'Homme et l'Oeuvre* (Lille & Paris, 2 vols, 1975)

Conrad, Joseph: *Letters from Conrad, 1895 to 1924,* ed Edward Garnett (1928)

——: *Collected Letters,* ed Frederick R. Karl and Laurence Davies (1983–)

Conway, Katharine St John: 'Life at Newnham', *Young Woman,* December 1894, 99–103

Crane, Stephen: *Letters,* ed R. W. Stallman and Lillian Gilkes (1960)

Crankshaw, Edward: *The Shadow of the Winter Palace: The Drift to Revolution: 1812–1917* (1976)

——: 'The Work of Constance Garnett', *Listener,* 30 January 1947, 195–6

Cronwright-Schreiner, S. C.: *The Land of Free Speech: Record of a Campaign on Behalf of Peace in England and Scotland in 1900* (1906)

Dudden, Arthur P., and von Laue, Theodore H.: 'The RSDLP and Joseph Fels: A Study in Intercultural Contact', *American Historical Review*, lxi, October 1955–July 1956, 21–47

E. T. [Jessie (Wood) Chambers]: *D. H. Lawrence: A Personal Record* (1935)

Farjeon, Annabel: *Morning Has Broken: A Biography of Eleanor Farjeon* (1986)

Galsworthy, John: *Letters from John Galsworthy 1900–1932*, ed Edward Garnett (1934)

Garnett, Angelica: *Deceived With Kindness* (1984)

Garnett, Anne: *Caught from Time, A Country Diary of the 1920s* (Padstow, 1986)

Garnett, Constance: (as Constance E. [*sic*] Black) 'New Career for Women: Librarians', *Queen*, 23 February 1889, 235

——: 'The Art of Translation', *Listener*, 30 January 1947, 195

Garnett, David: 'A Whole Hive of Genius' [review of *The Letters* of *D. H. Lawrence*], *Saturday Review of Literature*, New York, ix, No 11, 1 October 1932, 141–2

——: *Beany-Eye* (1935)

——: *The Golden Echo* (1953)

——: *The Flowers of the Forest* (1955)

——: *Great Friends: Portraits of Seventeen Writers* (1979)

Garnett, Edward: *The Paradox Club* (1888)

——: 'Behind the Isonzo: In the English Hospital', *Manchester Guardian*, 14 January 1916

——: *Turgenev* (1917)

——: *Friday Nights* (1922)

Garnett, Olive: *Tea and Anarchy! The Bloomsbury Diary 1890 – 1893*, ed Barry C. Johnson (1989)

Garrett, Sebastian: *A. I. Ertel: Letters to His Daughter*, thesis, University of Birmingham, 1982

Gerhardi, William: *Chehov: A Critical Study* (1923)

Gielgud, John: *Early Stages*, new and revised ed (1953)

Gifford, Henry: On Translating Tolstoy' in *New Essays on Tolstoy*, ed Malcolm Jones (Cambridge, 1978)

Gindin, James: *John Galsworthy 's Life and Art: An Alien's Fortress* (1987)

Glage, Liselotte: *Clementina Black, a Study in Social History and Literature* [in English] (Heidelberg, 1981)

Glendinning, Victoria: *A Suppressed Cry: Life and Death of a Quaker Daughter* [Wilhelmina Seebohm] (1969)

Haley, Sir William ['Oliver Edwards']: 'Constance Garnett', *Times*, 6 June 1957

Hambourg: Mark: *From Piano to Forte: A Thousand and One Notes* (1931)

Harcave, Sidney: *First Blood: The Russian Revolution of 1905* (1965)

Harrison, Jane Ellen: *Russia and the Russian Verb* (Cambridge, 1915)

Heilbrun, Carolyn G.: *The Garnett Family* (1961)

Hollingsworth, Barry: 'The Society of Friends of Russian Freedom: English

Liberals and Russian Socialists, 1890–1917', *Oxford Slavonic Papers*, ns, iii, 1970

Holt, Catherine Durning: *Letters from Newnham College, 1889–1892* (privately printed, nd)

James, Henry: *Letters*, ed Leon Edel, 4 vols (1974–84)

Jefferson, George: *Edward Garnett: A Life in Literature* (1982)

——: 'The Pseudonym Library', *Private Library*, 1:1, spring 1988, 13–26

Kapp, Yvonne: *Eleanor Marx* (1972)

Karlinsky, Simon: *The Sexual Labyrinth of Nikolai Gogol* (1976)

Kaye, Peter Paul: *A Monster in the House of Fiction: Dostoevsky and Modern English Novelists*, dissertation, Stanford University (1989)

Khrabrovitsky, A.: 'V. G. Korolenko, Konstantsiia Garnet, i S. M. Stepnyiak-Kravchinskii', *Russkay a Literatura*, No. 4 (1962) 167–71

Kochan, Lionel: *Russia in Revolution, 1890–1918* (1966)

Komisarjevsky, Theodore: *Myself and the Theatre* (1929)

Korolenko, V. G.: *The History of my Contemporary* translated and abridged by Neil Parsons (London, 1972)

——: 'V Golodnyi God', *Sobranie Sochinenii*, ix (Moscow, 1955), 100–336

Lawrence, D. H.: *Letters*, ed Aldous Huxley (1932)

——: *Letters*, ed James T. Boulton, i, *1901–13* (Cambridge, 1979); ii, *1913–16* (Cambridge, 1981); iii, *1916-21* (Cambridge, 1984)

Lineff, Eugenie: *The Peasant Songs of Great Russia as They are in the Folk's Harmonization* (Imperial Academy of Science, St Petersburg, 1905)

Mackenzie, Donald A.: 'Arthur Black: a forgotten pioneer of mathematical statistics' (Studies in the History of Probability and Statistics. XXXVI), *Biometrika* (1977), lxiv/3, 613–16

MacKenzie, Norman and Jeanne: *The First Fabians* (1977)

McCrimmon, Barbara: *Richard Garnett, the Scholar as Librarian* (Chicago, 1989)

Maevskaya, T. P.: *Slovo i Podvig: Zhizn' i Tvorchestvo S. M. Stepniaka-Kravchinskogo* [Word and Deed: The Life and Works of S. M. Stepniak-Kravchinskii] (Kiev, 1968)

Mahomed, Sake Deen: *Shampooing; or, Benefits resulting from the use of the Indian Medicated Vapour Bath . . .* (Brighton, 1826)

Mansfield, Katherine: *The Collected Letters*, ed Vincent O'Sullivan and Margaret Scott, 2 vols (1984, 1987)

Marshall, Mary Paley: *What I Remember* (Cambridge, 1947)

Marrot, H. V.: *The Life and Letters of John Galsworthy* (1935)

Melville, Lewis: *Brighton, its History, its Follies and its Fashions* (1909)

Miles, Patrick: *Chekhov on the British Stage, 1909–1987* (Cambridge, 1987)

Mills, M. G.: *Brighton and Hove High School, 1876–1972* (Brighton, 1953)

Mirsky, D. S.: *A History of Russian Literature* (1927)

Moser, Charles A.: 'The Achievement of Constance Garnett', *American Scholar* lvii, No 3, Summer 1988, 431–8

Moss, G. P., and Saville, M. V.: *From Palace to College: An Illustrated Account of Queen Mary College* (1985)

Motyleva, T.: *'Voina i Mir' za Rubezhom: Perevody, Kritika, Vliianie* [War and Peace Abroad: Translations, Criticisms, Influence] (Moscow, 1978)

Muchnic, Helen: *Dostoevsky's English Reputation* (Smith College Studies in Modern Languages, xx, April–July 1939, Nos 3, 4)

Nehls, Edward, ed: *D. H. Lawrence: A Composite Biography*, 3 vols (1957)

Newnham College Register: 1871–1950 (Cambridge, 2 vols, 1964)

Norman-Butler, Belinda: *Victorian Aspirations: The Life and Labour of Charles and Mary Booth* (1972)

Olivier, Sydney: *Letters and Selected Writings*, edited with a memoir by Margaret Olivier, with some impressions by Bernard Shaw (1948)

Partridge, Frances: *A Pacifists War* (1978)

—: *Memories* (1981)

—: *Hanging On* (1990)

Peel, Robin: *'Literary' Oxted and Limpsfield, 1895–1937: The Edward Garnett Years* (privately printed, 1984)

Phelps, Gilbert: *The Russian Novel in English Fiction* (1956)

Phillips, Ann (ed): *A Newnham Anthology* (Cambridge, 1979)

Raverat, Gwen: *Period Piece* (1952)

Robbins, Richard, jr: *Famine in Russia, 1891–1892* (1975)

Rodgers, W. R.: 'W. B. Yeats: A Dublin Portrait' in A. Norman Jeffares and K. G. W. Cross (eds): *In Excited Reverie: A Centenary Tribute to William Butler Yeats 1865–1939* (1965)

Rubenstein, Roberta: 'Genius of Translation' [Constance Garnett], *Colorado Quarterly*, xxii, No 3, winter 1974, 359–68

St John, John: *William Heinemann: A Century of Publishing* (1990)

Senese, Donald: *S. M. Stepniak-Kravchinskii: The London Years* (Newtonville, Mass. 1987)

Shaw, Bernard: 'A Word About Stepniak', *To-Morrow*, i, January–June 1896, 99–107

—: *Collected Letters* [i] *1874–1897*, ed Dan H. Laurence (1965); [iii] *1911–1925* (1985)

—: *The Diaries*, ed Stanley Weintraub (University Park & London, 2 vols, 1986)

Stallman, R. W.: *Stephen Crane: A Biography* (New York, 1968)

Stephenson, Graham: *History of Russia: 1812–1945* (1969)

Stepniak: *Underground Russia: Revolutionary Profiles and Sketches from Life* (1883)

Swinnerton, Frank: *The Georgian Literary Scene: A Panorama* (1935)

—: *Background With Chorus* (1956)

Taratuta, Evgeniya: *S. M. Stepniak-Kravchinskii – Revoliutsoner i Pisatel* [S. M. Stepniak-Kravchinskii – Revolutionary and Writer] (Moscow, 1973)

Tarn, John Nelson: *Five Per Cent Philanthropy* (1973)

Tomalin, Claire: *Katherine Mansfield: A Secret Life* (1987)

Tove, A. [Augusta Tovey]: 'Konstantsiia Garnet – Perevodchik i Propagandist Russkoi Literatury' [Constance Garnett – Translator and Propagandist of Russian Literature], *Russkaia Literatura*, No 4, 1958, 193–9

—: 'Perevody Chekhova v Anglii i SShA' [Translations of Chekhov in England and the USA], *Nauchnye Doklady Vysshei Shkoly: Filologicheskie Nauki* No 1, 1963, 144–51

Tracy, Robert: *The Flight of the Seagull: Chekhov on the English Stage*, thesis, Harvard University (1959)

Turgenev, Ivan: *Turgenev Letters*, ed David Lowe (Ann Arbor, 1983)

Turton, Glyn: *Turgenev in the Context of English Literature, 1850–1900* thesis, University of Warwick, 1984

Visram, Rozina: *Ayahs, Lascars and Princes: Indians in Britain 1700–1947* (1986)

Waddington, Patrick: *Turgenev and England* (1980)

Waterfield, Lina: *Castle in Italy* (1961)

Webb, Beatrice: *My Apprenticeship* (1926)

—: *Diaries 1873–1892* (1982)

Whyte, Frederic: *William Heinemann* (1928)

Wilson, A. N.: *Tolstoy* (1988)

Woolf, Virginia: 'The Russian Point of View', *The Common Reader* (1925)

367

Notes and References

Works listed in the Bibliography are cited by author, or by author and short title if there are more than one by the author. The following abbreviations are used:

Correspondents, etc.
AVG: Angelica Garnett
CB: Clara Black
CG: Constance Garnett (Constance Black)
DB: David Black
DG: David Garnett
EG: Edward Garnett
EMH: Ellen Maurice (Nellie) Heath
FS: Fanny Stepniak
LP: Lucy Patten
MAM: Margaret A. Marshall
ND: Natalie Duddington
ONG: Olivia Narney Garnett
ORG: Olivia Rayne (Olive) Garnett
RAG: Rachel Alice Garnet
RDG: Richard Garnett (the author)
Rev. RG: Rev. Richard Garnett
RG: Richard Garnett, CB, LLD
SS: Sergei Stepniak

Locations
BBC: BBC Written Archives, Reading
Berg: Henry W. and Albert A. Berg Collection, The New York Public Library, Astor, Lenox and Tilden Foundations
Birmingham: Birmingham University Library
BL: British Library
Bodleian: Bodleian Library, Oxford
Brunt: Martin and Katharine Brunt
Clark: William Andrews Clark Memorial Library, University of California
Eton: Eton School Library
Farrington: Veronica Farrington
Garrett: Anna Garrett
GBL: Gosudarstvennaia Biblioteka imeni Lenina (Lenin State Library), Moscow
Gielgud: Sir John Gielgud

Goldsmiths': Goldsmiths' Library, University of London
Gregory: Marion Gregory
Guildhall: Guildhall, City of London
Hilton: Estate of the late David Garnett at Hilton Hall
HRHRC: Harry Ransom Humanities Research Center, the University of Texas at Austin
Illinois: University Library, University of Illinois at Urbana-Champaign
King's: King's College, Cambridge
MacEwen: Ann MacEwen
Malinskaya: Nelly Malinskaya
Newnham: Newnham College, Cambridge
Nuffield: Nuffield College, Oxford
OPGL: Octopus Publishing Group Library
de la Potterie: Christine de la Potterie
PRO: Public Record Office
RDG: the author
Reading: Reading University Library
Rubenstein: Professor Roberta Rubenstein
Tolstoy: Muzei L. N. Tolstogo (L. N. Tolstoy Museum), Moscow
TsGALI: Tsentral'nyi Gosudarstvennyi Arkhiv Literatury i Iskusstva (Central State Archive of Literature and Art), Moscow
Turnbull: Alexander Turnbull Library, Wellington, New Zealand
UCL: University College, London
White: Caroline White

Other
nd: no date
os: Old Style date
pc: postcard
pm: postmark

Chapter 1: Antecedents

1 Baptised Patrick on 13 July 1783 at Pan-bride, but always known to the family as Peter, because his wife disliked the name Patrick. This account of his career relies heavily on Jane Gregory's researches (undertaken originally for DG's novel *Up She Rises*), the *Journal de St.-Pétersburg, 1827–31*, and memoirs by DB (Gregory) and Ernest Black (Hilton). His burial is recorded in Cronstadt Church Register (Bishop's transcript) Guildhall MS 11, 196/1.

2 DB, Memoir, [12] (Gregory)

3 Ibid

4 For details of his career see *The Engineer*, 13 February 1863

5 DB, Canadian experiences, in EG's hand (Gregory)

6 CG, Memoir, [6] (Hilton)

7 DB, Memoir, [26] (Gregory)

8 CG, Memoir, [6] (Hilton)

9 Prince Albert to Queen Victoria, 10 January 1840, *Letters*, 50, original in Royal Archives, Windsor, Z296/46. Wagstaff's mezzotint of Patten's portrait is reproduced as the frontispiece to *Letters*.

10 Royal Archives, Windsor, text provided by Sir Robin Mackworth-Young

11 *Letters*, 57

12 Schenck to Patten, 14 February 1840 (Gregory)

13 Ibid

14 Schenck to Patten, 21 June 1840 (Gregory)

15 Thackeray, 'A Pictorial Rhapsody: Concluded', *Works* (1885), xxv, 182

16 Arthur Black, 'Biographical Anecdotes' of George Patten (Gregory)

17 CB's annotated copy of *Catalogue of . . . the Remaining Pictures and Sketches of the Late George Patten*, Christie Manson & Woods, 18 January 1867 (Gregory)

18 CG, Memoir, [13] (Hilton)

19 CG to EG, 'Sunday' [spring 1906] (Eton)

20 George Patten to LP, 'Sund Aft' [1836] (Gregory)

21 CB, Diary, 29 August 1837 (Hilton)

22 CG to DG, nd, inserted in John A. Heraud, *The Life and Times of Girolamo Savonarola* (1843) (Jane Gregory)

23 The vicissitudes of their protracted courtship are recorded in two boxes of CB's letters to DB (Hilton).

24 CB to Miss Hine, 13 September [1848] (Hilton)

Chapter 2: Poor Connie

1 CG, Memoir, [36] (Hilton)

2 CB to LP, 23 October 1870 (Gregory)

3 CB to LP, 27 June 1869 (Gregory)

4 This has led to her year of birth being sometimes given – even by DG – as 1862.

5 CG, Memoir, [33] (Hilton)

6 DG, *Golden Echo*, 4, is mistaken in thinking it was No 57.

7 CG, Memoir, [33] (Hilton)

8 DB, Memoir, [10] (Gregory)

9 Jane Viney to DB, 1 January [? 1851] (Gregory)

10 Elizabeth Viney to DB, 30 March [1850s] (Gregory)

11 DB to 'young David', 23 October 1864, draft (Gregory)

12 DB to 'young David', 23 October 1864, nd, 1 May 1864, drafts (Gregory)

13 CB to LP, 16 February 1868 (Gregory)

14 CB to LP, 14 February 1869 (Gregory)

15 CB to LP, 21 February 1869 (Gregory)

16 CB to LP, 31 July 1870 (Gregory)

17 CG, Memoir, [14] (Hilton)

18 Ernest Black, 'Letters received' (Gregory)

19 CG, Memoir, [15] (Hilton)

20 Ibid, 15–16

21 CB to LP, 11 October 1868 (Gregory)

22 CG, Memoir, [16] (Hilton)

23 Ibid, 17

24 Quoted in *The Girl' Public Day School Trust, 1872–1972*, a Centenary Review, 9

25 Clementina Black, 'The Mind of One Child', 2 (Hilton)

26 Ibid

27 Ibid, 3

28 Ibid, 6

29 CG, Memoir, [16] (Hilton)

30 CB to LP, 19 June 1870 (Gregory)

31 Clementina Black, 'The Mind of One Child', 10 (Hilton)

32 CG to Arthur Black, 2 February 1873 (Eton)

33 CB to LP, 9 January 1870 (Gregory)
34 CB to LP, 13 November 1870 (Gregory)
35 CG, Memoir, [20] (Hilton)
36 Ibid
37 CB to DB, 17 August 1846 (Hilton)
38 CB to DB, 17 August 1846 (Hilton)
39 CG, Memoir, [20] (Hilton)
40 Ibid
41 Ibid
42 Ibid
43 Ibid
44 Ibid, [21]
45 CB to LP, 5 July 1870 (Gregory)
46 CG, Memoir, [37] (Hilton)
47 CB to LP, 5 September 1869 (Gregory)
48 CB to LP, 26 September 1869 (Gregory)
49 CB to LP, 4 July 1869 (Gregory)
50 CB to LP, 27 December 1869 (Gregory)

51 CG, Memoir, [10] (Hilton)
52 CB to LP, 10 June 1970 (Gregory)
53 CG, Memoir, [26] (Hilton)
54 Ibid
55 Ibid, [27]
56 CB to LP, 28 June 1868 (Gregory)
57 CG, Memoir, [28] (Hilton)
58 CB to LP, 5 September 1869 (Gregory)
59 CB to LP, 31 October 1869 (Gregory)
60 CB to LP, 2 January 1870 (Gregory)
61 Ibid
62 CB to LP, 'Account of the beginning of Mr. Black's illness' (Gregory)
63 CG, Memoir, [7] (Hilton)
64 CB, 'Dr. Radcliffe's opinion of Mr Black' (Gregory)
65 CG, Memoir, [17–19] (Hilton)
66 Ibid, [19]

Chapter 3: The Youngest Girl in the College

1 CG, Memoir, [24] (Hilton)
2 Ibid, [21–2]
3 Ibid, [34]
4 Ibid, [16–17]
5 Ibid, [29]
6 Ibid, [23]
7 Ibid, [22]
8 Ibid, [23]
9 Ibid
10 Ibid
11 Ibid, [24]
12 Ibid, [25]
13 'Concerning Two Public Institutions', *Brighton Gazette*, 10 June 1876
14 Phillips, 1
15 'North Hall Diary', January [1876] (Newnham)
16 Mills, 16
17 CG, Memoir, [41] (Hilton)
18 Ibid
19 Ibid
20 Glendinning, 67
21 Holt, 9
22 Conway
23 Holt, 11
24 Ibid, 40

25 Phillips, 12
26 CG, 'Art of Translation', MS, [7], omitted from published text (Hilton)
27 CG to DG, 1 October 1930 (Hilton)
28 Ibid
29 Phillips, 12
30 Raverat, 193
31 Partridge, *Memories*, 17
32 CG, Memoir, [42] (Hilton)
33 Marshall, 20
34 CG, Memoir, [42] (Hilton)
35 Marshall, 20
36 'Tennis Courts', inserted in Out Students' Minutes (Newnham)
37 CG, Memoir, [48] (Hilton)
38 Ibid, [43]
39 Ibid
40 Old Newnham Students' Club, Cambridge Letter, November 1882, 8
41 *Newnham College Roll*, 'Letter', January 1935; 37–9
42 Dollie Maitland to Ernest Radford, 7 June [1883] (MacEwen)
43 CG, Memoir, [43] (Hilton)
44 CG to DG, 1 October 1930 (Hilton)
45 Glendinning, 65

Chapter 4: The Nicest Set of People

1 *Newnham College Register*, i, 62–5
2 CG, Memoir, [46] (Hilton)
3 Ibid
4 Ibid, [48]
5 Ibid
6 DG, *Golden Echo*, 7–8

7 CG, Memoir, [46] (Hilton)
8 DG, *Flowers of the Forest*, 250
9 Anne Lee Michell, quoted in Glage, 38
10 Cover of Mahomed
11 Melville, 134–7; see also Visram, and for a portly likeness of Mahomed in front of

his baths, Peggy Hickman, *Silhouettes: A Living Art* (Newton Abbot, 1975), 33.

12 CG, Memoir, [38] (Hilton)
13 Ibid, [37]
14 Ibid
15 Ibid, [38]
16 Ibid, [33]
17 ORG, Diary, 26 November 1892 (White)
18 DG, *Golden Echo*, 125
19 D. H. Lawrence, *Kangaroo* (1923), 277–8
20 DG, *Golden Echo*, 125
21 Dollie Radford, Diary, 19 May 1885 (Clark)
22 Ibid, 22 January, 19 February 1884
23 Rules of the Club (MacEwen)
24 Dollie Radford, Diary, 22 February 1884 (Clark)
25 Ibid, 29 February 1884
26 N. and J. MacKenzie, 30
27 Edward R. Pease, 'Recollections for my Sons', [16] (Brunt)
28 Ibid, [7]
29 Quoted in N. and J. MacKenzie, 41–2
30 N. and J. MacKenzie, 28
31 Ibid, 42
32 Ibid, 37
33 Ibid, 38
34 *Fabian Tracts No. 1*
35 *Fabian Tracts No. 3*
36 Crankshaw, *Shadow of the Winter Palace*, 259
37 Ibid
38 CG, Memoir, [44] (Hilton)
39 Ibid
40 Ibid, [45]
41 Ibid, [45]
42 DG, 'Brief Memoir of CG', 4 (Hilton)
43 Ibid
44 Webb, *Diaries*, 26 April 1890, 329–30
45 N. and J. MacKenzie, 59
46 Ibid
47 Olivier, 9
48 Quoted in N. and J. MacKenzie, 28

49 ORG, Diary, 26 May 1895 (White)
50 Ibid, 21 June 1903
51 Ibid, 30 June 1893
52 N. and J. MacKenzie, 20
53 W. B. Yeats, *Memoirs*, ed Denis Donoghue (1972), 20
54 Dollie Radford, Diary, 30 November 1884 (Clark)
55 Grace Black to Shaw, 24 May 1887, BL Add MSS 50511 f321
56 *Letters from Conrad*, xxx
57 DG, *Golden Echo*, 9. He says this happened after Constance got to know Edward in 1886–7; but the few references in Shaw's *Diaries* (February 1885–November 1886) are before this date.
58 Grace Black to Shaw, 25 May 1887, BL Add MSS 50511 f323
59 Grace Black to Shaw, 31 March 1889, BL Add MSS 50512 f117
60 CG, Memoir, [47] (Hilton)
61 Webb, *My Apprenticeship*, 219
62 RG to W. J. Garnett, 8 December 1857, BL Add MS 37489
63 Samuel Butler, *Further Extracts from the Note-Books*, ed A. T. Bartholomew (1934), 195
64 For a full biography see McCrimmon
65 Osbert Sitwell, *The Scarlet Tree* (1946), 223 n1
66 ORG, Diary, 12 June 1892 (White)
67 Nickalls, 'The Time is Past and Gone', 51 (White)
68 Anne Garnett, 70
69 CG to DG, 23 October [1924] (Hilton)
70 CG, Memoir, [49] (Hilton)
71 CG to Ada Galsworthy, 30 March 1937 (Birmingham)
72 CG, Memoir, [49] (Hilton)
73 Ibid
74 Ibid, [50]
75 Ibid, [55]
76 Ibid
77 Ibid, [50]

Chapter 5: Romance in Whitechapel

1 EMH, MS notes (White)
2 CG, Memoir, [52] (Hilton)
3 Ibid
4 CG, Memoir, [51] (Hilton)
5 Ibid
6 Mary Cameron, 'Clementina Black: A Character Sketch', *Young Woman*, 1892, 515–16
7 EMH, MS notes (White)

8 CG to DG (as from EG), nd, see p. 247 (Eton)
9 CG, Memoir, [53] (Hilton)
10 Ibid
11 Ibid, [52]
12 Ibid, [51]
13 Ibid, [50]
14 I am almost certain that I have seen the original of this drawing, framed and hang-

ing, probably at the Cearne, but cannot find what has happened to it.

15 EG, *Paradox Club*, 83
16 ORG, Diary, 30 June 1893 (White)
17 Besant, i, 11
18 Grace Black to Shaw, 8 March 1887, BL Add MSS 50511 f293
19 *DNB*, 'Besant'
20 *More Letters of Oscar Wilde*, ed Rupert Hart-Davis (1985), 62
21 CG, Memoir, [56] (Hilton)
22 Ibid
23 Mary Booth to Charles Booth, 19 August 1887 (Goldsmiths')
24 CG, Memoir, [47] (Hilton)
25 Ibid, [48]
26 Ibid
27 Ibid, [54]
28 Ibid
29 Tarn, 87
30 *Builder*, 13 November 1886, 713. Only a thin slice of the original building remains, the rest having been supplanted by the plain utility brick of Attlee House. But a drawing in Henry Walker's *East London: Sketches of Christian Work and Wonders* (1896), 39, shows the whole façade with its fretted balconies and gothic arches.
31 CG in Booth, ii, 270
32 Ibid, 271
33 Ibid, 270–1

34 Ibid, 273
35 Ibid, 270
36 Edwin Pugh in George R. Sims (ed), *Living London* (1902), i, 365
37 J. Isaacs in Sir John Adcock (ed), *Wonderful London* [nd], iii, 801
38 EG, *Paradox Club*, 98–9
39 Crankshaw, *Shadow of the Winter Palace*, 266
40 *Encyclopedia Judaica* (1971), xix, 446
41 CG, Memoir, [54] (Hilton)
42 Ibid
43 Shaw to William Morris, 22 November 1887, *Letters*, i, 177
44 EG, *Paradox Club*, 87
45 CG to EG 'Saturday morning' [?24 December 1887] (Hilton)
46 CG, 'New Career for Women'
47 *Palace Journal*, 13 February 1889, 898
48 Tarn, 87
49 CG in Booth, ii, 271
50 Ibid
51 Ibid
52 DG, *Golden Echo*, 10
53 'The Librarian of the People's Palace', *Women's Herald*, 29 June 1893, 292
54 CG, 'New Career for Women'
55 Ibid
56 CG to RG, 17 September 1890 (Hilton)
57 *Palace Journal*, 17 July 1889, 111
58 ORG, Diary, 4 June 1892 (White)

Chapter 6: Marriage and Motherhood

1 DG, *Golden Echo*, 10
2 EG to RG, 14 September 1889 (Hilton)
3 CG to RG, 2 May 1890 (Hilton)
4 CG, Memoir, [54] (Hilton)
5 Ibid
6 ORG, Diary, 9 [10] April 1894 (White)
7 CG to RG, 23 January 1890 (Hilton)
8 Clementina Black to RG, 2 June 1890 (HRHRC)
9 ORG, Diary, 4 [5] May 1892 (White)
10 CG to ONG, 15 April 1890 (Hilton)
11 CG, pocket diary for 13 September 1890 (Hilton)
12 Nickalls, 'The Time is Past and Gone', 124, 71 (White)
13 Quoted in Grace Black to Ernest Radford, 16 September 1889 (MacEwen)
14 CG to RG, 13 September 1889 (Hilton)
15 RG, *DNB*, 'Levy, Amy'
16 Levy, *A London Plane-Tree* (1889), [7]
17 Levy, *A Minor Poet* (1884), [95]

18 CG to DG, 27 October 1927 (Hilton)
19 Ibid
20 CG to RG, 15 January 1890 (Hilton)
21 *Athenaeum*, 21 December 1889, 851
22 CG to RG, 15 January 1890 (Hilton)
23 EG to RG, 11 January 1891 (Hilton)
24 EG to RG, 19 July 1890 (Hilton)
25 CG to RG, 28 February 1890 (Hilton)
26 CG, Memoir, [31] (Hilton)
27 CG, pocket diary, 31 March 1890 (Hilton)
28 CG to RG, 21 December 1891 (Hilton)
29 ORG, Diary, 6 November 1891 (White)
30 Ibid, 19 April 1893
31 Ibid, 19 January 1893
32 Ibid, 22 February 1895
33 Ibid, 26 November 1891
34 EG to RG, 22 December 1890 (Hilton)
35 EG to RG, 14 July 1891 (Hilton)
36 ORG, Diary, 28 November 1891 (White)
37 Sean O'Faoláin quoted in Rodgers, 1
38 Ibid
39 EG to RG, 22 December 1890 (Hilton)

40 DG, *Familiar Faces*, 171–2
41 Introduction to RG, *The Twilight of the Gods* (1924), xii
42 EG to RG, 12 July 1890 (Hilton)
43 CG to EG, 'Thursday Morning 10.30' [summer 1890] (Hilton)
44 EG to RG, 10 March 1891 (Hilton)
45 Ibid
46 CG to RG, 10 March 1891 (Hilton)
47 ORG, Diary, 20 October 1892 (White)
48 CG to RG, 28 September 1891 (Hilton)
49 Ibid
50 CG, Memoir, [58] (Hilton)
51 *Speaker*, 1 March 1890, 241, unsigned but attributable from references in CG's pocket diary for 1890
52 *Saturday Review*, 18 January 1868
53 DG, *Golden Echo*, 12
54 Hambourg, 28
55 CG, Memoir, [58] (Hilton)
56 ORG, Diary, 4 November 1891 (White)
57 CG, Memoir, [58] (Hilton)
58 ORG, Diary, undated scrap ca 20 January 1893 (White)
59 EG, *Turgenev* (1917), 65
60 ORG to RG, 17 November 1891 (Hilton)
61 CG, Memoir, [58] (Hilton)
62 Ibid, [59]
63 ORG to RG, 17 November 1891 (Hilton)
64 Rev. RG, *Philological Essays* (1859), 208–9
65 Harrison, 10–11
66 CG, Memoir, [78] (Hilton)
67 CG to RG, 5 January 1892 (Hilton)
68 CG, Memoir, [74] (Hilton)
69 CG to EG, 6 February [1892] (Hilton)
70 ORG, Diary, 2 March 1892 (White)
71 Ibid, 10 March 1892 (White)
72 EG to RG, 10 March 1892 (Hilton)
73 James R. Wallace, 'The Horoscope of a Male born 9th March 1892 . . .at Brighton', 25 (Hilton)
74 Ibid, 32
75 Ibid, 33
76 CG to EG, 'Wednesday 6 o'clock' [1892] (Hilton)
77 DG, *Golden Echo*, 25–6
78 Information from Anne Lee Michell
79 ND to Tovey, 14 September 1963 (in Russian) (Malinskaya)
80 CG to RG, 18 March 1892 (Hilton)
81 In a letter to me
82 CG to EG, 'Thursday 6 o'clock' [1892] (Hilton)
83 CG, Memoir, [74] (Hilton)
84 CG to EG, 'Thursday morning' [March 1892] (Hilton)
85 Ibid
86 CG, Memoir, [32] (Hilton)
87 Ibid, [74]
88 Ibid, [75]
89 Ibid
90 Ibid
91 Ibid
92 DG, *Golden Echo*, 21
93 CG to EG, '11 o'clock Thursday' [1892] (Hilton)

Chapter 7: The Gentle Nihilist

1 CG, Memoir, [78] (Hilton)
2 CG to EG, 11 August [1892] (Hilton)
3 CG, typescript tribute to Stepniak [1944] (Hilton)
4 CG, Memoir, [79] (Hilton)
5 Ibid, [80]
6 Ibid
7 Senese, 37
8 ORG, Diary, 9 November 1892 (White)
9 Ibid, 28 December 1893 (White)
10 Shaw, 'A Word About Stepniak', 103–4
11 DG, *Golden Echo*, 14
12 ORG, Diary, 11 March 1893 (White)
13 Ibid, 26 November 1892
14 Ibid, 2 July 1893
15 Ibid, 14 March 1894
16 Shaw, 'A Word About Stepniak', 104
17 ORG, Diary, 15 December 1891 (White)
18 Taratuta, 11; most sources say 1852.
19 Bergman, 35–58
20 Ibid, 54
21 Stepniak, 40–1
22 Ibid, 41
23 Taratuta, 163
24 Report of police chief Selivertsov quoted from Russian archives by Taratuta, 171; DG, *Golden Echo*, 12–13, gives a rather different version.
25 Quoted in Hollingsworth, 48
26 *New York Times*, 31 December 1890, 8; the report in the *New York Tribune*, 31 December 1890, 4 does not include this exchange.
27 DG, *Golden Echo*, 11
28 DG, 'Brief Memoir of CG', [5] (Hilton)
29 EMH, MS Notes (White)
30 DG, 'Burst Balloons', [8] (Hilton)

31 EMH, MS Notes (White)
32 ORG, Diary, 26 November 1892 (White)
33 Ibid. Studies by Taratuta and Maevskaya make it clear that this story was in fact begun in 1889, but Stepniak recast it later.
34 It is quoted in Taratuta, 441–2 (in Russian)
35 ORG, Diary,?23 January 1893 (White)
36 Ibid, 20 October 1892
37 Ibid, 2 March 1893
38 DG, *Golden Echo*, 46, is mistaken in thinking she was the wife of the revolutionary, Peter Lavrov.
39 DG, MS Memoir of CG, [14–16] (Hilton)
40 Ibid, [17]
41 ORG, Diary, 20 August 1899 (White)
42 DG, MS Memoir of CG, [17] (Hilton)
43 ORG, Diary, 20 December 1891 (White)
44 Ibid, 25 February 1895
45 Ibid, 10 January 1895
46 Jefferson, EG, 177
47 DG, *Golden Echo*, 49–50
48 CG to RG, 6 October 1892 (Hilton)
49 EMH to EG, undated scrap (Hilton)
50 ORG, Diary, 18–22 January 1893 (White)
51 CG to RG, 18 December 1891 (Hilton)
52 CG, Memoir, [62] (Hilton)
53 ORG, Diary, 18–22 January 1893 (White)
54 DG to Donald A. MacKenzie, 12 March 1975 (Hilton)
55 *Brighton Herald*, 21 January 1893
56 EG to RG, 19 January 1893 (Hilton)
57 *Brighton Examiner*, 24 January 1893
58 Ibid
59 *Brighton Herald*, 21 January 1893
60 Ibid

61 EG to RG, 20 January 1893 (Hilton)
62 *Brighton Herald*, 21 January 1893
63 *Brighton Examiner*, 24 January 1893
64 Ibid
65 Ibid
66 Ibid
67 *Brighton Herald*, 21 January 1893
68 *Brighton Examiner*, 24 January 1893
69 Ibid
70 EG to RG, 20 January 1893 (Hilton)
71 *Brighton Examiner*, 24 January 1893
72 ORG, Diary, loose scrap preceding 24 January 1893 (White)
73 Ibid, 15 January 1893
74 (Gregory)
75 Karl Pearson to Francis Galton, 4 June 1894 (Galton Papers, UCL)
76 CG to Karl Pearson, 21 April 1897 (Pearson Papers, UCL)
77 Donald A. MacKenzie, *Biometrika*, (1977) lxiv 3 613–16
78 CG to RG, 31 August 1901 (Hilton)
79 Ibid
80 ORG, Diary, loose scrap preceding 24 January 1893 (White)
81 Waddington, 188
82 Turgenev, *Letters*, ii, 73
83 Barbara McCrimmon, 'W. R. S. Ralston (1828–78): Scholarship and Scandal at the British Museum', *British Library Journal*, 14 (Autumn 1988), 178–98
84 Mirsky, 218
85 EG, introduction to Turgenev, *A Lear of the Steppes* (1898), xiv
86 CG to ORG, 10 January 1894 (White)
87 CG to EG, [?1893] (Hilton)

Chapter 8: 'You must go to Russia'

1 ORG, Diary, 20 October 1892 (White)
2 Ibid, 18 April 1893
3 Ibid
4 Ibid, 20 April 1893
5 Ibid, 18–22 January 1893
6 Ibid, 17 March 1893
7 Ibid, 6 April 1893
8 Ibid, 12 May 1893
9 EG to RG, 20 January 1893 (Hilton)
10 ORG, Diary, 16 May 1893 (White)
11 DG, *Golden Echo*, 10
12 Ernest Radford to Dollie Radford, 30 May 1893 (MacEwen)
13 CG to ORG, 4 June 1893 (White)
14 ORG, Diary, 12 June 1893 (White)
15 Ibid, 12 May 1893

16 Ibid, 15 June 1893
17 Ibid, 21 July 1893
18 Ibid, 24 February 1893
19 N. and J. MacKenzie, 149
20 Ibid, 92
21 ORG, Diary, 12 June 1893 (White)
22 DG, MS Memoir of CG, [12] (Hilton)
23 ORG, Diary, 14 November 1894 (White)
24 Ibid, 11 November 1893 (White)
25 CG to EG, 6 July [1893] (Hilton)
26 ORG, Diary, 29 July 1893 (White)
27 SS to ORG, 29 July 1893 (Hilton)
28 CG, Memoir, [67] (Hilton)
29 ORG, Diary, 29 July 1893 (White)
30 Ibid, 22 May 1895
31 Ibid, 29 July 1893

32 Ibid
33 Ibid
34 Ibid, 30 July 1893
35 Ibid, 1 August 1893
36 Ibid, 2 August 1893
37 Nickalls, 3–4 (White)
38 EG to RG, 8 March 1891 (Hilton)
39 ORG, Diary, 12 June 1892 (White)
40 Ibid, 19 May 1893
41 Nickalls, 4 (White)
42 CG to EG, 3 August 1893, 24 August 1893 (Hilton)
43 CG to EG, [? 1893] (Hilton)
44 CG to EG, nd (Hilton)
45 CG to EG, 3 August 1893 (Hilton)
46 ORG, Diary, 20 October 1892 (White)
47 H. E. Bates, 31
48 See *Free Russia*, 1 January 1894, 4
49 ORG, Diary, 2 August 1893 (White)
50 Ibid, 20 July 1893
51 Ibid, 29 July 1893
52 Chalmers Mitchell quoted in Whyte, 33
53 CG, Memoir, [79] (Hilton)
54 'Tolstoi's New Novel', *Speaker*, 11 November 1899, 145
55 Wilson, 301
56 CG to RG, 22 October 1893 (Hilton)
57 CG to RG, 26 October 1893 (Hilton)
58 Ibid
59 CG to FS, [1893], fond 1158, op 1, ed, khr 238, No 5 (TsGALI)
60 CG to RG, 22 October 1893 (Hilton)
61 CG to SS, 11 October 1893, fond 1158, op 1, ed khr 238, No 3 (TsGALI)

62 ORG, Diary, 7 December 1893 (White)
63 Ibid, [18 December 1893]
64 Ibid
65 Ibid
66 Ibid, 28 December 1892
67 CG to RG, 26 October 1893 (Hilton)
68 CG to FS, 25 December 1893 (Hilton)
69 ORG, Diary, [28 December 1893] (White)
70 Ibid
71 *Daily Chronicle*, 26 December 1893, 3
72 Tolstoy to Heinemann, 5/17 January 1894, *Polnoe Sobranie Sochinenii*, lxvii (1955), 14
73 Tolstoy, *The Kingdom of God is Within You* (1894), vol i, x
74 Olga Novikoff, 'A Russian View of "Government by Journalism"', *Pall Mall Gazette*, 13 July 1886, 2
75 *Daily Chronicle*, 28 February 1894, 3
76 SS, *Underground Russia*, 41
77 ORG, Diary, [28 December 1893] (White)
78 Ibid, [29 December 1893]
79 Ibid
80 Ibid
81 Ibid
82 Ibid
83 *New Review*, February 1894, 214–22
84 ORG, Diary, 13 January 1894 (White)
85 Ibid, 31 December 1893
86 Ibid
87 Ibid
88 Ibid

Chapter 9: Russia in Winter

1 CG, Memoir, [63] (Hilton)
2 Ibid
3 Ibid
4 DG, *Golden Echo*, 11; but there is no other mention of it, and when she wanted money for herself she drew it on her father-in-law's bank.
5 CG, Memoir, [63] (Hilton)
6 Ibid
7 Ibid, [63–4]
8 CG to EG, 5 [4] January 1894 (Hilton)
9 Ibid
10 CG to EG, 5 January 1894 (Hilton)
11 CG to EG, '5' [4] January 1894 (Hilton)
12 *Novosti i Birzhevaia Gazeta*, 23 December 1893 os, No 353, 3 (trs Tatiana A. Wolff)
13 CG to EG, 5 [4] January 1894 (Hilton)
14 Ibid
15 Ibid

16 CG, Memoir, [64] (Hilton)
17 CG to EG, 5 January 1894 (Hilton)
18 CG to EG, 5 [4] January 1894 (Hilton)
19 CG to ORG, 10 January 1894 (White)
20 CG to EG, 10 January 1894 (Hilton)
21 CG to EG, 15 January 1894 (Hilton)
22 ORG, Diary, 30 January 1894 (White)
23 CG to EG, [11 February 1894] (Hilton)
24 CG to RG, 8 January 1894 (Hilton)
25 CG to EG, 15 January 1894 (Hilton)
26 CG to ORG, 10 January 1894 (White)
27 *Letters of Anton Tchehov* (1920), 11
28 Ibid, 11–12
29 Ibid, 12
30 CG to EG, 10 January 1894 (Hilton)
31 Ibid
32 ORG, Diary, [18 December 1893] (White)
33 CG to EG, 15 January 1894 (Hilton)

34 ORG, Diary, 20 October 1892 (White)
35 CG to EG, 15 January 1894 (Hilton)
36 CG to EG, 16 January 1894 (Hilton)
37 CG, Memoir, [65] (Hilton)
38 Ibid, [66]
39 Ibid
40 CG to RG, incomplete [January–February 1894] (Hilton)
41 CG to EG, 'Sunday evening' [11 February 1894] (Hilton)
42 CG, Memoir, [66–7] (Hilton)
43 CG to EG, 'Sunday evening' [11 February 1894] (Hilton)
44 CG to RG, 28 January 1894 (Hilton)
45 Ibid
46 Ibid
47 CG to RG, 15 January 1894 (Hilton)
48 CG to RG, 28 January 1894 (Hilton)
49 Ibid
50 CG to EG, 11 February 1894 (Hilton)
51 *Voyage en Russie* (1966 ed), 558
52 CG to EG, 1 February 1894 (Hilton)
53 Korolenko to SS, late January 1894 os, printed in Khrabrovitsky
54 Ibid
55 CG to EG, 1 February 1894 (Hilton)
56 Ibid
57 CG, Memoir, [68]
58 CG to EG, 1 February 1894 (Hilton)
59 Ibid
60 Ibid
61 Ibid
62 Ibid
63 Ibid
64 Ibid
65 Ibid
66 Ibid
67 Ibid
68 Ibid
69 Ibid
70 DG, *Golden Echo*, 15, has mistakenly transferred this adventure to Constance herself.
71 CG to EG, 1 February 1894 (Hilton)

72 Ibid
73 Ibid
74 Ibid
75 Ibid
76 CG, Memoir, [69] (Hilton)
77 Ibid
78 CG to EG, 1 February 1894 (Hilton)
79 Ibid
80 Ibid
81 Ibid
82 Ibid
83 CG, Memoir, [70] (Hilton)
84 CG to EG, [3 February 1894] (Hilton)
85 CG, Memoir, [70–1] (Hilton)
86 Ibid, 71
87 DG, *Golden Echo*, 14–15
88 CG, Memoir, [71] (Hilton)
89 Ibid, [72] (Hilton)
90 *Russkaia Zhizn'*, 15 February 1894, os, reprinted in Khrabrovitsky
91 Korolenko to SS, late January 1894 os, in Khrabrovitsky
92 CG to EG, [11 February 1894] (Hilton)
93 Ibid
94 Ibid. DG, *Golden Echo*, 15, is mistaken in thinking that she visited Tolstoy at Yasnaya Polyana.
95 CG to Tolstoy, 7 February 1894 [?os] (Tolstoy)
96 CG to Tolstoy, 27 September 1894 (Tolstoy)
97 CG to EG, [11 February 1894] (Hilton)
98 CG to EG, 5 January 1894 (Hilton)
99 CG's entry in ND's album, 'Confessions, Opinions, and Autographs of My Friends' (Garrett)
100 CG to EG, 13 February 1894 (Hilton)
101 Ibid, [11 February 1894] (Hilton)
102 Korolenko, however, had kept a copy, see Khrabrovitsky.
103 DG, MS Memoir of CG [26] (Hilton)
104 ORG, Diary, 25 February 1894 (White)

Chapter 10: An Unsettled Year

1 RG, 'Of One in Russia', *The Queen and Other Poems* (1901), sonnet xliv
2 ORG, Diary, 25 February 1894 (White)
3 Ibid
4 ORG, Diary, '3' [2] March 1894 (White)
5 Ibid
6 Ibid
7 Ibid

8 Ibid, 24 March 1894 (White)
9 Ibid, '3' [2] March 1894
10 *Academy*, 24 March 1894, xlv, No 1142, 245
11 DG, *Golden Echo*, 53–4
12 Interview with Kyle S. Crichton, *The World* (New York), 11 October 1925, section 3, page 4m
13 EMH to RDG, 4 March 1958 (RDG)

14 ORG, Diary, 14 March 1894 (White)
15 CG to EG, 7 January 1894 (Hilton)
16 ORG, Diary, 20 March 1894 (White)
17 Ibid
18 Ibid
19 ORG, Diary, 27 March 1894 (White)
20 Ibid
21 ORG, Diary, 'Saturday, Sunday, Monday' [31 March, 1, 2 April 1894] (White)
22 Ibid
23 ORG, Diary, 23 April 1894 (White)
24 Shaw, *Letters, 1874–1897*, 422
25 *Fabian News*, April 1894, 7
26 N. and J. MacKenzie, 182
27 FS to ORG, 22 April 1894 (Hilton)
28 Dollie Radford, Diary, 21 April 1894 (Clark)
29 N. and J. MacKenzie, 210
30 *Palgrave's Dictionary of Political Economy*, ed Henry Higgins (1925), i, 689
31 *Daily Chronicle*, 7 May 1894
32 ORG, Diary, 6 May 1894 (White)
33 *Daily Chronicle*, 7 May 1894
34 ORG, Diary, 6 May 1894 (White)
35 Ibid
36 Ibid
37 DG, Brief Memoir of CG, 5 (Hilton)
38 CG to SS, 16 March 1893, fond 1158, op 1, ed khr 238 (TsGALI)
39 ORG, Diary, 4 May 1894 (White)
40 Eventually put on by the Stage Society as *Mrs Maxwell's Marriage* on 21 January 1900
41 ORG, Diary, 24 May 1894 (White)
42 Sale catalogue, T. G. Wharton, 29, 30, 31 May 1894, marked up by Robert Garnett (White)
43 FS published a Russian text in Geneva in 1897. It was put on at the Avenue Theatre, London, on 14 June 1898 as a benefit for her, with no indication that it was not originally written in English, but in 1899

Duckworth advertised at the back of CG's translation of *The Storm* by Ostrovsky her forthcoming translation of *The Convert*. It did not appear, but a translation by Thomas B. Eyges as *The New Convert* was published by Stratford of Boston in 1917.
44 ORG, Diary, 16 'June' [July] 1894 (White)
45 Ibid
46 Ibid
47 *Daily Chronicle*, 16 February 1894, 3
48 Ibid, 14 July 1894
49 ORG, Diary, 14 July 1894 (White)
50 August 1894, 151
51 *Academy*, 27 October 1894, 325
52 Ibid
53 *Speaker*, 8 September 1894, reprinted in *Uncollected Prose of W. B. Yeats*, ed Frayne (1970), 341–3
54 Quoted in Jefferson, 'Pseudonym Library', 13
55 Ibid
56 Jefferson, *EG*, 56
67 DG, 'Brief Memoir of CG', [6] (Hilton)
58 EG, introduction to *Letters from Conrad*, vi
59 Ibid, vii
60 Ibid
61 CG to EG, 2 August 1894 (Hilton)
62 Ibid
63 ONG to CG, 7 August 1894 (Hilton)
64 CG, Memoir, [77] (Hilton)
65 Ibid
66 Ibid
67 Ibid
68 DG, MS Memoir of CG, [10] (Hilton)
69 ORG, Diary, 16 'June' [July] 1894 (White)
70 DG, *Great Friends*, 162
71 CG to DG, 24 February 1925 (Hilton)
72 CG to EG, 12 August 1894 (Hilton)
73 CG to RG, 26 October 1894 (Hilton)
74 CG to ONG, 10 October 1895 (Hilton)

Chapter 11: The Dear Little Cearne

1 ORG, Diary, 24 January 1895 (White)
2 CG to Pinker, 12 October 1919 (Berg); FS to ORG, 10 January 1898 (Hilton)
3 ORG, Diary, 24 January 1895 (White)
4 Ibid
5 Ibid, 16 February 1904
6 Ibid, 28 January 1895
7 Ibid, 7 October 1894
8 DG, *Golden Echo*, 18
9 ORG, Diary, 28 January 1895 (White)
10 N. and J. MacKenzie, 39–40
11 DG, *Golden Echo*, 16
12 Ibid, 17
13 Ibid, 17–18
14 Peel, 8
15 ORG, Diary, 15 March 1895 (White)
16 Ibid, 20 May 1895
17 DG, *Golden Echo*, 20
18 ORG, Diary, 20 May 1895 (White)
19 CG to RG, 25 November 1895 (Hilton)
20 CG to RG, 1 September 1895 (Hilton)
21 ORG, Diary, 5 May 1895 (White)

22 Ibid, 24 February 1895
23 Ibid, 20 May 1895
24 Ibid, 22 May 1895
25 Ibid, 15 August 1895
26 Ibid, 22 May 1895
27 Ibid, 23 May 1895
28 Ibid
29 Ibid
30 CG to EG, nd (Hilton). *The Awkward Age* was published on 25 April 1899.
31 ORG, Diary, 24 May 1895 (White)
32 Ibid, 23 February and 9 March 1895
33 Ibid, 24 May 1895
34 Ibid, 20 May 1895
35 CG to RG, 1 September 1895 (Hilton)
36 DG, *Golden Echo*, 19
37 Ibid
38 Ibid
39 ORG, Diary, 18 November 1895 (White)
40 Ibid, 19 November 1895
41 DG, *Golden Echo*, 19
42 Ibid, 19–20
43 ORG, Diary, 9 November 1892 (White)
44 Volkhovsky to Ada Radford, 25 December 1895 (Wallas papers, Newnham)
45 *Times*, 30 December 1895, 9
46 *Weekly Sun*, 29 December 1895
47 Ibid
48 ORG to Lazarev, 24 December [1895] (RDG)
49 Michell, 'Bloomsbury Girlhood', 374 (White)
50 DG, *Golden Echo*, 20
51 Michell, 'Bloomsbury Girlhood', 331 (White)
52 CG, Memoir, [81]
53 DG, *Golden Echo*, 21
54 CG, Memoir, [81]

55 CG to ONG, 8 April 1896 (Hilton)
56 CG to RG, Saturday morning' [pm 4 April 1896] (Hilton)
57 CG to FS, 'Saturday morning' [April 1896] (Hilton)
58 Ibid
59 CG to RG, 'Saturday morning' [pm 4 April 1896] (Hilton)
60 CG to RG, 'Easter Monday' [6 April 1896] (Hilton)
61 CG to RG, 27 April [1896] (Hilton)
62 CG to ONG, 10 April [1896] (Hilton)
63 Ibid
64 Conrad to EG, [13 April 1896], *Letters*, i, 213
65 CG to RG, 'Saturday' pm 9 May 1896 (Hilton)
66 ORG to RG, 5 May 1896 (Hilton)
67 CG to RG, 13 April [1896] (Hilton)
68 CG to RG, 'Saturday' [pm 9 May 1896] (Hilton)
69 EG to ONG, 2 June 1896 (Hilton)
70 ORG to RG, 5 May 1896 (Hilton)
71 EG to RG, 2 June 1896 (Hilton)
72 ORG to RG, 5 May 1896 (Hilton)
73 ND to Tovey, 16 June 1959 (in Russian) (Malinskaya)
74 FS to ORG, 10 January 1898 (Hilton)
75 CG to RG, 2 June 1896 (Hilton)
76 DG, *Golden Echo*, 22
77 Ibid, 53
78 Ibid, 23
79 CG to RG, 6 November 1896 (Hilton)
80 DG, *Golden Echo*, 31
81 Ibid, 66
82 'Broad Church', *New Statesman*, 15 June 1979, 874
83 E. g. CG to EG, 21 July 1904 (Hilton)

Chapter 12: Visitors and Colonists

1 CG to Volkhovsky, 17 September 1896 (RDG)
2 CG to RG, 4 January 1896 [1897] (Hilton)
3 CG to RG, 22 December 1896 (Hilton)
4 Clyman, 210
5 I am indebted to Patrick Miles for a copy of the original in GBL, Chekh, 40, 14; published by N. A. Alekseev in *Vestnik Istorii Mirovoi Kul'tury*, 1961, No 2, 103
6 *Russkaya Mysl*, No 12, 1896, 117–61
7 CG to RG, 4 January 1896 (Hilton), from which it is not absolutely clear whether the letter was from Chekhov himself or from his publisher, Suvorin. In either case the letter has not been traced.

8 Ibid
9 DG, *Golden Echo*, 8
10 Fabian Society Minutes, 14 April 1893 (Nuffield)
11 DG, MS memoir of CG, [8] (Hilton)
12 N. and J. MacKenzie, 250
13 Senese, 53
14 CG to RG, 21 April 1897 (Hilton)
15 CG to RG, 28 June 1897 (Hilton)
16 Ibid
17 CG to RG, 18 August 1896 (HRHRC)
18 CG to RG, 11 October 1897 (HRHRC)
19 Quoted in Beer, 160
20 Anonymous American lawyer quoted in Beer, 175

21 EG, *Friday Nights*, 203
22 Ibid, 206
23 Ford Madox Ford, *New York Herald Tribune Books*, 2 January 1927, 1
24 EG, *Friday Nights*, 203
25 Ibid, 202
26 EG, *Letters from Conrad*, xvi
27 Ibid, xxiv
28 CG to RG, 4 March 1898 (Hilton)
29 EG, *Letters from Conrad*, xxv
30 CG to RG, 4 March 1898 (Hilton)
31 EG, *Letters from Conrad*, xvi–xvii
32 Ibid, xvii
33 Ibid, xix
34 DG, *Golden Echo*, 62. EG, *Letters from Conrad*, xvi, has a slightly different version. EG says David was six; he says he was five. On 3 March, when Conrad's visit ended, he would have been six days short of his sixth birthday.
35 FS to ORG, 3 May 1898 (Hilton)
36 CG to ORG, 7 September 1898 (White)
37 Conrad to EG, [2 May 1917], *Letters from Conrad*, 268
38 EG, *Letters from Conrad*, xxxii
39 Conrad to EG, [2 May 1917], *Letters from Conrad*, 268–9
40 CG to Conrad, 30 December 1897, *Letters from Conrad*, 111 n1
41 Typed 'List of Conrad Manuscripts, Typescripts, and Original Letters, Presentation Copies of Conrad's Works and Others Inscribed to Edward Garnett by Joseph Conrad, etc.' (Hilton)
42 Turton, 273
43 *Daily News*, 10 August 1908, 3
44 CG to RG, 4 March 1898 (Hilton)
45 ORG, Diary, 26 March 1892 (White)
46 Ibid, 9 June 1892
47 DG, *Golden Echo*, 35–6
48 Ibid, 36
49 Quoted in Stallman, 299
50 Ibid
51 Douglas Goldring, *The Last Pre-Raphaelite: A Record of the Life and Writings of Ford Madox Ford* (1948), 93; Ford, *Mightier than the Sword* (1938), 54, has a slightly different version.
52 DG, *Golden Echo*, 64. This story is not in ORG's surviving diaries, some pages of which about James have been removed.
53 DG, *Golden Echo*, 37
54 Ibid, 37–8
55 Ibid, 38
56 Ibid
57 CG to DG, 4 July 1927 (Hilton)
58 DG, *Golden Echo*, 45
59 Ibid, 23
60 Ibid, 40
61 CG to RG, 15 January 1898 (Hilton)
62 EG to ONG, pc, 20 May 1898 [pm 20 April 1898] (HRHRC)
63 CG to EG, 24 January [1899] (Hilton)
64 CG to EG 'Tuesday' [13 December 1898] (Eton)
65 CG to EG, 18 December [1898] (Eton)
66 DG, *Golden Echo*, 46
67 CG to EG, 21 December [1898] (Eton)
68 DG, *Golden Echo*, 46
69 CG to EG, 14 January 1899 (Hilton)
70 CG to RG, 15 February 1899 (Hilton)
71 Ibid
72 Ibid
73 CG to EG 'Wednesday' [?15 March 1899] (Hilton)

Chapter 13: Fin-de-Siècle

1 ORG, Diary, 20–23 March 1899 (White)
2 DG, *Golden Echo*, 48
3 CG to RG, 31 October 1899 (Hilton). Although CG thought it very good, I cannot find any other reference to this portrait, or anyone who has seen it.
4 EMH to EG, nd, from 9 Endsleigh Terrace WC (Hilton)
5 EMH to EG, 26 September 1896 (Hilton)
6 Stebbing, 'Notes on Nellie Heath', 1 (Hilton)
7 CG to EG, pc, 28 January 1899 (Hilton)
8 CG to EG, 'Wednesday' [?15 March 1899] (Hilton)
9 CG to EG, pc, 28 January 1899 (Hilton)
10 EMH note 'Oct 19' of what seems to have been a recurring dream, but could have been an actual event (White)
11 EG to EMH 'Friday Night' (Hilton)
12 DG, 'Russian Women', [2] (Hilton)
13 Nickalls, 'The Time is Past and Gone', 2 (White)
14 DG, *Golden Echo*, 55
15 Ibid
16 N. and J. MacKenzie, 269
17 DG, *Golden Echo*, 209, 210 (taken out of order)
18 DG, 'Burst Balloons', [8] (Hilton)

19 Ibid, [9]

20 ORG, Diary, 20 June 1900 (White)

21 CG to Volkhovsky, nd (RDG)

22 DG, *Golden Echo*, 61

23 Ibid

24 CG to RG, 26 December 1899 (Hilton)

25 Philip Unwin, *The Publishing Unwins* (1972), 46

26 CG to RG, 26 December 1899 (Hilton)

27 CG to EG, 8 January 1899 (Hilton)

28 CG to Volkhovsky, 1 January 1898 (RDG)

29 EG in Turgenev, *The Jew and Other Stories* (1899), ix, xiv

30 *Academy*, 20 January 1900, lvi, 63

31 Ibid

32 Ibid, 64

33 Unidentified press cutting on greenish paper (Hilton)

34 CG to RG, 18 June 1897; *Manchester Guardian* review untraced – perhaps only in earlier editions?

35 CG to J. L. L. Hammond, 28 February 1940 (Bodleian)

36 DG, 'Brief Memoir of CG', [7] (Hilton)

37 CG, 'Art of Translation'

38 CG to Volkhovsky, 22 December 1896 (RDG)

39 CG to RG, 15 January 1898 (Hilton)

40 27 November 1897, 178

41 CG to RG, 2 December 1897 (Hilton)

42 Heilbrun, 192 n4

43 No 3501, 1 December 1894, 741

44 CG, 'Art of Translation'

45 Ibid

46 Turton, 313

47 DG to CG, [February 1930] (HRHRC)

48 Kaibunsha, Tokyo (1961)

49 ND to Tovey, 26 October 1959 (in Russian) (Malinskaya)

50 ND to Tovey, 16 May 1959 (in Russian) (Malinskaya)

51 Crankshaw, 'Work of Constance Garnett', 196

52 Haley

53 CG, 'Art of Translation'

54 Conrad to EG, 26 October 1899, *Letters*, ii, 209; *Letters from Conrad*, 154

55 It is not difficult to find these in her early translations; e.g. 'three hundred and three' for 'thirty-three (*Smoke*, 118), or *vpolgolosa* as 'in a loud voice', when it actually means 'in an undertone' (*Smoke*, 110)

56 Turton, 319

57 Now in Stanford University Library. No doubt she corrected other volumes, but I have not come across them.

58 CG, 'Art of Translation'

59 Turton, 232

60 Bennett, *Letters*, ii, 80–81

61 Marrot, *Galsworthy*, 88

62 DG, *Great Friends*, 103–4

63 DG, *Golden Echo*, 71

64 EG in *Letters from Galsworthy*, 5

65 DG, *Golden Echo*, 70

66 Galsworthy, 'Six Novelists in Profile: An Address', *Castles in Spain* (1927), 150

67 Reader's report (Berg) quoted in Jefferson, *EG*, 109–10

68 Ibid, no

69 EG in *Letters from Galsworthy*, 5

70 DG, *Beany-Eye*, 14–15

71 DG, *Golden Echo*, 70

72 CG to EG, 7 January 1910 (Eton)

73 ORG, Diary, 6 February 1901 (White)

74 CG to RG, 3 March 1901 (Hilton)

75 *New York Herald Tribune*, 24 November 1935

76 DG, *Beany-Eye*, 14–15

77 ORG to her sister Narney ('Patty'), 3 March 1937 (White)

Chapter 14: Tolstoy by Candlelight

1 CG to RG, 2 March 1900 (Hilton)

2 Ibid

3 CG to RG, 10 May 1900 (Hilton)

4 CG to RG, 2 March 1900 (Hilton)

5 ORG, Diary, 9 June 1900 (White)

6 St John, 79, says she was paid 'only £300' for *War and Peace*, which would work out at this rate. I have found no further confirmation of this in her papers or in the Heinemann Archive.

7 CG to RG, 3 May 1901 (Hilton)

8 FS to ORG, 9 June 1901 (Hilton)

9 CG to RG, 27 August 1900 (Hilton)

10 Ibid

11 Ibid

12 vi, 1900, 150–65

13 Russian translation in Tolstoy, *Polnoe Sobranie Sochinenii*, lxxii, 398

14 Ibid, lxxii, 397, letter 322

15 *North American Review*, April 1901, 504–19

16 *Bookman*, March 1901, 184–7

17 EG to RG, 5 July 1901 (Hilton)

18 *Alpine Journal*, October 1901, xx, No 153, 490

19 EG to RG, 'Friday' [26 July 1901] (Hilton)

20 CG to RG, 31 August 1901 (Hilton)

21 Ibid

22 CG to RG 'Wednesday' [?16 October 1901] (Hilton)

23 CG to RG, 19 September 1901 (Hilton)

24 *Academy*, 8 June 1901, 447

25 Heilbrun, 207, is mistaken in saying 'Chelkash' was translated by CG. In the book the title is spelt 'Tchelkash', and the translation is attributed to S. K. Michel. She did, however, translate The Prisoner and the Kitten', MS (Hilton), but it seems not to have been published.

26 ORG to RG, 28 September 1897 (Hilton)

27 CG to RG, 15 July 1901 (Hilton)

28 DG to RG, nd, enclosed with CG to RG, 8 January 1901 (Hilton)

29 Text from *The Poetry of Cats*, ed Samuel Carr (1974), 91

30 ORG, Diary, 5 February 1902 (White)

31 EG to RG, 4 October 1901 (Hilton)

32 CG to RG, 4 October 1901 (Hilton)

33 Leonard Woolf, *Downhill All the Way* (1967), 68

34 Anthony Powell, *Keep the Ball Rolling*, ii *Messengers of Day* (1978), 6

35 Ibid, 5

36 EG in *153 Letters from W. H. Hudson* (1923), 1

37 DG, *Great Friends*, 28

38 Ibid, 29

39 CG to RG, 5 July 1900 (Hilton)

40 CG to RG, 16 July 1902 (Hilton)

41 DG, *Golden Echo*, 94

42 CG, scrap of diary, 17 November 1902 (Hilton)

43 ORG, Diary, 21 May 1905 (White)

44 CG's entry in ND's album, 'Confessions, Opinions, and Autographs of My Friends' (Garrett)

45 CG, scrap of diary, November 1902 (Hilton)

46 ORG, Diary, 23 June 1903 (White)

47 Ibid

48 Ibid, 24 June 1903

49 Ibid

50 Ibid, 26 June 1903

51 Ibid, 27 June 1903

52 DG, *Golden Echo*, 57–8

53 Ibid, 58

54 Ibid, 103

55 CG to RG, 2 May [1903] (Hilton)

56 ND to Tovey, 8 May 1959 (Malinskaya)

57 Blach, Jay and MacFaul, 'The Concept of Degenerate Myopia', *Proceedings of the Royal Society of Medicine*, lviii, February 1965, 109–12

58 CG to RG, 20 September 1903 (Hilton)

59 Ibid

60 Ibid. Short of printing a facsimile, it is not practicable to reproduce all the typing errors in this letter, which have therefore been corrected.

61 Galsworthy to EG, 6 April 1903, *Letters from John Galsworthy*, 48

62 CG to EG, 28 May 1904 (Hilton)

63 CG, 'Art of Translation', 195

64 CG to EG, 14 January [1910] (Eton)

65 ND to Tovey, 16 June 1959 (in Russian) (Malinskaya)

66 CG to RG, 12 November 1901 (Hilton)

67 Gifford, 22

68 Ibid

69 Ibid

70 Ibid, 21

71 *Anna Karenin*, i, 143, Gifford's italics, Ibid, 21

72 Gifford, 21

73 Motyleva, 94

74 St John, 448–9

75 CG to EG, 'Thursday' [pm 17 November 1910] (Eton)

Chapter 15; Russia in Summer

1 DG, *Golden Echo*, 74

2 CG to RG, 9 May 1904 (Hilton)

3 DG to EG, [13 May 1904] (Hilton)

4 DG, *Golden Echo*, 75

5 DG, *Golden Echo*, 75

6 CG to EG, 20 May 1904 (Hilton)

7 CG to EG, 'Wednesday' [18 May 1904] (Hilton)

8 CG to EG, 21 May 1904 (Hilton)

9 CG to EG, 'Wednesday May 24' [25 May 1904] (Hilton)

10 DG, *Golden Echo*, 77

11 Ibid, 77–8

12 CG to EG, 12 June [1904] (Eton)

13 Quoted in Bunin, 127–8

14 CG to EG, 9 July [1904] (Eton)

15 DG, *Golden Echo*, 78
16 Ibid
17 Ibid
18 Ibid, 84
19 CG to EG, 12 June [1904] (Eton)
20 CG to EG, 24 June [1904] (Hilton)
21 DG, *Golden Echo*, 84
22 CG to EG, 9 July [1904] (Eton)
23 Ibid
24 DG, *Golden Echo*, 78–9
25 Ibid, 79–80
26 DG to EG, nd (Hilton)
27 CG to EG, 18 June [1904] (Eton)
28 Ibid
29 DG, *Golden Echo*, 83
30 CG to EG, 10 June [1904] (Hilton)
31 Ibid
32 Ibid
33 Ibid
34 DG, *Golden Echo*, 86
35 CG to EG, 3 July [1904] (Eton)
36 Ibid
37 Ibid
38 DG, *Golden Echo*, 89
39 Ibid, 88–9
40 CG to EG, 3 July [1904] (Eton)
41 CG to EG, pc, 3 July [1904] (Eton)
42 CG to EG, 3 July [1904] (Eton)
43 CG to EG, 9 July [1904] (Eton); DG, *Golden Echo*, 90, says he lost twelve pounds.
44 CG to EG, 3 July [1904] (Eton)
45 *Annual Register, 1904*, 305
46 DG, *Golden Echo*, 89–90

47 CG to EG, 10 June [1904] (Hilton)
48 CG to EG, 6 July [1904] (Eton)
49 Robert K. Massie, *Nicholas and Alexandra* (1968), 88
50 CG to EG, 9 July [1904] (Eton)
51 Ibid
52 DG, *Golden Echo*, 82
53 CG to EG, 28 July [1904] (Hilton)
54 CG to EG, 29 July [1904] (Hilton)
55 Ibid
56 DG, *Golden Echo*, 85
57 CG to EG, 29 July [1904] (Hilton)
58 Crankshaw, *Shadow of the Winter Palace*, 277
59 Ibid, 318
60 Ibid, 319
61 CG to EG, 5 August [1904] (Eton)
62 CG to EG, 'Sunday – 7 o'clock' [7 August 1904] (Hilton)
63 DG, *Golden Echo*, 76, calling her 'Madame Lenev', says that CG collaborated with FS in translating the words of the songs. The English prose text does not look as if CG had much hand in it.
64 DG, *Golden Echo*, 93
65 Ibid
66 Crankshaw, *Shadow of the Winter Palace*, 340
67 A. I. Ertel to N. A. Ertel, 18 February 1905 os, Garrett, 80
68 A. I. Ertel to N. A. Ertel, 16 February 1905 os, Garrett, 70
69 Trotsky, quoted in Harcave, 244

Chapter 16: Bad Eyes and Good Friends

1 CG to RG, 'Friday morning' [pm 30 September 1904] (Hilton)
2 CG to RG, 5 July 1900 (Hilton)
3 Hermine Priestman (Bréal), Brunt notes on Auguste Bréal, 10 (Brunt)
4 CG to RG, 26 June [1905] (Hilton)
5 Galsworthy to CG, 14 June 1905, *Letters from Galsworthy*, 87
6 CG to Galsworthy, 14 January 1906, *Letters from Galsworthy*, 104
7 Gindin, 169
8 EG to Galsworthy, 8 May 1905, *Letters from Galsworthy*, 60
9 CG to RG, 8 September 1905 (Hilton)
10 CG to RG, 3 October 1905 (Hilton)
11 Ibid
12 DG, *Golden Echo*, 125
13 Ibid
14 Ibid

15 Ibid
16 Ibid, 126
17 Farjeon, 109
18 Ibid, no
19 DG, 'Journal and Notebook', 'Thursday' [31 December 1908] (Hilton)
20 CG to EG, 'Saturday' [29 September 1906] (Eton)
21 CG to EG, 17 December [1907] (Eton)
22 ORG, Diary, 13 April 1906 (White)
23 EG, note on Neale correspondence, 26 October 1906 (Hilton)
24 EG, note on Neale letter of 30 June 1904 (Hilton)
25 CG to EG, 'Friday' black-edged [1906] (Eton)
26 EG, note on Neale correspondence, 26 October 1906 (Hilton)

27 Ibid
28 Archer, 25
29 DG, Golden Echo, 123
30 Ibid
31 Ibid (mistakenly making Lily Elsie the star of *The Spring Chicken*)
32 Ibid
33 Ibid, 124
34 CG to EG, 'Friday' [?1909] (Eton)
35 DG, *Golden Echo*, 72
36 Ibid
37 Ibid,   73
38 Conrad to EG, 17 November 1906, *Letters from Conrad*, 201–2
39 Gindin, 195
40 Galsworthy to Mrs Dawson Scott, 17 December 1931, Marrot, 219
41 Archer to Lady Mary Murray, 1 November 1907 in C. Archer, *William Archer* (1931), 321
42 DG, *Golden Echo*, 133
43 ORG, Diary, 5 April 1908 (White)
44 Ibid, 7 April 1908
45 CG to EG, 'Sunday' [March–April 1906] (Eton)
46 EG to *Galsworthy*, 8 March 1906, *Letters from Galsworthy*, 111–12
47 CG to EG, 'Saturday' [29 September 1906] (Eton)
48 Gindin, 193
49 CG to EG, 27 September 1907 (Eton)
50 Marrot, 214
51 DG, 'Journal and Notebook', 9 March 1909 (Hilton)
52 CG to EG, 'Saturday' [pm 14 September ?1907] (Eton)
53 DG, *Golden Echo*, 163
54 N. and J. MacKenzie, 328–9
55 DG, *Golden Echo*, 163, says that EG resigned a month after Wells was defeated. Fabian records in Nuffield College show that he did not resign till 1926.
56 'A Poisonous Book', *Spectator*, 20 November 1909, 846–7
57 CG to DG, 10 November 1928 (Hilton)
58 CG to EG, 'Saturday' (Eton)
59 DG, *Golden Echo*, 165
60 Ibid
61 CG to EG, 10 February 1914 (Eton)
62 J. A. Spender, *The Life of Sir Henry Campbell-Bannerman* (1923), ii, 261–3

63 *Daily News*, 15 November 1906, 9
64 Ibid, 16 November 1906, 8
65 Ibid, 15 November 1906, 6
66 ORG, Diary, 9 February 1907 (White)
67 Ibid
68 Ibid
69 Ibid
70 DG, *Golden Echo*, 116
71 Ibid
72 Peter Struve, 'My Contacts and Conflicts with Lenin', *Slavonic and East European Review*, xii, No 36, April 1934, 591
73 maxim Gorky, *Days with Lenin* [1932], 4–6
74 Dudden and von Laue, 31
75 ORG, Diary, 9 December 1899 (White)
76 Hambourg, 32
77 Dudden and von Laue, 35
78 Ibid
79 DG, *Golden Echo*, 118; Bruce Chatwin must have been thinking of quite a different family when he described CG and EG as 'Lenin's English friends' and asserted that DG 'used to keep in his wallet Lenin's bus ticket from Tottenham Court Road to their house in Putney', *What am I Doing Here* (1989), 180 – what indeed!
80 Ibid
81 Ibid
82 Clark, 119
83 Clark, 120
84 DG, *Golden Echo*, 118
85 Ibid
86 DG, 'Journal and Notebook', 18 December 1908 (Hilton)
87 CG to EG, nd (Eton)
88 EMH to Louise Bréal, 26 December 1908 (Brunt)
89 G to EG, 12 May 1913 (Hilton)
90 CG to EG, 16 May 1913 (Hilton)
91 CG to EG, 'Saturday' [17 May 1913] (Hilton)
92 Ibid
93 CG to EG, 16 August 1908 (Eton)
94 CG to EG, 'Tuesday' [?18 August 1908] (Eton)
95 CG to EG, 'Sunday' [pm 7 June 1909] (Eton)

Chapter 17: Two Painful Episodes

1 CG to EG, nd, black-edged [1906] (Eton)
2 ORG, Diary, 2 November 1905 (White)
3 CG to EG, nd (Eton)
4 ORG, Diary, 19 January 1906 (White)

5 *Daily News*, 23 January 1908, 7
6 CG to EG, 'Friday' [pm 5 October 1906] (Eton)
7 *Albany Review*, April–May 1907, i, 86–101, 204–40; there is a typescript, corrected by CG, in HRHRC.
8 *Nation*, 13 June 1908, 383
9 DG, *Golden Echo*, 115
10 Crankshaw, *Shadow of the Winter Palace*, 326
11 CG to EG, 'Thursday' [ca May 1907] (Eton)
12 DG, 'Journal and Notebook', 8 December 1908 (Hilton)
13 Ibid
14 Ibid, 10 March 1909
15 Ibid, 3 January 1909; Robert Drury, *Madagascar: or, Robert Drury's Journal During Fifteen Years Captivity on that Island* (1729), 229–30
16 DG, *Golden Echo*, 141
17 Ibid, 140
18 CG to EG, nd [? April 1909] (Eton)
19 DG, *Golden Echo*, 143
20 Ibid
21 Ibid, 144
22 Ibid, 145
23 Ibid, 146
24 Ibid, 147
25 *Daily News*, 6 July 1909, 5
26 DG, *Golden Echo*, 149
27 CG to EG, nd [pm 15 March 1900] (Eton)
28 DG, *Golden Echo*, 153
29 CG, draft letter, 20 April 1910 (Hilton)
30 CG to 'Audrey' (Ada Radford), 5 July 1910 (Wallas papers, Newnham)
31 DG, *Golden Echo*, 119
32 Ibid, 155
33 EG to EMH, '8 o'clock' [29 May 1910] (Hilton)
34 EG to EMH, 30 May 1910 (Hilton)
35 DG, *Golden Echo*, 160
36 EG to EMH, nd (Hilton)
37 CG to EG, nd (Eton)
38 DG to CG, 'The Cearne, Wednesday' (HRHRC)
39 CG to EG, 'Monday' [pm 10 January 1910] (Eton)
40 ORG, Diary, 23 January 1910 (White)
41 CG to EG, 'Monday' [pm 10 January 1910] (Eton)
42 Ibid
43 DG, Savarkar MS, chap v (Hilton)
44 Ibid
45 DG, *Golden Echo*, 171
46 Ibid
47 CG to DG, draft letter as from EG, nd (Eton)
48 Ibid
49 Ibid
50 Galsworthy to Ernest Radford, 23 October 1909 (MacEwen)
51 Quoted in CG to EG, nd [1910] (Eton); the relevant Treasury file, PRO 1910/4727, appears to have been destroyed.
52 CG to EG, nd (January 1910] (Eton)
53 CG to EG, 'Wednesday' [?5 January 1910] (Eton)
54 Ibid
55 CG to EG, 'Thursday' [?6 January 1910] (Eton)
56 Galsworthy to EG [January 1910]; present whereabouts unknown, quoted by Jefferson, *EG*, 187
57 CG to EG, 'Monday' [pm 10 January 1910] (Eton)
58 DG to EG, nd, copy in EG's hand with a correction by EMH (Hilton)
59 CG to EG, 'Friday' [?7 January 1910] (Eton)
60 CG to EG, 'Saturday' [?8 January 1910] (Eton)
61 CG to EG, 'Monday' [pm 10 January 1910] (Eton)
62 Ibid
63 CG to Ernest Radford, 6 March 1910 (MacEwen)
64 CG to EG, 14 January [1910] (Eton)
65 CG to EG, 'Friday night' [14 January 1910] (Eton)
66 CG to EG, 'Monday' [?31 January 1910] (Eton)
67 DG to CG, nd (HRHRC)
68 DG, 'Journal and Notebook' 20 December 1908 (Hilton)
69 Ursula Cox to CG, incomplete (Eton)
70 Ursula Cox to CG, incomplete (Hilton)
71 ND to Tovey, 8 May 1959 (in Russian) (Malinskaya)
72 CG to ND, 'Saturday' [in envelope pm 1 September 1919 with 5 others] (Garrett)

Chapter 18: Chekhov Spurned, Dostoevsky Beatified

1 CG to Galsworthy, 14 January [1908], *Letters from Galsworthy*, 104
2 CG to EG, 'Friday' [?February 1909] (Eton)

3 CG to EG, Saturday' [?8 January 1910] (Eton); she refers to Mrs Roberts, but it was Mrs Grant Richards who was editor of the *Englishwoman*.

4 CG to EG, 'Thursday morning' [spring 1906] (Eton)

5 Ibid

6 Galsworthy to CG, 19 April 1906 (HRHRC)

7 CG to EG, 'Saturday' [before 5 March 1906] (Eton)

8 CG to EG, 'Saturday' [pm 29 April 1911] (Eton)

9 W. Somerset Maugham, *The Vagrant Mood* (1952), 199–200

10 *Teatr i Iskusstvo*, 29 May 1911 os, No 22, quoted in Miles, 4

11 Ibid

12 ORG, Diary, 29 May 1911 (White)

13 [A. B. Walkley], *Times*, 30 May 1911, 13

14 *Saturday Review* (London), 13 April 1912, 454

15 'Jacob Tonson' in *New Age*, 8 June 1911, 132

16 Ibid

17 Swinnerton, *Background with Chorus*, 143

18 CG to EG, 'Whit Monday' [pm 6 June 1911] (Eton)

19 *World*, 6 June 1911, 853

20 Archer to Shaw, 20 June 1923, C. Archer, *William Archer* (1931), 392

21 Shaw to Archer, 22 June 1923, *Letters*, [iii], 837

22 *Academy*, 1 September 1906, 202

23 'Jacob Tonson' in *New Age*, 31 March 1910, 519

24 See Bennett, *Journals*, i, 346

25 'Jacob Tonson' in *New Age*, 31 March 1910, 519

26 Ibid

27 'Jacob Tonson' in *New Age*, 9 February 1911, 349

28 DG, 'Journal and Notebook', 18 December 1908 (Hilton)

29 *Living Age*, 19 June 1909, 738–48

30 Max Beerbohm, *Letters*, ed Hart-Davis (1988), 90

31 *Daily News*, 15 November 1910, 2

32 'How it Strikes a Russian', *Daily News*, 19 November 1910, 4

33 CG to EG, 'Monday' (Eton)

34 Heinemann to CG, 10 March 1911 (Hilton)

35 'Jacob Tonson' in *New Age*, 23 March 1911, 492

36 CG to EG, nd [?1911] (Hilton)

37 CG to EG, nd (Eton)

38 Ibid

39 Quoted in CG to EG, nd (Eton)

40 Kropotkin, *Daily News*, 23 April 1912, 7

41 Ibid

42 Ibid

43 CG, *Times*, 13 May 1912, 5

44 Ibid

45 *Times*, 24 June 1912, 5

46 Ibid, 26 June 1912, 5

47 FS to CG, 'Tuesday' [26 June 1912] (Eton)

48 *Daily News*, 3 May 1912, 3

49 Ibid

50 *Spectator*, 28 September 1912, 452

51 Ibid

52 Conrad to EG, 27 May 1912, *Letters from Conrad*, 260

53 Galsworthy to EG, 5 April 1914, *Letters from Galsworthy*, 217

54 Rupert Hart-Davis, *Hugh Walpole* (1952), 91

55 James to Walpole, 19 May 1912, *Letters*, iv, 618–19

56 Swinnerton, *Georgian Literary Scene*, 296

57 *Living Age*, 15 May 1916, 436

58 Exhibition catalogue quoted in Virginia Woolf, *Roger Fry* (1940), 177

59 CG to EG, 9 August 1912 (Eton)

60 CG to EG, 'Wednesday' [August 1912] (Eton)

61 CG to EG, 17 August 1912 (Eton)

62 DG, *Flowers of the Forest*, 182

63 CG to EG, 17 August 1912 (Eton)

64 CG to Heinemann, 5 April 1915 (Heinemann Archive, OGPL)

65 Heinemann to CG, 10 September 1913 (Hilton)

66 CG to Pinker, 12 October 1919 (Berg)

67 Muchnic, 62

68 Ibid, 62–3

69 CG, 'Art of Translation'

70 DG, 'Brief Memoir of CG', [6–7] (Hilton)

71 Ernest Hemingway, *A Moveable Feast* (1964), 119

Chapter 19: D. H. Lawrence: 'Little Demon of Perversity'

1 E. T. [Jessie (Wood) Chambers], *D. H. Lawrence: A Personal Record* (1935), 92

2 Lawrence to Ernest Collings, 14 November 1912, *Letters* (1932), 72

3 DG, *Golden Echo*, 182

4 CG to EG, 'Thursday' [summer 1915] (Eton)

5 EG, introduction to Lawrence, *A Collier's Friday Night* (1934), vii

6 Lawrence to Louie Burrows, 16 October 1911, *Letters* (1979), No 321, i, 314

7 Ibid, 315

8 Scott-James, 'Edward Garnett', *Spectator*, 26 February 1937, 362

9 Lawrence to Helen Corke, 1 February 1912, *Letters* (1979), No 379, i, 360

10 Lawrence to EG, 17 December 1911, *Letters* (1932), 14

11 Low, quoted by Nehls, 216

12 Lawrence to EG, 17 April 1912, *Letters* (1932), 32–3

13 Lawrence to EG, 21 May 1912, *Letters* (1932), 38

14 Lawrence to EG, 22 March 1913, *Letters* (1979), No 560, i, 530

15 Lawrence, 'At the Cearne', *Complete Poems* (1964), 886–7

16 Lawrence to EG, 18 February [1913], *Letters* (1979), No 549, i, 517

17 Lawrence to DG, [23 July 1912], quoted in DG, introduction to *Love Among the Haystacks* (1930), v

18 DG, *Golden Echo*, 242

19 Ibid, 243

20 Lawrence to EG, 4 August 1912, *Letters* (1932), 46–7

21 DG, *Golden Echo*, 243

22 Lawrence to DG, 5 December 1912, *Letters* (1979), No 523, i, 485

23 Lawrence to EG, 19 May 1913, *Letters* (1979), No 577, i, 551

24 Lawrence to EG, 12 January 1913, *Letters* (1932), 91

25 Low, quoted by Nehls, 218

26 Lawrence to Arthur McLeod, 17 January 1913, *Letters* (1932), 93

27 Low, quoted by Nehls, 220

28 CG to EG, [in envelope pm 24 February 1913 with one other] (Eton)

29 DG, *Golden Echo*, 226

30 Ibid, 227

31 CG to EG, 'Wednesday', [1912] (Eton)

32 CG to EG, nd [early June 1912] (Eton)

33 CG to DG, 'Monday' [February 1913] (Eton)

34 Ibid

35 Lawrence to EG, 3 March 1913, *Letters* (1932), 111

36 CG to EG, 28 March [1913] (Eton)

37 CG to EG, 'Monday' [pm 1 April 1913] (Hilton)

38 Frieda Weekley to DG [25 March 1913], *Letters* (1979), No 562, i, 533

39 CG to EG, 'Monday' [pm 1 April 1913] (Hilton)

40 CG to EG, 7 April [1913] (Hilton); the letter to David is not in *Letters* (1979), unless it be No 564, in which Lawrence says they should be in England 'about the 13th'.

41 Ibid

42 Ibid

43 Lawrence to EG [21 April 1913], *Letters* (1979), No 572, i, 542

44 Ibid

45 Ibid

46 Ibid

47 CG to EG, 'Monday' [pm 16 June 1913] (Eton)

48 DG, 'A Whole Hive of Genius', 142

49 Lawrence to EG, 21 June 1913, *Letters* (1932), 126

50 DG, *Golden Echo*, 254

51 Ibid

52 CG to EG, 'Saturday' [?28 June 1913] (Eton)

53 Ibid

54 CG to EG, nd [ca 1 July 1913] (Eton)

55 CG to EG, 'Monday' [7 July 1913] (Eton)

56 CG to EG, 'Tuesday' [?15 July 1913] (Eton); the letter also refers to reviews of *The Idiot* and *Sons and Lovers* in the *Nation*, both of which were on 12 July.

57 Lawrence to CG, 'Friday' [11 July 1913], *Letters* (1981), No 596, ii, 33

58 DG, 'A Whole Hive of Genius', 142

59 Lawrence to EG, 'Monday' [28 July 1913], *Letters* (1981), No 619, ii, 51

60 Lawrence to Elsie Jaffe, [2 August 1913], *Letters* (1981), No 627, ii, 183

61 Lawrence to EG, 5 June 1914, *Letters* (1932), 198

62 Lawrence to Lady Ottoline Morrell, 'Wednesday' [24 March 1915], *Letters* (1981), No 892, ii, 311

63 Lawrence to Catherine Carswell, 27 November 1916, *Letters* (1984), No 1320, iii, 41

64 *Daily News*, 20 October 1913, 9

65 CG to EG, 'Tuesday', [21 October 1913] (Hilton)

66 Lawrence to EG, 30 September 1913, *Letters* (1932), 141

67 Lawrence to CG, 23 January 1914, *Letters* (1981), No 698, ii, 139
68 CG to DG, 31 January [1914] (Eton)
69 CG to EG, 'Monday' [pm 27 January 1914] (Eton)
70 Ibid
71 Ibid
72 Shelley to Byron, 3 May 1822, *Letters*; ed F. L. Jones (1964), No 702, ii, 415
73 CG to EG, 'Monday' [pm 27 January 1914] (Hilton)
74 CG to DG, 31 January [1914] (Eton)
75 Ibid
76 CG to EG, 'Monday' [pm 27 January 1914] (Hilton)
77 CG to DG, 31 January [1914] (Eton)
78 Ibid
79 Ibid
80 Ibid
81 CG to EG, 5 February [1914] (Eton)
82 Ibid
83 Ibid
84 Ibid
85 Waterfield, 137
86 CG to EG, 31 January [1914] (Eton)
87 CG to EG, 5 February [1914] (Eton)

88 CG to EG, 24 February [1914] (Eton)
89 CG to EG, 31 January [1914] (Eton)
90 DG, 'Brief Memoir of CG', [3] (Hilton)
91 Lawrence to EG, 22 April 1914, *Letters* (1932), 190
92 Frieda Weekley to EG, [? March 1914], *Letters* (1981), No 708, ii, 151
93 CG to Li Whale, 11 February 1914 (Eton)
94 CG to EG, 'Monday' [23 February 1914] (Eton)
95 CG to EG, 4 July 1914 (Eton)
96 CG to EG, 'Tuesday' [? autumn 1914–spring 1915] (Eton)
97 Lawrence to Lady Ottoline Morrell, 'Monday' [pm 19 April 1915], *Letters* (1932), 224
98 Lawrence to Ernest Collings, 17 January 1913, *Letters* (1932), 94
99 DG, 'A Whole Hive of Genius', 142
100 bid
101 Ibid
102 Ibid
103 Lawrence to DG, [19 April 1914], *Letters* (1981), No 901, ii, 321
104 Lawrence to Katherine Clayton, 2 February 1916, *Letters* (1981), No 1159, ii, 524

Chapter 20: Lost Causes

1 CG to EG, nd, [spring 1910] (Eton)
2 EMH to Louise Bréal, 20 March 1916 (Brunt)
3 DG, *Flowers of the Forest*, 180
4 CG to Louise Bréal, 29 June 1914 (Brunt)
5 DG, *Flowers of the Forest*, 180
6 CG to EG, 9 September 1912 (Eton)
7 CG to EG, July [1914] (Eton)
8 CG to EG, 3 August 1914 (Eton)
9 CG to DG, 8 August [1914] (King's)
10 Dickinson, 'The Holy War', *Nation*, 8 August 1914, 699–700
11 CG to DG, 8 August [1914] (King's)
12 CG to DG, 5 August 1914 (King's)
13 CG to DG, 14 August 1914 (King's)
14 CG to DG, 5 August 1914 (King's)
15 CG to DG, 7 August [1914] (King's)
16 CG to DG, 5 August 1914 (King's)
17 CG to DG, 6 August [1914] (King's)
18 CG to DG, 7 August [1914] (King's)
19 Ibid
20 CG to DG, 5 August 1914 (King's)
21 CG to DG, 7 August [1914] (King's)
22 Békássy to CG, 29 July 1914 (Hilton); these letters make it clear that DG's circumstantial account (*Golden Echo*, 270–1) of Békássy returning to Hungary on 11

August, the day before Britain declared war on Austria-Hungary, must be wrong.
23 Heinemann to CG, 11 June 1914 (Hilton)
24 CG to EG, 'Tuesday' [autumn 1914–spring 1915] (Eton)
25 Ibid
26 CG to EG, 18 August 1916 (Eton)
27 DG, diary, 31 January 1915 (Hilton)
28 EMH to Louise Bréal, 5 December 1914 (Brunt)
29 EG to Louise Bréal, 4 October 1914 (Brunt)
30 EMH to Louise Bréal, 5 December 1914 (Brunt)
31 EMH to Louise Bréal, 21 December 1914 (Brunt)
32 EMH to Louise Bréal, 13 February 1915 (Brunt)
33 CG to Louise Bréal, 29 June 1914 (Brunt)
34 DG, *Flowers of the Forest*, 55
35 Ibid, 58–9
36 EMH to Louise Bréal, 1 September 1915 (Brunt)
37 EG, 'Behind the Isonzo', 3
38 EG to CG, 5 September [1915] (Hilton)
39 EG to CG, 13 and 14 October [1915] (Hilton)

40 CG to Louise Bréal, 13 September 1915 (Brunt)
41 CG to EG, 14 September 1915 (Eton)
42 DG to CG [pm 16 September 1915] (Hilton)
43 Partridge, *Hanging On*, 73
44 DG, *Flowers of the Forest*, 28
45 CG to DG, nd, incomplete (Hilton)
46 DG, *Flowers of the Forest*, 95
47 Ibid, 98
48 Ibid
49 Ibid, in
50 CG to EG, nd [June 1916] (Eton)
51 CG to EG, 17 August [1915] (Hilton)
52 CG to EG, 16 August 1915 (Hilton)
53 CG to EG, nd (Eton)
54 CG to ND, 3 November 1917 (Garrett)
55 CG to EG, 7 September 1915 (Hilton)
56 CG to EG, 23 September 1915 (HRHRC)
57 DG, *Flowers of the Forest*, 113
58 CG to EG, 4 May 1916 (Eton)
59 DG to CG, 'Wissett Lodge, Monday' [1916] (HRHRC)
60 DG to CG, 'Wissett Lodge', nd [1916] (HRHRC)
61 Vanessa Bell to Lady Ottoline Morrell, 'Saturday' [20 May 1916] (HRHRC)
62 Ibid
63 DG to CG from the Ram, Firle, 'Friday night' [October 1916] (HRHRC)
64 DG, *Flowers of the Forest*, 124
65 DG to CG, 'Wissett Lodge', nd [1916] (HRHRC)
66 DG to CG, 19 September 1916 (HRHRC)
67 CG to EG, 'Charleston, Friday' [autumn 1916] (Eton)
68 DG, 'Trouble', MS (Hilton)

69 Ruth Hall, 'Bloomsbury Group Survivor', *Observer Colour Supplement*, 5 March 1972, 25
70 DG, diary, 'Monday' [18 January 1915], 11 (Hilton)
71 DG, diary, 'Saturday' [23 January 1915], 14 (Hilton)
72 DG to CG, nd, ?incomplete [April 1918] (HRHRC)
73 CG to EG, 'Tuesday' [?1915] (Eton)
74 CG to EG, 'Brighton, Tuesday' [summer 1917] (Eton)
75 Kochan, 200
76 Quoted in Kochan, 200
77 Kochan, 205
78 CG to EG, 29 June 1917 (Eton)
79 CG to EG, 27 June 1917 (Eton)
80 CG to EG, 29 June 1917 (Eton)
81 Ibid
82 CG to ND, 14 July 1917 (Garrett)
83 DG, *Flowers of the Forest*, 165
84 CG to ND, 26 November [1917] (Garrett)
85 DG to CG, 1 February [1918] (HRHRC)
86 Ibid
87 *Annual Register*, 1918, 228
88 DG to CG, 1 February [1918] (HRHRC)
89 Ibid
90 DG, *Flowers of the Forest*, 167
91 Ibid, 168
92 Ibid
93 CG to ND, 24 September 1917 (Garrett)
94 CG to ND, nd, in envelope with letter of 10 December 1917 (Garrett)
95 CG to ND, 20 September [1918] (Garrett)
96 CG to ND, 'Tuesday' [pm 18 November 1918] (Garrett)
97 Ibid
98 CG to RDG, 25 February 1944 (RDG)

Chapter 21: Chekhov: 'A Perfect Flower'

1 H. E. Bates, 29
2 Phelps, 171
3 *Times*, 23 December 1914, 10
4 DG to CG, 'Sunday' [late autumn 1916] from Charleston on 46 Gordon Square paper (HRHRC)
5 DG to CG, nd (HRHRC)
6 DG to CG, 'Sunday' [late autumn 1916] from Charleston on 46 Gordon Square paper (HRHRC)
7 ND to Tovey, 26 October 1959 (in Russian) (Malinskaya)
8 Swinnerton, *Background with Chorus*, 142–3

9 CG to EG, nd [1916] (Eton)
10 *New Statesman*, 18 November 1916, 159 –60
11 Spalding to CG, 19 March 1919, Letter-book No 123 (Reading)
12 CG to ND, nd [in envelope pm 10 December 1917 with a letter of that date] (Garrett)
13 DG, 'Brief Memoir of CG', [6] (Hilton)
14 CG to EMH, 24 September [1914] (Eton)
15 DG, *Flowers of the Forest*, 197
16 Ibid, 169
17 CG to Spalding, 26 March 1921 (Reading)

18 Miles, 7

19 *New Statesman*, 24 August 1920, 446

20 CG to ND, pc [pm 14 July 1920] (Garrett)

21 Naomi Royde-Smith, *Outlook*, lvii, 27 February 1926, 150

22 *Athenaeum*, 16 July 1920, 91, unsigned but attributed to Katherine Mansfield by Murry in *Adelphi*, August 1925, 214–15

23 CG to ND, 30 August [1919] (Garrett)

24 EG, *Friday Nights*, 44–50

25 *Nation and Athenaeum*, 8 April 1922, 57

26 Mansfield to Koteliansky, nd [? July 1919], *Letters*, ii, 341

27 Mansfield to Koteliansky, [mid-August 1919], ibid, ii, 349

28 Mansfield to CG, 8 February 1921 (HRHRC)

29 CG to Mansfield, 19 February 1921, Murry Ms Papers 4003, folder 36 (Turnbull)

30 CG to EG, 'Thursday' [April 1922]; the letter refers to sending off the last of *Dead Souls*, which Spalding acknowledged on 2 May 1922 (Hilton)

31 Ibid

32 Tomalin, 228

33 Affable Hawk' [Desmond MacCarthy], *New Statesman*, 15 January 1921, 450

34 Tomalin, 209

35 Gerhardi, 8

36 Tovey, 'Perevody Chekhova', 146, 151

37 Quoted by Eugene K. Bristow, *Quarterly Review of Speech*, October 1966, iii, No 3, 292

38 Leighton, 'Chekhov in English', Clyman, 294–5

39 Miles, in a letter to me, 13 December 1989 (RDG)

40 *Capajon: Fifty-four Short Stories Published in 1921–1933* (1933); republished (after checking the number!) as *Fifty-three Short Stories* in 1937

41 Galsworthy, 'Four Novelists in Profile: An Address', *English Review*, lv, November 1932, 488

Chapter 22: Dear Granny

1 CG to ND, 'Monday' [spring 1921] (Garrett)

2 Partridge, *Memories*, 21

3 DG to CG, nd [spring 1921] on Birrell and Garnett paper (HRHRC)

4 Partridge, *Memories*, 21

5 DG to CG, nd [spring 1921] on Birrell and Garnett paper (HRHRC)

6 Ibid

7 DG to CG, nd [spring 1921] on Birrell and Garnett paper (HRHRC)

8 Ibid

9 MAM to CG, 17 March 1921 (Hilton)

10 DG to CG, nd [spring 1921] on Birrell and Garnett paper (HRHRC)

11 MAM to CG, 17 March 1921 (Hilton)

12 Ibid

13 DG, *Flowers of the Forest*, 234

14 Ibid, 233

15 Partridge, *Memories*, 21

16 RAG to MAM, 'Saturday' [July 1913] (Hilton)

17 Partridge, *Memories*, 21

18 CG to ND, 4 October 1921 (Garrett)

19 Spalding to CG, 15 March 1921, Letterbook No 589 (Reading)

20 CG to Spalding, 16 March 1921 (Reading)

21 CG to ND, 15 August 1921 (Garrett)

22 Mirsky, 191

23 CG to ND, 10 October 1921 (Garrett)

24 CG to DG, 'Sunday', [pm 5 October 1924] (Hilton)

25 CG to ND, 23 September 1921 (Garrett)

26 CG to ND, 4 October 1921 (Garrett)

27 CG to ND, 'Sunday' [in envelope pm 9 May 1922 with one other] (Garrett)

28 Ibid

29 CG to EG, 6 September 1922 (Hilton)

30 CG, Family notes [8] (Hilton)

31 ND to Tovey, 19 August 1959 (in Russian) (Malinskaya)

32 Ibid

33 *Times Literary Supplement*, 23 November 1922, 760

34 *New Statesman*, 20 January 1923, 460

35 Tovey to Rubenstein, 7 December 1974 (Rubenstein)

36 CG, 'Art of Translation'

37 *The Complete Tales of Nikolai Gogol*, ed Leonard J. Kent, 2 vols (Random House, 1964). A spot check of the opening of 'The Tale of How Ivan Ivanovich Quarreled with Ivan Nikiforovich' reveals: two sentences omitted altogether; 'Victorian' terms modernised ('persons' to 'people'; 'nether garments' to 'underwear', though it is clear that Gogol is

referring to trousers); 'British' terms altered to American ('mowers' to 'hay cutters', 'kitchen garden' to 'vegetable garden'); stylistic changes for the worse ('the air was dry and quivering' to 'the air was arid and vibrating'); a few errors corrected; others introduced. Constance expressed her disgust when an earlier editor 'whose taste and conception of the English language are utterly unlike my own' did a similar job of work on *Notes from the Underground* – CG to Miss Callender of Heinemann, 21 March 1945 (Heinemann Archive, OPGL).

38 Karlinsky, 318
39 CG to RAG, 4 March 1923 (Hilton)
40 CG to EG, 'Thursday' [November 1922] (Hilton)
41 DG, *Flowers of the Forest*, 249
42 CG to ND, 29 December [1921] (Garrett)
43 Ibid
44 CG to EG, 'Thursday' [?winter 1922–3] (Hilton)
45 DG to CG, 9 January 1923 (HRHRC)
46 CG to ND 'Tuesday' [pm 6 March 1923] (Garrett)
47 CG to Spalding, 8 February 1923 (Reading)
48 CG to DG, 10 February 1923 (Hilton)
49 CG to ND, 17 February 1923 (Garrett); two phrases taken out of order
50 CG to ND 'Tuesday' [pm 6 March 1923] (Garrett)
51 Spalding to CG, 9 June 1922, Letterbook No 521–2 (Reading)
52 CG to Spalding, 26 June 1922 (Reading)
53 CG to ND, 3 March 1924 (Garrett)
54 Mirsky, 275
55 CG to ND, 4 March 1925 (Garrett)
56 CG to ND, 23 January 1925 (Garrett)
57 CG to Spalding, 20 October 1923 (Reading)
58 Spalding to CG, 22 October 1923, Letterbook No 746 (Reading)
59 CG to ND, 26 August 1923 (Garrett)
60 CG to Spalding, 23 November 1923 (Reading)
61 CG to Spalding, 28 May 1924 (Reading)
62 Chekhov to 'E. M. S.', November 1896 [os], *Letters to his Family and Friends*, 342
63 *Times*, 29 November 1921, 8
64 CG to DG, 16 July 1925 (Hilton)
65 Komisarjevsky, 135–6
66 Duke of York's Theatre, 18 February
67 *Daily Herald*, 18 February 1926
68 Gielgud, 86
69 Ibid, 86–7
70 Ibid, 70
71 Miles, 18
72 CG to ND, 11 February 1927; Russian text printed by E. M. Sakharova in A. G. Golovacheva (ed), *Chekhovskie chteniia v Ialte* (Chekhov Readings in Yalta) (Moscow, 1987), 21
73 CG to ND, 'Thursday' [May 1926] (Garrett)
74 CG to DG, 11 June 1926 (Hilton)
75 Ibid
76 Ibid
77 Spalding to CG, 9 October 1924, Letterbook No 329 (Reading)

Chapter 23: The Empty Years Ahead

1 CG to EG, 'Thursday', [ca 1908] (Eton)
2 CG to DG, 12 October 1926 (Hilton)
3 AVG, 'Connie', 3 (RDG)
4 CG to ND, 16 March [1924] (Garrett)
5 CG to DG, 2 July 1926 (Hilton)
6 CG to ND, 3 March 1924 (Garrett)
7 CG to DG, 8 May 1925 (Hilton)
8 CG to ND, 11 September 1936 (Garrett)
9 CG to ND, 23 November 1923 (Garrett)
10 CG wrote that it was a stoat, but a stoat is far from being 'as big as a cat', or it could have been a pine marten; DG tells a similar story ('Burst Balloons', 13–14) as having occurred around 1940 and identifies the beast as a polecat, or rather as a 'polecat ferret' gone wild. Whether this is a recollection or a repetition of the earlier event I cannot say.
11 CG to ND, 23 November 1923 (Garrett)
12 Ibid
13 CG to ND, 30 July 1937 (Garrett)
14 Ibid
15 CG to ND, 19 August 1927 (Garrett)
16 Ibid
17 CG to EG, 'Monday' [August 1927] (HRHRC)
18 CG to ND, 30 August 1927 (Garrett)
19 CG to DG, 9 May 1929 (Hilton)
20 CG to DG, 27 October 1927 (Hilton)
21 Ibid
22 Grace Human to CG, 5 September 1924 (Hilton)
23 CG to ND, 19 August [1927] (Garrett)

24 DG to Sylvia Townsend Warner, nd, present whereabouts unknown
25 DG to Sebastian Sprott, 'Wednesday' [autumn 1924] (King's)
26 CG to DG, 'Sunday' [pm 5 October 1924] (Hilton)
27 Ibid
28 DG to Sebastian Sprott, 'Wednesday' [autumn 1924] (King's)
29 CG to DG, 'Thursday night' (Hilton)
30 DG to CG, nd [spring 1925] (HRHRC)
31 CG to ND, 'Saturday' [pm 5 June 1926] (Garrett)
32 EG to DG, 'Sunday night' [pm 18 July 1927] (Hilton)
33 CG to ND, 22 August 1937 (Garrett)
34 CG to EMH, 'Saturday' (Hilton)
35 CG to ND, 22 August 1937 (Garrett)
36 CG to ND, 3 November 1917 (Garrett)
37 DG, *Great Friends*, 204
38 H. E. Bates to CG, 26 September 1929 (HRHRC)
39 H. E. Bates to CG, 24 February 1929 (HRHRC)
40 H. E. Bates, 29–30
41 CG to DG, 1 May 1930 (Hilton)
42 CG to DG, 11 June 1926 (Hilton)
43 H. E. Bates, 12–13
44 CG to EG, 25 January [1927] (HRHRC)
45 Jane Harrison to CG, nd (Hilton)
46 CG to ORG, 10 July 1928 (White)

47 DG to CG on Nonesuch Press paper [February 1930] (HRHRC)
48 Ibid
49 CG to Prentice, 3 April 1930 (Reading)
50 DG to CG, nd [?1932] (HRHRC)
51 Prentice memo, 10 March 1931, folio 6152 (Reading)
52 Prentice to CG, 12 March 1931, Letterbook No 950 (Reading)
53 CG to DG, 7 February 1928 (Hilton)
54 CG to DG, 31 October 1931 (Hilton)
55 Sasha Yershov to CG, 8 August 1923, incomplete (Hilton)
56 CG to ND, 28 February 1927 (Garrett)
57 CG to ND, 16 March [1934] (Garrett)
58 Ibid
59 Woolf, *New Statesman*, 11 November 1933, 606
60 Ibid
61 This incident is described in CG to ND, 26 July 1933 (Garrett)
62 CG to Woolf, November 1933, transcript in ND's hand; the more obvious transcription errors have been corrected.
63 DG to CG, 30 November 1932 (HRHRC)
64 *New Statesman*, 25 November 1933, 666
65 Personal knowledge
66 CG to DG, Christmas day 1928 (Hilton)
67 CG to ND, 7 September 1936 (Garrett)

Chapter 24: The Last Adventure

1 AVG, 'Connie', 1 (RDG)
2 CG to ND, 'Sunday' [pm 18 July 1937] (Garrett)
3 CG to DG, 16 January 1935 (Hilton)
4 CG to DG, 28 February 1928 (Hilton)
5 EMH to Stella Stebbing, 15 January 1957 (transcript by Stebbing supplied by Jefferson)
6 H. E. Bates, 82
7 Ibid, 83
8 MacDonald to CG, 22 February 1937 (Hilton)
9 EMH to DG, 6 May 1937 (Hilton)
10 Stebbing, 'Notes on Nellie Heath', 23 October 1977 (supplied by Jefferson)
11 CG to Gielgud, 26 December 1937 (de la Potterie)
12 Ibid
13 Miles, 26
14 CG to St-Denis, 10 February 1938 (de la Potterie)
15 Ibid

16 CG to Gielgud, 10 February 1938 (Gielgud)
17 Gielgud to CG, 13 February [1938] (Hilton)
18 St-Denis to CG, 14 February 1938 (Hilton)
19 Winston S. Churchill, *The Second World War* (1948), 235
20 Ibid
21 CG to ND, 15 September [1938] (Garrett)
22 *Times*, 3 October 1938, 19
23 Ibid
24 CG to Wells, 11 October 1938 (Illinois)
25 Ibid
26 CG to Wells, 17 October 1938 (Illinois)
27 CG to J. L. L. Hammond, 28 February 1940 (Bodleian)
28 CG to ND, 31 August 1939 (Garrett)
29 CG to DG, 1 June 1940 (Hilton)
30 CG to DG, 11 June 1940 (HRHRC)
31 CG to DG, 1 June 1940 (Hilton)

32 CG to DG, 4 June 1940 (HRHRC)
33 Ibid
34 CG to DG, 1 June 1940 (Hilton)
35 CG to DG, 20 May 1940 (Hilton)
36 CG to DG, 9 July 1940 (Hilton)
37 DG, 'Burst Balloons', [11] (Hilton)
38 CG to DG, 6 September [1940] (Hilton)
39 DG, 'Burst Balloons', [10] (Hilton)
40 CG to ND, 'Thursday', [May 1926] (Garrett)
41 DG, 'Burst Balloons', [14] (Hilton)
42 DG to CG, 'Christmas day' [1918] (HRHRC)
43 Partridge, *A Pacifist's War*, 89
44 Ibid
45 DG to CG, 18 September 1940 (HRHRC)
46 AVG, 'Connie', 1 (RDG)
47 DG to CG, 18 September 1940 (HRHRC)
48 DG, 'Burst Balloons', [15] (Hilton)
49 AVG, 'Connie', 3 (RDG)
50 Ibid
51 CG to DG, 16 July 1930 (Hilton)
52 AVG, 'Connie', 1 (RDG)
53 Ibid, 3
54 Partridge, *A Pacifist's War*, 112; also DG to AVG, 7 November 1941 (AVG)
55 DG, 'Burst Balloons', [40] (Hilton)
56 AVG, 'Connie', 4 (RDG)
57 H. E. Bates, *EG*, 31
58 AVG, 'Connie', 3 (RDG)
59 AVG, *Deceived With Kindness*, 146
60 DG, 'Burst Balloons', [13] (Hilton)
61 Ibid
62 Information from Gerard Gould
63 Marjorie Pease to Veronica Pease, 3 May [1944] (Farrington)
64 Partridge, *A Pacifist s War*, 184
65 Ibid
66 DG, 'Burst Balloons', [10] (Hilton)
67 CG to ND, pc 30 October 1946 (Garrett)
68 CG, 'Art of Translation'
69 Ibid
70 DG to George Barnes, 22 November 1946 (BBC)
71 CG to E. M. Layton, 10 October 1946 (BBC)
72 Barnes to DG, 20 November 1946 (BBC)
73 DG to Barnes, 22 November 1946 (BBC)
74 E. S. Bates, 85

Index